THE RAILWAY GAZETTE

SPECIAL GREAT WAR
TRANSPORTATION NUMBER

The Naval & Military Press Ltd

Published by

The Naval & Military Press Ltd
Unit 5 Riverside
Bellbrook Industrial Estate
Uckfield, East Sussex
TN22 1QQ England

Tel: +44 (0) 1825 749494
www.naval-military-press.com

THE RAILWAY GAZETTE

SPECIAL WAR TRANSPORTATION NUMBER.

THE RAILWAY GAZETTE is published weekly at

QUEEN ANNE'S CHAMBERS, WESTMINSTER, LONDON, ENGLAND.

Registered at the General Post Office, London, as a Newspaper.   Telegraphic Address :—" Trazette, Vic., London."

Annual subscription, Inland and Abroad, £2 5 0 post free.   Special issues extra.

Special Issue.   SEPTEMBER 21, 1920.   Price 5s.

CONTENTS.

IN issuing this special number describing the work of the Directorate of Movements and Railways, and of railway and inland water transport in the various theatres of war, the *Railway Gazette* publishes the first connected account in a single issue of war transportation both at home and abroad. We would add that this review has been compiled from official facts and figures, and with the co-operation of the Directorate of Movements and Railways. Transport has always been an important factor in war, but never in the history of the world has it played such a great part as in the war now terminated The movement of large armies on a scale hitherto unrealised, the work of maintaining them in the field, and the handling of unwieldly and terrible engines of war, brought into play every known means of transportation—from the primitive pack transport of man himself to the high-capacity motor vehicle ; and even the aeroplane, developed primarily as a means of offensive, was utilised to some extent. Reliable, regular and adequate means of communication were essential, and it was speedily found that this could only be ensured through a specialised organisation which could co-ordinate the many means of transportation. This specialised organisation developed into the Directorate of Movements and Railways, which, as described in the following pages, was the avenue through which the Army Council worked its transportation in such a successful manner.

The Organization of War Transportation.

Throughout the whole course of the war the demand for railway material of all descriptions was enormous, and it speaks volumes for those who were responsible for meeting the requisitions that the situation was handled in such a satisfactory manner. The fact that more urgent work rendered it impossible to meet the makers of rails and rolling-stock to turn out sufficient to meet all requirements led, as is well known, to a great deal of track being lifted from existing lines both at home and in the Colonies, whilst hundreds of locomotives and thousands of wagons were diverted from their peace-time occupations to meet the emergency requirements. Full particulars of the railway material supplied to the various theatres of war are given in subsequent pages, but it might here be said that nearly 10,000 miles of track of all gauges, over 3,500 locomotives and tractors and over 80,000 wagons were shipped to France and other theatres of war for constructional and operating purposes. These are tremendous figures, but they do not tell the whole story. A large quantity of material was captured from the enemy at various times and places, and this was all turned to good use. Even in those cases where the enemy had attempted to render the plant of no utility, our engineers very ingeniously patched up both locomotives and wagons in such a way that they could be placed in traffic. It will never be possible to give full credit for the magnificent work performed, often under conditions militating against best results, but it is hoped that the facts recorded in the following pages will go far to indicate that the British transportation effort was a gigantic one, and that its successful performance had much to do with the military success.

Railway Material.

The paper read before the British Association at Bournemouth on September 10, 1919 (reproduced elsewhere in this issue), by Sir George Beharrell, D.S.O., Director-General of Finance and Statistics, Ministry of Transport, who was for some time Assistant Director-General of Transportation in France, and before that Assistant Goods Manager of the North Eastern Railway, affords full justification for the relatively elaborate nature of the statistics compiled by the Transportation Services during the continuance of war conditions in France. It is pointed out that while ordinary economic conditions did not apply, there were other factors, notably shortage of men and material, which caused the operations of transportation to be watched with a most critical eye. Operations were remarkably diverse in character and scattered over a very wide and varying field. Statistics constituted the only means whereby the Director-General of Transportation could satisfy himself that the services for which he was responsible were being managed efficiently. More-

Statistics of War Transportation in France.

over, conditions and demands changed so quickly that rapidity of compilation was essential, and the maintenance of a standard whereby preliminary statistics were available on the Tuesday evening for the week ended the previous Friday midnight, followed by complete statistics ready for circulation on the Thursday following, was no mean achievement, bearing in mind the conditions under which the work was done. Sir George Beharrell points out that these statistics not only told each responsible officer what he was doing, where he was going backward or forward, and how he compared with his opposite number in other places, but also informed other branches of the service what transportation was doing for them and where they fell short in assisting transportation to obtain the best results.

The general public were very much impressed during the war when the fact leaked out that a large and well-equipped port had been **"The Mystery** hurriedly developed for war purposes. In the **Port."** early days of the war, Richborough was merely a small depôt from which barges, acquired for service on the French waterways, were manned, equipped and despatched. By the end of 1917, however, the port comprised an area of 2,200 acres, and was replete with all sorts of modern appliances for the rapid handling of traffic. It served as a base for inland water transport operations, classes being inaugurated for training the personnel, whilst it was the principal terminal on this side for the cross-channel train ferry and barge services. The railway network in the area comprised some 60 miles of line, served by a military line linked up with the South Eastern & Chatham main line. Richborough also became an important centre for the re-erection of barges, and the construction of tugs, seaplane carriers and other small craft, whilst it served a very useful purpose as a " base workshop." It will be recalled that this port was recently offered for sale by the Government.

The Mediterranean Line of Communication, which was inaugurated in 1917 in order to save shipping tonnage and minimise sea risks, proved of great service during the war. **The Overland** The distance between the terminals of Cherbourg **Route to the** and Taranto is nearly 1,500 miles, and a vast **East.** amount of work was required at both terminals and at certain places along the route to make the line of communication satisfactory. Apart from yard and siding accommodation at Cherbourg and Taranto, a number of rest camps and *haltes repas* had to be arranged *en route* for the convenience of the troops, as the scheduled timing for the journey was 180 hours. The French and Italian authorities co-operated heartily with the British in the arrangements, and whilst, from one cause and another, the line did not reach its expected traffic density, it carried a relatively large traffic and proved a great boon to the troops stationed in the Near East. From the commencement of the service until February 8, 1919, some 380,000 passengers and 184,000 tons of goods were transported over the line, the " record " month being June, 1918, when 70 trains were run in 28 days. A description of the route and particulars of the work performed are given on page 97, *et seq.*, and it need merely be added that the overland route to the East, taken all in all, proved of considerable benefit.

In order to assist the anti-Bolshevist forces operating in Siberia, the Allies supplied a number of troops, a considerable quantity of equipment and material, and also undertook **Working of the** the control of the Trans-Siberian Railway. A **Trans-Siberian** certain amount of dissension arose as to the form **Railway.** of organisation, but in 1918 this was overcome by the constitution of an Inter-Allied Committee, consisting of representatives from each Allied Power having military forces in Siberia and Russia. Under this Committee was a Technical Board of railway experts, which administered the technical and economical affairs of the railway and a Military Transportation Board which co-ordinated military movements. The working of

the railway very speedily improved on arrangements being made for the respective Allies to supervise definite sections of line. The British controlled that portion running westwards from Omsk through Ekaterinburg and Chelyabinsk.

No railway history of the Great War, however brief, could possibly ignore the great part played by light railways. By light railways we mean narrow gauge lines built of light-weight **Light Railways** rails, which can be laid quickly over any ground **in War.** on which railway construction and operations are at all feasible. Lines of this nature were used in all the main theatres of the campaign, and their employment ranged from the transport of troops and guns, shells and foodstuffs, to the conveyance of water supplies and the speedy evacuation of the wounded. Motive power was—according to circumstances—steam, electricity, petrol, and even horses, while in certain instances ordinary road motor cars were fitted with flanged metal wheels and thus used for railway purposes. On page 30 *et seq.* of this number we publish an account of light railway working on the Western Front, which indicates the difficulties and triumphs of the light railway personnel. The light railways on the Western Front were developed as a system from 1916 when the Commander-in-Chief decided that a well-planned network of such lines was essential. By the end of 1917 well over 1,000 miles were being operated and the weekly traffic figures often reached 200,000 tons. The lines were splendidly operated, often under hazardous conditions, and their efficiency, as reflected in the statistics collated, continued to the end.

The remarkable development of Basra from an area of swamp and desert into a well-equipped port was one of the noteworthy features of the Mesopotamian campaign. In 1916, trans-**The Port** ports were compelled to discharge their cargoes **of Basra.** to native craft which conveyed the traffic to temporary jetties. By 1918, however, modern wharfage accommodation had been provided at Basra to the extent of 1,500 ft., and at Nahr Umar, 25 miles north, to a length of 700 ft. These wharves were equipped with first-class mechanical appliances, gantry cranes (numbering 50 at Basra), runways, elevator conveyors and other labour-aiding devices. The capacity of the port was thus increased from 40,000 to 150,000 tons a month. In addition, an extensive dockyard, several slipways, and marine workshops with power-driven machinery were constructed and equipped. From July 29, 1917, to March 29, 1919, the stores discharged from sea transports at this port exceeded 2,245,000 tons, and upwards of 1,600 sea-going vessels were berthed and unloaded. The average weekly discharge during 1918 was nearly 30,000 tons, the number of ships berthed being about 20 a week, and the number of men on the wharves averaging over 1,500 at work. In addition to the port developments, a very comprehensive light railway system was laid down in and around Basra. This served all the depôts in the vicinity, and was operated on a commercial basis as the Basra Light Railway, fares being in operation and ordinary passengers carried.

The city of Paris probably furnishes the best example in the world of railroads centering in a big city properly organised for harmonious co-operation in war time. It has taken **Paris as a** the war to prove this fact, as well as the value **Military** of such railway organisation. It is not too **Railway** much to say that, without the co-ordination of **Centre.** the systems about Paris, Verdun certainly could not have been kept supplied with artillery, munitions and troops, and, in short, could not have been held. It has long been patent that, but for the railways making possible quick movements of troops early in the war, Paris herself would have fallen. Each of the big lines has a central passenger station near the centre of Paris, with freight and engine yards a little further removed from the passenger station, and, finally, car yards and shops just beyond the city suburbs. The six lines, 25,000 miles in length, which handle the transportation of a nation of 40,000,000 people are able to work together as a single unit by means of a little bit of double track, 75 miles long, that circles Paris at an average distance of 10 miles. This strategic railway, so important in wartime, is all but unknown to the ordinary traveller. Its name is the Grande Ceinture, as opposed to the 19-mile Petite Ceinture which circles Paris just within the old, and to-day useless, line of fortifications. The building of the Grande Ceinture came about as a result of the Franco-Prussian war of 1870–71, when both the French and German nations realised in some measure how much better that war might have been conducted, either as a defensive or offensive instrument, had railroad facilities been more complete. While Bismarck was working to this end in Germany, the French were not idle. Indeed, the Petite Ceinture about the fortifications had been built before that war, during the reign of Emperor Napoleon III. The possession by all the railroads of France of an ample passenger and freight terminal within the city, thereby making possible their use as a single unit for national defence by the connecting link of the Grande Ceinture, must, however, be attributed in some measure to the ambition to make Paris the foremost capital of Europe.

When the Allied forces landed at Salonica with the object of affording aid to Serbia, the three railway lines radiating from Salonica were found of great utility. For some

Railway Operations in Macedonia. months the Greeks continued to operate these lines, but in June, 1916, their working proved so unsatisfactory that General Sarrail compulsorily took them over. In due course the necessity of securing economy of administration and co-operation in working between the French and British forces led to the formation of a Railway Commission which, for executive purposes, consisted of one French and one English member. The former dealt particularly with the operation of the Oriental and the Salonica-Monastir lines, and the latter with the Jonction Salonique Constantinople line, and, in our account of " Railways and the Salonica Campaign," published on pages 106–114 herein, special reference is naturally paid to British methods of operation. It was speedily found that the existing accommodation was insufficient to deal with the traffic, and a large yard was established at Dudular, some 6 km. from Salonica. Very efficient methods of operation were soon installed, and the facts recorded in our account of railway work in Salonica will prove that those responsible for the railway arrangements performed a difficult task in a splendid manner. There was always a shortage of locomotives and rolling-stock, and no less a shortage of trained railwaymen, yet the turn-round of wagons was very satisfactory.

Even those writers who realise the essential importance of railways in modern warfare often overlook one particular aspect of railway interest. That is, the extent to which the

Railways and the Wounded. control of a railway system leads to the conservation of the man-power of an army. It is a truism that only a relatively small proportion of the deaths of soldiers in any campaign take place in battle. Disease and inability to attend speedily and promptly to wounds claim a far greater number. Thanks to the railway, the percentage of wounded men who recover and who can be sent back to the firing line again is very high. A sufficient and well-organised system of hospital trains, operating from suitable bases, nowadays enables the worst cases to be brought in a few hours from the field to the hospital best suited to the circumstances of the case, and in this way prompt medical attention or surgery has saved thousands of lives which would have been lost in an earlier period. Much suffering and death is also avoided by the fact that a modern Red Cross train provides one of the most perfect methods of transporting wounded that has yet been devised. And not only does the railway thus conserve the fighting strength of an army, but it also enables men to be returned to the firing line in quicker time. It is pleasing to reflect that, in addition to its rôle as a weapon of offence,

the railway also serves as an instrument for the reduction of death and suffering.

The railways of Mesopotamia came into being under the impulse of war necessities. They were originally introduced on a very modest scale during 1916 for the purpose of

The Military Railways of Mesopotamia. supplementing river transport. After the recapture of Kut, however, and the victorious drive beyond Baghdad, it speedily became apparent that additional railways would have to be constructed, as the fighting front extended so widely that troops had to be maintained at points far distant from the rivers. This led to a very rapid expansion of the railway system which, at the beginning of 1919, or within 24 months after the opening of the first railway, comprised nearly 1,000 miles of track. When it is remembered that the tremendous difficulties experienced in obtaining permanent way, locomotives and rolling-stock necessitated a great deal of additional work in conversion to wider gauges, it must be held that the Mesopotamian railways were developed in a wonderful manner. It is true that they are somewhat roughly laid ; the signalling is of the most primitive character and the facilities generally are by no means what could be desired, but it is indisputable that the railway system of Mesopotamia, constructed and developed under the stress of war conditions, will have a very important effect on future communications in the Middle East, and play a great part in the regeneration of Mesopotamia and Southern Persia. The recent completion of the Basra-Baghdad through railway is of some importance, as this leaves but a small section of the original Constantinople-Basra line to be completed—between Nisibin and Mosul. When this is linked up, and linked up it will be at an early date, the through overland route will be an accomplished fact, and the dreams of many farseeing Englishmen fulfilled.

The construction of a standard gauge line from the Suez Canal to Haifa, a distance of 412 km., was one of the most remarkable achievements of war railroading. The development of

Railway Construction in Palestine. this line followed the decision to advance in Palestine during 1916, and speedy construction was desired in order that there should be effective communications between the front and the base. By the summer of 1916 the line had reached Romani, 41 km. from Kantara, whilst El Arish, 155 km. from Kantara, was reached in January, 1917, a new station being opened for traffic at this place exactly one month after it had been occupied by the advancing army. Two months later Rafa was reached, and in June El Belah, 219 km. from Kantara, was served by railway. At about this time, moreover, the question of doubling the Kantara line became an important question, and it was eventually decided that this should be done as far as Rafa, opportunity being taken in the doubling to ease serious gradients and otherwise improve the line. The rapid advance of General Allenby and his victorious troops soon placed him in possession of sections of the Turkish lines, and it became essential to connect up with these and, as it became possible, to convert them to standard gauge. Meanwhile the main line was progressing, and by the end of March, 1918, Ludd, 308 km. from Kantara, was passed, Haifa eventually being reached in December, 1918.

One of the most interesting transportation developments of the war was the inauguration of a cross-channel train ferry service. The

The Cross-Channel Train Ferry Services. idea of developing a train ferry service between England and France was first pressed forward towards the end of 1916, when the shipping question was becoming a serious one, owing to the enormous losses sustained as a result of enemy submarine activities. The War Cabinet finally approved of the scheme as an urgent war measure and, early in 1917, gave instructions for terminal ports to be selected, the necessary special berthing accommodation provided, and three ferry steamers built. The work was so energetically pressed forward that the inaugural service from Richborough to Calais was run on February 10, 1918, whilst the Southampton-Dieppe service followed on February 22, 1918. The train ferries contributed very handsomely to the remarkable transportation effort of this country, as their utilisation avoided the necessity of transhipment on both sides of the Channel.

RAILWAYS AND THE GREAT WAR.

IN his final despatch Sir Douglas (now Lord) Haig pointed out that the wonderful development of transportation had an important influence upon the course of events, and that no war had been fought with such ample means of transportation as were available during the recent struggle. This is a striking testimony to the value of railways in military operations ; with due regard to the splendid work performed by other means of transportation, it is indisputable that the brunt of the transport burden was borne by the railways.

While the railway cannot claim the speed of the aeroplane, nor the mobility of the motor vehicle, it can definitely be affirmed that, for any prolonged transport function, the railway has proved to be the most satisfactory means, and this fact was abundantly established during the Great War. In many cases, moreover, especially in those areas where roads were poor or non-existent, motor transport had to give place to the railway. A typical instance of this was found in the case of the Seres Road, along which motor vehicles carrying supplies for the British Salonica force travelled in a constant stream. The road became so battered and the rate of repair unable to keep pace with the wear and tear that a railway became imperative. Once this was constructed and opened for traffic there was a great improvement in the transportation arrangements.

Moltke is said to be the first man who foresaw the value of railways in military operations, and there can be no doubt that the Germans speedily recognised the importance of this new " weapon." From 1870 onwards, both Germany and France paid special attention to the development of their railway systems to fit them for effective use in war time. They extended the number of lines to the frontiers, built lateral lines to facilitate speedy transfer from one point to another, and arranged suitable concentration and marshalling yards to meet emergencies. It was undoubtedly due to the splendid arrangement of their railway operating facilities that the Germans were enabled to throw huge armies into Belgium in an incredibly short space of time. The value placed by the Germans on effective railway operation in war was also exemplified by the fact that they were fully prepared to take over the Belgian lines—lock, stock and barrel—their pre-arranged programmes being put into operation as soon as they had occupied Belgian territory.

From the British standpoint, the fact that the war was fought outside these islands, meant that they had at first to rely upon the railways of their Allies, and, when it was found that these would not suffice, to build up, as expeditiously as possible, a railway organisation and a railway system for their own purposes. The facts recorded in the following pages will go far to show that they accomplished this task in a strikingly satisfactory manner. In France alone over 2,300 miles of standard gauge track and 1,300 miles of narrow gauge track were laid by the British, whilst something like 509,000 tons of traffic per week were carried. This great effort proved to have an important bearing upon the military operations, as it was possible, despite the huge increase in the size of the armies, to effect great concentrations of troops with great speed. Having regard to the numbers of men and bulk of material moved, and the necessity of an incredibly heavy traffic to supply and maintain the forces, the speed of transport has never before been equalled.

It was not only in France, however, that railways proved to be so vital to the military success. In Mesopotamia, it was originally considered that water transport on the Tigris and Euphrates Rivers would suffice to meet all requirements, but, following the downfall of Kut, and the reorganisation and reinforcement of the British forces that ensued, it became abundantly clear that railways must be introduced. The great utility of the railways, constructed under enormous difficulties, in Mesopotamia is clearly brought out in the special chapter dealing with the subject, and it need merely be added

that, at the end of the war, there was a railway system comprising some 1,000 miles of track in Mesopotamia, and that the development of railways in that inhospitable region coincided with the progress of the sustained offensive which led to the complete capitulation of the Turkish forces operating in that area.

In Palestine, moreover, the decision to take the offensive led, as a natural sequence, to the development of railways to support and maintain the forces as they advanced. The main line from Kantara along the coast eventually reached Haifa, 412 km. from the base, and was connected up to various Turkish lines as they were captured. The construction of this line was a splendid piece of work, and like the development of the railway system of Mesopotamia, is a striking tribute to the hard work and indomitable energy of the railway personnel in the arrangement and maintenance of the communications upon which everything depends.

Throughout the course of the Great War the railways—both at home and abroad—successfully met the heavy obligations imposed upon them. Both in trench warfare and in the wars of movement, they performed astonishing transport feats, and it is hoped that this brief review of war transportation, which is based on official facts and figures, will serve to show how magnificently the Directorate of Movements and Railways arranged and conducted the British transportation effort.

RAILWAYS AND FOREIGN POLITICS.

RAILWAYS played an important part in those events in the Near East which exercised so great an influence on the making of the Great War. Owing to racial jealousies and Turkish domination, the Balkan peninsula remained devoid of railways until the second half of last century, and it was not until after the Crimean war that the Sultan authorised the construction of two lines, one from Constantinople to Belgrade, via Roumelia and Serbia, and the other from Salonica into Macedonia. The Russo-Turkish war, which led to the independence of Serbia, to the creation of the Principality of Bulgaria, and to the granting of autonomy to Eastern Roumelia, caused great political changes in the Balkans ; but in order to mollify Turkey, the Congress of Berlin specifically left the Porte with rights over the railways of the Balkan peninsula and the Oriental Railways Company. Germany and Austria insisted on the insertion in the Treaty of Berlin of a proviso calling on Austria, Serbia, Bulgaria and Turkey to settle the question of connecting the lines of the Oriental Railways Company with those of the main Austrian system.

The immediate outcome was the Convention of 1883 between the four Powers concerned, which laid down the route of the Constantinople-Belgrade and Nish-Salonica lines. Serbia and Bulgaria reserved to themselves the right of operating the railways in their own territory, but the Oriental Railways Company, whose previous rights were safeguarded by the Treaty of Berlin, took over the working of new sections constructed in Turkish territory—in Thrace and Macedonia—as well as in Eastern Roumelia, which, at that time, had not been formally united to Bulgaria, although its autonomy was accorded by the Treaty of Berlin.

After the armistice the control and administration of the railways in Asia Minor, Thrace, Bulgaria and Macedonia had to be arranged very carefully. They were placed in the hands of a Superior Commission with headquarters at Constantinople, and branches at Sofia, Smyrna and Salonica. The Roumanian railways were managed by the Roumanians themselves assisted by a British Commission ; the Transylvanian Lines by the local civil authorities with French assistance ; the lines in Old Serbia by the Serbian authorities, with the railway department of the Serbian staff administering the lines in Bosnia and Herzegovinia. The railways of Hungary were provisionally controlled by separate Serbian Commissions at Temesvar and Neusatz, by a Franco-Serbian-Italian Commission at Agram, and by the civil authorities at Budapest. Early in 1919, British and French railway officers were placed in executive control of the Turkish lines in the respective spheres of their Governments, the Allied Railway Commission co-ordinating control as between Asia Minor and Europe.

BRITISH RAILWAYS AND THE WAR.

A Summary of their Emergency Organisation and the Methods of Operation.

While the outbreak of war in August, 1914, found the country in general unprepared for any such emergency, it did not fail to find the British railways, at least, equal to any immediate demands that might then be made upon them ; and this fact was well established by the perfect smoothness with which all the initial transport movements were operated, whatever the difficulties that subsequently arose by reason of developments and complications which no one, in all the circumstances of the situation, could possibly have foreseen.

This initial smoothness was directly due to the fact that in the pre-war period nothing had been left to chance so far as concerned railway preparations for naval and military movements, the need for which might arise at any moment owing to some crisis in our relations with other countries. Just as time-tables must be drawn up in advance to meet ordinary traffic arrangements, so had it been regarded as a matter of course, many years before any suggestion arose as to a possible war with Germany, that arrangements should be made, and an effective organisation created, as a precautionary measure for dealing with mobilisation movements and emergency schemes of all kinds, no matter how suddenly the need for them might occur.

Hence it was that, whereas the British public in general had heard nothing about a Railway Executive Committee until the outbreak of war, that body had been in existence, in a consultative capacity, since November, 1912. It then succeeded a still earlier peace-time organisation known as the War Railway Council and consisting of representatives of the War Office and the Admiralty, together with the members of the Engineer and Railway Staff Corps, which body, in turn, had been originally constituted in 1865, its purpose being to provide an organisation of railway managers, engineers and contractors who in case of invasion and under the direction of the military authorities, would superintend the operation of the railways and carry out such additional works as might be necessary. Railway preparations for the special needs of transport in time of war had thus a record of close on half a century prior to the autumn of 1914.

Railway Executive Committee.

The Railway Executive Committee itself was formed exclusively of the General Managers of certain leading railways. Its function was to be to control, on behalf of the Board of Trade, such railways as might be taken possession of in the name of His Majesty in the event of an emergency arising of the nature contemplated by Section 16 of the Regulation of the Forces Act, 1871, under which it was enacted :—

" When Her Majesty by Order in Council declares that an emergency has arisen in which it is expedient for the public service that Her Majesty's Government should have control over the railways in the United Kingdom or any of them, the Secretary of State may by warrant under his hand empower any person or persons named in such warrant to take possession in the name or on behalf of Her Majesty of any railroad in the United Kingdom and of the plant belonging thereto, or any part thereof ; and may take possession of any plant without taking possession of the railroad itself, and to use the same for Her Majesty's service at such times and in such manner as the Secretary of State may direct, and the directors, officers and servants of any such railroad shall obey the directions of the Secretary of State as to the use of such railroad or plant as aforesaid for Her Majesty's service."

On the formation of the Railway Executive Committee in 1912 it was explained by Mr. Buxton, who was then President of the Board of Trade, that the Government did not propose to supersede in any way the existing management of the railways during the time they were taken over by the State. What was aimed at was, not that the State should itself manage the lines, but that it should be in a position to give binding instructions and to require separate railways to co-operate as part of a single system. He went on to say :—

" This working of the lines as one would be essential if heavy calls for naval, military and civil purposes were to be made on them at one and the same time, as might possibly happen. The control of this system would be vested in the Executive Committee, and one of their principal duties is to prepare now all necessary arrangements, in consultation, if necessary, with the Board of Trade, for the joint working of the lines to the best possible advantage."

Following on certain representations made by the railway managers, the creation of this Railway Executive Committee was supplemented by the formation of a Communications Board, which, presided over by the Quartermaster-General of the Forces, was formed by representatives of various State departments and the members of the Railway Executive Committee, a guarantee of harmony of working as between those departments and the railways in regard to all transport questions affecting His Majesty's Forces being thus secured.

The President of the Board of Trade became nominal Chairman of the Railway Executive Committee ; but there was no suggestion that he would himself preside over its meetings. He was, rather, to constitute a court of appeal for the Committee, in the event of their experiencing difficulties in dealing with any individual company, and he was, also, to act as an intermediary, whenever this might be necessary, as between the Committee and the Government. The first Acting-Chairman of the Executive Committee was the late Sir Frank Ree, General Manager of the London & North Western Railway Company, on whose death, in April, 1914, Mr. H. A. Walker (now Sir Herbert A. Walker, K.C.B.), General Manager of the London & South Western Railway Company, was appointed Acting-Chairman in his place. As originally formed, the Railway Executive Committee consisted of the General Managers of nine Railway Companies ; but subsequently the General Managers of three other companies were added.

The Controlled Railways.

On the outbreak of the war a public announcement of the taking over of the railways by the State was issued by the War Office in the following terms :—

" An Order in Council has been made under Section 16 of the Regulation of the Forces Act, 1871, declaring that it is expedient that the Government should have control over the railways in Great Britain. This control will be exercised through an Executive Committee composed of General Managers of railways, which has been formed for some time and has prepared plans with a view to facilitating the working of these provisions of the Act.

" Although the railway facilities for other than naval and military purposes may for a time be somewhat restricted, the effect of the use of the powers under this Act will be to co-ordinate the demands of the railways upon the civil community with those necessary to meet the special requirements of the naval and military authorities.

" More normal conditions will, in due course, be restored, and it is hoped that the public will recognise the necessity for the special conditions, and will, in the general interest, accommodate themselves to the inconvenience involved."

A further notification issued at the same time by the Railway Executive Committee said :—

" The control of the railways has been taken over by the Government for the purpose of ensuring that the railways, locomotives, rolling-stock and staff shall be used as one complete unit in the best interests of the State for the movement of troops, stores and food supplies. . . ,

" The staff on each railway will remain under the same control as heretofore, and will receive their instructions through the same channels as in the past."

The lines passing under State control at this time were exclusively those of England, Wales and Scotland. Irish railways were not dealt with until some time later, nor did the Order in Council apply to the whole of the British lines, without exception. The number owned by separate companies or by joint companies included in the list of those over which the State control was to be exercised was 130. These had a mileage of 21,331 and a capital value of 1,200 millions. The lines not taken over numbered 46. Their mileage was 499, and their capital value 41½ millions.

The working of the railways as one complete unit had been rendered possible of attainment by the fact that for many years prior to the war the railway companies had, in the interests of ordinary commercial transport, adopted the policy of establishing physical connections with each other's lines at points where this could be done to their mutual benefit. The facilities thus brought about were now to be of great advantage to the Government from the point of view of the movement of troops or supplies in any direction and for strategical purposes generally; and they were already so complete that very little more in the establishment of further connections between the lines of different companies became necessary. Two instances, however, in which such works were found expedient might be mentioned, namely, (1) the laying of a double junction at Gospel Oak between the Hampstead Junction Railway of the London & North Western and the Midland and Great Eastern, Tottenham and Hampstead Joint lines; and (2) a short connection between the Great Central main line and the South Leicester branch of the London & North Western Railway, thus forming a means of direct communication between the main lines of the Great Central Railway and the Midland Railway.

Docks, Steamships, &c.

What the Government took over from the railways, however, was not simply their lines, their locomotives and their rolling-stock, but, in addition, many of the largest and best-equipped docks and harbours in Great Britain, together with, approximately, 100 of the 164 steamships owned by the railway companies on the outbreak of the war and used by them for their services on the Scottish coast, with Ireland, with the Channel Islands or with the Continent of Europe. The value of these docks and steamships to the Government for the purposes of the war was incalculable. Then the State also got the use of railway workshops, railway warehouses, railway hotels and other railway property, together with the services of the railway staffs and the advantages of the whole railway organisation.

Financial Arrangements.

The basis of the financial arrangements made between the Government and the railway companies was that the amount of the compensation to be paid should be the ascertained deficiency in the aggregate net receipts of all the railways taken over as compared with the aggregate for the corresponding period of 1913, " provided that if the aggregate net receipts for the first half of the year 1914 are less than the aggregate net receipts for the first half of the year 1913, the ascertained deficiency shall be reduced in the same proportion." In the official announcement of these terms made by the President of the Board of Trade, and published in the press of September 16, 1914, it was added :—

" The compensation to be paid under this arrangement will cover all special services, such as those in connection with military and naval transport rendered to the Government by the railway companies concerned, and it will, therefore, be unnecessary to make any payments in respect of such transport on the railways taken over."

A modification was made in the original arrangement in February, 1915, when, on the railway companies agreeing to pay 25 per cent. of the war bonus then conceded to railway workers to meet the higher cost of living, it was agreed that they should be relieved, as from January 1, 1915, from the proviso quoted above. Subsequent bonuses and " war wages " were met by the Government.

In August, 1915, the Government accepted the principle of making allowances to the railway companies (supplementing the periodical compensation payments) in respect to deferred maintenance and renewal, and in November, 1916, a clearer definition was arrived at as to the particular services in regard to which the companies were or were not to receive direct payment from the Government, as distinct from the compensation paid to them on the basis already stated.

The Executive and its Work.

The members of the Railway Executive Committee settled down to their labours at the Westminster offices of the London & North Western Railway Company, 35, Parliament Street; and here their meetings were held and their chief business carried on, though much was also done at the Parliamentary offices of the Midland and the Lancashire & Yorkshire Railway Companies, as well as at the Railway Clearing House. While the Executive Committee itself took supreme control and direction, much of the detail work for which the occasion arose was delegated, in the first instance, to special or sub-committees formed of members of the Executive Committee, of railway officers and of representatives of the Army, the Navy, and of various State Departments in such combinations as the particular subjects to be dealt with might render expedient.

Initial Troop Movements.

The first of the many traffic problems arising out of the war, so far as the railways were concerned, was that which related to the work of mobilisation and the despatch of the first Expeditionary Force to France. These two operations were carried out simultaneously, and they subjected to a severe test the aforesaid precautionary peace-time preparations. The following figures deal with the mobilisation movements, which extended over a period of about fifteen days— approximately the first half of the month of August, 1914 :—

Number of						Tonnage of Stores.
Trains.	Troops.	Guns.	Horses.	Vehicles.	Cycles.	
1,408	334,500	700	58,522	5,155	793	5,332

The corresponding movements in connection with the despatch of the Expeditionary Force to France between August 9 and 26 may be shown thus :—

Number of							Tonnage of Stores.
Days.	Trains.	Troops.	Guns.	Horses.	Vehicles.	Cycles.	
16	689	126,496	354	42,284	6,151	2,007	4,937

Each of these operations was a complete success. As regards the latter the Official Press Bureau announced on August 18, 1914.

" The Expeditionary Force, as detailed for foreign service, has been safely landed on French soil. The embarkation, transportation and disembarkation of men and stores were alike carried through with the greatest possible precision and without a single casualty."

Lord Kitchener, then Secretary for War, said in the House of Lords on August 25, 1914.

" The railway companies, in the all-important matter of the transport facilities, have more than justified the complete confidence reposed in them by the War Office, all grades of railway service having laboured with untiring energy and patience. And it is well to repeat that the conveyance of our troops across the Channel was accomplished, thanks to the cordial co-operation of the Admiralty, with perfect smoothness and without any untoward incident whatever."

Lord French afterwards added his testimony to the same effect, writing from France in his despatch of September 9, 1914 :—

" The transport of the troops both by sea and by rail was effected in the best order and without a check. Each unit arrived at its destination in this country well within the scheduled time."

Later Movements.

Following on mobilisation and the despatch of the first Expeditionary Force came the constant flow of reinforcements and of fresh armies for overseas. The movement of men to and from their depôts and the training centres set up all over the country, or to and from these places and their homes, when they were on leave, became an enormous business in itself. The railways had to provide, also, for the transport here, not alone of British armies, in their manifold movements, but for that of all the Colonial and American Forces landed in this country and spending certain periods in training camps before going on to France. Special leave trains for men from the Western Front became an established daily institution. With the setting up of the Ministry of Munitions, the impetus given to shipyard activities, and the vastly increased output of war manufactures generally, many thousands of workpeople had to be carried daily by rail between their work and their homes. Great numbers of other persons besides, coming under the definition of "war workers," travelled either on free "warrants" or reduced-fare "vouchers" granted by one or other of the numerous departments of the State which had authority to issue them.

Enlistment of Railwaymen.

So many reservists, territorials and volunteer recruits left the railway service to join the Colours that as early as September, 1914, the prospect already seemed to be arising of a serious impairment of the railway service at a time when the maintenance of its complete efficiency was being regarded as a matter of vital importance. Yet on the occasion of each successive special appeal from that time onwards for more and still more recruits the railway companies were urged to make a generous response thereto by releasing either a further definite number of their staff or as many as they could, and the drain upon their resources in the way of personnel became practically continuous.

The places of many men of military age working on railways could be filled by substitutes, male or female, though these were far from having the experience or the physical powers of those whom they succeeded. There were, also, many skilled railwaymen—drivers and signalmen, for example—for whom, beyond a certain number, it was a very difficult matter, indeed, to find substitutes. Then there came a time when railwaymen were especially wanted overseas to construct, repair and operate military railways or to engage in other essentially railway work at the various fronts, and more especially in France. To some extent this want was supplied by transferring from the fighting forces men who were already experienced in railway work. Others, similarly experienced, were drafted from the Colonial contingents; but there still remained the need to send many more railwaymen from this country to do the work for which they were specially fitted and urgently required.

In the result the total number of railwaymen who had been released for service with the Colours down to the end of December, 1918, was no fewer than 184,475, or over 30 per cent. of the total pre-war staff of about 600,000.

Among the 184,000 in question were some 25,000 who joined railway units of the Royal Engineers formed for the carrying out of railway or analogous duties on the Lines of Communication. Such duties included the Railway Construction Corps, which consisted of civil engineers, platelayers and others engaged in laying both broad and narrow gauge military railways for the use of our troops overseas; the Railway Operating Division, comprising civil engineers, engine drivers, firemen, shunters and signalmen, who were concerned partly in the construction and the repairing of locomotives and partly in the working of the traffic in the various theatres of war; the Railway Transport Establishment, the members of which, largely composed of the railway supervisory staffs, co-ordinated and supervised military traffic arrangements on the Western Front, in addition to undertaking at railway stations, &c., the duties devolving in England upon railway transport officers; and the Military Forwarding Establishment, which, recruited from station-masters, checkers and the clerical staffs of the railways, dealt with parcels and comforts sent out to the troops and undertook a variety of other duties besides.

Railwaymen "Loaned."

In addition to losing the services, for the time being, of so large a proportion of their staffs by reason of enlistment, the companies "loaned" those of various general managers, of deputy-general managers, of chief officers and of some 2,000 employees of all grades, though chiefly clerks, to various Government departments, including many of those specially created for the purposes of the war.

Among the railway officers undertaking positions or duties of exceptional importance in connection with Government departments were Sir Albert Stanley, appointed President of the Board of Trade; Sir Guy Granet, late General Manager of the Midland Railway, who became Director-General of Movements and Railways, and afterwards, at the request of His Majesty's Government, visited the United States, in connection with food and transport problems there; Sir Sam Fay, General Manager of the Great Central, appointed to the control of military and munition movements in Great Britain in connection with the Department of Military Railways, and subsequently successor to Sir Guy Granet as Director-General of Movements and Railways; Sir Guy Calthrop, General Manager of the London & North Western Railway, who died in harness as Controller of Coal Mines; and last, though certainly not least, the Rt. Hon. Sir Eric Geddes, G.C.B., G.B.E., M.P., late Deputy-General Manager of the North Eastern Railway, who, among other positions, became successively Deputy Director-General of Munitions Supply; Director-General of Military Railways; Inspector-General of Transportation; First Lord of the Admiralty; representative of the War Cabinet in the co-ordination of activities of various Government departments in regard to demobilisation; and First Minister of Transport, under the terms of the Ministry of Transport Act (1919).

Manufacture of Munitions of War.

Within one month of the outbreak of war the railway companies were appealed to by the military authorities to undertake the supply from their locomotive and carriage workshops of various necessaries urgently required but not procurable from the ordinary manufacturers with the speed and on the scale that had alike become indispensable. The first of these requests was for 12,000 ambulance stretchers. It was received on September 2, 1914, and by September 5 the announcement was made that eleven companies had divided the work between them and would be ready to send in the first deliveries by September 12. Then there came repeated orders for general service wagons, which, again, were promptly supplied; and after this there were received so many orders for different articles, either from the War Office direct, from Woolwich Arsenal, or from manufacturers in want of help, that the railway workshops began to be actively employed on Government work to the neglect of their ordinary activities. Thereupon the Railway Executive Committee appointed a Railway War Manufactures Sub-Committee in order that the whole business should be properly organised. The railway companies were to undertake no manufactures which could be supplied by ordinary business firms, and it was arranged that what they did for the Government should be done at cost price, plus workshop expenses and an allowance for supervision and establishment charges, though in the case of Government work done for private firms a further 10 per cent., for profit, was to be added.

As time went on and the need for munitions overseas became urgent, the Executive Committee suggested that the facilities offered by the railway workshops might be further utilised in the supply of these particular needs. This was prior to the creation of the Ministry of Munitions, and the offer made was warmly accepted by the Government. So the railway companies, depending to a considerable extent on women workers, developed into producers of shells and every other possible kind of munitions on a scale which, when the Ministry of Munitions had attained its full strength, assumed enormous proportions. This fact will be sufficiently appreciated from the statement that the total value of the munitions and military necessaries produced by them during the course of the war amounted to no less a sum than £15,250,000.

Construction and Repair of Engines and Wagons.

The manufacture of this immense volume of munitions, coupled with the shortage of both materials and of workshop staffs, reacted to a very serious extent on the construction and repair of engines and rolling-stock. So far was this the case that by the end of August, 1918, the companies were short of about 2,000 new locomotives and about 33,000 wagons which, under normal conditions, they would have built since the beginning of the war. In addition to this there were awaiting repair, at the same date, 5,000 locomotives, or more than one-fifth of the total stock owned by the companies; 37,000 wagons, or 5 per cent. of the total stock; and 8,000 carriages, constituting 10 per cent. of the total.

Permanent Way.

By reason of a like combination of causes, the railway companies were greatly troubled by the diminution in their supply of rails; though here, no doubt, the main factor in the situation was the enormous demand for steel for munitions and other exclusively naval or military purposes. Normally the railways require somewhat over 200,000 tons of steel per annum for the maintenance and renewal of their permanent way; but from the beginning of the war until towards the end of 1918 probably not more than about 100,000 tons altogether had been available for them. Hence the companies got considerably behind in their relaying work, one result of which was that many of the trunk lines had to limit the speed of their trains over long sections of line. Subsequently, however, a certain amount of steel was allocated to the railways to enable them to relay the more important sections of their lines.

Railway Material for Overseas.

At the end of 1916 the companies were called on to send 300 locomotives to France, to assist in the transport of the British armies there. From this time down to the beginning of 1919 no fewer than 675 locomotives of various types were sent to the various theatres of war in order to meet War Office requirements. These locomotives were supplemented by 30,000 open goods wagons supplied from the railway companies stock (apart from a large number of privately owned wagons), together with 100 special rail-carrying wagons and 40 up-to-date 30-ton coal wagons. Of 20-ton covered wagons, specially designed, 2,500 were constructed in the railway companies' workshops and sent to France, for the use of our armies there. These were subsequently followed by 20 passenger trains for use as leave and demobilisation trains on the extended lines of communication.

Strong appeals were also made to the railway companies from time to time to supply material for the construction in France of additional lines, broad gauge and narrow gauge, which were most urgently needed by our armies, and more especially so to enable them to follow up the enemy on his retirement. The companies responded to these appeals to the very best of their power, having regard to all those demands which absolutely had to be met at home. So it was that they were able to send across the Channel 72,000 tons, otherwise 204 miles of rails and 20,000 sleepers; though in a number of instances these supplies were obtained only by closing certain local lines altogether or by reducing other lines from double to single track.

Among the railway material supplied might be mentioned 2,500 platelayers' trolleys, 19 high-power cranes and 2 electric gantry-cranes, the last-mentioned being built by the London & North Western Railway for use on the lines in France. Nor should the fact be overlooked that railway workshops erected in various parts of France for the purposes of the war were not only designed and constructed with the aid of British locomotive engineers but were, to a great extent, equipped with machinery taken from the locomotive workshops of British railway companies.

Ambulance Trains.

Considerable demand was made on the activities of the railway companies by reason of the provision and the running of ambulance trains.

For the conveyance of sick and wounded soldiers to hospitals or other destinations in this country, the companies supplied the War Office with 20 ambulance trains, the cars for which had been mostly adapted from existing stock and fitted up with every comfort and convenience necessary for the journeys undertaken. Five other ambulance trains were provided at the request of the naval authorities for sick and wounded seamen, the internal fittings of the latter trains being of a somewhat different type from those of the former. Then the companies furnished 30 ambulance trains—comprising, with spare coaches, 499 vehicles, mostly of bogie stock—for the use of our troops overseas; they provided 19 other ambulance trains, having 304 vehicles, for the American armies overseas, while the construction of 29 other ambulance trains for the United States armies was being proceeded with when the armistice was signed.

The building of the ambulance trains actually supplied meant, in the first place, the taking of over 800 vehicles, constituting some of the very best types of rolling-stock, from available supplies; and, in the next place, the absorption of a considerable amount of time on the part of the diminished staffs in the railway workshops; though, as against these considerations, the advantages conferred on the sick and wounded by the provision of the trains were, of course, incalculable.

Thanks to these ambulance trains, supplemented by the hospital ships, it was possible to bring the wounded to this country with such speed that they were on various occasions landed here the same day that the engagement in which they got their wounds had been fought in France, and to distribute them, mainly from Southampton or Dover, among the hospitals throughout England, Wales and Scotland, many of them going as far north as Aberdeen or Strathpeffer. Once more, therefore, the railways rendered good service; yet, as a matter of working detail, the fact had to be recognised that the running of all these ambulance trains throughout the war, and so often for such long distances, did, inevitably, tend to complicate a traffic situation already presenting difficulties in many other directions.

Railway Material Supplied for Home Use.

In addition to the railway material sent abroad, in whatever shape or form, and to the rolling-stock utilised for ambulance trains at home, the companies lent many locomotives to the War Office, the Admiralty, the Ministry of Munitions or other State departments for use in arsenals, munition factories, &c., or for the internal working of the various camp railways. No fewer, also, than 3,000 wagons were supplied under like conditions. In one instance, at least, the rails of a local line on the Highland Railway were taken up in order that they could be utilised for other lines urgently wanted elsewhere in Scotland for special purposes in connection with Government traffic.

Much material and much time were further absorbed by the construction in railway workshops of wagons specially adapted to the conveyance of heavy guns, tanks, aeroplanes and many other kinds of exceptional traffics. At an early stage of the war, two complete armoured trains were built for use on the East Coast in case of invasion.

Restrictions on Travel.

As the combined result of so many locomotives being sent abroad, of the depletion of the staffs by enlistments, of the trouble experienced in regard to coal supply, and of the magnitude of the Government traffic, for which preference had necessarily to be shown, various restrictions were imposed from time to time— beginning with the end of 1916—in order to reduce the volume of ordinary passenger travel to what was then regarded as the absolutely essential. Nearly the whole of the cheap travel facilities were, in successive instalments, swept away; the ordinary train services were drastically reduced; express trains were decelerated; many stations, together with certain local lines, were closed; passenger fares were increased by 50 per cent., and the amount of personal luggage allowed per passenger was limited to 100 lb. per head.

For a time these various restrictions, and especially the increase of 50 per cent. in the fares, did have an appreciable effect in reducing travel; but, in the later stages of the war, what with the number of people who had become well-to-do as the result either of their work on munitions or of their war-time profits as manufacturers or traders, and what, also, with the number of soldiers and sailors on leave who paid their own fare, the amount of passenger traffic to be carried by the railways, in spite of their decreased resources, and in spite of the fact that, by the autumn of 1918, there had been brought about a reduction of above 40 per cent in the main line services, assumed greater proportions than ever before. The deterrent effect of the 50 per cent. increase had practically disappeared by the early part of 1919, and absolutely so by August in that same year.

Regulation of Passenger Travel.

At one time there was brought under consideration a scheme for the issuing of " permits " for travel in respect to other than what would be practically suburban traffic. It was seen that the 50 per cent. increase in fares had practically no effect on those who could well afford to pay the difference, and it was argued that the only effectual restraint upon such people as these would be obtained if everybody who wanted to travel beyond a certain distance were required first to secure a " permit " to be granted only for journeys which could be shown to be thoroughly justifiable.

The scheme was subjected to an exhaustive investigation by a committee of railway experts. The conclusion arrived at was that the adoption of it would necessitate the setting up of an elaborate and widespread organisation for examining the claims of those who sought to procure the " permits," and it was felt that the railway companies, at least, with their depleted staffs, could not possibly undertake such an addition to their already abnormal tasks. If, alternatively, the Government undertook the working of the system, this would involve the creation of a new State department having headquarters in London and branches in every populous centre throughout the United Kingdom. The creation of a large staff would be necessary, much trouble and time would be involved in elaborating and setting up the necessary machinery, and many practical difficulties in working the proposal would arise. So the idea of travel permits was abandoned ; but the Lancashire & Yorkshire Railway Company brought into operation on its own account a system under which tickets limited in number to actual seating capacity were put on sale at leading stations for certain trains some days in advance of the running thereof, holders of the tickets so issued being alone carried by those trains. The method thus adopted was found to be of great practical advantage in the handling of holiday traffic. It was also declared by patrons of the trains to be a complete success from the point of view of their own comfort and convenience.

Luggage in Advance.

Down to December, 1916, the railway companies had in operation a system under which they collected in advance, from residence, the baggage of persons proposing to travel by their lines, conveyed it by rail, and delivered it at destination for an inclusive and prepaid charge of 1s. 3d. per package, not exceeding 112 lb. in weight.

With the further object of reducing labour, the suspension of this practice followed the other restrictions on travel recorded above.

Carted Luggage.

A like course was, at the same time, adopted in regard to what was known as " carted luggage "—that is to say, luggage which the passenger himself took to the departure station and, while saving the company any need to collect, left them to carry it by rail and deliver it at destination for an inclusive and prepaid rate of 9d. per package, again not exceeding 112 lb.

Traffic Difficulties.

The closing of certain ports on the east coast to trading vessels ; the risks to shipping resulting from the naval policy of the enemy ; the consequent increase in marine insurance, and the commandeering of so many merchantmen for the purposes of troop transport, &c., combined to divert to the railways a great amount of traffic that had previously gone by coasting steamers, the already heavy demands upon the facilities at the disposal of the companies being swollen proportionately.

Another set of difficulties soon began to arise inasmuch as there was developed a tendency on the part of almost everyone concerned in the sending of traffic by rail—whether traders, Government officials, or naval and military authorities—to reduce very seriously the proportions of the available transport by failing to unload wagons promptly ; by causing them to stand idle for what were often considerable periods ; by inadequate loading of wagons ; by forwarding for short distances consignments they might very well have sent by road, and by a resort in various other ways, besides, to what the railway people themselves regarded as wholly unnecessary rail journeys.

As a means of ensuring a better use of the wagons, the Railway Executive Committee enforced demurrage penalties against traders who exceeded the free period allowed to them for unloading, and they secured the appointment of joint committees comprising railway officers and representatives of Government departments concerned in naval, military or munitions traffic, arrangements being made that all cases of undue detentions of wagons, inadequate loading, &c., should be reported and at once investigated by inquiries made on the spot or otherwise. The adoption of this principle produced excellent results. It led to the checking of most, though by no means all, of the abuses which had arisen through the, perhaps natural, failure of contractors, naval and military officers, Government officials and others to appreciate technicalities essential to the efficient working of the railway system, and it also facilitated the inauguration of a system of traffic regulation which aimed at checking congestion and ensuring priority to consignments according to their various degrees of urgency.

Increase in Goods Traffic.

One inevitable consequence of the reduction in shipping facilities, due in part to the commandeering of merchantmen by the Government, though still more to the submarine campaign of the enemy, was a great falling off in the volume of imports. Any decline in railway traffic in this direction was, however, more than counterbalanced by increases in other directions. Absolute necessaries which could no longer be imported at all, or only in diminished quantities, had to be produced at home instead. This was the case with many of our food supplies, to the conveyance of which the railways had to give a preferential treatment not to be regarded as in any way " undue." It was the case, also, with timber, wanted for pit-props, hutments, sleepers, cases in which to send munitions overseas, and a thousand other purposes besides. In the days before the war we depended for timber mainly on imports. We were now to learn that for the duration of the war we should have to depend mainly on the timber already available at home. This was certainly plentiful, but there was a shortage of men. Happily our kith and kin from overseas came to the rescue by supplementing the available forces of the British timber trade. Forestry Corps were formed in Canada and Newfoundland. They were formed also in the New England States. They crossed to this country with all possible despatch, and before long the forests, more especially of Scotland, became scenes of great activity in the felling and the preparation of timber at the camps and the mills that were set up, while the railways carried prodigious loads, and, in some instances—notably the Highland Railway—found their wagon resources severely taxed for the conveyance even of this one commodity alone.

In the same way we had to depend more on home supplies of steel and iron. Then the munition works set up in so many parts of Great Britain led to a vast amount of traffic of an exceptionally varied type. The railways had first to convey the building material wanted for constructing new works or for extending old ones. They had next to carry the machinery needed for fitting up the works. Then came the raw materials for manufacture, followed, possibly, by several movements of partly-finished munitions and of transport of the finished articles to some other part of the country for " inspection," before they were finally sent off to a port for despatch overseas. That the output of munitions in this country was stupendous is known to all the world ; but from a railway point of view it was a matter, not only of conveying practically the whole of this output by rail, but, having regard to all these preliminary processes, of carrying it by rail many times over.

There was the traffic, again, that became necessary in connection with training camps and in supplying the wants of our own armies and the armies of our allies either passing through this country or looking to us to meet requirements which all needed rail transport together with more or less handling at the railway termini.

Another leading item on the list of war-time traffics was represented by coal—the coal that went in a steady and apparently never-ending succession of " specials " from South Wales to North Eastern or to Scottish ports for the Fleet, or the coal wanted for commercial or domestic purposes that would formerly have gone by water but was now conveyed almost entirely by rail.

There is no need to mention all the other items that might be added to the list; but one especially significant cause of traffic troubles on the railways should not be overlooked—namely, that, which arose from the fact that, inasmuch as the railways became the only form of transport which maintained its pre-war rates throughout, traders of every possible class thought to save money in consigning their commodities by rail even when transport by coasting vessel or by canal was available and might just as well be adopted by them, apart from what had now become the greater cost of the water route.

As the result of all these and of other analogous conditions, the railways found that, in spite of their depleted resources in men and material, they were actually dealing with a greater volume of traffic than they had done under normal conditions; and the question as to how the difficulties which arose were to be efficiently surmounted was one that became, almost from the very outset, one of steadily increasing gravity.

Exceptional Traffics.

Apart from the tonnage of the traffic carried, there were various circumstances or conditions which led to the work done frequently involving a much greater effort on the part of the railways than would be necessary for the conveyance of an equivalent tonnage under peace-time conditions.

There were, for example, traffics of such exceptional weight or size, or. both, that no ordinary railway wagon could accommodate them, and special vehicles had to be made, or at least adapted, for their transport. Among many other consignments of this type were "tanks," aeroplanes, heavy guns, armour plates, boilers, traction engines and ships' machinery.

Dislocation of Traffic.

Then, also, as against the reduction in the sum total of the imports there was to be put the fact that, owing to the greater gravity of the enemy submarine campaign, and to the changes made in the flow of shipping, beginning with the end of 1916, a considerable proportion of the traffic which had formerly been dealt with at ports on the East Coast was transferred to those on the West Coast, throwing alike upon them and upon the railway facilities there a greater strain than they had originally been designed to bear. Relief in one direction was thus secured at the cost of greater effort and increased difficulty in another.

Pooling of Railway Wagons.

The "shortage" of railway wagons which, at the outset of the war and under the conditions already narrated, was mainly due to other causes than an inadequate supply, tended to become a reality when so many were being sent overseas, were used on Government property at home, or were falling out of repair on account of inadequate labour and material, and when also the traffic demands were assuming such greatly increased proportions. So the problem arose as to the best way in which this now actual and steadily increasing shortage could be met.

The popular remedy for overcoming any difficulties arising in respect to wagon supply was the creation of a vast "pool" of railway wagons of all kinds in order that these could be used indiscriminately without regard to ownership or locality.

Similar proposals had been heard long before the war broke out; but, in proportion as the traffic situation became more acute, the "pooling" theory was advocated with increased persistence in many different quarters, and the whole question was subjected to exhaustive examination by the Board of Trade and the Railway Executive Committee in combination with traffic experts and representatives of the different interests concerned.

The further, however, that the investigations were carried, the greater did the complexities of the situation appear to be.

Private Owners' Wagons.

The total number of railway wagons in use on the outbreak of the war was, approximately, 1,450,000; but of these only about one half belonged to and were under the control of the railway companies, the remainder being the property of private owners, mainly colliery companies or coal merchants, who, under the early railway laws of

England, still retain the right to run their wagons on the railways, subject to certain conditions. These actual owners, together with wagon-building companies and associations or federations for the defence of private owners' rights and privileges, represented trading and financial interests on an exceptionally large and powerful scale, so that the carrying through of any proposals threatening a serious dislocation alike of these interests and of the trading customs and conditions which have grown up in connection with them was a matter not to be entered upon even as a war-time emergency measure without adequate consideration.

Apart, also, from the complicated financial questions involved, there was the fact that a large proportion of the privately-owned wagons had been so constructed that, although well adapted to the special traffics for which they were designed, they were not suited for the carriage of other commodities, while the bringing of all of them under a common-user scheme might involve a serious interference with the coal industry.

Very great difficulties in an indiscriminate user of private owners' wagons would have arisen in the carrying out of repairs upon them, the practice of the owners generally being to make contracts with repairing firms which keep in stock the spare parts necessary for a particular type among the great variety of wagons. These spare parts might not be obtainable elsewhere, and if the wagons, instead of being run only on their regular routes, were sent to distant parts of the country, and there got in need of repair, the necessity might arise of loading them on to other wagons in order to bring them back to the workshops where the repairs could alone be effected. A variety of other more or less serious difficulties were also indicated.

Certain advantages were obtained when, in March, 1916, the President of the Board of Trade made an order under the Defence of the Realm Act authorising the railway companies to load up private owners' wagons on their return journey when but for this the wagons would travel empty. Other steps were subsequently taken for enabling still further use to be made of such of the private owners' wagons as were suitable for ordinary goods transport purposes. The railway companies thus secured some degree of compensation for the wagons they had sent overseas. They were also placed in a somewhat better position than they would otherwise have been in to respond to the transport needs not only of the Government but of the traders of the country in general.

Railway-Owned Wagons.

Apart from the possibility or otherwise of bringing private owners' wagons into a pool of all railway wagons of whatever kind, there was the question as to whether railway-owned wagons, at least, might not be formed into a pool by themselves; and here, again, an investigation into all the points at issue was made. Once more, however, it became evident that a really indiscriminate user even of all railway-owned wagons was impracticable owing, among other causes, to the absence of standardisation in the construction of the wagons; to the fact that certain wagons were necessarily kept for particular classes of commodities, and to the consideration that many railway-owned coal wagons built to suit the discharging appliances at certain groups of ports or works would be unsuited to others where the appliances provided were of a different type.

A limited form of common-user of railway-owned wagons was nevertheless agreed to, there being brought into operation by the Railway Executive, as from January 2, 1917 (though subject to certain exceptions), a common-user of ordinary open goods wagons having sides of three or more planks and doors on both sides the full depth of the wagon. In this way about 300,000 wagons, of a generally useful type belonging to the controlled companies of Great Britain, were made available for use in any direction on the lines of any of those companies.

Subsequently the situation was further relieved by an arrangement under which the companies obtained the use, on hire, of wagons belonging to the private owners.

Goods Traffic "Restrictions."

In quite the early days of the war much congestion of lines, sidings and terminals, together with difficulties and delays in handling traffic, arose by reason of the fact that goods were being sent forward in quantities beyond the capacity either of their destination points or of their consignees to accept delivery and release the wagons promptly for further service elsewhere. These conditions were, no doubt, due in many instances to shortage of staffs on the part of the traders; but the result was none the less a source of great trouble to the railway companies and a leading cause of the traffic troubles in general which were then arising.

As a means of meeting the situation, the expedient was resorted to of putting "stops" on traffic in certain directions until it could be shown that the consignees would be able to deal with it on delivery. A similar principle was afterwards applied to shipping traffic, the railway companies declining to accept such traffic for transit until the shipping company or the dock authority concerned had intimated that they were in a position to receive it.

Good results followed from the adoption of this system, among the advantages derived from it being a better user of wagons, less waste of engine power in shunting and diminished risk of congestion. It was found, however, that the benefits gained were not so great as they might and should have been, the reason therefor being that the application of the principle was intermittent, and not regular. So it was that, under the combination of difficulties by which the companies were faced, in various directions—culminating in the adoption of the eight-hour day, the increased diversion of coasting traffic to the railways and the heavy traffic still passing on Government account—there was adopted a further scheme which provided for certain places a daily programme for the acceptance of traffic from any and every part of the country, such programme varying from day to day, as might be necessary, to suit changing conditions due to such factors as heavy consignments either of Government traffic or of food supplies.

All these measures, whatever the amount of inconvenience caused by them to individual traders, were designed to ensure traffic regulation rather than to bring about traffic restriction; and the effect of them was to prevent much greater trouble arising on the railways than that actually experienced and, also, to improve the traffic situation so far as it concerned the traders of the country in general.

Unloading of Wagons.

Mention has been made of the fact that, in the early days of the war, the Railway Executive Committee sought to ensure a prompter unloading of wagons by a more rigid enforcement of demurrage penalties. As time went on, however, it became obvious that this remedy would be ineffectual since in many instances it was to the advantage of the trader to pay demurrage in order that he could retain the wagons until it suited his convenience to unload them.

In December, 1916, an addition ("7b") to the Defence of the Realm Regulations gave power to the Board of Trade, "for the purpose of making the most efficient use of railway plant for the prosecution of the war," to issue orders for, amongst other purposes, enforcing the prompt loading or unloading of wagons by making failure to load or unload in accordance with such order a summary offence against the Defence of the Realm Regulations. Further power was given, in February, 1917, for the making of similar orders "for enabling wagons which are not promptly unloaded by the consignee to be unloaded, and their contents to be dealt with, at the risk and expense of the consignee."

Orders in accordance with these powers, applying to (1) unloading of wagons and (2) detention of wagons and sheets, in regard to England and Wales and Scotland respectively, and reducing the "free period" previously allowed before the imposition of demurrage charges, were made by the President of the Board of Trade in March, 1917.

Coal Transport.

Among still other measures adopted with a view to relieving the strain upon the railways and utilising engine power and rolling-stock to the best advantage was the resort to a scheme of coal transport re-organisation.

In February, 1917, following on certain labour troubles in the coal industry and on a decline in the output of coal owing to enlistments and other causes, the Government announced their intention to take control over all the coal mines of the country as from March 1 of that year; and Mr. (afterwards Sir Guy) Calthrop, General Manager of the London & North Western Railway, was appointed Controller of Coal Mines, to act under the Board of Trade with the assistance of an advisory board formed by representatives of both coal owners and miners.

One of the earliest problems which thus arose was that of distribution. A large proportion of the coal raised went to districts themselves raising coal and sending it elsewhere, and, even allowing for special qualities the importation of which into these other districts was indispensable, there was a great amount of cross traffic that might very well be considerably reduced. The Coal Controller accordingly devised a Coal Transport Re-organisation Scheme under which Great Britain was divided into 20 areas, 16 in England and Wales, and 4 in Scotland, and, by virtue of a Board of Trade Order made with the authority of the Defence of the Realm Regulations, he directed that on and from September 8, 1917, coal for inland consumption should be forwarded by railway from any one of these areas only to such other area or areas as were specified by him, though movement within the area of production was not interfered with.

It was anticipated that, apart from a saving in labour in regard to the handling of empty trucks and in the marshalling and shunting both of empty and loaded ones, there would be a saving of 700,000,000 ton-miles per annum, in railway haulage. This expectation may have been unduly sanguine, and all railway companies may not have gained equal advantages, proportionately to the amount of coal traffic they carried; but there is reason to believe that the saving in ton-miles was, in the aggregate, very considerable and of much service in helping to improve the railway situation.

Allocation of Traffic.

Under peace-time conditions traders claimed, and exercised, the right to forward their traffic by such company, or such route, and to such terminal station, as they thought fit; and they were naturally encouraged in this tendency by companies competing one with the other for traffic which two or more of them might carry.

With a view to economising engine power, securing better loading of wagons, and saving mileage under the variety of traffic difficulties and complications already told, the further expedient was adopted, in May, 1917, of allocating goods traffic between certain definite points to stated companies and by stated routes, information as to which could be obtained by the trader at his local station. The adoption of this principle, which subsequently underwent further developments, was quite consistent with the idea at the basis of State control, namely, that the railways of the country should be worked as a single unit, while it was rendered practicable by reason of the disappearance of competition.

The results may not have been quite satisfactory from the point of view of the trader who could no longer receive his traffic at the particular station which might be the one most convenient to himself; but for the railways they meant that the wagons were loaded to better advantage, and that the traffic went by shorter routes, with a consequent reduction in haulage, and also with less shunting. Against, therefore, any inconvenience caused to individual traders there was to be put a material advantage for the community, and one from which the individual trader himself stood to gain through the betterment effected in the general transport conditions.

From June, 1918, arrangements were made from time to time to allocate, on the same principle, parcels passing in large number between important towns. Once more the objects aimed at were to concentrate the traffic as far as possible and to forward it by the most direct route, thus securing better loading and avoiding circuitous conveyance, unnecessary transfer, handling at junctions and delays in transit. The working of the system was, on the whole, found to be very satisfactory.

Prepayment of Passenger-Train Traffic.

On April 2, 1917, there was brought into force a regulation under which all parcels forwarded by passenger train had to be paid for in advance. Here the advantages gained included greater expedition in delivery of the parcels, inasmuch as the carmen had no longer to collect carriage charges ; the avoidance of disputes (often causing much correspondence) as to the responsibility for payment at destination, and the simplification of book-keeping at the stations.

Transport Workers' Battalions.

Congestion in the leading docks of the country, akin to that which became acute in the summer of 1919, began to develop in quite an early stage of the war. By November, 1915, it had increased to such proportions that a Committee known as the Port and Transit Executive Committee was appointed by the Government to deal with it. Deficiency in the available labour was found to be one of the causes of the trouble, and in February, 1916, it was decided to create a Transport Workers' Battalion in order that an organised body of men, working under the control of the said Committee, might be available to assist, whenever necessary, with the loading, discharging and handling of traffic at docks. The members of this battalion were to be men from the Home Army who had previously been engaged in occupations which qualified them to undertake dock work. They would be " lent " for this purpose as the occasion required, would have the status of a military unit, and be subject to military law ; though it was understood that they were to be used only to supplement the available supply of local labour, that they might be moved about from place to place according to requirements, and that while at work in any port they would receive the same rates of pay as civilians engaged on similar duties.

So successful did the scheme become that, after a time, it was extended in order to permit of men belonging to the battalion being sent to inland industrial centres to assist in the loading or unloading of railway wagons. Once more success was scored, and eventually the original battalion expanded into a series of battalions comprising a membership of about 10,000 men. Great Britain was divided into areas, each area having its local committee, with a railway officer for its chairman, and an additional means of much practical utility was afforded for surmounting difficulties arising on railways in connection, more especially, with the handling of sudden rushes of traffic by otherwise inadequate staffs.

Government Control of Canals.

The condition to which the railways had been reduced led to the belief that their difficulties would be considerably mitigated if only a greater use could be made of such of the canals and waterways as were still available for traffic.

Those owned by the railway companies, or in which railway companies had the controlling influence had already passed, together with the railways themselves, under Government control by virtue of the arrangements made in August, 1914, and the Railway Executive Committee were able to give such directions for their utilisation as circumstances and conditions would permit. The staffs, also, on the railway-owned canals shared in the various advantages gained by other railway employees. The position, however, on the independently-owned canals was altogether different and very much to their disadvantage. The canal companies lost a large proportion of their staffs through the earlier enlistments, voluntary or compulsory, without their having the same means of retaining indispensable men as had been conceded to the railway companies ; they had no State aid in the way of giving war bonuses to men who might still have remained with them but for the temptation of higher rates of pay elsewhere, while, owing to the consequent shortage of boatmen, crews, boat-builders and boat-repairers, a large number of vessels remained idle, either because there was no one to work them or because they could not be put into a fit condition to be worked. The canal carriers and bye-traders also lost a large number of their men through enlistment. Then, not being under statutory restrictions in the same way as railway companies, they increased their rates in order to meet their higher working costs, whereas the railway-owned canals, owing to the Government control, could pay war bonuses and, at the same time, avoid any increases in rates.

It was sought in March, 1917, to meet this position by bringing the more important of the privately-owned canals under the control of a Canal Control Committee (Board of Trade). By the end of 1918 the number of separate companies thus dealt with was 31, namely,

26 in England and Wales and 5 in Ireland. Numerous advantages were realised from the adoption of this course. The Government undertook to place the canal companies thus taken over on practically the same footing as the controlled railway companies in guaranteeing to them their net revenue of 1913. Later on a similar guarantee was given to canal carriers who kept in commission as many boats as they were working in 1913. Canal men in the employ of independent canal companies were to have bonuses similar to those paid to canal men employed by the railway companies.

Indiscriminate enlistment of canal men (and especially those over 25 years of age) was checked, as it had been in the case of railwaymen. A number of men of low medical category, but possessing a knowledge of canal work, who had already joined up, were released from the Army and allowed to go back to their former employment. In order still further to meet the labour difficulty, it was arranged that men belonging to the Transport Workers' Battalion should be available for service on the canals, and steps were taken to put them through a course of training in canal operation.

Concurrently with these measures, efforts were made to organise the traffic on the canals. Sub-committees of the Central Control Committee were formed for the Northern, Midland and Southern districts of England and also for Ireland, with headquarters at Leeds, Birmingham, London and Dublin respectively. Active steps were taken to induce State departments and private traders to send their traffic by canal, whenever they could do so, in order that the railways might have a proportionate degree of relief.

So far as the State departments—and notably the Ministry of Munitions and the Ministry of Food—were concerned, a good deal of traffic that might otherwise have been put on railways was sent by canal, instead ; but the results in the way of inducing private traders to consign by water were much less successful than had been desired. Theoretically, there were many more traders who might have used, or made more use of, the canals. When, however, for one or other of a variety of reasons, the railway was regarded as the better or the more convenient form of transport from the point of view at least, of the particular works or establishments concerned, it was often found impossible to secure the desired transfer, and the traffic was put on the rail as before.

Employment of Women.

Railway companies were among the first of the country's greatest employers of labour to engage women as a definite means both of meeting the shrinkage in male staffs owing to enlistment and of enabling them to accomplish the special war work—more particularly in the making of munitions—which they undertook. Begun on a small scale, the resort to this expedient rapidly broadened out until eventually there was scarcely a single branch of the railway service offering scope for woman's work in which women were not to be found.

Women were, of course, employed on British railways long before the war began. The total number thereof in the early days of August, 1914, was, in round figures, 13,000. Of these approximately one-third were on railway work proper—mainly clerical work—while two-thirds came under " other categories," including hotel staff, waitresses, charwomen, &c. By the end of January, 1917, the total had increased to 49,086, namely, railway work, 36,570 ; munitions, 2,637 ; other categories, 9,879. A maximum in the number of women employed on munitions was reached in October, 1917, when the figure stood at 4,698. The maximum in the sum total of women engaged on railways in whatever capacity was attained in September, 1918. It amounted to 68,801—an increase of 55,755 over the total for August 4, 1914—and was made up thus : Railway work, 55,942 ; munitions, 2,182 ; other categories, 10,677.

Financial Results.

Complete figures as to the financial results of operation of the railways under conditions of Government control are not yet available ; but there was issued from the Board of Trade, under date April 30, 1919, a statement on " Railway Working during the War " which showed, in the first place, that the estimated value of Government traffic carried on the railways of Great Britain (exclusive of those in Ireland), if such traffic had been charged for at authorised pre-war rates, had been as follows for the periods stated :—

	£
August 5 to December 31, 1914 ..	3,500,000
Year 1915	10,279,104
Year 1916	20,649,126
Year 1917	35,698,554
Year 1918	41,917,024
Total	112,043,808

It was added that these figures were in respect to railway transit only, and that the railway companies had, by means of steamboats, docks, canals, &c., performed a number of additional services for which no charges had been raised. The value of these further services could not be ascertained, but it might be estimated at, roughly, from £10,000,000 to £15,000,000.

The statement further showed that the compensation paid to British railway companies in respect to control periods, on the basis of their net receipts in the year 1913, had been :—

	£
August 5, 1914, to December 31, 1915 ..	15,946,839
Year 1916	14,039,674
Year 1917	24,075,768
Year 1918	41,251,326
Total	95,313,607

Here, again, it was admitted that the figures are incomplete. They include provisional allowances for deferred maintenance of permanent way, rolling-stock and plant, but do not include any provision for " extra wear and tear." " This item," it was added, " cannot be ascertained at present ; but the auditors advise that the cost of making good the ' extra wear and tear ' will be considerable."

Taking, however, the figures as given in the statement, and putting down £12,500,000 as the approximate value of the " additional services " estimated at between £10,000,000 and £15,000,000, we get the following net result :—

	£
Estimated value of Government traffic carried	112,043,808
Estimated value of other services (say)	12,500,000
Total value of services rendered	124,543,808
Compensation paid	95,313,607
Excess value of services rendered over compensation paid	29,230,201

While the last of these items would suggest that the Government made what was indeed, for themselves, a most advantageous " bargain " with the companies on the outbreak of the war, there is to be set against it the payment by the Government of interest at 4 per cent. on capital expenditure which became productive for the first time during or subsequent to the year 1913.

The increased cost of working the railways for the financial year ending March 31, 1920, as compared with 1913, was estimated by the statement as follows :—

	£
War wage and other concessions	57,000,000
Eight-hour day and new concessions recently granted or still under discussion	20/25,000,000
Extra cost of materials and coal	27,000,000
Total	104/109,000,000

Further details as to the financial results of the Government control of railways since the beginning of the war are shown in four statements contained in a Parliamentary Paper [Cmd. 402] dated October 31, 1919.

Summary of Results during Controlled Period.

Below is a summary of the figures showing the results for the whole of the controlled railways in the United Kingdom :—

	Total Revenue Earned. £	Total Expenditure. £	Balance. £
1914 (August 5 to December 31) ..	47,918,000	31,783,000	16,135,000
1915	130,358,000	85,028,000	45,330,000
1916	145,871,000	95,757,000	50,114,000
1917	169,701,000	113,503,000	56,198,000
1918	183,775,000	137,137,000	46,638,000
1919 (to June 30)	87,099,000	79,672,000	7,427,000

The estimated value of all services rendered to the Government free of charge by the railways from August 5, 1914, to June 30, 1919, is £136,000,000 to £141,000,000, according to the value put on services other than actual railway working, the value of the latter being put at £126,192,000.

Railway Deficit.

For the financial year ending March 31, 1920, the estimated deficit was £45,000,000, but it was expected that some slight improvement might be shown by reason of the fact that it had been decided to apply, from April 1, 1919, to Government traffic the same rates of increase as were made to the public. It was considered that this amount would result in a credit to the railway account of £5,000,000. Additionally, it was pointed out that, in the framing of the figures, no allowance was made for any growth of revenue from increases in goods rates which might become operative before the close of the 1919-20 financial year.

New Railway Rates.

A step was soon taken in the direction of increasing the revenue by means of higher charges for freight traffic. In December, 1919, the Minister of Transport, acting in pursuance of his powers under the Ministry of Transport Act, 1919, directed the railway companies of the United Kingdom to advance their goods rates. Accordingly, on December 29, 1919, the Railway Clearing House issued the customary public notification to the effect that increased railway rates and tolls and charges would come into force on January 15, 1920. These increases ranged from 25 per cent. to 60 per cent. on " smalls," on which 100 per cent. increase was imposed. In addition flat rate increases varying between 3d. and 3s. per ton were added, and it was expected that the resultant increased revenue would yield between £40,000,000 and £50,000,000 per annum.

Position at end of Financial Year.

In April, 1920, a White Paper (Cmd. 654) was published in connection with the Ministry of Transport estimates for the financial year 1920-21 and incorporated a statement as to railways. The increase of freight rates, which had been operative from January 15, had brought in approximately £9,000,000 increased revenue, but the actual deficiency for the financial year was £40,500,000. It became necessary, therefore, for the Government to take steps to restore the financial equilibrium, and it was obvious that a further revision of rates and charges would be required.

The Rates Advisory Committee, which was then inquiring into the general question of railway rates and charges, was thereupon instructed to make recommendations for an interim revision in railway charges in order to make good a deficiency which, as from April 1, 1920, was estimated at the rate of £54,500,000 per annum.

In July last, the first report of the Rates Advisory Committee on the interim revision was submitted to the Minister of Transport. This dealt with passenger fares and recommended that new ordinary fares should be $16\frac{2}{3}$ per cent. higher than those then in force, i.e., 75 per cent. above the pre-war level ; season tickets of all descriptions were recommended for an increase of 50 per cent. above the pre-war level, and traders tickets in future were to be issued at the uniform rate of 20 per cent. below the season ticket rates. Workmen's fares, which had been allowed to remain at pre-war rates, were to be based on a scale according to distance. The Cabinet adopted the recommendations and the increase in ordinary fares and season tickets came into operation on August 6, while the new workmen's fares were charged as from September 1.

The report of the Rates Advisory Committee dealing with the increase in freight rates and charges was submitted in August last, and the recommendations followed very closely the suggestions made by the railway companies to meet the situation. The new basis is that all rates in force prior to the last interim revision (i.e., January 14, 1920), with the exception of those for coal, coke, patent fuel (for which special proposals are made) are doubled, while certain flat rate additions are authorised. An exception was, however, made in the case of " smalls," which traffic was increased 150 per cent. above the old level. The rates were brought into operation on September 1.

The result of the increases in passenger fares and freight rates is expected to restore the financial equilibrium of the railway companies by the end of the control period. As, moreover, the increases recommended have been based upon a higher level than was really necessary, in order to meet the accumulated deficit, it is expected that a further revision will be made before the termination of Government control.

ORGANISATION AND WORK OF THE TRANSPORTATION DIRECTORATE.

An Account of the Introduction of a separate Directorate for the Control of Transportation.

The first step towards the establishment of a department for the co-ordination of all transportation was taken in the autumn of 1916, when the Secretary of State for War, Mr. Lloyd George, appointed Sir Eric Geddes, who held the position of Deputy-General Manager of the North Eastern Railway, and was then serving in the Ministry of Munitions, to inquire into the organisation and working of transportation in France.

The outcome of Sir Eric Geddes' report, in which he suggested a thorough re-organisation of all transportation services, was his appointment as Director-General of Transportation in France, with authority to look after all questions of railways, roads, docks and inland water transport. In reply to a question in the House of Lords on November 30, 1916, the Earl of Derby explained the appointment of Sir Eric Geddes in the following words:—

"The Secretary of State for War, knowing that there would be a large and ever-increasing amount of ammunition to be sent to France, was anxious to satisfy himself that the transportation of such ammunition from the ports to the front would be adequate, and with that view he sent Sir Eric Geddes over with instructions to make a full report on the subject. This was done with Sir Douglas Haig's full consent, and the report was given to him for consideration. It impressed him very much, and he adopted the suggestions made therein, and himself asked that Sir Eric Geddes should go to France to carry out his own suggestions. The position, therefore, can be summarised as follows:—The proposal for inquiry came from the Secretary of State for War, and was approved by Sir Douglas Haig. Its adoption and the appointment of Sir Eric Geddes came from Sir Douglas Haig and was approved by Mr. Lloyd George. In common fairness to Sir Eric Geddes I would ask the House to believe that he was not the least anxious to undertake the work—very much to the contrary. He only did it from purely patriotic reasons. I may mention that this answer has been shown to Sir Douglas Haig, and he entirely approves of it, his idea being (to use his own words) that 'the principle underlying it is to employ individuals in war on work which they have been accustomed to perform in peace. Thus the plan aimed at employing in the service of the country in the field a skilled railway manager and staff of assistants, experienced road engineers, dock managers, &c.' Sir Eric Geddes arrived in France just at the moment when the need for the services of such a man was keenly felt, and, as Sir Douglas Haig says, he 'recognised in him the very qualities which the army in the field required.'"

It might also be mentioned that, in his final despatch, dated March 21, 1919, Sir Douglas Haig makes reference to the appointment in the following words:—

"The successful co-ordination and economic use of all the various kinds of transportation requires most systematic management, based on deep thought and previous experience. So great was the work entailed in the handling of the vast quantities, of which some few examples are given above, so complex did the machinery of transport become and so important was it that the highest state of efficiency should be maintained, that, in the autumn of 1916, I was forced to adopt an entirely new system for running our lines of communication. The appointment of Inspector-General of Communications was abolished, and the services previously directed by that officer were brought under the immediate control of the Adjutant-General, the Quartermaster-General and the Director-General of Transportation. The last mentioned was a new office created with a separate staff composed for the greater part of civilian experts to deal specifically with transportation questions."

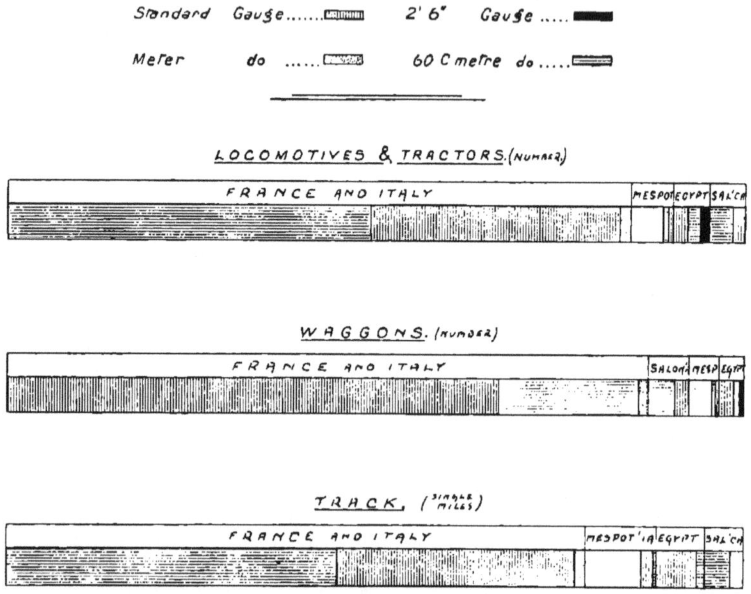

SUMMARY.

	LOCO'S AND TRACTORS.						WAGGONS.				TRACK.		
	LOCO'S			TRACTORS									
	S.G.	Metre	60 c.m.	S.G	2·6"	60 c.m.	S.G.	METRE	2'·6"	60 c.m.	S.G.	METRE	60 c.m
	No.	No.	No.	No.	No.	No.	No.	No.	No.	No.	Miles	Miles	Miles.
FRANCE & ITALY....	1.224	50	687	11	·	1.123	53255	1.200		15761	2990	178	3927
MESOPOTAMIA.....	22	156	25	·	·	6	113	3140	·	138	175	700	10
SALONICA.........	.54	·	69	·	·	47	1.784	·	·	2922	110	·	281
EGYPT............	75	·	25	3	33	45	1.675	·	321	767	625	·	128
	1.375	206	806	14	33	1.221	56827	4340	321	19.588	3900	878	4346
TOTALS	(No.) 3655						(No.) 81,076				(Miles) 9.124		

Fig. 1.—Railway Material Supplied to Various Theatres of War.

Evolution of Transportation Directorate.

It was in August, 1916, that Sir Eric Geddes was entrusted with an investigation into the transport arrangements connected with the British Expeditionary Force, both in this country and overseas, and from September 25, 1916, all papers and letters relating both to railway stores and establishments for overseas, and to inland water transport, were passed to him.

In order that he might direct and organise transport services in France under the G.O.C.-in-C. he was appointed Director-General of Transportation, but, in addition, he was detailed to act as deputy to the Quartermaster-General, War Office, in matters of transport, and for this purpose assumed the title of Director-General of Military Railways. The organisation of the department was as shown in the following charts :—

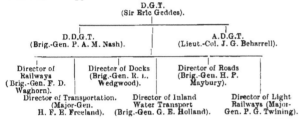

The Director-General of Transportation extended the organisation in France very considerably on taking over the whole of the functions and appended is an outline of the main divisions :—

In January, 1917, however, he ceased to be a deputy to the Q.M.G., and was authorised to report direct to the Secretary of State, and to attend those meetings of the Army Council at which matters pertaining to his department were under discussion. At the same time, in accordance with the principle of appointing technical experts, a civilian Director of Movements, in the person of Sir Sam Fay, was appointed under the Director-General of Military Railways, and took over the duties formerly embodied in the Directorate of Transport and Movements at the War Office.

In March, 1917, Sir Eric Geddes ceased to be Director-General of Military Railways and was made Inspector-General of Transportation for all theatres of war, but was subsequently transferred to the Admiralty as Controller.

Coincident with Sir Eric's appointment as Inspector-General, Sir Guy Granet was made Director-General of Movements and Railways and became a civilian member of the Army Council. An Army Council Instruction, dated April 20, 1917, contains the following reference to the D.G.M.R. :—

(g) The D.G.M.R. shall be responsible to the Secretary of State for so much of the business relating to the transport by rail or inland waterways at home or abroad of the personnel and material of the army as may be assigned to him from time to time by the Secretary of State.

To him was allotted the duty of dealing with all questions of movements to and from the United Kingdom and between the various theatres of war, i.e., Mesopotamia, East Africa, India, Egypt, Salonica, &c.

In March, 1918, Sir Guy Granet resigned his appointment, in order, at the request of the British Government, that he might visit the U.S.A. on food and transport problems. Sir Sam Fay, who, in his capacity of Director of Movements, had been assisting Sir Guy from the beginning of December, 1916, was then appointed Director-General of Movements and Railways.

Functions of the D.G.M.R.

In brief, the Director-General of Movements and Railways was responsible for the general supervision and co-ordination of railway, light railway, road and inland waterway and dock requirements overseas, and policy in regard thereto in all theatres of war. He was also responsible for the provision of railway, light railway and road plant, material and rolling-stock, as well as other waterway, port and dock plant and material, and the personnel for these services. He exercised War Office control on ports and overseas movements in the United Kingdom and movements by sea, and not the least of his duties was the co-ordinating of control over home railways under Act of Parliament, and maintaining a channel of communication with the Railway Executive Committee and the Admiralty.

Before Sir Sam Fay was appointed to the position of D.G.M.R., the organisation of the Directorate was as shown in broad outline on the chart below :—

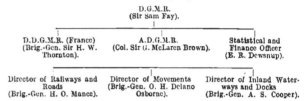

As the scope and work of the department grew in relation to the increasing activities in the various theatres of war, it was necessary to make certain extensions in the scheme of organisation, and the following chart will serve to indicate the broad divisions of the work of the Directorate at the signing of the armistice :—

```
                        D.G.M.R.
                       (Sir Sam Fay).
             |               |              |
  D.D.G.M.R. (France)   A.D.G.M.R.      Statistical and
  (Brig.-Gen. Sir H. W.  (Col. Sir G. McLaren Brown).  Finance Officer
    Thornton).                            (E. R. Dewsnup).

  Director of Railways and   Director of Movements   Director of Inland Water-
        Roads               (Brig.-Gen. O. H. Delano    ways and Docks
  (Brig.-Gen. H. O. Mance).    Osborne).          (Brig.-Gen. A. S. Cooper).
```

The Directorate of Railways and Roads.

This Directorate, under the control of Brig.-General H. O. Mance, was divided into three main sections, i.e., M.R.2 (a), M.R.2 (b) and M.R.2 (c), as shown on the chart below :—

```
            Director of Railways and Roads
                (Brig.-Gen. H. O. Mance).
          |                 |                 |
     M.R.2 (a)          M.R.2 (b)         M.R.2 (c)
  (Lt.-Col. E. Woodhouse,  (Col. H. A. Micklem,  (Lt.-Col. R. H.
    D.A.D.R.R.)            D.D.R.R.)          Cunnington).
```

The section M.R.2 (a), under the control of Lieut.-Colonel E. Woodhouse, was responsible for all questions of policy governing the construction or development of railways in the various theatres of war. It collated railway and road intelligence outside the United Kingdom, and dealt with questions other than those affecting the supply of material and personnel. It was responsible for the co-ordination of arrangements for the maintenance of the Mediterranean Line of Communication, and latterly dealt with transportation questions in connection with the Peace Conference.

The section M.R.2 (b), under Colonel H. A. Micklem, controlled the supply of material for railways, light railways and roads, including the supply of all special road making, maintenance and repairing equipment, plant and materials.

The section M.R.2 (c), under Lieut.-Colonel R. H. Cunnington, covered the supply of personnel for all railways, light railways, roads and quarries.

The Directorate of Movements.

This Directorate, under the control of Brig.-General Osborne, dealt with a most extensive range of subjects, and, as has already been mentioned, existed in the Quartermaster-General's branch before the formation of the separate Directorate-General of Movements and Railways. As its name implies, it was responsible for the movement of all personnel and stores by land and sea, excepting local movements in the United Kingdom, and the handling of the various classes of traffic.

The procedure laid down was practically as follows :—

(1) Q.M.G., France, to prepare for D.G.T. an estimate of stores required through French ports for three months ahead.

(2) D.G.T. to prepare a schedule of distribution of each class of stores to be imported through each of the ports in use by the British Expeditionary Forces ; this to be prepared in consultation with the Q.M.G. Directorate concerned.

(3) D.G.T. schedule of distribution to be circulated to Admiralty, War Office and Q.M.G., France, and taken as a basis for the regulation of shipping.

(4) Loading of all stores in England to be made in accordance with the schedule after making allowance for cargoes expected

to arrive at French ports from overseas, arrears to be made up by additions to subsequent months' distributions.

(5) Arrangements were agreed for the passing of information of ship movements, &c., by the Admiralty to the War Office, and details of daily progress (quantities loaded, &c.) by War Office to Admiralty, with a corresponding organisation on the French side by means of telegraphic advices in cipher "agreed" by the representatives of Admiralty and War Office at the ports.

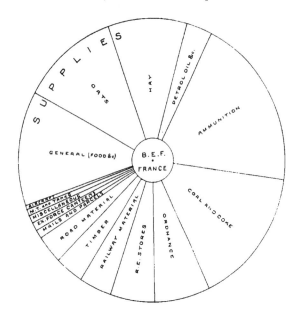

Fig. 2.—War Department Material Shipped to B.E.F., France.

Description.	TONS (d.w.)	
	Details.	Total.
Supplies:- General (Food)	3,438,851	
Oats.	3,105,326	
Hay.	2,648,096	
Petrol, Oil etc..	819,574	9,906,847
Ammunition		5,256,722
Coal and Coke - Army & R'ys..		4,158,061
Ordnance - Guns & Stores. ...		1,794,932
R.E. Stores.		1,408,065
Railway Material (other than Timber).		1,024,346
Timber. - R.E. and R'ys & Roads.		956,372
Road Material. -Shoe, Slag, Tar.		761,540
Mails and Parcels..(from U.K.only)		303,600
Exped' Force Canteens.. ...		284,345
Miscellaneous. ...		266,057
M.T. ...	165,432	
Tanks...	69,259	234,691
Aircraft Stores.		128,495
TOTAL.		26,384,073

The Director of Movements kept records in deadweight tons of stores despatched to the French ports from ports in the United Kingdom and stores received at French ports from overseas, setting these against D.G.T.'s schedule from week to week.

The various Directorates of the Q.M.G., War Office, acted upon advices from France as to quantities required, and conferred with the Directorate of Movements as to the most convenient port from which the stores were to be shipped to France; arising out of this, an allocation was made for each of the ports in the United Kingdom. In practice, ports were set apart for the shipment of certain commodities, the stores shipped from these ports remaining more or less constant, e.g., supplies (food) for Calais were shipped from Deptford; for other French ports from Newhaven.

The movement of military stores over the railways from places of origin to ports of shipment in the United Kingdom was controlled

by the Director of Movements, who received information each morning from the ports of the number of wagons and the quantity of stores received. Where necessary, he also facilitated the transit from places of origin. The control and supply of ships was in the hands of the Ministry of Shipping, and demands were made by the Director of Movements upon that Ministry to meet the requirements of the D.G.T. schedule, ships being broadly allocated to particular stores services, e.g., ammunition, hay, railway material, R.E. stores, &c. At the ports the Director of Movements was represented by embarkation officers, who were responsible for the receiving and shipping of stores, the actual loading in the ships being controlled by the Admiralty staffs.

A statistical section was formed for the purpose of keeping records of the shipment of stores at ports in the United Kingdom; each day's totals were drawn from daily returns and set against the day's proportion of the weekly schedule, thus showing, in addition to the total shipped, the surplus or deficiency compared with the schedule; these were circulated to all concerned. At the end of each week a return was similarly made up for the seven days and distributed. These statements were brought up for discussion by the sectional officers of the Directorate of Movements at meetings held each day, and also at joint meetings of the representatives of Q.M.G. and the Directorate of Movements. The state of affairs was thus considered in relation to the immediate future.

In regard to the economical use of shipping, the statistical section accumulated records from day to day of ships' time occupied in United Kingdom ports, and abnormal delays were dealt with each day by the officer concerned. A weekly return of operations at United Kingdom ports set out the time occupied in the various operations of loading, discharging, waiting berth, &c., at each United Kingdom port. The position in United Kingdom ports in summary form showing total ships in each of the ports was prepared and distributed in the directorate. Similarly, information drawn from telegrams received from the Directorate of Docks, France, enabled the Directorate of Movements to be acquainted with the shipping position at each of the French ports.

Considerable shipments of commodities, mainly supplies (food), oats, petrol, railway material, &c., were made from overseas ports direct to the French ports, and the Directorate of Movements also followed up the movements of these ships.

A weekly memorandum on the working at United Kingdom ports reviewing the week's operations generally was submitted to the D.G.M.R. In order to keep the Director of Movements and his assistant director acquainted with the work done at the United Kingdom ports, the statistics were set out in convenient form in loose leaf books, and were made up each week to date.

It should be mentioned that, in addition to the shipment of stores to France, the Directorate was responsible for the conveyance by the overland route, via French ports, of stores for theatres of war in the East, the necessary statistical information also being compiled.

Sections of Directorate of Movements.—The Directorate of Movements was divided into five main sections as shown below :—

Director of Movements
(Brig.-Gen. O. H. Delano Osborne).

S.R.1
(Lt.-Col. B. Way,
A.D.M.).
All shipping questions
other than stores to
France.

S.R.1 (a)
(Lt.-Col. C. R. Bond,
D.A.D.M.).
Moves of formations
and despatch of
troops, &c.

S.R.3
(Col. A. S. Redman,
D.D.R.T.).
Questions concerning
railways and canals in
the United Kingdom.

S.R.2
(Lt.-Col. A. B. Foster,
A.D.M.).
Movement of war
material and stores
to and through France.

S.R.4
(Lt.-Col. Clow).
Working of military
railways for camps
and War Department
Depôts.

S.R.1 (a) was a separate section under the control of Lieut.-Colonel C. R. Bond, D.A.D.M., who controlled the moves of formations between all theatres other than from United Kingdom to France, and dealt with individual passage claims to and from India. He was responsible for the despatch of troops as under :—

(1) Units from the United Kingdom to India and Mesopotamia, and drafts to all places abroad other than France.

(2) From and between various theatres of war.

(3) Inter-colonial moves.

(4) Passages to and from India.

(5) Colonial and allied contingents.

With the conclusion of the armistice he also dealt with demobilisation and repatriation arrangements.

The sub-section S.R.1 (b), in charge of Bt. Major C. Deakin, D.A.D.M., dealt with all moves from the United Kingdom to France. It covered the despatch of troops, including United States army, Labour Corps, and remounts to France, Holland and Russia ; cross-Channel hospital ships and leave service ; and home moves, including prisoners of war.

Sub-section S.R.1 (c), under Major M. J. M. Makalua, D.A.D.M., supervised all questions regarding despatch of W.O. and R.A.F. stores, supplies, ammunition, coal, &c., in requisitioned or commercial ships (1) from the United Kingdom to theatres of war and other ports abroad (except all hired transports to N. France, Belgium, Holland and Scandinavia) ; (2) from and between ports abroad (except N. France, Belgium and Holland). Previous to the armistice it also supervised the stores service from United States of America and Canada to the United Kingdom.

Sub-section S.R.1 (d), under Major E. C. Russell, dealt with the provision of booked passages and individual passage claims other than to and from India, also remount services from United States of America and Canada to the United Kingdom and Mediterranean, as well as questions in connection with the provision of passports from United Kingdom.

The fourth sub-section, S.R.1 (e), was responsible for the internal economy of the Directorate, for the keeping of the war diary, and records of rewards and other miscellaneous questions.

S.R.2.—At the head of section S.R.2 of the Directorate of Movements was Lieut.-Colonel A. B. Foster, A.D.M., who was responsible for the movement of war material and stores to and through France. His section was divided into seven sub-sections.

The first, i.e., S.R.2 (b), under Lieut.-Colonel W. Blomefield, D.A.D.M., exercised general control and supervision of the despatch of war material and stores to France, and through France to other theatres of war, and also controlled the working of ports in the United Kingdom. The second sub-section, S.R.2 (c), dealt with the despatch to France of ammunition, ordnance supplies, R.E. and R.A.F. stores. The third sub-section, S.R.2 (d), covered the forwarding and shipment of military railway stores, M.T. and tanks stores, road metal, slag, timber and coal to France, and allotted cargoes to cross-Channel barge and ferry services.

The fourth sub-section, S.R.2 (e), controlled the rail movements of all stores to ports in the United Kingdom, and the despatch of stores to Salonica and Egypt overland. The fifth sub-section, S.R.2 (f), dealt with shipping statistics under Mr. Allaway (N.E.R.), the Statistical Assistant to the Director of Movements, and the sixth, S.R.2 (g), with the despatch to France of supplies, ammunition and stores from overseas, and hay from the United Kingdom. The seventh sub-section, S.R.2 (h), under Lieut.-Colonel W. Parish, D.A.D.M., made arrangements in connection with the return of all salvage and ammunition empties from all theatres of war.

S.R.3.—This section, under the control of Colonel A. S. Redman, D.D.R.T., dealt with all questions concerning railways and canals in the United Kingdom. It was divided into three sub-sections, S.R.3 (a), S.R.3 (b), S.R.3 (c), but, subsequent to the armistice, an additional section was added, S.R.3 (d), under Major L. F. Lanyon, dealing with all question of procedure and irregularities in connection with demobilisation as affecting movements.

The first sub-section, S.R.3 (a)—Lieut.-Colonel C. L. M. O'Malley —dealt with appointments to the railway transport staff, claims for travelling by land, and issue of railway warrants not connected with embarkation. The second, S.R.3 (b)—Major R. Micklem— dealt with railway engineering questions, such as construction of War Department railways, all sidings and other works services carried out by railway and dock companies, and accounts for works services. The third, S.R.3 (c)—Major F. Bedford Glasier—controlled stores traffic in the United Kingdom, except to ports, and dealt with the issue of priority certificates for naval, military and munitions traffic, as well as loss of, and damage to, W.D. stores by rail.

S.R.4.—This section was in the charge of Lieut.-Colonel W. Clow (Superintendent of the Line, Great Central Railway), and dealt with all questions affecting the administration, operation, maintenance, &c., of the temporary military railways, serving camps

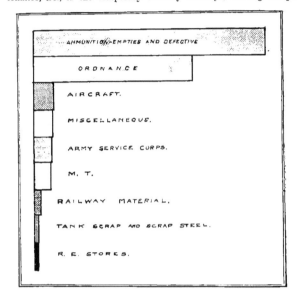

Description	TONS (aw)	
	Details	Total
Ammunition Empties and Defective Ammun? }		366,957
Ordnance	...	251,683
Aircraft		30,021
Miscellaneous	... 26,381	
R A M C	659	
Naval Stores	... 1,457	28,497
Army Service Corps	...	26,109
M. T.		25,037
Railway Material	..	10,931
Tank Scrap and Scrap Steel	..	6521
R. E. Stores	..	6437
TOTAL		752,193

Fig. 3.—Salvage, Empties, &c., Returned from France to United Kingdom.

and W.D. depôts at home. Technical, civil and mechanical engineering questions in both S.R.3 (b) and S.R.4 were dealt with by Captain (afterwards Major) W. Gregson.

The Directorate of Inland Waterways and Docks.

The Inland Water Transport Corps of the Royal Engineers was formed on December 28, 1914, as part of the railway troops to take over and develop transport on the canals and waterways of Belgium and Northern France. The organisation was originally operated directly under the Quartermaster-General, War Office, but was subsequently transferred to the control of the Director-General of Transportation when that department was formed. The Deputy-Director of Inland Water Transport took charge of the I.W.T. operations in France towards the end of 1914 ; the I.W.T. was constituted a separate Directorate overseas in October, 1915.

In September, 1916, when the new Directorate-General of Military Railways was formed at the War Office, the Inland Water Transport Department was transferred to it, and formed the Directorate of

Inland Waterways and Docks under the D.G.M.R. This change brought under its control not only inland water transport operations and the supply of personnel and material, but the equipment and working of the docks. At the conclusion of the armistice, Brig.-General A. S. Cooper was at the head of the directorate; this officer in civil life was the General Manager of the Nigerian Railways, and had, therefore, very extensive experience with regard to inland water transport. Assisting him as deputy-director was Mr. O. R. H. Bury, a former General Manager of the Great Northern Railway, who subsequently became the director.

Sections of I.W.D.—The Directorate was divided into nine sections, which are shown on the chart below :—

Director of Inland Waterways and Docks
(Brig.-Gen. A. S. Cooper).

D.D.I.W. and D.
(O. R. H. Bury).

| M.R.3 (a) (Lt.-Col. E. A. Weston). | M.R.3 (b) (Lt.-Col. W. G. Clarke). | M.R.3 (d) (Lt.-Col. C. H. W. Francis). | M.R.3 (e) (Lt.-Col. H. Clarke). | M.R.3 (g) (Lt.-Col. A. T. Andrews). |

M.R.3 (f)

M.R.3 (h) (C. E. Dale, C.M.G.).   M.R.3 (j).   M.R.3 (l).   M.R.3 (o).

The first section comprised M.R.3 (a) and M.R.3 (f), and dealt with questions of policy and matters affecting the administration of I.W. and D. establishments, also general arrangements for the

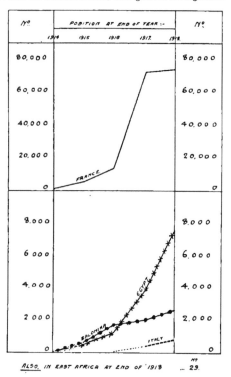

Fig. 4.—Personnel on Railways and Roads.

supply of personnel. M.R.3 (b) covered mechanical engineering and dock equipment for overseas, whilst M.R.3 (d) attended to the fulfilment of requisitions for plant, stores and material for home and abroad. M.R.3 (e) controlled the movement of I.W. and D. craft, the operation of cross-Channel services, and the movement by rail and water of I.W. and D. stores and material. It attended to the co-ordination of craft requirements for overseas, the alteration, repair and maintenance of the home service fleet, and the equipment and outfit of new vessels. M.R.3 (g) was the civil engineering section; it covered designs, plans and supervision of I.W. and D. construction work in England, also engineering questions arising from I.W. and D. construction work overseas, and technical records.

M.R.3 (h) was the finance section. It supervised finance and prepared statistics, and scrutinised and checked accounts before submission for payment; it also prepared works costs of I.W. and D. works. M.R.3 (j) kept records of working statistics and all traffic operations, and co-ordinated working with financial statistics. It also compiled statistics showing the commercial aspect of I.W. and D. undertakings and prepared the periodical returns. M.R.3 (l) covered the record and control of all loose and fixed plant, and supervised the hire and transfer of plant. It was responsible for the periodical inspection of all plant and insurance of steam boilers. M.R.3 (o) was the engineering inspection branch.

Personnel.

An important function of the Directorate was the supply of personnel for transport requirements, and Fig. 4 gives particulars of the development of personnel on railways and roads. At the end of 1918 the personnel provided under the supervision of the Directorate and employed on railways, inland waterways and roads, numbered the following :—

Raised in England	62,344
Colonial Corps sent from England ..	22,608
Units raised overseas	23,390
Total officers and other ranks..	108,342

Officers.—Approximately half the technical officers were furnished by the British railway companies on recommendation from the Railway Executive Committee, and the other half were men from overseas employed on Colonial or foreign railways who offered their services. A few regular officers serving were mostly drawn from the Indian army and numbered about 40.

The officers for the new road and quarry companies formed at the end of 1916 and beginning of 1917, were selected on the recommendation of the Road Board from lists submitted by them containing some 1,300 serving officers and 1,300 civilians, and, as far as possible, the units formed entirely by counties and county boroughs were officered by local men, who were given rank suitable to their technical qualifications, but subject to at least one trained officer joining each company as a transfer.

At the request of the Military Secretary, the road section of the Directorate also undertook the selection of officers with technical qualifications for the Labour Corps. Applications amounting to 1,600 were considered during 1917 and 400 candidates appointed to temporary commissions. A large number of officers with technical experience were transferred to the Royal Engineers for the technical railway or road units.

Other Ranks.—With regard to other ranks prior to the war, arrangements were in hand for the formation of a reserve of 1,000 men from the British railways for operating railways in war, but were not complete, and the only railway personnel in being when war broke out consisted of two regular and three special reserve construction companies. In addition, one railway transport section had been provided for and was immediately formed, the other ranks being regular Royal Engineers troops.

The French had given an assurance that they would undertake all railway transportation for the B.E.F. in France, but it was felt that this would not last long, and, immediately on mobilisation, Colonel Twiss, Director of Railway Transport, was instructed to organise additional railway construction units.

In October, 1914, the Railway Executive Committee formed a sub-committee for recruiting purposes. Sir William Forbes (London, Brighton & South Coast Railway) was responsible for personnel for the railway construction companies, Mr. (afterwards Sir) Francis Dent (South Eastern & Chatham Railway) for railway operating personnel, and Mr. Arthur Watson (Lancashire & Yorkshire Railway) for railway transport personnel. These gentlemen kept closely in touch with the requirements and made all arrangements with the railway companies concerned in the selection and recruiting of men.

There was then a very large number of the employees of the British railway companies volunteering for military service, and the men for railway troops were selected from them, provided they obtained permission to enlist. All the men not so selected, and who could be spared, were allowed to enlist in other branches of the service, and out of 180,000 enlistments from the English railway companies, only some 40,000, or approximately 20 per cent., were serving in railway units at the end of 1917. The following year the percentage had risen to approximately 25 per cent.

Until May, 1915, all enlistments were passed through the Railway Executive Committee, who issued intending recruits with special forms to ensure correct posting. It was then found necessary to obtain a certain number of men who were not available in the British railway companies, and independent enlistment was undertaken.

After the railway companies had been asked, under compulsory service conditions, in January, 1917, to release as many men as possible for the Army generally, a new system of obtaining recruits from the Railway Executive Committee came into force, the railway companies drawing up statements by trades of the men available for release, which were duly considered and men selected as required.

With respect to the enlistment of men for roads and quarries, special methods had to be adopted towards the end of 1916 for recruiting. General Maybury, Chief Engineer of the Road Board, who was appointed Director of Roads in France, convened conferences of the chief officials of the local road authorities in Great Britain with a view to the enrolment of men, it being decided that the more important counties and county boroughs should endeavour to raise complete companies of 250 men, while the less populated should combine in forming companies. Recruiting for the quarry companies was carried out in a similar manner by approaching the quarry officials and masters of the British Isles, and a special depôt was opened at Buxton, whilst one company was formed in Ireland and two by transfers in France.

Arrangements were made for recruits for the railways, roads and canals to pass through recognised trade test centres, the numbers so passing during 1917 being 2,550 and during 1918 3,805. A Railways and Roads training centre was established at Longmoor, which, before the war, was the headquarters of the railway troops, which consisted of the 8th and 10th regular companies Three special reserve companies also came to Longmoor annually for training on the Woolmer Constructional Military Railway. On the outbreak of war these five companies mobilised at Longmoor, and the 8th company proceeded at once to France. Longmoor, and subsequently part of Borden, became the centre for all railway and road personnel, and at one time was also the centre for the I.W.T. From the outbreak of war until the end of November, 1918, nearly 1,700 officers and 66,000 other ranks were sent overseas from this

centre, including 30 officers and 3,000 other ranks from Colonial units.

Conclusion.

The brief history of the Directorate of Movements and Railways is one of development. Its inauguration was the result of a decision that a purely military organisation of railways could not result in a working satisfactory alike to military and civilian needs. The railway had to be subordinate to combatant authorities to the extent that war requirements had to be given preference, and that it should be utilised to the furtherance of the national effort, although post-war necessities were at all times borne in mind. The growing needs of the campaigns in the various theatres of war necessitated a tremendous and rapid increase in transportation to maintain the troops. The total number of personnel embarked in the United Kingdom for France from August, 1914, to December, 1918. numbered more than 10,000,000, details of which are shown in Fig. 5. It should be pointed out that these figures do not represent merely fresh personnel, but journeys backwards and forwards of reinforcements, leave parties, sick and wounded, &c.

The entry of America into the war necessitated still further transportation to the extent shown by the following figures, which

Description.	To France.	Through France—						Total to and through France.
		To Italy.	To Salonica.	To Egypt.	To Mesopotamia.	To India.	To other Stations.	
	No.	No.	No.	No.	No.	No.	No.	No.
Drafts and units ..	5,254,411	27,928	57,237	90,603	16,912	9,427	7,602	5,464,120
Leave ..	3,664,516	37,141	28,085	6,560	251	84	625	3,737,862
Royal Navy	42,952	9,515	3,357	3,749	13	821	10,808	71,215
Red Cross—relatives of wounded, &c. ..	45,729			..			..	45,729
Labour Corps—Chinese, South African, &c. ..	110,058							110,058
United States Forces ..	1,015,731							1,015,731
Belgians ..	299,156							299,156
Other Allies ..	48,558	..		..			..	48,558
Miscellaneous ..	4,994	118		1,047	11		1,509	7,679
Total personnel ..	10,486,105	74,702	89,279	101,959	17,187	10,332	20,544	10,800,108
Animals	804,203	8	..	2,265	1,887	..	..	808,363

Fig. 5.—Personnel (Officers, Nurses and other Ranks) and Animals Embarked in the United Kingdom for France, and through France for other Theatres of War, from August, 1914, to end of December, 1918.

are the totals of American troops transported to the United Kingdom and France by British and American tonnage from May 17, 1917, to December 28, 1918 :—

To United Kingdom	..	..	1,019,886
Direct to France	..	..	1,079,434
Direct to Italy ..	..	..	1,653
Total	..	..	2,100,973

The total stores shipped to France for the British Forces up to December, 1918, in deadweight tons totalled over 26,000,000 tons, whilst 400,000 tons were shipped through France for onward conveyance ; large quantities of troops and stores were also shipped by the long sea route to the Eastern theatres of war. The number of vehicles shipped on own wheels reached a prodigious total, and details are shown below, whilst Fig. 2 graphically illustrates the proportions of the main classes of traffic.

Number of Vehicles, &c., Shipped on Own Wheels for Use of B.E.F., France—August, 1914, to December, 1918.

Description.				Number.
Aeroplanes	..	..	..	3,087
Barrows ..	..	..	..	44,995
Bicycles ..	..	..	..	62,805
„ motor ..	..	..		26,284
„ cycle cars	..	..		2,957
Guns and carriages	..	..		15,880
„ trench and bomb throwers				27,466

Description.	Number.
Pontoons and pontoon wagons	1,152
Pumps, trench	1,413
Tanks	1,976
Trucks, hand	14,040
,, miners'	380
Vehicles, railway—	
Locomotives	791
Tenders	768
Carriages	200
,, ambulance ..	635
Wagons, &c.	38,831
Vehicles, road—	
Four-wheeled	45,592
Two-wheeled	71,472
Limbered	12,103
Ambulance wagons	557
Telegraph and cable wagons	129
Travelling kitchens and field oven wagons ..	3,595
Water tanks, carts and trailers	1,172
Trailers, vans and tenders (R.A.F.)	2,325
Motor ambulances	4,918
,, buses and chars-a-banc	370
,, cars and chassis	13,043
,, lorries, store and workshop, &c. ..	38,547
,, tractors	1,572
Sundry vehicles, &c.	4,839
Total	442,994

A tremendous amount of railway material was essential to meet the needs in the various theatres of war, and Fig. 1 is interesting as indicating the quantities supplied to each theatre. In all, some 3,655 locomotives and tractors, over 80,000 wagons and more than 9,000 miles of track were supplied. The extent to which the question of salvaging serviceable material was taken up is admirably shown by the chart at Fig. 3, which indicates that over three-quarters of a million tons of salvage and empties were returned from France to the United Kingdom up to the end of 1918.

These facts and figures will serve to show the value of the work performed by the Directorate of Movements and Railways. Under no other system would it have been possible for the work to have been done in such a wonderfully efficient manner. The co-ordination of transportation requirements, under the direction of recognised experts, was a war innovation that synchronised economy and efficiency. It is not too much to say that the transportation effort, that had so much to do with the success of the Allied cause, received its greatest stimulus on the inauguration of a Directorate devoted to the specialised work of transportation.

THE RAILWAY TRANSPORTATION OF "TANKS."

A Description of the Vehicles used and the Methods of Loading and Unloading.

There has been some misconception as to the transport of our fighting Tanks, and those actually responsible for their transport during the war. Primarily, of course, credit should rightly be given to the railway companies concerned for the working and haulage, but as regards loading and unloading, and the control of the movements in England of all tanks, tank components, spare parts and general material moving between manufacturers, stores depôts and testing grounds, and the final movement through British ports to the Tank Corps overseas of the completed tanks, together with stores and equipment in bulk, credit must be given to the Transportation Branch of the Mechanical Warfare Department.

Special Railway Trollies Built.

Among the claimants appearing during the course of the recent "Tanks" inquiry we find none in connection with the designing and production, in an incredibly short time, of 200 specially strong and suitable flat-topped rail "Rectank" trollies for the conveyance of the larger and heavier machines, weighing approximately 35 tons each, to France. These trollies answered their purpose so admirably from the outset that no modifications were subsequently required. It may interest many to know that the word "Rectank" is built up of the initials of the Railway Executive Committee and the load the vehicle was intended to carry.

Seven hundred and eighty seven wagons were also built by the Leeds Forge Company, Limited, and proved quite satisfactory in service.

The special feature in connection with the designing of them was to get sufficient strength at the centre of the wagon and also over the bogie bolster. It will readily be understood that if the jacks were screwed down on to the rails whilst the wagon was without its load and the Tank were then placed in position at the centre, the chief supports of the wagon would be at the ends instead of at the bogie centres, thus greatly increasing the bending moment in the centre. Again, the underframe had to be specially strengthened over the bogie centre in order that it might not be crippled in the event of a Tank being placed on a wagon with its centre of gravity over the end of the wagon without the jacks having been screwed down, the bending moment at the bogie bolster under such condi-

tions being very considerable. As a matter of fact the Tank, when right over the end of the wagon, placed the underframe in equilibrium about the centre of the bogie nearest to the Tank, and it was found possible to make the underframe swing when in this position, the weight of the Tank on one side of the bogie centre counterbalancing the weight of the underframe and bogie on the other side.

The illustrations on pages 83 and 84 show the "Rectank" trolley loaded or in process of loading. The vehicle is 37 ft. 2 in. in length over the buffers. The tare is 15½ tons, and the carrying capacity 35 tons. By its means the railway companies were enabled to arrange the conveyance of even the largest "Tanks" over all the required routes, as the exceptionally low platform, 3 ft. 6½ in. from rail level, reduced the projections beyond the railway companies' gauges at the top to the smallest limit practicable in view of their dimensions. Several thousands of the machines were thus successfully conveyed, notwithstanding their cumbersome and weighty character.

Method of Loading.

In loading, the machines are usually worked over the sides of the trollies, and afterwards turned to a central position, under their own power, but when they are passed over the ends in the process of either loading or unloading, the screw jacks seen in the illustrations are brought into use. These novel appliances serve to relieve the end bogies of the considerable strain they would otherwise suffer during the passage of the machines, as they can be lowered to rest on the rails and thus act as supports.

In the early days all Tanks were transhipped from their trucks at the English ports and taken across to France by special boats set aside for that purpose, but after the introduction of the Train Ferry the Tanks were carried right from manufacturers and testing centres to Tank Corps headquarters in France on the wagons upon which they were originally loaded. During the first month, when sent by the Train Ferry, the average time taken for the vehicles, from leaving Birmingham to arriving back again at that centre from France, was 14 days, which, by the end of the third month, was reduced to an average of 5·5 days, reflecting credit upon all concerned in their movement.

RAILWAYS AND ROADS ON THE WESTERN FRONT.

An Outline of the Development of Railway and Road Communications in France and Belgium.

In Sir Douglas Haig's final despatch on the operations on the Western Front, dated March 21, 1919, he observes that it "is impossible to apprehend the full course of the war unless the long succession of battles which commenced on the Somme in 1916 and ended in November of last year are viewed as forming part of one great and continuous engagement." The conditions, therefore, were essentially different from those operating in every other theatre of war—and, indeed, different from those of any previous war.

The "locking together" of gigantic armies on extended fronts renders it impossible clearly to distinguish the particular objects of individual transportation developments in the manner found practicable in the "wars of movement," whilst the enormous extent of transportation development on the Western Front obviously renders any detailed survey impracticable. It has, therefore, been deemed advisable in the following pages more or less broadly to review the development of rail and road communications in France and to confine the scope to a brief sketch of the transportation effort. A map of the area is given in Fig. 6.

First German Sweep.—Aided by her splendid system of strategic lines, Germany was able to throw immense forces into Belgium, whose neutrality she violated in August, 1914, and, despite the valiant resistance of the Belgians, reinforced by French and British armies, the Germans rapidly advanced. The battle of Mons was fought on August 23, 1914, but overwhelming enemy forces impelled a retirement to the Cambrai-Le Cateau line, this subsequently being evacuated after a great German massed attack on our line. The terrific pressure exerted by the enemy impelled a still further retirement, the Allies finally taking a definite stand in front of Paris. At this point the German onrush was stayed, and as the Allies "made good the Aisne" in the early part of October, 1914, the enemy had to effect a readjustment of his line. The Allied counter-attack continued, and the German line was rolled back north and east, the general position after the battle of the Marne being that the Germans were held on a line running southwards from Nieuport through Lens, thence curving south-east through Clermont, Chateau Thierry and Vitry upwards to Verdun.

The Germans thus acquired control over the major portion of the Belgian railway system and important sections of the French railways running north of Paris.

Early Developments.—In the early days of the war it was the intention that the French railway administration should be responsible for the maintenance and operation of all railway lines of communication, and for a time the arrangement worked satisfactorily. As, however such proposals were based on a British force of limited size and took no account of the enormous requirements in the way of supplies and material such as were subsequently required by the greatly augmented British forces, nor of the extensive railway demands in connection with offensive operations, it speedily became evident that assistance would have to be given to the French in the matter of railway transport.

As early as March, 1915, the French Transportation Authorities asked the British to supply rolling-stock and to afford assistance in other directions. The extent of this assistance was at first on a comparatively small scale, but the great increase of the British Army during the year 1916, and the strain thrown upon transportation resources by the Somme offensive in the autumn of that year, proved conclusively that additional help would be required. In the autumn of 1916, therefore, the necessity of obtaining reliable information as to the additional provision required led to an investigation of the general transportation situation by Sir Eric Geddes, who, as previously stated, was subsequently appointed Director-General of Transportation.

Position at End of 1916.—At the time of this investigation, which coincided with fresh demands for transport assistance from the French, very little railway work had been done by the British Army. It is true that nearly 600 miles of standard gauge track had been sent to France, but this was primarily utilised for the construction of additional running lines and sidings in connection with regulating stations, ammunition depôts, &c. The responsibility for working traffic to railhead rested with the French, and as the regulating stations for the distribution of traffic had been laid out with a view to future development, it was expected that they would be equal to the demands made upon them so long as the distribution arrangements for the Army were divided into the proportions that were then in operation. Any material change in the disposition of the Forces would, of course, influence the question, and steps had to be taken to meet this contingency.

The running line (apart from regulating stations and depôts) laid by the British to the end of September, 1916, was confined to the Hazebrouck-Ypres section (19 miles), the Candas-Acheux section (14½ miles), the Contay line (8 miles) and extensions of line in the Somme area to open up additional railheads in the direction of Montauban and Guillemont. After the laying of these lines, the British stock of track in France was no more than 65 miles, which length, together with 200 further miles on order, was the only provision made for additional railway facilities.

The rolling-stock and locomotives on hand were also very limited. Practically the whole of the rolling-stock for the British Army traffic was supplied by the French, but Great Britain was in course of supplying 13,000 wagons towards the estimated 22,000 required for an advance through Belgium. Only 34 steam and 7 internal combustion locomotives were in France for British Army purposes by the end of September, 1916, although 100 locomotives were on demand and the short-notice supply of a further 70 from British railways had been arranged. The engines then in service were mainly occupied in performing shunting and marshalling operations at the various regulating stations, ammunition depôts, &c., whilst they were also used for working short sections of line operated by British troops. In addition, there were a few Belgian locomotives used for working the lines of communication behind the Army zone.

Rolling-Stock Requirements.—In deciding the question of rolling-stock requirements for British Army purposes, the Allied position was divided into two zones, namely :—

(1) The French zone—comprising all lines south-west of a line drawn from Hazebrouck through Lille, Valenciennes and Maubeuge.

(2) All railways north-east of that line up to the Rhine with the exception of the working of British depôts.

The original intention was that the French should work the French zone and that the second zone should be worked by an International Commission which would have a "pool" of locomotives contributed by the Allies, but mainly by the Belgians. Rolling-stock, so far as the British Armies were concerned, was to be provided by the French. The French, however, found it utterly impossible to provide for the requirements, and made heavy demands upon Britain, their estimate of the requirements on the existing alignment of Armies being some 40,000 wagons, i.e., 10-ton units (all types and capacities of wagons are reduced to 10-ton units). This estimate was critically examined by British experts, who reduced the figure to 27,000, which, however, was sufficiently alarming. Again, on the possibility of an advance to the German frontier, the French suggested that Britain would have to supply 54,000 wagons, a figure reduced by our experts to 41,000.

The locomotive question was, if anything, more serious, as the French had requested that the British should undertake all transport working for British Army traffic up to the Hazebrouck-Maubeuge line, a task that involved the provision of some 900 additional locomotives with crews and repairing facilities. As, moreover, the French difficulties were such that they desired Britain to take over the complete working (including civilian traffic) of a portion of their lines, to maintain certain sections of the railway and to provide additional skilled personnel to work in the Nord workshops on engine repairs, the transportation question assumed a most serious aspect.

The immediate requirements were summarised in a report dated November 24, 1916, and called for the provision of between 200 and 300 locomotives, some 20,000 wagons, together with about

vision of additional locomotives, wagons and personnel, whilst he very strongly recommended the development of the light railway system, which was suggested by the Commander-in-Chief in the middle of 1916.

As mentioned previously, the investigations and recommendations of Sir Eric Geddes led to his appointment as Director-General of Transportation in France, with control over all means of communication. This resulted in very speedy development in all branches. By the end of February, 1917, or within three months of the formation of the new Transportation Directorate, permanent way, locomotives, rolling-stock and all kinds of railway material, plant

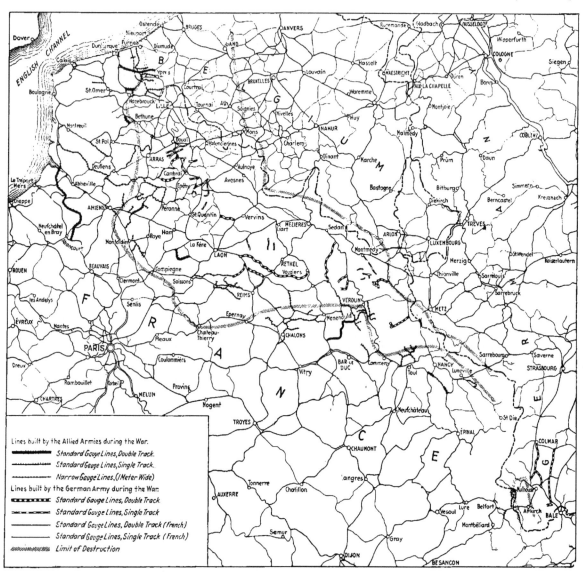

Fig. 6—The Western Front— showing Railway Developments.

1,000 miles of track and necessary personnel within a short time. It was this crisis that led to the withdrawal of locomotives and rolling-stock from British railways and to the cutting down of passenger traffic, as no other means existed of meeting the urgent transportation requirements of the British Forces in France.

Speedy Provision of Material.—The result of Sir Eric Geddes's investigation proved that considerable development of railway facilities would be essential to deal with the estimated 300,000 tons of traffic weekly to supply the British Armies during 1917. In a comprehensive report on the subject Sir Eric recommended a very considerable amount of new construction, together with the pro-

and tools for standard and light railways were being poured into France, the assistance given by overseas Dominions and the travel restrictions on British railways having much to do with the prompt supply.

Standard and Metre Gauge Railways.

The burden placed on the British Transportation Directorate steadily grew, and it became clear that the existing facilities and organisation would be inadequate to meet the requirements of the 1917 operations. Extensive orders for locomotives, wagons and track were placed, whilst a very extensive track-laying programme, including the doubling of existing lines, building of new lines, laying of sidings, and the equipment of yards, depôts, &c., was decided upon.

Track.—In the year 1916 only 417 miles of track were laid by British troops, but over 800 miles were put down during 1917. Of this mileage, 442 miles were laid during the months of March, April and May, the rate averaging 32 miles per day. The maximum was laid during the week ending May 19, when 45 miles of track were built. This extensive construction followed the retirement of the enemy early in 1917, and was occasioned by the rapid rebuilding of the lines in following up the advance.

Despite the heavy consumption of track, the stock in the country increased considerably during the year. Whereas, at the end of 1916, there were only 95 miles of standard gauge rails in stock, this rose to 745 miles by the end of 1917, the latter figure including 94 miles of track, dismantled after the advance and put back into stock.

The enemy advance in the spring of 1918 threatened the important railway centres of Amiens, St. Pol and Hazebrouck, and created a situation of extreme gravity. To ensure the maintenance of communications in Northern France, therefore, a comprehensive programme of construction was undertaken, in conjunction with the French. This comprised the provision of three separate routes, independent of Amiens, for north and south traffic, and involved extensive doublings and quadruplings of existing railways and the construction of new lines. At the same time a system of railheads had to be developed for the maintenance of the Army on the new front and to prepare for a prospective advance.

These measures involved the building, with attendant appurtenances and bridging, of some 200 miles of track during the period from April to July. During the whole of this period the work was rendered extremely difficult owing to the activity of enemy aircraft, which was particularly directed against important junctions and points on the main railway system. Special protective and precautionary measures, therefore, had to be taken on bridges, whilst, for the same reason, deviations were constructed at junctions. As an instance of the utility of these precautionary measures, it might be mentioned that the bombing by aircraft of the viaduct at Etaples cut this most important line of communication, but as a deviation had been linked up just previously, only slight delay resulted in the middle of important troop movements. As our troops fell back under the terrific pressure of the enemy, every measure was taken to hinder the German advance. The main lines of communication were effectively destroyed, and all rolling-stock and guns on railway mountings cleared in good time.

With the commencement of the successful counter-offensive in August, 1918, this position was reversed, and the energies of all concerned were centred upon the reconstruction of the railway system recaptured from the enemy. In the withdrawal the Germans employed every possible artifice for the destruction of the railways; nearly all the bridges and water supplies were destroyed and a very large proportion of the track rendered useless. In certain sections, moreover, delay-action mines had been placed in the track, and special steps had to be taken for their discovery and removal. Those not located made huge craters on explosion causing considerable damage to both track and formation—and frequently disaster to personnel.

In addition to the destruction caused by delay-action mines, extensive damage was wrought on the railway as far back as Namur by the burning of rolling-stock and the explosion of train loads of ammunition in stations. Most serious damage was caused in this way at Luttre, where about 2,000 wagons were blown up and completely wrecked the station and yard. Considerable damage was also caused at Monceau, another large goods yard in the vicinity of Charleroi. In fact, after the retirement of the enemy, it was found that the railways had been totally destroyed up to a line Sotteghem - Grammont - Ghislenghien - Jurbise - Mons-Fontaine-Valmont.

In the last quarter of the year over 1,100 miles of line were re-constructed, whilst over 100 miles were dismantled. Thus, even after the armistice, the work of the construction troops was in no way relieved, as it was of the utmost importance to link up the French and Belgian systems as speedily as possible in order to provide for the armies and also the civilian population. The reconstruction of the 1,581 miles of railway involved the entire relaying of nearly 600 miles of track, so that there were actually 1,348 miles of new track laid during 1918. Figs. 7 and 8 indicate the development of track in France.

The carrying out of the enormous construction of 1918 called for the greatest zeal on the part of the British and Canadian railway construction troops. Often employed continuously through day

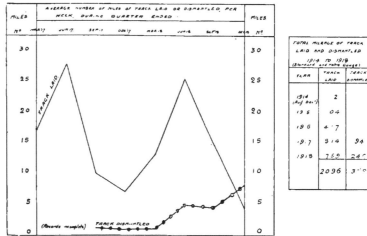

Fig. 7.—Rate of Construction &c., of Standard and Metre Gauge Railways.

and night, it was solely their magnificent work that rendered possible the successful advance of our armies. The extent of the work and the rapidity with which it was carried out created a phenomenal record of railway construction, and some remarkable performances were achieved. The following are a few examples :—

On November 11, 1918, a stretch of 20 miles was destroyed on the Arras-Douai-Valenciennes-Mons line. On this length there were 13 bridges, totalling 650 ft. in length, to be reconstructed. Within 15 days a single track was connected through to Mons, and through railway traffic to the armies was commenced. Beyond

Fig. 8.—Rate of Construction of 60 c.m. Gauge Lines.

this point the track was in fair condition, although extensive preparations had been made for its destruction. Double tracking was completed throughout by December 13, and double line working was brought into operation the following day.

Another valuable piece of work was performed on the Courtrai-Audenarde-Sotteghem-Grammont line, on which the destroyed length consisted of a stretch of 30 miles. The bridge over the Scheldt, which is 100 ft. wide, was totally destroyed and had to be spanned with a trestle bridge, whilst several minor bridges of 30 ft. span had to be repaired. The Scheldt bridge was completed in 4½ days and through running resumed on December 6, three weeks from the commencement of the work. A somewhat similar piece of bridge construction work was performed near Lille, which was evacuated by the Germans on October 17, 1918. Before railway traffic could pass into Lille a new bridge had to be thrown over the Lys at Armentières. This was completed within four days, and the first train of supplies for the civil population was taken into the city on October 25.

As a last example mention might be made of the magnificent work performed on the Lille-Tournai-Ath line, on which there was a destroyed gap of 27 miles. The single track was completed to Tournai and the station there opened for supplies on November 28, 1918, 11 days from the commencement of the work. Double tracking to Tournai was completed on the last day of 1918 and linked throughout by the end of January, 1919.

Rolling-Stock.—At the end of 1916 only 62 standard gauge locomotives had been imported for British use, but during 1917 this number increased to 753. In addition, 32 other locomotives were available but not put in traffic, whilst 62 were awaiting erection. The following year witnessed further large supplies of locomotives, and at the end of 1918 the total number imported for British use was 1,205, this figure being exclusive of engines hired or captured.

The special gravity of the situation arose in connection with wagons, and, to meet the extreme urgency, 20,000 wagons were obtained from service on British railways. Whereas, at the end of 1916, there were only 3,849 imported wagons (representing 6,286 10-ton units) in traffic, the number increased to 34,845 (46,004 10-ton units) by the end of 1917. The total number of wagons ordered was based on an estimate of the number considered necessary to cover the requirements of the British Forces in the event of an advance across Belgium. This, however, was soon found to be an under-estimate, as the estimated requirement of 27,000 units to meet the requirements of the then existing front was quickly exceeded by nearly 11,000 units.

Throughout 1918 the supply of locomotives and wagons continued, and, as will be noticed from the following table giving the comparative position at the end of each year, very large supplies were delivered during that year :—

	At December 31—		
	1916.	1917.	1918.
Standard gauge locomotives—			
Imported	62	753	1,205
Hired	198	215	229
Captured	—	—	6
Total	260	968	1,440
Petrol tractors—			
Imported	—	7	8
Wagons—			
Imported	3,849	34,845	52,597
Captured or built from scrap	—	—	67
Equivalent 10-ton units	6,286	46,317	69,146

In addition to the above, 50 metre gauge locomotives and 1,200 wagons were supplied to France, the whole of the rolling-stock on hand at the end of 1918 being more than sufficient to meet the full requirements of the British Army. Of the rolling-stock imported into France, some 387 locomotives and 14,550 wagons were erected at the Chief Mechanical Engineer's shops in France.

Traffic.—At the beginning of 1917 considerable anxiety was felt as to whether it would be possible to comply with the demands on transportation during the projected operations, but the prompt supply of locomotives, rolling-stock and other assistance to the French enabled the enormous volume of traffic which developed in connection with the operations to be handled satisfactorily. After the Somme battle there was serious congestion on the

French railways, and this naturally resulted in a shortage of rolling-stock. Traffic working was rendered difficult, an unsatisfactory condition accentuated by the severe weather experienced during the first two months of 1917. To meet the situation, both military and civilian traffic was reduced to a minimum, and an embargo was placed upon certain traffics. Normal conditions were resumed during March, when the number of trains run to railheads and on lines of communication averaged 179 per day, this increasing to an average of 261·2 per day when the October operations in Flanders were in operation.

The following table gives the daily average number of trains run to railheads and on lines of communication during the months when the various battles were being fought, and also the maximum week during the course of the various operations :—

Month. 1917.	Operations.	Average per day.			On L. of C.	Total.	Maximum week.
		Zero day. 1917.	To railheads.				
April	Arras	April 9	121·1		73·5	194·6	197·5
June	Messines	June 7	127·0		97·8	224·8	242·3
August October	Passchendaele	July 31 {	148·7 159·9		85·8 101·3	234·5 261·2	261·2 270·6
December	Cambrai	Nov. 20	129·7		82·1	211·8	241·7

Owing to the concentration of traffic on sectors of the line where offensive operations were in progress, the increase shown by the above figures represents a much greater effort than appears at first sight, as an enormous concentration of men, ammunition and material upon the area immediately behind the front of an offensive entails traffic problems of very great complexity. The average daily number of loaded trains run for the B.E.F. is shown over various periods in Fig. 9.

It will be seen from the above table that there was a continuous increase in the volume of traffic, culminating in a maximum during the fighting in Flanders in October. Subsequently there was a considerable decline, this being accentuated during the last two weeks of 1917 by weather conditions of frost and snow, which necessitated a reduction in the traffic programme for the British armies.

At the end of 1917 the whole of the British and French front from St. Pol downwards to the Swiss frontier was served by three independent double lines of railway available for the lateral move-

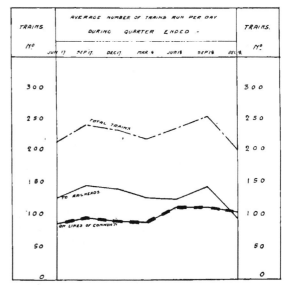

Fig. 9.—Average Daily Number of loaded Trains Run for B.E.F.

ment of troops, whilst another independent double-tracked line was available for moves between Peronne and Rheims. Each of the three routes mentioned above included a section of the Ceinture railway system encircling Paris, a most disadvantageous feature in the event of heavy movement owing to emergency.

The rapid advance of the enemy offensive during April and May, 1918, rendered the railway situation extremely difficult for three main reasons :—

(1) The territory occupied between the front and the sea was considerably narrowed by the enemy advance.

(2) The lateral line between Amiens and Arras was occupied by the enemy, and the second lateral from Ypres via Chocques and St. Pol was unworkable through Hazebrouck, precarious through Chocques and difficult through St. Pol.

(3) Communication from north to south of the Somme was rendered dangerous owing to the loss of Longeau and the main lines running from the east of Amiens towards Paris.

In consequence, army railheads, depôts, &c., were thrown back into the lines of communication area, thus producing considerable congestion, which was enhanced by the necessity of finding storage accommodation for material evacuated from the forward areas. The demands upon the railways, therefore, were largely increased, whereas the facilities were greatly reduced.

During this period constant enemy aircraft activity and the repeated interruption of telephone communications made the maintenance of an efficient control of train movements a very hazardous business, and movements by night were temporarily paralysed. The reduction in the train service between north and south of the Somme, moreover, necessitated severe traffic restrictions, and, added to the heavy troop movements thrown on to the coast line, caused considerable congestion between Calais and Abbeville, this being further complicated by the urgent demands for reinforcements for the front. The enemy offensive against Chateau Thierry at the end of May impelled the withdrawal of a large number of wagons from the British zone for the evacuation of military and civil stores from this front and from Paris to the south of France. In consequence certain of the ports allotted to the British Forces ran very short of wagons.

Relief was not obtained until the opening of newly-constructed lines in July, and the Allied counter-attack on the Marne in the same month, which resulted in a considerable reduction in the organised air attacks on the railways. The attack of the Fourth Army on the Amiens front in August changed the whole position, and, by freeing the great railway centres of Arras and Longeau, permitted the reconstruction and use of the main lines radiating therefrom, and effected easy communication between north and south. Every effort was then made to follow up the advancing army, the continuous fighting on all fronts causing very heavy demands on transport.

By the end of September and during October the railway situation again changed. The main trouble then was that of keeping pace with the rapid advance of the armies and providing for the needs of the civil population in the reconquered territory. The expansion of the railway lines and the necessity of meeting construction requirements, whilst simultaneously meeting the heavy demands for offensive operations, taxed railway resources to the uttermost.

After the armistice the advance of the British Army to the Rhine created great difficulties in regard to traffic working. In the destroyed area, which in parts was 60 miles in depth, all the railways had been totally destroyed. On the west of this gap, moreover, the lines for a distance of 16 to 20 miles were not in normal condition, whilst on the east side the lines right up to the German frontier had been left in a disorganised and congested condition and with most of the working facilities out of action. The resumption of civil traffic in France greatly intensified the problem of free circulation. The French and Belgian railways were called upon, not merely to carry essential military traffic, but also to provide for the feeding of the civil inhabitants in the zone recovered from the enemy, whilst at the same time there was an abnormal traffic in railway construction material required to bridge the gap in communications between France and Belgium.

Some idea of the immensity of the traffic that was handled will be appreciated from the following tonnage figures :—

1918.	B.E.F. France.	To Italy and the East.	Total.
January to March ..	4,339,770	130,440	4,476,216
April to June ..	3,132,181	52,044	3,184,225
July to September ..	3,723,150	64,413	3,787,563
October to December	3,535,696	46,494	3,582,190
Total	14,730,797	299,397	15,030,194

The number of loaded trains run for the B.E.F., France, during 1918 was as follows :—

	To railheads.	On L. of C.	Total.
January to March	11,805	8,240	20,045
April to June	11,451	10,323	21,774
July to September ..	13,116	10,301	23,417
October to December ..	8,993	9,451	18,444

It will be seen that the total for the September quarter is the highest on record, this being due to the heavy traffic in ammunition, personnel, railway and road material.

French Lines Worked by British.—At the end of 1916 the British Railway Operating Division worked no more than 160 km. of standard-gauge line, but by the end of 1917 the general extension of transportation activities increased this figure to 534 km. A considerable proportion of these lines had, however, to be abandoned in consequence of the enemy offensive early in 1918, and the length of line operated at the beginning of May, 1918, amounted to 334 km, Subsequently the figure rapidly advanced, and at the end of 1918 amounted to 1,312 km., or 8·2 times that operated at the end of 1916.

The volume of traffic on these lines increased monthly, and except for the early months in 1918, when traffic volume naturally decreased with the substantial loss of line, the quarterly figures given below show a sustained improvement. It will be observed that the total for 1918 represents an increase of 145 per cent. over that for the previous year :—

	Loaded wagon-km.	
	1917.	1918.
January to March ..	3,208,980	7,648,315
April to June ..	4,496,979	6,671,466
July to September ..	7,842,275	23,368,993
October to December	9,775,791	24,064,469
Total	25,324,025	61,753,243

British Engines Working Over French Lines.—At the commencement of 1917 the French requested the British to provide manned locomotives for working traffic over the Nord lines, and although this liability had never been contemplated, the R.O.D. started to furnish manned locomotives towards the end of February. The development of this traffic was extremely rapid and highly successful. In April, 1917, only 72 engines were allocated for working traffic over French lines, but this number increased to 267 by the end of the year, at which time British power was hauling 60 per cent. of the trains for the B.E.F. in France. Throughout 1918 the assistance given in this way was increased, as will be noted from the following table, giving the loaded wagon-kilometres hauled by British locomotives over lines operated by the French. It will be observed that the total traffic work during the last quarter of the period 1917-18 had increased to nearly five times that of the first quarter :—

	1917.	1918.
January to March ..	—	36,577,235
April to June ..	11,521,328	60,784,922
July to September ..	17,055,889	55,756,007
October to December	27,946,596	56,595,084
Total	56,523,813	209,713,248

The great assistance afforded to the French railways by the provision of British locomotive power will be appreciated from the fact that, whereas in the quarter ending June, 1917, the total traffic work measured 25 per cent. of the British Army traffic, the proportion for the final quarter was only a little below 100 per cent.

Movements to Italy.—In November, 1917, when the movement of British forces to Italy was ordered, the whole of the movements of British troops up to the Italian border was placed under D.G.T., France, whilst a separate D.G.T., Italy, was appointed to control the transportation services in that country.

The greater part of the supplies for the maintenance of the British Forces in Italy were despatched from bases in France, a certain proportion of the supplies, mainly meat, oats, hay, flour and coal being sent direct by sea. Traffic for Italy was routed *via* Ventimille, and the average haul from French ports and bases up to the Italian frontier was about 1,250 km. The movement of British troops commenced in the first week of November, and during that month trains for B.E.F., Italy, averaged 128 per week, the average for December being 52 trains per week and the total for the last two months of 1917 being 720 trains. During 1918, 1,676 trains were run from France to Italy and the East, 925 for the Italian Expeditionary Force, 603 to Taranto, and 148 to Marseilles.

Light Railways.

Until the middle of 1916 the 60 cm. (Decauville) lines were not developed to any great extent. Those in operation were constructed of very light rails (9 lb. per yard) and laid as tramways, upon which vehicles were propelled by man-power. Later in the year, however, a heavier type of rail was requisitioned for use on lines in advance of railheads, but it was not until towards the end of the year that any general development took place.

The Commander-in-Chief then decided to adopt a complete system of light railways for the distribution and conveyance of ammunition and other stores beyond railhead to the gun positions and towards the trenches, and also for the conveyance of roadstone. Accordingly, 1,000 miles of 20-lb. track were ordered, together with a large number of steam and petrol locomotives and wagons. This decision also led to the adoption of schemes for the provision of workshops and equipment for the erection and maintenance of light railway stock, whilst the question of water supply was taken in hand. The whole of the organisation was placed under the control of Brig.-General Twining, R.E., who was appointed Director of Light Railways and Roads.

Track.—The light railway system developed rapidly. Whilst only 96 miles of railway were being operated at the end of 1916, the mileage increased to 815 by the end of 1917, and whilst this was subsequently extended in the early months of 1918, the fluctuations in the campaign led to some being lost and then regained, the net result being that, in October, 1918, 800 route-miles were being worked.

During the year 1917, 1,022 miles of track were laid, whilst during 1918, 768 miles were laid, and 580 miles reconstructed. As the armies advanced, both in 1917 and 1918, sections of the line were dismantled if not required for salvage purposes, the track being replaced in stock or sent on ahead for new constructions. In December, 1916, there were no 20-lb. rails in stock, whereas, at the end of 1917, despite the large amount of construction, there was a reserve of 200 miles at the depôts.

In following up the advance, many remarkable performances were achieved. In the Fourth Army area, for example, a demolished timber viaduct, 250 ft. long, was reconstructed and available for traffic in 48 hours. On August 8, 1918, the attack in the Fourth Army area resulted in the recently-constructed system being left behind and becoming practically valueless for army purposes. Advantage was, however, taken of track and rolling-stock recovered from the enemy to open up a new system to follow up the advancing troops. Tractors were sent by road, and some 15 miles of line were being operated on August 11, six miles in advance of what had been the front-line trenches two days previously. In consequence of this rapid extension of lines, supplies were able closely to follow up the advancing troops. For instance, ammunition, supplies, &c., were conveyed to Passchendaele, and wounded brought back within 60 hours of the occupation. Again, ammunition was being delivered at Achiet le Grand four days after the first attack.

Rolling-stock and Traffic.—The development of traffic handled by light railways was very remarkable. In January, the traffic averaged 10,325 tons weekly, whereas, in September, this figure had risen to an average of 210,808 tons per week. The average haul was between four and five miles. Of course, this huge increase of traffic could only be handled by a large increase in rolling-stock, the actual figures of which are set out below :—

	1917.			
	January 1.	March 31.	June 30.	September 30.
Locomotives..	68	126	371	550
Tractors ..	27	68	252	360
Wagons ..	560	1,305	2,937	4,403

It is of further interest to note that some of the vehicles had been specially fitted for the carriage of heavy guns by light railway.

During the period of the battles of Passchendaele and Cambrai (August to November), ammunition carried by light railways averaged over 50,000 tons per week, whilst, during September, 1917, the light railways carried an average weekly traffic of 208,600 men. As a result of the thorough organisation of light railway working, the operating results improved considerably. In March, 1917, the turn-round of wagons averaged 1·7 days, whereas, from August to December, the turn-round averaged ·9 days. The ton-miles per route-mile per day, which, in February, 1917, averaged 56, rose to 225, this indicating an increased efficiency measured by 300 per cent. It might also be noted that the ton-miles per locomotive equivalent in traffic averaged 140 per day in February, 1917, whereas this figure worked out to 343 in September, 1917.

During the year 1918, light railways experienced several great changes of fortune. Just prior to the enemy offensive in March, a record traffic was being handled, but, in the course of the enemy advance, a large portion of the light railway network, together with a considerable amount of rolling-stock and power, were lost. This imposed a great strain on the organisation, and necessitated an almost entire re-arrangement of the system, though little could be done until a position of stability was established on the front. The re-organisation of existing facilities and construction of new lines was undertaken in June, and after the opening of the Allied counter-offensive, large mileages of light railway were uncovered in the extensive retreat of the enemy. These lines were immediately exploited in following up the advance. Between March 21 and the end of April, 1918, the route-mileage operated dropped from 920 to 360, but increased by October to 800 miles.

As the Allied Armies continued to advance across Belgium, the light railway system was left far behind, and traffic fell rapidly. In fact, the decrease was so pronounced that, in the quarter ending December, 1918, very little more traffic was handled than in the June quarter of 1917, although the mileage was much more extensive. The following figures indicate the tonnage carried in quarterly periods during 1917 and 1918, and it will be seen that during 1917 and up to March, 1918, the traffic shows a remarkable development. During the second half of 1918, it might be mentioned, the average haul increased considerably with the result that the total ton-miles for 1918 were one and a half times greater than for 1917.

	1917.	1918.
March quarter ..	228,334	2,458,629
June quarter ..	831,957	1,485,138
September quarter	2,276,749	1,889,779
December quarter	2,401,314	997,652
	5,738,354	6,831,198

It will thus be seen that the 1918 traffic was over a million tons in excess of the 1917 figures, and this would undoubtedly have been much greater but for the heavy fall occasioned by the great loss of track in the enemy offensive. Traffic increased rapidly after the opening of the Allied counter-offensive, and was maintained until the armies advanced beyond the limits of the light-railway systems.

In spite of the difficulties under which light railway working was conducted during 1918, the operating results markedly improved during the year. Whilst the loaded wagon-miles in January averaged 57·5 per power unit in traffic per day, this figure increased to 100·6 in August. Locomotives in steam, moreover, which averaged 28·3 miles per day in January, averaged 41·8 miles per day in July, whilst tractors in traffic increased their work from 26·4 miles per day to 33·8 in July.

Roads.

Owing to the inability of the French to continue to maintain the roads in the back areas of the British line, the mileage of roads to be kept up by the British increased very considerably during 1917. The responsibilities that necessarily had to be undertaken in this direction were far in excess of anything originally contemplated and included all roads of any military importance on the lines of communication.

At the beginning of 1917, a period of intense frost considerably hampered roadwork, and for a period of a month, an embargo was placed on the conveyance of all roadstone by rail, while traffic was considerably restricted for some time afterwards. When the frost broke, many of the roads were practically destroyed and very extensive reconstruction was necessary to make them fit for traffic. A great deal of very heavy roadwork had also to be done in connection with the advances made during 1917, as the roads over the destroyed zone had, in most cases, to be rebuilt.

Extent of Roadwork.—As an illustration of the increase in roadwork, it may be noted that during the first six months of 1917, the area of new and re-made roads and cours constructed averaged 50,736 sq. yards per week, whereas, during October, when operations were in full swing, this figure rose to over 100,000 sq. yards per week. The re-surfacing of existing roads and cours during the first six months averaged a little over 180,000 sq. yards per week, and rose in the month of September to an average of 273,000 sq. yards per week.

The greater portion of the road material used during 1917 was required for maintenance work, and the average mileage maintained in army areas was about 1,900 miles, whilst the total mileage in the back areas of the lines of communication averaged about 1,200 miles. The provision of sufficient material to meet the heavy demands taxed all available resources to the utmost, and numerous quarries, gravel pits and fosses were opened, equipped and worked during the year.

The introduction of properly-built sleeper and slab roads and " cours " greatly facilitated and expedited road construction in the forward areas, and, especially, in the shell-torn areas, these roads—which are quickly built and ready to take traffic—proved invaluable. The timber roads, of course, have the further advantage of being economical, as they can be taken up after serving their purpose in one place and be laid elsewhere, or be built into the foundation of the metalled road. A considerable amount of surface tarring was carried out during the summer and autumn months, this much abating the dust nuisance, and also preserving the road surfaces by waterproofing them. The roads were thus made more durable for travelling purposes, and less conspicuous to enemy observers.

Material.—Great difficulties were experienced in obtaining sufficient roadstone for the work, and it was not possible throughout 1917 to build up any reserves, as the supplies never coped with the demands. During January, stone, slag, gravel, sand, &c., used by the Director of Roads averaged 25,412 tons per week, this figure rising to an average of 61,224 tons per week in September. The Director of Roads was also responsible for the supply of roadstone to the French and Belgian Armies in the field and to several other services, and his total consumption of road metal during the latter half of 1917 averaged over 80,000 tons per week. The quantities of road timber used during 1917 were considerable, and the transport of this material was a very heavy item. During October, for example, the number of sleepers, pit-props and slabs received in army and lines of communication areas averaged 56,197 per week.

Road Plant.—To meet the increased requirements of road construction and maintenance, it became of vital importance during 1917 to increase the quantity of road plant available, and the following table shows the principal items at the end of 1916 and the end of 1917 :—

	1916.	1917.
Steam rollers	85	170
Steam wagons	11	395
Petrol rollers	—	35
Sweeping machines	57	175
Petrol lorries	—	235
Tarring machines	—	54
Water carts	72	132
Dump carts	91	930
Mud tumbler carts	16	132
	332	2,258

Increase in Roadwork.—The responsibilities of the Roads Directorate rapidly increased during 1918. Whereas, in June, 1917, the mileage of roads maintained was 1,640, and in January, 1918, 3,267, the mileage maintained in October, 1918, was 4,412 miles. It is interesting to note that the operations of the Roads Directorate eventually covered, not only the whole of northern

France from Havre to Dunkirk and from Boulogne to St. Quentin, but also the whole of the areas in which the Canadian Forestry Corps operated, such as Rouen, Orleans and Bordeaux, and as far afield as the northern slopes of the Jura and Vosges Mountains.

Important Road Scheme.—At the time of the German advance in the spring of 1918, a scheme was prepared for the provision of roads to accommodate the armies in the event of a move in a south-westerly direction. Very few roads run in this direction, and it was necessary to construct new roads in order to link up existing ones, and also to reconstruct and re-surface many miles of roads which had previously been of no importance to the British Army. The scheme comprised 28 separate roads, with a total mileage of 1,170, of which 700 miles comprised roads not previously maintained by the Directorate.

For close on two months, several road-construction companies and practically all the roads organisation in the back areas were concentrated on the work of making these roads fit for the traffic they might be called upon to bear. In addition, it was necessary to stock each route with sufficient material to permit of local repairs being effected in case of collapse. The further essential that these routes should be sign-posted demanded the provision and distribution of some 2,500 illuminated road signs to depôts conveniently situated to the routes, and arrangements were made that these sign-posts should be erected within three days of instruction to that effect. During this period, several miles of timber roads had also to be constructed across the flat country in the vicinity of St. Omar, in order to provide ways for troops moving across the country in the event of the necessity for flooding the areas for military purposes. One of these roads, from Tilques to St. Momelin, was 2 miles in length, and over 20,000 sleepers were laid down in the construction.

Roadwork after Advance.—After the great Allied advance, it was necessary to concentrate all labour and material on the upkeep of roads used in connection with the advance. This was successfully accomplished, and all roads were maintained in good condition and proved adequate to bear the weight of traffic. The maintenance of roads kept pace with the advance, and whilst the numerous delay-action mines laid by the enemy caused some trouble, the roads affected were made good with the least possible delay, and on no occasion was traffic seriously delayed through this cause. As the armies advanced across Belgium, road construction troops were moved forward to maintain the roads required. In addition, quarrying troops and plant had to be moved forward for the working of local quarries to provide the necessary roadstone.

The following figures will give some indication of the extent of road construction and maintenance during 1917 and 1918 :—

	Assuming the average width at 18 ft.		Assuming the average width at 18 ft.	
	1917. Sq. yds.	1917. Miles.	1918. Sq. yds.	1918. Miles.
New roads and cours	901,847	85	1,481,403	140
Reconstructed roads and cours	2,007,457	190	1,325,662	125
Resurfaced roads and cours	9,917,664	940	4,721,337	450
	12,826,968	1,215	7,528,402	715

Marquise Quarries.—In order to provide the vast amount of roadstone required, extensive quarrying operations had to be undertaken and developed, the output of the various quarries, &c., during 1918 being nearly 3,000,000 tons.

The Marquise Quarries supplied most of the roadstone, and every endeavour was made to develop these quarries. Whilst the output of the Marquise Quarries during March and April, 1917, averaged 14,000 tons per week, they were despatching 30,000 tons per week during September, and were dependent for further development on the provision of additional transportation facilities. During 1917, over 1,000,000 tons of roadstone were obtained from the Marquise Quarries and nearly 2,000,000 tons during 1918, the output for the September quarter of 1918 being nearly five times that of the first quarter of 1917.

Shops and Stores.

With the heavy importations of British rolling-stock, it became necessary to provide extensive facilities for the erection and repair of locomotives and wagons, and for this purpose works were constructed and equipped.

Standard Gauge Railways.—The erection of American and Canadian locomotives in France commenced in July, 1917, and up to the end of the year, 141 locomotives were erected ready for the road. In addition, 143 heavy and 675 light repairs to locomotives were carried out during 1917, part of which repairs were undertaken at the R.O.D. works and sheds, especially before the completion of the C.M.E. works. At R.O.D. works, also, shed repairs during the last quarter of 1917 averaged about 100 per week and washing out, 350 per week.

The erection of wagon stock was also performed in France, and during 1917, the shops at Audruicq assembled 8,474 standard gauge and 442 metre gauge wagons. The rate of erection during January, 1917, was 30 wagons per week, but this rate rapidly developed until, in July, 310 wagons per week were being turned out. The works were originally laid out for an output of 300 wagons per week, so the result more than satisfied the expectations.

The following figures show the rapid development in wagon repair work :—

	Weekly average—		
	April, 1917.	October, 1917.	December, 1917.
Heavy	33	93	78
Light	73	313	278
Total ..	106	406	356

The upkeep of the great quantity of rolling-stock under war conditions proved a big undertaking, and the table will be instructive as showing the output of the various repair shops and outstations during 1918 :—

Locomotives and tractors—

Erected	..	..	..			246
Repairs : Heavy and light	..					809
Repairs : Shed..	..	..				5,487
Washing out	..	..	..			25,813

Wagons—

Erected	..	..	..	..	..	3,434
Repairs : Heavy and light	..	..	..	..	22,039
Ambulance trains repaired	..	..	..	..	104
Leave train stock : Repairs, conversions, &c.		..	3,318

Light Railways.—Extensive workshops were also provided at Berguette for light railway work, and also for attending to the steam rollers and lorries working on the roads. In addition to these main workshops for erection and heavy work, repair trains were provided to facilitate the carrying out of light repairs in the army areas.

Evacuation of Shops and Depôts.—At the end of 1917, all the store depôts were concentrated in the northern areas, the reason for this being that as transportation material was imported *via* Dunkirk, this gave a shorter rail-haul from the port, and, additionally, the railway workshops were established in the north. Following the enemy offensive early in 1918, and his advance towards Hazebrouck, No. 2 depôt (Berguette), No. 3 depôt (Aire), and No. 4 depôt (Borre) had to be evacuated, this being effected with practically no loss of material. No. 2 was moved first to Zeneghem and then to Beaurainville, No. 3 first to Zeneghem, then to Richborough and afterwards back to Aire, and No. 4 to Audruicq.

Following the evacuation, new depôts were promptly commenced at Beaurainville, to which place the light railway workshops had been removed, and at Lory, south of the Seine. Both depôts were designed to hold track and general stores of all kinds in order to avoid having everything concentrated in one area. At the same time, the D.G.M.R. arranged to hold the main reserve of general stores and tractor spare parts at Purfleet and the reserve of I.W.T. material at Richborough. The forward locomotive shops at Borre were evacuated during April, 1918, whilst a large portion of the St. Etienne shops were later handed over to the Nord Railway, whose northern

shops were lost, to enable the French to cope with their repair work. The subsequent re-organisation carried out at St. Etienne, together with the loss of Borre, seriously affected the locomotive repair work and a large number of locomotives had to be sent to England for repairs.

New locomotive shops were hurriedly erected at Rang du Fliers, and by the end of September work was in operation at that place. As a precautionary measure, in case Audruicq had to be evacuated, a wagon repair depôt was built at Cissel. This proved very useful in connection with the maintenance of British wagons, and was supplemented by a large number of outstation repair depôts at various points to provide for the upkeep of W.D. stock.

The Beaurainville depôt was sufficiently forward to permit of the storage of material by June 6, 1918, but the Lory depôt was not completed, as the Allied counter-offensive in August rendered it unnecessary. Moreover, the Cissel depôt, although primarily for the use of workshops at St. Etienne and Cissel, was utilised for the storage of standard gauge locomotive spare parts, and general stores for D.G.T. units in the neighbourhood of Rouen.

Stores.—The rapid development of railway operations during 1917 resulted in a heavy increase in the work of the Stores Department. In order to cope with the demands, extensive additional storage capacity had to be built. Accommodation at the Main Depôt at Audruicq was doubled, and new depôts were formed at Berguette for light railway material only, at Borre for standard gauge locomotive spare parts, and at Aire primarily for I.W.T. stores. In addition, new warehouses were erected at Audruicq, and arrangements made at Zeneghem for a depôt for baulk timber, road sleepers and the overflow of standard gauge sleepers.

Small sectional stores were also provided in connection with the workshops at St. Etienne, and it was found necessary to have port storekeepers at Calais, Boulogne, Dieppe and Havre, and a Local Purchase Officer at Paris. Owing to the rapid increase of the storage requirements for the Transportation Services, the Stores Department was subsequently re-organised, all stores for all Directorates being placed under one central organisation, an A.D.G.T. (Stores) being located at G.H.Q., and administrating the whole of the Stores Department.

Personnel.

The great development of railways and roads naturally demanded the provision of additional personnel. When the D.G.T. took over the responsibility for the transportation services at the end of 1916, there were only 52 sections in the Railway Directorate, this comprising 20 operating, 20 construction, and 12 R.T.E. sections, the total establishment being just over 13,000. In January, 1917, therefore, it became desirable to obtain heavy reinforcements and to divide the railway personnel into Railways and a Light Railways and Roads Directorates. Over 1,000 officers and 60,000 men were asked for, whilst the formation of additional Directorates necessitated an additional demand for nearly 100 units, totalling 20,000 officers and other ranks in April. The establishment was further supplemented by a later demand for 2,000 men to reinforce construction and operating companies.

Transportation Establishment in 1918.—At the beginning of 1918, the effective strength of transportation troops in France was 2,290 officers and over 72,000 other ranks, this number subsequently being increased by heavy reinforcements following the enemy offensive in March. With the general retirement of the enemy during the autumn, the need for railway operating personnel was very acute, and the additional provision of skilled men from England became essential. In addition, arrangements were made to withdraw 3,000 men from the armies in France to form eight standard gauge railway operating companies and three standard gauge miscellaneous trade companies. By the time the first unit was formed, the need became less acute, owing to the fact that a certain amount of Belgian, French and German civilian labour had been obtained in the newly-occupied territory. As a result, only 1,300 men were withdrawn from the armies instead of 3,000 originally sanctioned.

The following statement shows the daily number of men working for the respective Transportation Services at various times during the year :—

	Daily average number of men working.			
	May, 1918.	August, 1918.	November, 1918.	December, 1918.
Roads	25,045	28,592	40,745	34,449
Construction (S. and M. gauge) ..	13,057	10,680	27,624	18,916
Docks	10,456	10,511	11,063	9,564
C.M.E.	671	902	2,713	2,816
I.W.T.	—	—	771	1,022
R.O.D.	1,323	1,162	1,915	1,797
Light railways..	2,265	5,909	1,541	1,663
Stores	1,552	1,660	2,103	2,084
C.E.P.C.	573	953	611	525
Total	54,942	60,369	89,176	72,836

As will be noted, there was a very marked increase up to November, this being accounted for by the increased demands for road and standard gauge construction work. After the signing of the armistice, however, these demands naturally declined, with the result that the personnel working shows a marked diminution.

Conclusion.

In his final despatch Sir Douglas Haig points out that the immense expansion of the Army from 6 to over 60 infantry divisions, combined with the constant multiplication of auxiliary arms, called inevitably for a large increase in the size and scope of the rearward services. He also furnished some interesting facts and figures with regard to transportation achievements, and so placed on record the valuable contribution which the railways, roads and inland waterways directorates made to the successful prosecution of the war. It will, therefore, be a fitting conclusion to repeat his remarks in this section :—

Volume of Traffic.—As the Army grew and became more complicated the total feeding strength of our forces in France rose until it approached a total of 2,700,000 men. The vastness of the figures involved in providing for their needs will be realised from the following examples :—For the maintenance of a single division for one day nearly 200 tons deadweight of supplies and stores are needed, representing a shipping tonnage of nearly 450 tons. In an army of 2,700,000 men the addition of one ounce to each man's daily rations involves the carrying of an extra 75 tons of goods.

Roads.—To meet the requirements of mechanical and horse traffic the upkeep or construction of a maximum of some 4,500 miles of roadway was entrusted to the Directorate of Roads. Some idea of the work involved may be obtained from the fact that for ordinary upkeep alone 100 tons of road material are required per fortnight

for the maintenance of one mile of road. Under this Directorate were organised a number of road construction companies, together with quarry companies to supply the necessary metal. In the month of October, 1918, over 85,000 tons of road material were conveyed weekly by motor transport alone, involving a petrol mileage of over 14,000,000 weekly. The total output of stone from the commencement of 1918 to the date of the armistice amounted to some 3,500,000 tons.

Railways.—For the working of the existing railways and for the construction or repair of many miles of track, both normal and narrow gauge, railway troops of every description, operating companies, construction companies, survey and reconnaissance companies, engine crew companies, workshop companies, wagon-erecting companies and light railway forward companies had to be provided. Under the Directorate of Railway Traffic, the Directorate of Construction, and the Directorate of Light Railways, these and other technical troops during 1918 built or reconstructed 2,340 miles of standard gauge and 1,348 miles of narrow gauge railway. Throughout the whole period of their operation they guaranteed the smooth and efficient working of the railway system. In the six months May to October, 1918, a weekly average of 1,800 trains were run for British Army traffic, carrying a weekly average load of approximately 400,000 tons, while a further 130,000 tons were carried weekly by our light railways. The number of locomotives imported to deal with this traffic rose from 62 in 1916 to over 1,200 by the end of 1918, while the number of trucks rose from 3,840 to 52,600.

Transportation Development.—The wonderful development of all methods of transportation had an important influence upon the course of events. No war has been fought with such ample means of quick transportation as were available during the recent struggle. Despite the huge increase in the size of armies, it was possible to effect great concentrations of troops with a speed which, having regard to the numbers of men and bulk of material moved, has never before been equalled. Strategical and tactical mobility has been the guiding principle of our transportation arrangements ; but this was itself at all times vitally affected by questions of supply and by the necessity of providing for the evacuation and replacement on a vast scale of the sick and wounded.

The enormous development of the transportation services in France was in great measure due to the valuable assistance afforded by the British railways in the provision of locomotives, wagons, track, &c. Similarly, much help was afforded from Colonial Governments which raised railway construction troops, and, in certain cases, lifted and sent to France a considerable mileage of track at a time when it was most urgently required.

The operations of the British transportation services necessitated the closest association with the French railway authorities, and the success which was achieved in providing for the British Army in France was largely due to the great efforts made by the French to assist in every possible way the task of developing the railway system behind the British Army.

DELAYS BY KING'S ENEMIES.

A case of considerable interest was heard at the Attleborough County Court, during which the Great Eastern Railway Company was sued for breach of contract by E. A. Fox, a master butcher, who claimed as damages, £24, the price of eight dead pigs consigned to a dealer in Smithfield, but delayed in transit and condemned as unfit for food. The goods were consigned at Company's risk on September 8, 1919, but, owing to an injury to the line caused by a Zeppelin raid, there was a congestion of traffic, and the goods were not delivered till September 13.

His honour, Judge Milligan, K.C., in giving judgment, said he was satisfied by the evidence and found, as a fact, that the railway company did not act either negligently or unreasonably. On the contrary, every effort was made by the company and its servants, working overtime night and day and on Sunday, to minimise the loss to traders consequent on the action of the King's enemies. This case was clearly within the rule of law laid down by Lord Watson in the case of Raymond v. Reid. " A reasonable time has invariably been held to mean that the party on whom it is incumbent duly fulfils his obligations, notwithstanding protracted delay, so long as delay is attributed to causes beyond his control, and he has neither acted negligently nor unreasonably." The company had carried out their contract as far as that was possible for them to do ; they had shown no negligence, but due care and diligence and what had happened had been altogether beyond their control. The action must, therefore, fail. Counsel for the company did not ask for costs. It may be noted that this case, being an instance where traffic was directly interfered with by the action of the King's enemies, differs from ordinary cases of delay which arose owing to war conditions, such as congestion caused by Government traffic.

LIGHT RAILWAY WORKING ON THE WESTERN FRONT.

An Account of the Construction and Operation of Light Railways in France, and a Description of the Plant and Equipment.

" Railways are the arteries of modern armies. Vitality decreases when they are blocked, and terminates when they are permanently severed."—*Imperial Strategy.*

The importance of the part played by railways in modern warfare has for long been realised by the high commands of all nations, and the excellence of the work performed by the standard gauge lines on all fronts during the great war is pretty generally recognised. Of the work of the light railways of 60-cm. gauge, however, little is generally known. This may be attributed partly to the fact that their work differed so vastly from anything met with in peacetime operation, and partly to the veil of secrecy which naturally hid their operations from public notice. Without doubt, the most striking feature of the campaign on the Western front, so far as transportation interests are concerned, was the importance of the part played by the 60-cm. lines in the transport of material and *personnel* in the zone lying between the standard gauge railheads and the infantry and artillery positions, and the story of their operation is full of interest to the student of transportation.

Establishment of a Directorate of Light Railways.

The home depôt of the Royal Engineers' railway troops has, for many years, been situated at Longmoor Camp, Hants, which is reached from Borden Station, on the London & South Western Railway, by a short standard gauge military line. In pre-war days the railway branch of the Royal Engineers consisted simply of two companies of men—the 8th and the 10th—and was therefore quite a small branch of that famous corps. Naturally, on the outbreak of war, these two companies were totally unable to cope with the working of the military railways at home and overseas, and so it came about that the various railway companies in the United Kingdom and in all corners of the Empire were asked to supply trained *personnel* to form new units.

These new units were, so-far as the Western front is concerned, really composed of construction troops, with a sprinkling of operating and locomotive men, and it was not until the spring of 1915 that the Railway Operating Division was formed to operate sections of French standard gauge line given over to the British authorities and such new standard gauge lines as had been laid by us in France. About February, 1916, the Railway Operating Division, in addition to its work on the standard gauge, began to operate certain narrow gauge lines taken over from the French; but towards the close of 1916, with the growth of the narrow gauge system, the Directorate of Light Railways came into being, and numbers of men were then transferred from the Railway Operating Division, where they had been engaged on both standard and narrow gauge working, to the Light Railway Directorate. With the light railway lines which had been taken over from the French authorities, and others which were gradually constructed, there became a regular network of narrow gauge railways behind the whole of the Western front operated entirely by the Directorate of Light Railways, leaving to the Railway Operating Division the operating of the standard gauge alone.

Organisation of Light Railway Working.

The light railway organisation in France was briefly as follows. Under the General Officer Commanding-in-Chief of the British Army came the Director-General of Transportation, to whom the Director of Light Railways at General Headquarters was directly responsible. For each army there was an Assistant Director of Light Railways and under him a Superintendent of Light Railways. Then came the Army Traffic Superintendent, the Locomotive and Tractor Superintendents, the various commanding officers of operating companies and the district traffic, locomotive and tractor superintendents. Each army also had a chief train controller, and numerous other officers such as an officer in charge of statistics and a stores officer. The organisation thus worked out on the following lines:—

G.O.C.-in-C.

Director-General of Transportation.
Director of Light Railways
Assistant Directors of Light Railways.
Superintendents of Light Railways.

Army Traffic Superintendents.
District Traffic Superintendents.
Army Locomotive Superintendents.
District Locomotive Superintendents.
Army Tractor Superintendents.
District Tractor Superintendents.
O.Cs. Operating Companies.
Statistical and Miscellaneous Officers.

It frequently happened that an operating company would be split up into two or three detachments situated at various points with an officer in charge of each detachment, all nominally under the commanding officer of the company, but in practice left almost entirely to their own devices. Each army corps also had a corps light railway officer attached to it, who acted as a kind of *liaison* officer between corps and the light railways.

The gauge of the light railway was 60-cm.—approximately 2 ft.—and for hauling trains steam, petrol and petrol-electric locomotives were utilised. In the rear areas steam locomotives were largely but not exclusively used; in the forward areas these were invariably replaced by petrol and petrol-electric tractors. Owing to the absence of escaping smoke, steam and sparks, the two latter types of locomotives were particularly suitable for work in the forward zones, where to have run a steam locomotive would have meant instant detection by the enemy and the consequent drawing of hostile fire.

Types of Steam Locomotives Employed.

The principal types of steam locomotives in use on the light railways were as follows, Hunslet 4-6-0, Hudson 0-6-0, Baldwin 4-6-0, Barclay 0-6-0 and American 2-6-2. All these locomotives performed excellent work, and as the details may be of interest they will be found tabulated on the following page.

Petrol and Petrol-Electric Locomotives.

The working of the petrol and petrol-electric locomotives in the forward zones forms a particularly interesting study, for the conditions there were naturally not of the best, and the demands made upon the locomotives as heavy as they very well could be. Until something like 15 years ago little attention had been paid by British engineers to the possibilities of petrol locomotives for commercial haulage. This may be attributed to the fact that there was already on the market a German-made petrol locomotive selling at such a low figure as to make it difficult for British makers to compete with it in the open market. There was no question of any superiority of design or high-class of manufacture. The working results of the German product were, however, such as to preclude our engineers seriously attempting to compete with it. The petrol locomotive, too, was looked upon by most engineers, to all intents and purposes, as an unknown quantity, and locomotive engineers preferred to devote their attention solely to the production of, and improvements to, the steam locomotive, in the manufacture of which engine British makers have attained such world-wide renown.

A few British firms did, however, about this time seriously begin to study the possibilities of petrol traction on rails, and as a result of many years of time, study and usage, the petrol locomotive has gradually grown to be the efficient engine it is to-day. Faults there naturally were in their early efforts, but thanks to the indomitable perseverance of the British manufacturers these were eventually

become in this direction that one great manufactory quickly increased its output to something like 30 times its pre-war turn-out in order to meet the phenomenal demand for its products. When one considers the severe conditions under which these petrol locomotives had to work, and the fact that the greater proportion of their army drivers were hurriedly trained and possessed little or no previous experience of this class of engine, or, in fact, of engines of any description, the wonderful results attained are little short of marvellous.

Utility of the Petrol Locomotive.

Many of the narrow gauge railways in France were originally laid for horse traction and man haulage, hence it was essential that the weight of the locomotives, particularly those which were intended for service in the forward areas, should be kept within reasonable figures, and provision was therefore made by the makers of petrol locomotives for war service to increase or reduce their adhesion by removable ballast weights, thus providing for the locomotive a much wider sphere of operation. One of the fundamental principles covering the design of the locomotives was that, while being comparatively simple to control, they should, in addition, be capable of withstanding a very considerable amount of rough usage and overloading.

The light railway lines on the Western front were often, of necessity, laid without due regard to symmetry or rigidity. These conditions alone were obviously not helpful towards the locomotives operating at their best. In the winter months the rails were frequently submerged in snow, water and mud, and, truth to tell, many suffered rough treatment at the hands of inexperienced drivers. Human nature being what it is, many of the locomotives were almost inevitably driven through shelled areas at considerably above the speed for which they were designed, and this, although speaking volumes for their capabilities in an emergency, was bound in time to impair the efficiency of any engine. Notwithstanding these adverse conditions, the petrol locomotive came out of the campaign with an established reputation.

The principal types of petrol locomotives used on the Western front were the 20 and 40 h.p. "Simplex" petrol locomotives manufactured by the Motor Rail & Tramcar Company, Limited, of Bedford, and the 40 h.p. petrol-electric locomotives manufactured by the British Westinghouse Company, Limited, and Dick, Kerr & Co., Limited. All of these performed excellent work and gave complete satisfaction.

		Hudson 0–6–0 Well Tank.	Hunslet 4–6–0 Side Tank.	Baldwin 4–6–0 Side Tank.	Barclay 0–6–0 Well Tank.	American 2–6–2 Side Tank.
Cylinders— Diameter		0′ 6¼″	0′ 9¼″	0′ 9″	0′ 6¼″	0′ 9″
Stroke		1′ 0″	1′ 0″	1′ 0″	0′ 10¾″	1′ 2″
Length of boiler		5′ 6″	5′ 0″	7′ 0″	5′ 10″	—
Diameter of boiler		2′ 1″	2′ 9″	2′ 9″	2′ 2¼″	2′ 8″
„ bogie wheels		—	1′ 6¼″	1′ 4″	—	1′ 4″
„ coupled wheels		1′ 11″	2′ 0″	1′ 11½″	1′ 10″	2′ 3″
Coupled wheelbase		4′ 2″	5′ 6″	5′ 10″	4′ 4″	5′ 0″
Total wheelbase		4′ 2″	13′ 0″	12′ 4″	4′ 4″	15′ 9″
Heating surface— Tubes	Sq. ft.	108·5	168	231	111	—
Firebox	„	17·5	37	23·5	20	—
Total	„	126	205	254·5	131	272
Grate area	„	3·25	3·95	5·6	3·5	5·5
Capacity of tank	Galls.	110	375	393	110	398
„ bunkers	Cwt.	3·5	15	15·7	3·5	15
Working pressure	Lb. per sq. in.	150	160	178	160	175
Tractive force	Lb.	2,970	5,415 (at 75 per cent. b.p.)	5,510	—	—
Valve gear		Walschaert	Walschaert	Walschaert	Walschaert	Walschaert
Brake		Hand	Steam and hand	Steam and hand	Hand	Steam and hand
Firebox		Copper	Copper Belpaire type	Copper	Copper Belpaire type	Copper
Tubes		Steel—45	Brass—86	Brass—83	Brass—45	Brass—54
Width overall		5′ 8″	6′ 3¼″	6′ 11″	5′ 5¼″	6′ 9″
Height overall		8′ 8¼″	8′ 11½″	9′ 3¼″	8′ 4¼″	9′ 0″
Length over buffers		15′ 5¼″	19′ 10¾″	19′ 6¼″	14′ 2¼″	—
Weight— Empty	Tons	5·775	10·9	11·04	5·9	—
In working order	„	6·8875	14·05	14·7	7·0	—
Maximum weight— On a pair of wheels	„	2·3875	3·5	3·46	—	3·5
Per foot of wheelbase	„	1·653	1·08	1·14	—	—
Per foot run over buffers	„	0·446	0·708	—	—	—
On coupled wheels	„	6·887	10·5	10·38	—	—
Tubes—external diameter and length		1⅝″ ×	1½″ × 5′ 0¼″	1½″ × 7′ 2″	1⅝″ × 6′ 0″	2″ × 8′ 5″

Details of principal types of Light Railway Engines used on the Western Front.

overcome, and to-day the British petrol locomotive is a perfect engine, far ahead of its German competitor. Its introduction has placed a new means of haulage—speedy, reliable and economical—at our command.

The war was responsible for enormous improvements in this form of traction, just as it was for a hundred-and-one other valuable developments in the engineering world, and no branch of our engineering industry was quicker to respond to the demands made upon it than that of the petrol engine manufacturers. Large quantities of petrol locomotives were called for by the War Office, having for their especial task the hauling of the heavy ammunition trains on the light railways to the guns. So successful did these locomotives

The "Simplex" Petrol Locomotive.

These petrol locomotives were used in greater numbers than any other types of tractor, and were constantly to be seen hauling long trains in the forward zones, and frequently also in the rear areas. The machinery of both locomotives as a whole is carried upon two pairs of wheels and axles, both of which are driven from the engine. The prime mover consists of an internal combustion engine, which may be of either two, four or more cylinders, and is similar in many respects to that adopted in the construction of heavy commercial motor lorries.

The engine is placed across the centre of the frame, and is fitted with an extra large flywheel carrying a specially-designed friction clutch. The clutch is directly coupled to the driving shaft in the gearbox, and from this power is taken to operate the locomotive. Upon the locomotive frame are mounted the necessary fuel tank, radiator and silencer, and the radiator is kept cool by means of a fan driven from the engine. Sanding gear is also provided, with the necessary foot pedals. The wheelbase is remarkably short, and the centre of gravity low, thus permitting of the roughest track and the sharpest gradient being safely negotiated.

Three types of the 40 h.p. "Simplex" petrol locomotive were used on the Western front—the open, protected and armoured types. The first type did not give the driver great protection from shell fragments and shrapnel, but the two other types provided considerable protection, and this protective armour was the means of saving the life of more than one driver in France.

Light Railway Rolling-Stock.

Almost the whole of the rolling-stock in use on the light railways on the Western front was specially built by English wagon makers to the order of the War Office, and the total stock of trucks of all types in use numbered many thousands. The wagons were all of substantial construction, with, in many cases, pressed-steel underframes, bogie trucks predominating. The types of wagons in most frequent use were the open bogie trucks of from 12 to 17 ft. inside length, and the open box wagons with an inside length of 6 and 8 ft. respectively. Another useful type of truck was a well-wagon fitted with detachable iron stanchions for the transport of ammunition, rails, timber, &c. These trucks had an inside length of 17 ft. 8½ in., with a well 7 ft. 4 in. in length and 1 ft. 7¾ in. deep. Bogie tank wagons, having a capacity of 1,500 galls., were also used extensively for the transport of drinking water to the artillery and infantry. A smaller type of tank wagon was also utilised for journeys on very exposed routes. Special types of open and covered trucks were also used for the transport of wounded from the battlefield, as break-down vans, and on the tractor repair trains. Steel tip trucks were also extensively made use of for construction work, train loads of 20 or so of these cars loaded with ballast being a common sight in all the army areas. There were also numerous odd types of wagon, many built overseas, for special purposes, such as inspection cars, ration wagons and the like. The First Army possessed a most attractive covered inspection car lettered outside "F.A.L.R." (First Army Light Railways), and many notable passengers travelled on inspection trips over the light railways in that army area in this comfortable coach.

High speeds were naturally impossible on the narrow gauge lines, and 10 m.p.h. was considered a good running speed for loaded trains over most lines. On good stretches of track, however, speeds of 15 and even 20 m.p.h. were not uncommonly attained. Train loads varied very considerably, according to circumstances, but there was rarely more than 150 tons behind the locomotive. Wagon loads would be anything from 1 to 10 tons, according to the type of wagon utilised and the nature of the traffic. Ammunition naturally provided the best loads.

Method of Working Trains.

Time-tables were practically non-existent on the narrow-gauge lines, except for special large troop movements, trains simply running as and when required. The "rush" hours for traffic were usually from 6 p.m. to 6 a.m., or thereabouts. The running of trains was controlled entirely by telephone, and there were no fixed signals on the line. Any number of trains could travel in the same direction from one telephone post to another at the same time, the only stipulation being that sufficient distance was maintained between the engine of the second train and the rear wagon of the first to permit of the second pulling up clear of the preceding one if necessary. In the forward area at busy times there was one almost continuous string of trains travelling through the section at the same time.

The train crew consisted of a locomotive driver, fireman and guard, although on trains drawn by petrol locomotives the fireman was dispensed with. There was no guard's brake van on the train, the guard riding in between the last wagon and the last wagon

but one, from which position he manipulated the wagon brakes as necessary, this frequently entailing him working his way along the train as it was in motion. On several light railway wagons captured from the enemy we found small hinged seats of wood about 1 ft. square fixed on to either end of the truck for the use of the guard. As, however, the guard was constantly on and off the train at control posts and sidings, and journeys of more than an hour's duration were not frequent, we did not consider any useful purpose would be served by adopting a similar arrangement, especially as it would have meant foreshortening the wagon in order to provide room for the seat.

Headlights were carried on the locomotives after dark, and usually a tail lamp on the last wagon of the train, except in the forward area, where, owing to the danger of drawing enemy fire, head and tail lamps were in many cases replaced by luminous discs, which could not be distinguished at any considerable distance. On very exposed portions of the line no lights whatever were carried, and there was no daylight working on these branches, whilst occasionally the lines were camouflaged with cloth covers during the daytime. The greater part of the track was single line, with passing places at each telephone box or control post. All behind the front was one vast network of light railway lines, so that if one section of line happened to be blown out by enemy shell fire, it was often possible to divert traffic to another route for the time being. The whole system of traffic working was naturally very free and easy, and much latitude was allowed officers and men in working. Difficulties were constantly cropping up, especially in night working in the forward areas, where, for instance, it was no unusual thing to have three or four derailments in one section in one night, and it was usually the "man on the spot" who had to decide how the difficulty should be overcome.

Extension of Light Railway System.

For the first three years or so of war, the light railways simply covered the district from the front to about 10 miles behind, but as time went on the desirability of having lines of light railway leading back for, say, 20 miles became evident. Particularly was this noticed after the German advance towards Amiens in the spring of 1918. Many locomotives and tractors, together with much rolling-stock, then fell into the hands of the enemy—who also worked with a 60-cm. gauge—which might have been saved had we possessed one single line of light railway track leading far enough back from the front. As it was, locomotives and rolling-stock were in several cases brought as far as the terminus of the light railways, and there abandoned or destroyed, owing to the inability of the standard gauge to get them away in time. After this, lines of escape to the back areas were constructed at suitable points.

The First Army light railway system, shown on page 33, consisted of (1) a main line running roughly north to south from Bethune to Marœuil, 4 miles west of Arras ; (2) numerous branch lines running from various points on this main line eastwards towards our front-line infantry positions ; and (3) an "escape" line running westwards from the southern end of the main line back to Savy, Ligny and Dieval, all on the standard gauge railway. The whole of the line was made up of single track, with the exception of a short stretch of main line at Gouy, where separate "up" and "down" roads had been laid, and, of course, at stations and passing places. The portion of main line at the southern end, from Bray Loop to Artillery Corner, was at one time worked by the Third Army, but was taken over from them by the First Army in April, 1917.

How the Operating Personnel Lived.

The headquarters of the operating company with which I was connected were situated at Marœuil, near Arras, and when I arrived there the town was very badly damaged. The Chemin-der-fer du Nord standard gauge station was damaged very considerably, and the standard gauge railhead had, therefore, been moved back a couple of miles to Mont St. Eloi. A few days prior to my arrival a shell had twisted the substantial water column on the station platform like so much scrap iron. The *personnel* of the operating company at Marœuil lived in wooden huts, sandbagged a portion of the way up as a protection against shrapnel and shell fragments. Dug-outs were available for shelter in the event of enemy shelling or air raids. The company's locomotive sheds and wagon shops were at Maroeuil, while the district traffic control office was located at Artillery Corner, near the village of Anzin, and midway between Maroeuil and Arras. At that time our front line positions were located roughly 4 miles east of Arras. It was at Artillery Corner that I made my home. All of us there lived in dug-outs constructed in the hillside, at the foot of which the River Scarpe placidly flowed eastwards, through Arras and towards the German lines. Behind us were the big guns, and in front the field guns.

Traffic Control.

For the district traffic control office we had a roomy dug-out built in the hillside. Down the centre of the place ran a plain wooden table, at which sat the controllers and clerks. Along one wall was fixed the control board—a huge board painted black, with white grooves running along it to represent the railway system over which we worked, and with the name of each station, siding, dump, &c., painted in white letters in its proper place. Wire clips, to which a wooden tag was affixed, with the number of the engine painted thereon, were moved along the grooves on the board to coincide with the actual movements outside, as advised to district

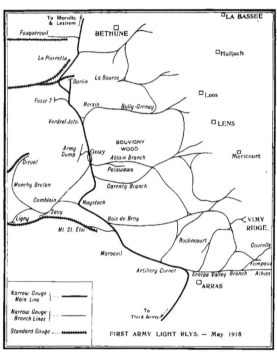

First Army Light Railway System, May, 1918.

control over the telephone by the various outside control posts. Into these clips were placed specially printed slips of paper—one for each wagon—giving details as to wagon number, contents and station from and to. The information given on these slips was also transferred to the wagon books daily, and it was thus possible to tell at a glance what traffic had been dealt with on any particular date.

The staff in the district control office worked in three shifts of eight hours each. On each shift were one sergeant in charge, two traffic controllers, two clerks and one telephone operator. The district went forward—that is, in an easterly direction—from Artillery Corner, through St. Nicholas just north of Arras, to Roclincourt, and so on to the foot of the Vimy Ridge, with a branch going off at St. Nicholas along the Scarpe Valley to Athies and Fampoux. Behind, it extended to Bois-de-Bray, from which point another operating company took over the traffic. Altogether there were about 20 miles of track, with extensive sidings at Artillery Corner and Maroeuil. Something like 16 outside control posts at

different points on the line were staffed by us, and reported by telephone to the district control office at Artillery Corner the movements of all trains in their sections. Almost all of these control posts were located in dug-outs, varying in depth from 4 to 20 ft. One of these dug-outs—that at Plateau, beyond Roclincourt and in sight of the enemy front line—in addition to serving as the light railway control post, also at times accommodated wounded walking cases from the trenches. During my stay in the district we inaugurated a system whereby the outside control staffs were given alternate spells of duty in the more advanced posts and those located further behind the front. The staff in the district control office were specially skilled, and remained on duty there throughout.

Traffic Working Incidents.

In the rear areas behind Artillery Corner traffic was worked by steam locomotives, and on the forward lines beyond that point by 20 and 40 h.p. petrol and petrol-electric tractors. About 1,000 tons of traffic was handled every 24 hours, consisting principally of ammunition, *personnel*, guns, rations, engineering material, poison gas cylinders, salvage and ballast for railway and road construction. Whatever happened, the batteries served by the light railway had, at all costs, to be fed. Their appetite, too, was phenomenal.

We had some rather exciting times running up shells for the guns at night. Looking backwards, it appears miraculous how sometimes the light railway trains managed to get through at all, for, often enough, enemy shells landed all around, on more than one occasion half burying the train crew in flying *débris*. Our casualties were remarkably light: on one occasion a shell landed clean in the middle of a train of six wagons, smashing two of them to bits. The driver of the tractor hauling the train and the guard riding on the rear wagon, escaping unhurt, coolly set to and cleared the line, re-railed the tractor, which had come off the road, and carried on with the remaining four sound trucks.

Working in the dark on a derailment, not daring to show a light, and with enemy shells landing in the neighbourhood, and our own batteries firing right under our nose, was not exactly a picnic. It frequently happened that, after working on a derailed tractor or wagon for some time, it was found impossible to re-rail it before daylight, and so it had to wait until the following night, when a party would set off and finish the job, wondering the whole time whether the enemy would have noticed the tractor or wagon lying there during the day, and open up fire on the assumption that a party would go out at night to get the derailed vehicle on the line again.

Description of Traffic.

During my stay at Artillery Corner many thousands of troops were carried to and from the front. As many as 35 men were conveyed in an ordinary narrow gauge open wagon, and eight wagons usually formed a train load in this district. For the conveyance of artillery special steel gun bogies were utilised, and a train load of these would be made up of four, five or six loaded bogies, according to the size of the guns. The batteries invariably provided escorts to travel with each gun, and also labour to assist in loading and unloading. In times of stress the narrow gauge lines performed much useful work in conveying the guns back to a place of safety.

The ration traffic dealt with in the district travelled principally over the Scarpe Valley line towards Athies and Fampoux, skirting *en route* the northern suburbs of Arras. This line was under direct observation from enemy balloons, and could only be worked at night. Four ration trains were loaded up daily at Maroeuil and Mont St. Eloi, and were hauled thence to Artillery Corner yard by steam locomotives. As soon as darkness fell, petrol locomotives conveyed the trains to their destination, which at one point was within rifle and machine gun range of the enemy line. On arrival there the wagons were unloaded by the infantry, and the empties hauled back to Artillery Corner or used for bringing troops back to rest billets.

The engineering material handled consisted principally of "elephant iron," wire netting, and cement for the construction of dug-outs and "pill boxes," iron stakes, barbed wire and defence timber, and concrete slabs. All this was important traffic, but like everything else it had to give preference at times to ammunition.

The conveyance of loaded poison gas cylinders formed an interesting but rather dangerous part of the work performed by the light railways, and thousands of train loads of deadly gas were worked up to the liberating points by their aid. Much salved material, also, was brought down from the front by light railway to salvage dumps at standard gauge railheads, and considerable economics thereby effected.

A Traffic Exchange.

At Artillery Corner traffic was exchanged with the Third Army, who held the adjoining portion of the front. The junction with that Army system was situated about half a mile east of Artillery Corner, the line branching off in a southerly direction, skirting the western portion of Arras and running thence through Dainville to Simencourt. A most efficient telephone system enabled us to keep in touch with the Third Army controls in regard to traffic on and off that line.

Whilst on the subject of telephonic communication, mention should be made of the excellent work performed by the Signal Section of the Royal Engineers in this and other districts. To keep traffic moving, and so keep the guns going, and the front line positions supplied with men and material, it was at all times absolutely essential that telephonic communication from the district control office to the outside controls should be maintained. Time and again our telephone lines were severed by hostile shell fire, and no matter at what hour of the day or night this happened, the signal staff set out and made good the damage. How hazardous was their work may readily be realised.

The men at Artillery Corner, like so many other light railway units on detachment, away from company headquarters, were unfortunate by reason of the lack of facilities for amusement and recreation in the off hours at their disposal. Notwithstanding this, and the natural tendency to melancholia inseparable from dug-out life, they remained wonderfully cheerful. All were old railwaymen, and over occasional copies of the home railway publications they had many interesting discussions. Never once did they lose their interest in home railway affairs, and always were they eager for "shop talk." Out in the control posts on the line there was usually a tattered copy of some railway publication or other lying about, and on the walls photographs galore of locomotives, stations and so on, clipped from magazines from time to time.

Arming of the Railway Operating Troops.

In view of the possibility of a sudden enemy break-through, the whole of the *personnel* of the First Army Light Railways were early in 1918 provided with rifles and bayonets, and opportunity taken to give them practice on the range. In connection with the possibility of a German break-through, our plans for the evacuation of the light railway locomotives and rolling-stock were all cut and dried, and every officer and senior non-commissioned officer was given an outline of the form this evacuation would take, and more definite instructions as to his own particular part in the operation. Had the Germans succeeded in breaking through the First Army positions in 1918, the chances are they would have secured little, if any, light railway rolling-stock; all stock would have been withdrawn behind our retiring troops, the lines blown up in vital places, and such works on the line as pumping stations, water tanks, locomotive sheds and the like rendered useless before the enemy arrived.

Gouy Marshalling Yards.

At Gouy, some miles north of Artillery Corner, were situated the First Army Light Railway central marshalling yards. Here was the only stretch of double track on the whole of the main line in the Army area, and something like 800 loaded wagons per day were dealt with in the yards in addition to empties, traffic for all parts of the system passing through. The loaded wagons were sorted at Gouy and assembled in train loads for their various destinations. The yard was of the usual flat type; no gravitational yards existed, so far as I could learn, anywhere on the British light railways in France. It consisted of two portions—an "up" and a "down" yard—the former dealing principally with traffic going towards the front, and the latter with the return traffic. In the "up" yard there were five roads, each capable of accommodating about 30 wagons; and in the "down" yard four slightly shorter lines. Empties were collected into train loads in the "down" yard, and any slight damages made good on the spot by the wagon repair staff, serious damages being left to the wagon shop staff at Barlin, 5 miles to the north, where the headquarters of the First Army Light Railways were situated. Shunting operations were performed by the ordinary train engines.

All kinds of traffic passed through Gouy, and as it was no infrequent occurrence for a stray enemy aeroplane to come over in the daytime, the yards were invariably kept as free from traffic as possible. Often at busy times, however, there would be as many as 80 or 100 wagons of high-explosive shells standing in the "up" sidings at the same time waiting engine-power to lift them. A very large troop movement in the district or the working of trains of gas cylinders up to the front in preparation for a big attack, which drew the locomotives away from their ordinary work, usually resulted in congestion at Gouy. We were most fortunate, however, as regards our freedom from enemy shell fire. If a shell from the enemy had dropped on our yard at times of pressure, there would have been very little left of Gouy. Only once, however, did a shell land anywhere in the immediate vicinity, and this demolished a well which had been sunk in the "down" yard to obtain water for the locomotives, smashing up in addition the pump-house alongside. It always struck me as an inexplicable thing why the enemy did not shell the Gouy yards in earnest, for he must have known quite well of their existence. In addition to the observation aeroplanes which came over, it was possible on a clear day to see his balloons, and from them he could not have failed to watch the movements of trains in and out.

"Camouflage."

In connection with enemy observation from the air, and consequent shelling, an interesting occurrence arose at Bois-de-Bray, a little to the south of Gouy. The enemy frequently used to shell a duckboard track there leading to an old, disused infantry camp, and we often wondered at his partiality for this target, for the light railway a short distance away was rarely hit. Eventually a photograph came into our possession taken by an enemy airman, and on the explanatory notes alongside being examined, it was discovered that the duckboard track in question had been mistaken by the German "intelligence" staff for an "important light railway." No reference was made on the map to the light railway proper.

The ballast for the First Army light railways was obtained from a colliery near Barlin called Fosse 7, the slag heaps being reached by a line of light railway about half a mile in length, leaving the main line between Verdrel and Cairo Junction. The slag, which was loaded into light railway trucks both by hand and by means of a steam navvy manufactured by Ruston & Hornsby, Limited, Lincoln, made excellent light railway ballast, and loadings often touched 1,000 tons per day.

Light Railway Reorganisation.

On the Fifth Army being reorganised after the retirement on the Amiens front in the spring of 1918, it took over the portion of front lying between Bethune and Armentieres, and the light railway system was quickly developed in this area. The northern section, with which the writer was connected, made its headquarters at La Lacque, about 2 miles north-west of Berguette. As shown on page 35, the light railway system then consisted of a main north to south line running from La Lacque to Bethune, with a connection at its southern end with the First Army system, and branch lines running eastwards from this lateral towards the infantry positions. At the outset the northern section simply served an engineering dump on the standard gauge at La Lacque and an ammunition dump further west at Neufpré, which had also standard gauge connection, and which was situated on the outskirts of the town of Aire-sur-le-Lys. The last portion of track between Neufpré and Aire was only suitable for the passage of trucks pushed by hand, and was used for the transport of material to a bridging school of the Royal Engineers on the Lys Canal, and an R.E. electric power-station. The engineering dump at La Lacque was formed on what had been the site of the central light railway workshops. These shops were enormous places, full of costly machinery of every description for the repair of steam and petrol locomotives, and rolling-stock, and when first laid down our front line infantry positions were 20 miles distant. When the enemy made his advance there in the spring of 1918 the place was evacuated, and the shops transferred to a safer site at Beaurainville, between Hesdin and Etaples. The

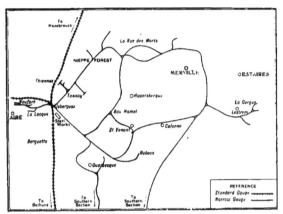

Fifth Army Light Railways (Northern Section).
August 31, 1918.

enemy shelled the La Lacque workshops at the time of his advance, but practically the whole of the shops and their contents were safely transferred to Beaurainville.

About a couple of miles to the south-east of La Lacque were situated the Isbergues steel works, run by the French, the second largest works of its kind in the country. These works continued to employ many hands, and turned out large quantities of steel—approximately one-sixth of their pre-war output—despite daily enemy shelling and bombing. Soon after our arrival at La Lacque we commenced to open up a light railway line running from that point, and passing through Isbergues, to the south-western corner of the Nieppe Forest and through the forest towards Merville. The forest was entered about 2 miles north-east of Isbergues steel works, near the village of Tannay. Just prior to entering the forest a branch left the main line and went to Thiennes, on the Hazebrouck-Isbergues standard gauge line. At Thiennes there was at first simply an R.A.M.C. casualty clearing station and an engineering dump, but as time went on the place was opened out as a standard gauge railhead, and troops and ration traffic were dealt with in considerable quantities.

Although the line from La Lacque to the Nieppe Forest had been in existence some time, little had been done prior to our arrival to develop traffic over it. The ammunition dump at Neufpré and the La Lacque engineering dump were, however, soon opened up seriously ; numerous light railway locomotives were put into traffic and a stock of wagons got together, and in a couple of weeks or thereabouts we were carrying well over a thousand tons of traffic daily. There was only one main road through the Nieppe Forest, and along-side this was laid the light railway track. On either side was dense forest with thick, tangled vegetation under the trees, with here and there narrow, winding footpaths leading into the heart of the forest. Along many of these paths the light railway track was laid for the purpose of conveying shells to the batteries concealed in the forest. After passing the " Street of the Dead," the light railway line continued to within about a mile of the eastern edge of the forest opposite Merville.

Light Railway Extension on Enemy Retirement.

About the middle of August the enemy commenced to retire on this front, and by the beginning of September we had pushed ahead with the narrow gauge line as far as the northern outskirts of Merville, the enemy being then back at Estaires. Until this retirement took place the main road through the forest, along which ran the light railway line, was under direct observation from the enemy balloons, and to conceal to some extent our movements strips of canvas about 6 ft. wide were stretched from tree to tree across the road at a height of about 10 ft. from the ground. As the enemy retired, we quickly pushed the light railway forward, and by the beginning of September opened up a line which branched off in a south-easterly direction at Isbergues, and after following the Aire Canal for some 3 miles, proceeded to St. Venant, Calonne, Lestrem, the southern outskirts of Merville, and on to La Gorgue. Huge quantities of light railway and road material were rushed up the light railway to keep pace with the retreating enemy, and new traffic controls were constantly established further east as the line grew. After passing Calonne the new line was laid on our old light railway formation, and alongside the new track were the old rails, broken, twisted and torn up by the enemy to hamper our pursuit. On our old lines we came across numerous British wagons which had been captured by the enemy in the spring, many of them quite intact, and these were quickly put into traffic.

The construction of the light railway lines in this district presented a good many engineering difficulties, for although there were practically no gradients, canals, streams and marshy ground abounded. During September, 1918, heavy rains seriously interfered with the work of construction and played havoc with newly-ballasted track.

Fifth Army Light Railways Left Behind.

The retreat of the enemy, begun in August, continued throughout September, 1918, and by the end of that month the Fifth Army light railways were left high and dry miles behind the front, in spite of the efforts of the construction troops to lay steel. As, however, the main ammunition and engineering material dumps, and infantry rest-camps, were also situated at an equally great distance from the fighting line, the light railways continued to carry considerable quantities of traffic, including large numbers of troops, up to the end of steel, from which point road transport was employed. New dumps were gradually made further forward, but as our fighting forces were almost daily moving eastward on the heels of the retreating enemy, no permanent dumps could be made, as an advanced dump with light railway connection laid

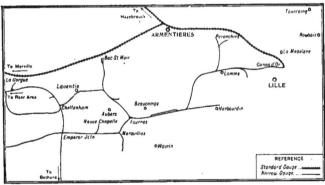

Fifth Army Light Railways (Northern Section).
October 31, 1918.

out one day would be miles behind the front the next. The light railway line by the end of September was being operated as far as Laventie and Fromelles, almost within sight of Lille.

With a haul from standard gauge railhead at La Lacque to end of steel of nearly 20 miles, over a considerable proportion of newly-laid track, it was somewhat difficult to meet all traffic requirements, particularly as the power and wagon-stock remained the same as had been employed on a small self-contained system with an extreme haul of 8 or 10 miles. At this period train crews worked exceptionally long hours, and if two trips per day per train from standard gauge railhead to end of steel were obtained it was considered good work, especially as labour for loading and unloading trucks was particularly scarce. We had been an exceptionally long way behind the infantry since the beginning of September, but with the capture of Lille on October 18, 1918, our light railways were hopelessly out of the fight. The lay-out at the end of October is shown on page 35. Headquarters were then moved up to Lestrem, and steam working introduced as far as Fournes, 6 miles south-west of Lille, while trains drawn by petrol locomotives travelled to Lomme on the town's north-western outskirts.

German Light Railways.

The light railway line from Lestrem to Lomme consisted mainly of German track. As the enemy retired he did not damage the track to any extent. Here and there sections of rail had been removed, but these were quickly restored, and thus he left at our disposal a most useful light railway system, which we at once commenced to use for the transport of ammunition and material.

After leaving Lestrem the line passed through the ruins of the town of Laventie, and then turned in a south-easterly direction over the Aubers Ridge to Fournes, on the La Bassee-Lille road. Here it turned off to the north-east to Harbourdine and Lomme, to the west of Lille. Between Fournes and Harbourdine the enemy left an excellent double track some 3 or 4 miles in length, equipped with semaphore signals worked from substantially-built brick signal-boxes alongside. Every signal-box and station had its name-board outside in German, and all along the line were speed indicators, warning boards and the like. Everywhere were spurs leading to various camps and artillery positions, indeed, the whole district was one vast network of light railways, completed and in course of construction.

At Lomme was an extensive light railway yard with large, brick-built locomotive and wagon shops lit by electricity, and full of tools and spare parts. Huge stocks of coal had been left behind, a hundred light railway wagons, and immense quantities of rails, sleepers and ballast. From Lomme the line branched off in two directions. The line to the north went to Perenchies and the other branch to Canon D'or, just outside the citadel of Lille. Here the line was blocked by the standard gauge railway, which had been blown up by the enemy. These lines were all being operated when news was received of the signing of the armistice, and on November 13 ammunition traffic began to be worked back from Lille to Lestrem. All along the light railway system the same backward movement was soon in progress.

General Utility of Narrow Gauge Lines.

Narrow gauge lines were not confined exclusively to the forward area, for there was an extensive light railway system on the lines of communication in France. At Oissel, near Rouen, timber was worked by 60-cm. railway from the Rouvray Forest to standard gauge. At Brotonne, midway between Rouen and Le Havre, a short narrow gauge line served to convey timber from forest to Inland Water Transport barges on the River Seine. At Havre light railways dealt with petrol and general stores, and a small system at Trouville-sur-Mer served convalescent depôts and hospitals.

From the date of their inception light railways were concerned in every success of our arms, and played no small part in civilisation's struggle. I should like, in conclusion, to take this opportunity of paying a tribute to the loyalty of the whole of the light railway staff—most of them drawn from the home railways—with whom I came in contact in France. Always cheerful, always anxious to put their last ounce of energy into whatever task they might be allotted, it was indeed a pleasure to command a body of such men. Casualties were inevitable, but the memory of those very gallant railwaymen who paid the supreme sacrifice will ever be with us.

RAILWAY FACILITIES AT LILLE, LENS AND VALENCIENNES.

During the war special interest was taken in the railway facilities at various places in the battle areas, and it will be worth while to recapitulate a few of the published details. Lille, for instance, is on the Nord Railway, and through it passes the traffic to and from Brussels via Calais or Boulogne, the frontier being 8 or 10 miles east of Lille. The line from Calais is joined by one from Douai, which gives a connection with Paris. There also runs into this station the Nord line from Roubaix, which is joined on to the Belgian State Railway for Ghent. The station has 12 platform roads, all signalled for arrival and departure. Trains from Calais can enter any platform road, and trains for the Calais direction can leave from any line. The engine shed is alongside the down Calais line, and there is direct access between the engine siding and every platform. The Roubaix trains can only use platforms 6 to 12. The western end of the station is protected by a signal-box—Lille No. 1—over the running lines and at right angles thereto, which contains 76 levers. In normal times there used to be 189 train movements in 2 hrs. 40 min. between 4 and 7 p.m.

At Lens railways from four directions meet. There is a triangle, the apex of which is the line from Hazebrouck, also the station. On the left side of the triangle is the line from Arras, whilst in the lower right hand corner is a junction between the lines from Armentieres and Ostricourt. These are joined at Sallau Junction, whence they form the right side of the triangle. From Sallau Junction, and forming the base of the triangle, there is a loop connecting the Armentieres-Ostricourt lines with the Arras line and joined at D'.vion Junction. In the middle of the yard there are two sets of sorting sidings, each set having six roads, served by an arrival and departure road and a shunting neck. By the side of the Hazebrouck-Sallau line there are 24 sidings, which are served by six gravitation sidings. Access to and from the Arras and Sallau lines is made with all the 24 sidings. Quick access to the sorting and gravitation sidings is given off all the main lines by means of numerous facing points. There are three platform faces in the passenger station. The main station buildings are alongside the Hazebrouck-Sallau line. The trains to and from Arras can, however, use the Sallau-Hazebrouck platform by passing through a facing connection in the line from Arras at that end of the station.

Valenciennes station is approached by a double line from the north, into which converge connections from Douai, Lille, Peruwelz and Blanc-Misseron, the two latter being in the direction of Belgium, and by a double line from the south into which lines from Maubeuge, Aulnoye and Lourches converge. Outside the station the two goods lines are diverted and run separately on the west side. There are four through platform faces and two dock lines at each end, and there are five passenger lines, three being on the east side and two on the west side. The latter two are through lines of the usual type, with a scissors crossing in the centre of the station. The easternmost of these is known as No. 7 at the north end and as No. 8 at the south end, and the westernmost as No. 10 at the north and as No. 9 at the south. Trains arrive from the north at No. 7 and depart therefrom for either north or south, and arrive from the south and depart for the north or south at No. 10. Trains arrive from the south and depart for north or south at No. 8 and depart for north or south from No. 9. The other three through lines are peculiarly arranged. They are at the north end known as Nos. 1, 4, 5 and at the south end as 2, 3, 6. Nos. 4 and 3 are one continuous middle road, but Nos. 1, 2, 5, 6 only serve the platform for one-half of the station and are diverted in the centre of the station into the middle road. The arrangements are, to a degree, like those which are to be found in the London, Brighton & South Coast Company's terminus at Victoria.

THE VALUE OF FULL AND ACCURATE STATISTICS
As Shown under Emergency Conditions in the Transportation Service in France.

A Paper read by Sir George Beharrell, D.S.O., Director-General of Finance and Statistics, Ministry of Transport, before the British Association at Bournemouth on September 10, 1919.

The conditions arising out of the war, involving the need for intensive production and a high state of efficiency in all operations, drove home to many minds probably more forcibly than ever before the necessity for exact and complete information, and emphasised the impossibility of successfully directing large organisations if such information is not forthcoming.

Elaborate statistics were necessary in connection with the production of all classes of war material to ensure that the various components were available in adequate and balanced quantities ; but these statistics do not call for special consideration in this paper.

It has been said on more than one occasion that the success of transportation in France was largely due to the fact that money was of no account and was spent like water. From this it is inferred that efficiency from the commercial point of view was disregarded, everything being subordinated to meeting the needs of the army. This is a complete misconception of the facts. Although the ordinary business tests of interest earned on capital expenditure or ratio of working expenses to gross receipts could not be applied, other considerations compelled the utmost economy and efficiency, and caused the operations of transportation to be watched with a most critical eye ; these were—shortage of men and material.

With operations so diverse in character and scattered over a very wide and varying field, how was the Director-General of Transportation to satisfy himself that the services for which he was responsible were being efficiently managed ? This could only be done by making full use of the science of statistics. Stale figures could be of little value under the changing conditions of war, so that rapidity of compilation was one of the first considerations. Preliminary information, giving a reliable guide to the position, was available on the Tuesday evening for the week ending the previous Friday midnight. Complete statistics, which never materially varied from the preliminary ones, were circulated by the Thursday following ; that is, on the sixth day after the completion of the period dealt with.

Informatory Value of Statistics.

The statistics told each responsible officer what he was doing, whether he was going back or going forward, and how he compared with his opposite number in other places. They also told the other branches of the service what transportation was doing for them, and where they fell short in assisting transportation to obtain the best results. There is little value in the mere compilation of statistics. Their value depends very largely on judicious circulation ; but this aspect is, I am afraid, sometimes overlooked.

The demand for statistics is rarely, if ever, enthusiastically received by those on whom it is made, and it is only by the circulation of the information so obtained that the sympathetic interest of those away from Headquarters can be secured and retained. Without statistics it is impossible to know with any certainty that there has been any improvement, and it is certainly impossible to measure such improvement. The spirit of emulation which developed was directly due to the circulation of detailed and accurate figures.

Before considering the statistics relating to the various phases of transportation work in France it may be of interest to explain in a few words the procedure with regard to new railways and works after the transportation organisation was adopted.

Measures Preliminary to Military Operations.

The General Staff in the case of major operations, or the Staff of the Army in the case of operations on a small scale, communicated as early as possible to the Director-General of Transportation the plan of campaign, giving at the same time a forecast of the numbers of troops and guns proposed to be employed, and estimates as to reliefs, casualties and so forth. This enabled calculations to be made as to the trains which would have to be provided for, and the Director-General was able to decide as to the new broad gauge lines and new railheads to be constructed, what use could be made of canals, whether the case would be better met by a system of 60 cm. lines, or whether roads should be built to enable full use of motor lorries to be made. Sometimes a combination of two or three or even all of these methods was decided upon. In considering all these cases regard was had to the available resources in men and material suitable for the various classes of work and the time in which the works had to be completed. There was no hard and fast rule that up to a certain point broad gauge lines were to be constructed, and thereafter light railways, and beyond that roads with motor lorries. Each scheme was carefully considered on its merits.

A system of statistics was introduced for each of the services for which the Director-General of Transportation was responsible, and will now be considered in detail.

Docks.

In the summer of 1916 the docks in France were congested and no more quay space could be allotted to the British Army. At that time the imports had not reached more than 130,000 tons per week, and having regard to the fact that the army was growing and that in the near future ammunition would be required at a greatly increased rate, it was obvious that the necessary imports could not be received unless the capacity of the docks was increased.

The first step was to remove congestion, as with congested quays the rate of import was bound to fall.

Careful programmes were prepared for one month and also for three months ahead, and sent to the War Office for guidance. The monthly programmes showed the weekly tonnage of various traffics which could be dealt with and the port to which it was allotted, and weekly statistics were circulated, showing how the allocation had been worked to. This programme was of immense benefit in avoiding congestion and waste of shipping.

Three main units of efficiency were adopted for testing the working of the various ports :—

1. The tonnage discharged per ship per hour in port.
2. The tonnage handled per man per hour.
3. Ship days lost awaiting berths.

275 per Cent. Increase in Tonnage Discharges.

The average tonnage discharged per ship per hour in port was arrived at by taking the total tonnage discharged from all ships which completed unloading in a particular week and dividing by the total number of hours the ships had been in port, i.e., from arrival to completion of discharge. In February, 1917, this figure was 10 tons per ship per hour in port. The figure steadily rose until in the spring of 1918 the tonnage discharged in certain weeks was $37\frac{1}{2}$ tons per ship per hour in port, an increase of 275 per cent. This improved rate of discharge was due to improved equipment and improved organisation. By improved equipment I mean not only the equipment on the quays but increased numbers of railway wagons and locomotives, which enabled the flow of traffic through the ports to be steadily maintained.

The rate of handling per man per hour was closely watched, each port being compared with its previous performance on similar cargoes. Comparison was also made with other ports handling similar traffics. The improvement in the rate of handling per man per hour could not show the same increase as the rate of discharge per ship per hour ; but after a year's experience it was found that for all ports the tonnage had gone up from ·51 to ·63, an increase of 24 per cent., and it must not be overlooked that the demands of the front line steadily reduced the category of men available for dock working. This improvement was due to better supervision and equipment.

Coloured labour was moved about until the most suitable form of work and the supervision necessary to secure the best results were ascertained.

Another important figure showed the number of ship days lost awaiting berths. This was a very good index of the efficiency of the working of a port, and also showed whether there was close touch with the forwarding departments at home. Early in 1917 in one week the equivalent of 100 ship days was lost ; but this was gradually reduced to only six ship days per week.

Without any addition to the accommodation the imports increased from 130,000 tons per week to a maximum of 225,000 per week.

I am not aware that similar operating figures are regularly available for any docks in this country. Their absence may be partly due to the lack of uniformity of practice in dealing with ships in home ports. In many cases dock authorities are in no way responsible for the discharge of the ship, the delivery of the goods to warehouses, or the removal of the goods from the quay to depôts in the ports, or for the delivery to railway. The work at the present time is in so many hands that a comprehensive statistical view of the position may be difficult to obtain ; but results in France show the value of fuller information as to dock working.

Cross-Channel Barge and Train Ferry Achievements.

Before leaving the question of imports it may be of interest to state that during 1918 just under 1,000,000 tons of traffic were conveyed across the Channel by barges, and that over two-thirds of this amount was able to proceed direct up the canals in France to depôts or canal-heads where required. The Channel ferry came into operation much later ; but in one quarter in 1918 it dealt with 80,000 tons. The outstanding feature of the ferries was the rapidity with which they were loaded and unloaded. During one month the time of loading and unloading in France averaged only 18 minutes per trip for each operation, which was one half the time occupied some months earlier. The ferry dealt with traffics such as tanks, locomotives and heavy guns, which would have occupied very considerable time in unloading if conveyed in ordinary cargo steamers, and in addition loss of time would have been experienced and additional labour required in taking down and re-erecting.

Broad Gauge Railway Construction.

The construction of broad gauge railways during the first two years of the war was comparatively small, but during the last two or three months of 1916 and the years 1917 and 1918 there was great activity in the construction of new lines, and in the later months of 1918 in the reconstruction of lines following up the German retreat. The total length of new lines constructed by the British Army in France was roughly 2,000 miles, and in addition, during the last six months of 1918, 1,581 miles were reconstructed, this latter work involving the entire relaying of 589 miles of track and the reconstruction of every bridge and culvert on the line of route. In destruction the enemy was undoubtedly thorough.

The construction of each line was carefully considered, plans were prepared, the work was properly authorised and given a reference number, and dealt with in every way in a regular manner. Requirements of men and materials were made out, and estimated dates given for the completion of each work. The progress of these works was reported weekly to Headquarters, showing the percentage of earthwork, the percentage of track and the percentage of the total work completed, and the number of men (skilled and unskilled) employed. Progress diagrams were compiled so that as the time for operations came near the General Staff were fully posted as to the progress which was being made with the various essential lines and depôts.

148 Miles of Railway Reconstructed in One Week.

Early in 1917, 8 miles of broad gauge and metre gauge railway were completed per week ; but in May of that year 45 miles of new

lines were completed and open for traffic in one week, the average for the whole month being 32·25 miles per week. This figure was, however, entirely put into the shade during the advance in October, 1918, when during one week 148 miles of railway were reconstructed, involving the use of 57 miles of entirely new material. The latter was, of course, reconstruction over the old roadbed, whereas the 45 miles was construction through virgin country involving, in some cases, cuttings, embankments and bridges. Reconstruction had, however, its own special difficulties. A single line was first laid which had to carry not only army supplies and food for the civilian population, but also material for the doubling. As a traffic factor the single line was probably out of action some six or eight hours a day.

Broad Gauge Railway Operation.

In the early days of the war it was expected that the French railways would be able to deal with the traffic for the British Army, with the exception of possibly a little shunting at certain depôts. The length of the war and the magnitude of the operations rendered it necessary for the War Office to have in France 1,400 broad gauge locomotives and wagons equivalent to 70,000 10-ton units, as well as 30 ambulance trains and 11 trains for personnel. Even after this amount of stock had been provided it would have been impossible to meet the demands if the stock had not been worked with the greatest efficiency. The number of trains worked to railheads and to depôts on the lines of communication rose from an average of 180 per day in March, 1917, to a maximum of 298 per day in August of 1918. This is exclusive of trains worked through France to Italy with traffic for the Mediterranean and Italian Expeditionary Forces

The army worked in close relationship with the civilian railway personnel in France. First—the Railway Operating Division were responsible for the operation of certain lines. Over these lines trains were mainly worked by that unit ; but also to a smaller extent by the French. Secondly—the R.O.D. worked trains over the systems maintained and generally operated by the French. Separate statistics for R.O.D. lines and French lines were compiled.

The lines operated and maintained by the British army grew from 160 kms. in December, 1916, to 1,312 km. in December, 1918. The average haul over the French lines increased from 37 km. to 65 km., and over the R.O.D. lines from 14 km. to 24 km. The loaded wagons per train went up from 31 to 37 on French lines, and from 21 to 33 on R.O.D. lines, increases of 19 per cent. and 57 per cent.

Improving Locomotive Mileage Efficiency.

A great improvement was effected in the working of locomotives. During 1918 the hours per locomotive in steam per day were reduced, but the mileage per locomotive per day was increased. At the same time a reduction in coal consumption was realised. The following is an interesting comparison of results of working over lines for which the British were responsible :—

	April, 1917.	August, 1918.	Improvement.
Kilometres per locomotive in steam per day	69·5	89·0	28 per cent.
Hours per locomotive in steam per day	14·3	10·9	24 ,,
Lbs. of coal per locomotive-km.	62	42	32 ,,

Importance of " Wagon-User " Statistics.

The closest attention was paid to wagon-user. In the first place returns were received from large depôts such as Boulogne, Audruicq, Rouxmesnil and Romescamps, showing the number of trains and wagons despatched and the average number of wagons per train. Naturally the weight could not be exactly ascertained, but the nature of the traffic and the standard size and weight of packages made it fairly easy to arrive at an approximate average load per train. The number of wagons awaiting despatch at the end of the day was very closely watched and materially reduced. Every effort was made to keep down the detentions at destination. Full returns were received from each railhead. These were analysed under various traffics, such as ammunition, supplies, roadstone, &c., showing the number of loaded trains and loaded wagons received and the time the train was at railhead. This figure was shown in three parts :—

Time before unloading commenced.

Time occupied in unloading.

Time from completion of discharge to return of train.

This division enabled the departmental responsibility for delay or lack of improvement to be readily fixed. Summaries for each army were prepared and circulated, and cases calling for explanation were specially noted. The total times at railhead became stabilised round 13 hours as an average for all armies. Actual unloading took about 6 hours. The figures were maintained in spite of materially increased attention paid to railheads by enemy artillery and aircraft. These times are very striking when the free time which is allowed in this country for the unloading of traffic under peace conditions is considered.

Repair shops for locomotives and wagons had to be constructed and equipped and organised. The output of work in terms of vehicles erected or repaired was shown in relation to the personnel employed.

Light Railway Construction.

The light railway system was designed to give the army mobility. Owing to the devastated nature of the country it was impossible to construct roads to carry the necessary traffic as the amount of roadstone involved would have taken up practically all the railway capacity available for army supplies.

In the end upwards of 1,000 km. were under operation at one time, and the traffic conveyed exceeded 250,000 tons in one week during the period of the German offensive in the spring of last year; but the usual amount of the traffic could be taken at something like 160,000 to 180,000 tons per week.

Light Railway Operation.

The efficiency of these lines was most closely watched. It was a new system and suitable statistics could be introduced. To facilitate comparison various types of locomotives and tractors were converted into a power unit, and the wagon stock was similarly converted into a unit of a bogie wagon.

The figures were often compiled in huts or dug-outs under artillery fire, but in time all concerned realised the benefit of the information which was produced, and objections to even ton-miles ceased. During the maximum week 1,341,000 ton-miles of work were performed.

The organisation provided for District Controls, and it was here that the figures were compiled in their initial stages. Little work in connection with statistics was thrown upon the train or yard staff and very few forms were involved. Telephonic advice was given the District Control of the despatch of each train with certain particulars, and from these advices summaries were prepared and the ton-miles and wagon-miles inserted at the Central Control.

Many instructive diagrams were produced showing the improvements in the various units of efficiency for each section, each army and the systems as a whole. It is only possible, however, to refer specially to the more important results obtained.

Ton-Miles per Power Unit per Day.

The first unit to be considered is the number of ton-miles worked per power unit in service per day. This was a most valuable figure, indicating the effective use made of the power available. In 1917 the average ton-miles per power unit per day were 242; but by July, 1918, this figure had risen to 658, an improvement of 172 per cent. Wagon-miles per power unit were also compiled.

Tonnage per Wagon Unit per Day.

Wagon user was tested by the tons per wagon unit in service per day. The daily average for the best week was 8·9 tons per day; but the figure never fell below 6 tons. The small systems varied in extent, and the average distance was affected by the position for the time being of the batteries served by the light railway. There was a general tendency for the average length of the loaded wagon trip to increase. The minimum was 4½ miles and maximum 6½ miles.

Traffic Density, Personnel and Running Results.

Density of traffic showed an almost unbroken progression from 1917 to the date of the armistice. The number of loaded wagon-miles per route mile per day rose from 23½ miles to slightly under 50. The loaded wagon-miles per effective (personnel) per day afforded

a very good index of efficiency. They rose from 2·4 to 5·4. The whole of the operating personnel were included in this figure.

Every effort was made to improve locomotive running and some success was achieved. The number of miles per locomotive in steam per day rose from 17·5 in February, 1917, to 41·8 in July, 1918. These figures do not include tractors.

The consumption of fuel was abnormally high at the commencement of the service, but a reduction of nearly 50 per cent. in coal and 30 per cent. in petrol was effected.

Records were kept as to the distribution of locomotives and tractors, and the numbers under repair, in the same way as for standard gauge plant, and the work of the light railway workshops was similarly scrutinised.

Waterways.

Inland waterways were made use of to the fullest possible extent. At the end of 1916 about 20,000 tons per week were being conveyed in British barges; but this rose to 75,000 tons per week before the date of the armistice. The average distance increased from 25·8 km. in October, 1917, to 37·8 km. in October, 1918. The ton-kilometres for one year reached nearly 100,000,000.

It is interesting to note that throughout the war the measure of the very large river traffic in Mesopotamia was invariably taken in ton-miles. During the quarter ended June, 1918, the work performed on the Tigris and the Euphrates amounted to 7,750,000 ton-miles.

Roads.

Very careful statistics had to be compiled in connection with the maintenance of roads. The bulk of the stone was quarried in France; but in spite of the relief afforded by light railways, roads required for construction and maintenance in some weeks nearly 90,000 tons of roadstone and, in addition, sleepers and pit-props to the extent of 30,000 to 40,000 in number in the same period. The work on the roads was very closely scrutinised in relation to the labour employed. The number employed per mile of road maintained fell from 19 in August, 1917, to 5·5 in August, 1918, although in the later period the proportion of new roads was greater than in the former. The work of the quarries was also watched in relation to the personnel employed. The output of stone per man rose from 7½ tons in March, 1917, to 12½ tons per man per week in the summer of 1918. The numbers employed on unloading trains with roadstone were also shown, so that so far as roads were concerned a complete picture was available as to the efficiency of the work.

Work of the Roads Department during 1918.

The following figures represented the work of the Roads Department during 1918 :—

	Sq. yards.
New roads and cours constructed ...	1,500,000
Roads and cours reconstructed ...	1,250,000
Roads and cours re-surfaced	4,750,000
Total	7,500,000

Assuming an average width of 18 ft. this represented 715 miles.

The working of the lorries conveying the roadstone was followed in relation to the tons moved, the distance carried and the hours worked. The ton-miles per lorry per day increased during 1918 from 32·3 to upwards of 51.

With such a wide subject it has only been possible to touch on the more interesting and salient figures which were produced. Many refinements were compiled so as to obtain the fullest value out of the figures. The statistical side of light railways alone would provide material for a long discussion.

Elaborate Statistics Fully Justified.

I think it must be admitted that the elaborate statistics which were compiled in connection with war transportation fully justified themselves. They were studied and copied by our Allies. It does not appear too much to hope that in the future our knowledge of all classes of transportation at home will be at least equal to the knowledge which was obtained under war conditions by the British Army in France.

THE B.E.F. BASE LOCOMOTIVE SHOPS.

An Account of the Construction, Arrangement and Work of large Locomotive Shops for the British Expeditionary Force at St. Etienne-du-Rouvray.

Before considering the task set before the British military railway repair shops in France, from December, 1916, when the question of providing heavy repair shops was first seriously entertained, till the conclusion of the war two years later, it might be interesting to consider the locomotive position behind the German lines.

Disillusioned as to the prospect of a speedy and victorious finish to the war, the Germans in 1915 took measures to deal adequately with the locomotive question. Repair shops were extensively organised and a critical situation was avoided. No material difficulties faced them in the execution of these measures. Belgium is sown with railway shops, and the existing repair shops in the occupied territories were fully developed by the enemy for their own purposes. Nor did he hesitate to add to his railway resources by the conversion of private workshops, where it seemed worth while.

Lille, though lost to us, was of no great use to the Germans for railway repair shops; but he held—and used—Liége, Namur, Marchiennes, Hasselt, Luttre, Ottignies, Landen, Marcinelle, St. Nicolas, Antwerp, Brussels, Manage, Haine-St. Pierre, Malines, and a dozen other repair shops. Behind these, and still no further from the front than London is from Leeds, were the three great repair shops of the Cöln area, Cöln-Nippes, Oppum, and later, the magnificent new shops at Jülich, built during the war.

Construction and Early Work.

During December, 1916, it was decided that the British Army must equip and operate heavy repair shops capable of dealing with a substantial volume of work, both erection and major repairs. No existing French railway shops could be handed over to the British for this purpose; but towards the end of January, 1917, an agreement was reached, whereby three unfinished bays of the projected locomotive workshops of the *Chemins de fer de l'Etat* were to be occupied by the British, who were to assist with the completion of the buildings and the installation of the cranes. The necessary track and connections, machine tools, plant and accessories, lighting and power had to be provided and installed by the British.

The detailed schemes, including lay-out and equipment estimates, were ready early in February, and arrangements were put in train at once for the construction of the works and for the supply and installation of equipment.

The works, which are located at St. Etienne-du-Rouvray, half-way between Rouen and Oissel, alongside the main line, inspired no visions of a large or early output of any sort, as seen by the first British officers who, with a borrowed retinue of P.B. men, commenced operations on the site towards the end of February, 1917. The main block, which was to comprise erecting, tender, boiler, machine and fitting shops and forge, was represented by the unfinished skeletons of two bays, each 830 ft. long, and the foundations of the third—a barren sight. With a number of P.B. men borrowed from the base, however, the first drafts of the 37th, 62nd and 63rd Workshop Companies, raised—partly in France, from skilled men withdrawn from line regiments—for operating the shops, the erection of the buildings made encouraging progress. Skilled fitters, turners, blacksmiths and boilermakers, pattern-makers and moulders themselves mixed the concrete or rigged stanchions, girders and roof trusses, and the job went on.

In April and May a few machine tools began to arrive, and soon engine parts also, from Canada and the States, began to accumulate —signs and tokens that cheered all ranks, and tended to confirm the wavering hopes of some who doubted if the shops would ever be ready to deal with locomotives. But locomotive erection had to commence, and machinery to be installed, with the shops still under construction, and with no overhead cranes yet in operation.

In July, 1917, the first two imported engines were completed and put into traffic. The shops began to look more useful. Two more companies—the 79th and 80th Broad Gauge Railway Workshop Companies, R.E.—arrived in July, and the 84th (S.A.) Miscellaneous Trades Company in October, 1917. Thus neither in respect of buildings, equipment nor personnel did the British heavy locomotive repair shop spring, fully-armed, Minerva-like, from Jove's (or the Director-General's) brain.

The power plant, comprising two 400-kw. D.C. generator sets, direct-driven by Belliss-Morcom engines, fed by Babcock & Wilcox boilers, ordered in March, 1917, was completed and started up in October of the same year. In the meantime a few machine tools had been operated by using temporary drives from small internal combustion engines.

By August a small pattern shop and foundry had been improvised in a little contractor's shop yard to the south of the main shop yard. The building was a rough shanty, the cupola an old cast iron curiosity with no air-belt. The drive was a venerable portable engine bought as scrap iron and patched up to do yet another spell of work. A Ford car at one time drove the blower. By such improvisations an output of locomotive spare parts began to turn out for running-shed requirements before complete repairs could be undertaken.

The latter were held up for some time for want of cranes. Of the electric overhead cranes only three 8-ton (in the erecting shop) and two 10-ton (in the boiler shop) were in operation by October, 1917, and it was not till February, 1918, that the two 60-ton erecting shop cranes could be used. By September, 1917, however, arrangements were in train for receiving locomotives for repairs, and in October night-shift working was commenced in the erecting shop.

The following is a summary of the work accomplished in the period from December 19, 1916, when the site was first inspected by a British officer, to the end of October, 1917. At this date the works were practically complete and in regular day and night operation:—

Plans, lay-out and estimates had to be prepared for the entire major and minor equipment, including machine tools and accessories, power, lighting, general tools and stores. These were projected for an output of an engine per day, or 350 to 360 engines per year, plus spares for running sheds.

The orders were placed in March, 1917. Most of the machinery was in actual operation in October the same year. By September 30 2,300 tons of concrete foundations had been put in for the plant, 6,056 cubic yards of ballast had been laid for floor level and tracks, and 2,650 yards of standard track laid for yard and shop lines and connections. The yard traffic office had dealt with 21,800 tons of incoming material, including 3,962 tons of locomotive parts for erection. Excluding the cranes, motors to a total rating of 473 h.p. had been installed and connected up to the generators. In addition to the main boilers, boilers approximating 140 h.p. were in position to serve the air compressor and steam hammers. By the same date (September 30) 34 locomotives had been erected, run trials, and been made over for traffic.

By the end of October the main block of buildings, 230 ft. wide by 830 ft. long, had been completed for occupation, including roofing and the erection, but not completion, of the overhead cranes. A new steel-frame shed for the brass and iron foundries, aggregating 8,000 sq. ft. floor area, entirely constructed from the raw material, had been almost completed and was occupied.

Concurrently with the construction and equipment of the shops and the erection of locomotives, it was necessary also to lay out the hutting and water supply for the workshop companies. This was

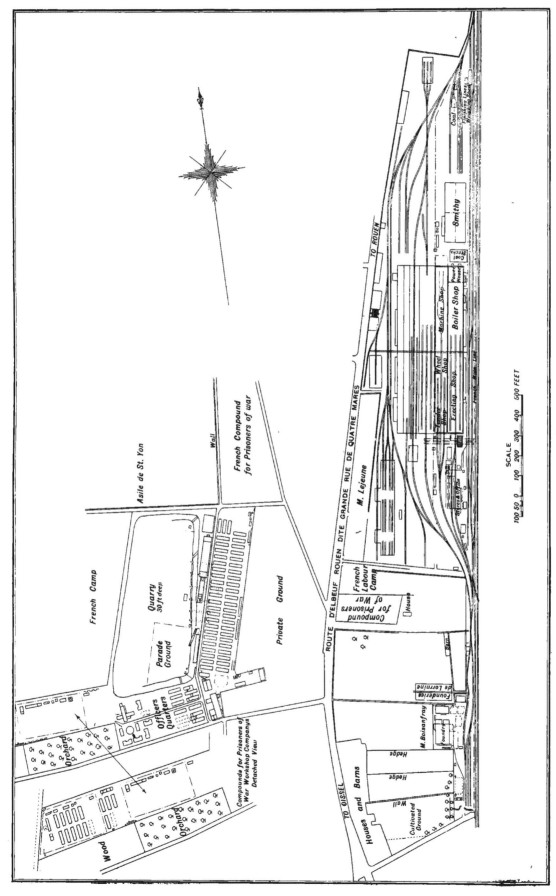

Fig. 10.—General Plan of Workshops, Yard and Camp in latter half of 1918. The chain dotted line indicates the yard boundary of the portion in British occupation.

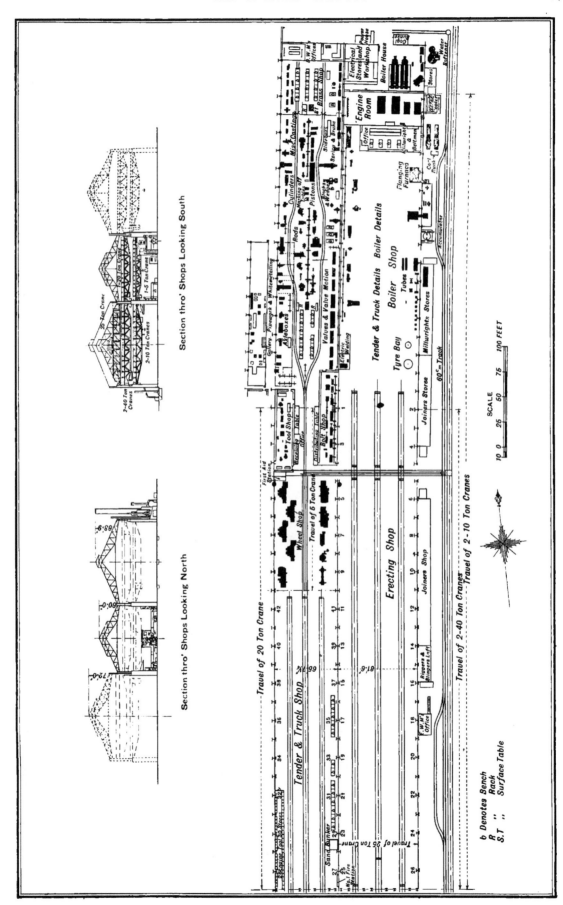

Fig. 11.—General Plan of Main Block in July, 1918, after re-arrangement.   The evacuated Erecting Shop is shown dotted in the end elevations.

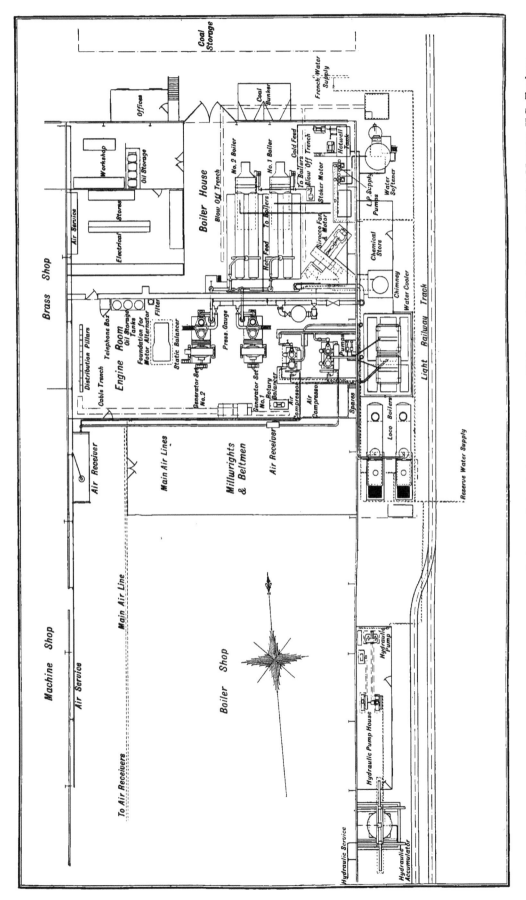

Fig. 12.—Plan of Power Station. Power Plant includes two 440-volt D.C. Generators, 400 kw. each, direct-driven by Belliss-Morcom H.S. Engines, fed by two Babcock and Wilcox Boilers, with Mechanical Stokers.

carried out by the companies themselves, owing to the pressure of construction with which R.E. works were already dealing elsewhere.

Output of Engines and Spares during 1917.

By the end of 1917, within a little over nine months after the arrival of the first company drafts from the Transportation Troops Depôt, Boulogne, not only had the shops been constructed and equipped, but 135 new engines had been erected, and five old engines repaired and returned to traffic. The wheel shop had turned up 74 pairs of wheels, the smiths' shop turned out 72 tons of forgings, and the foundries 23 tons of brass and 225 tons of iron castings. Over 11,000 tons of incoming locomotive parts alone had been handled through the yard by December 31, 1917.

From zero in February, the average strength on works rose gradually to 1,000 towards the end of October, and for the last two months of 1917 averaged 1,200 sappers and 300 German prisoners of war, allotted to the works at the end of October.

Locomotive Repairs and Re-arrangement of Shops during 1918.

The New Year—cheerily greeted by a strong night shift with a two-minutes' salute of clamorous American locomotive bells and a *feu-de-joie* of hammer-blows—opened with good prospects of an early harvest of results from the stiff work of the preceding 10 months. The heavy cranes were approaching completion. Working drawings—almost unobtainable at first, and prepared locally by direct measurement for most of the old Belgian and many of the old British engines that were arriving for repairs—were being turned out rapidly by the drawing office staff. The pattern shop, foundries, forge, machine and boiler shops were getting into stride. The routing and planning office organisation—built up, trained and developed *pari passu* with the work—was becoming increasingly effective as its functions, methods and objects became better understood. Best of all—the one-time heterogeneous mixture of Mons men and other veterans from the line, " C.3's," specially enlisted sappers, " Derbies " and Colonials, were crystallising into a homogeneous, solid and well-disciplined force, a result which reflects the greatest credit upon the company officers and the men themselves, in view of the fact that the R.E. Company administrative organisation was wholly unadaptable to the technical requirements of the workshops.

From January 1 to May 9, 1918, a further 97 engines were erected, after which erection ceased and the shops concentrated on locomotive repairs and spares, and—a serious blow to the output prospects for the year!—an entire re-arrangement and re-location of the erecting and boiler shops and of the smiths' shop and forge was necessitated by the result of the great German offensive from March to July, 1918. Nevertheless, although the big cranes were not in operation, due to delays of materials, till the middle of February, and in spite of the upheaval in May and June, which deprived the works of the whole of the erecting shop bay, involved the rooting up and re-location of the whole of the smiths' shop and forge equipment, the clearance of the boiler shop from the southern to the northern half of the last bay, and, within one month, the construction of new erecting shop pits in place of the boiler shop, and the evacuation and transfer from the original erecting shop of 40 locomotives in every stage of disrepair—yet the output for 1918 reached 365 engine repairs in addition to 97 erections.

The lowest output for any one week from March to December was 3 repairs; the maximum in any one week was 12, and the average for the whole 12 months was 7 repairs per week besides erections. The average capacity of crane-served pits available for locomotives during this period was under 28.

The excavation for the new erecting pits was commenced on May 15, simultaneously with the removal of boiler and smiths' shop plant to their respective new sites, according to an equipment transfer programme designed to enable the whole operation to be effected without a break and with the minimum possible reduction in the output of locomotive work. All ranks entered thoroughly into the spirit of the scheme, whole gangs voluntarily working extra hours, and a month later, though the concrete in the new pits was

still green, they were occupied and the original erecting shop placed at the disposal of the French.

As illustrating the proportion of casualties amongst " war " locomotives as compared with peace repairs, the following analysis of 400 engines repaired at these workshops is of interest :—

General repairs	..	..	..	249 engines or 62·25 per cent.
Collisions	..	..	..	87 ,, 21·75 ,,
Running accidents	..	..	42 ,, 10·50 ,,
Burnt fireboxes	..	..	..	22 ,, 5·50 ,,

Starting in February, 1917, with but the incomplete skeleton of a shop, no equipment even on order, and only the small nucleus of a personnel, with few drawings, less spares and no patterns, the outlook was not bright. In addition to engine erections and general repairs, however, the development of the several departments enabled very material assistance to be rendered to the running sheds with a considerable output of manufactured spares and repaired detail parts.

Output was continued for some months after the armistice, but the results up to December 31, 1918, were, exclusive of construction and reconstruction of shops, as follows :—

Item.			1917.	1918.	Total to end of 1918.
Engines erected, number	..		135	97	232
,, repaired, number	..		5	365	370
Brass castings, tons	..	..	22·7	145·3	168·0
Iron castings, tons	..	..	224·5	1,961·8	2,186·3
,, forgings	..	..	71·7	665·5	732·2
Wheels re-tyred, number	..		—	275	275
,, turned up, pairs	..		74	1,999	2,073
Loco. parts unloaded for erection of new engines, tons	..		11,186	3,651	14,837

Lay-out and Equipment.

The general lay-out—*i.e.*, the relative siting of erecting and machine shops, boiler shop, forge and foundries—was practically defined by the areas allotted.

The detailed lay-out of the machine shop and fitters' benches was based on the principle of work-groups, each set of related engine parts being dealt with by a suitable battery of tools located together, the number and grouping of the tools being planned originally for an output of 30 engines per month. Machines not estimated to be fully employed by any one group, but essential for operations required by other groups, were sited so as to be shared conveniently by two or more groups. With this reservation the bulk of the work connected with each series of engine parts was dealt with by a certain group of machines and benches with a minimum of traffic and handling, as indicated by the group-names on the machine shop lay-out.

This internal organisation into work-groups extended back to the locomotive stores and to the foundries, every detail having also a permanent engine class and part number from a prepared schedule of locomotive parts.

Development during 1918.

As already related, the general lay-out was completely transformed consequent upon the events of March to July, 1918. Fortunately it was found possible to accommodate our Allies to the desired extent without uprooting the machine shop equipment or the power station ; but everything else, with the exception of the foundry and pattern shop, and tender shop, was stripped and transferred.

To compensate for the reduction in the pit accommodation from 40 engines to 22, a second 20-ton crane was ordered for the tender shop. This was made with the utmost possible expedition by the London & North Western Railway Works at Crewe, but could not be put into operation till January, 1919, after which the tender shop became available to the extent of six to eight pits for the accommodation of the lighter classes of British and Belgian locomotives. But the critical period was already past.

In addition to the ordering of this crane a stripping pit to accommodate two engines was put in, located outside the stores to the south of the new erecting shop. Besides this, finishing lines were laid down in the north yard, to render it possible to release crane-served pit accommodation in the erecting shop with a minimum of delay.

The new smiths' shop and forge " building " was constructed

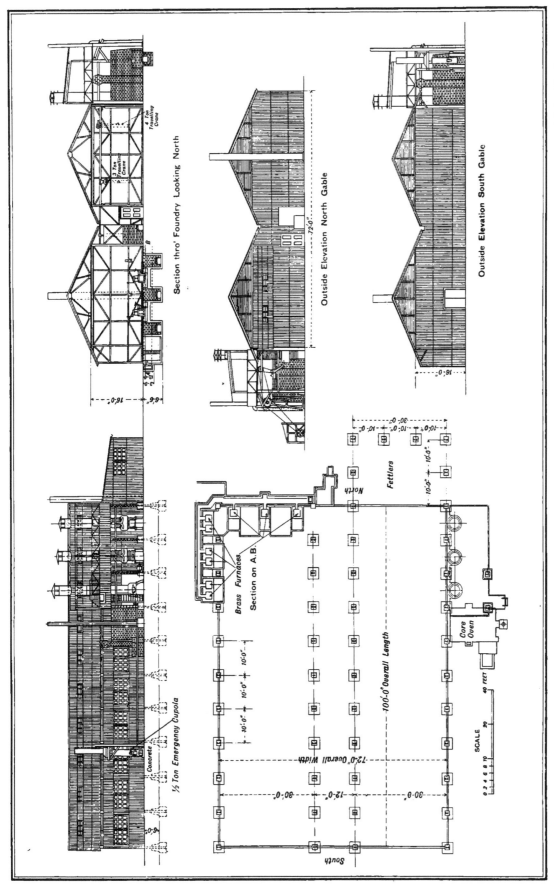

Fig. 13.—Foundry, built alongside old Contractor's Sidings South of Main Workshop Yard. The two Corrugated Cupolas were constructed locally from a Scrapped Corrugated Boiler Flue.

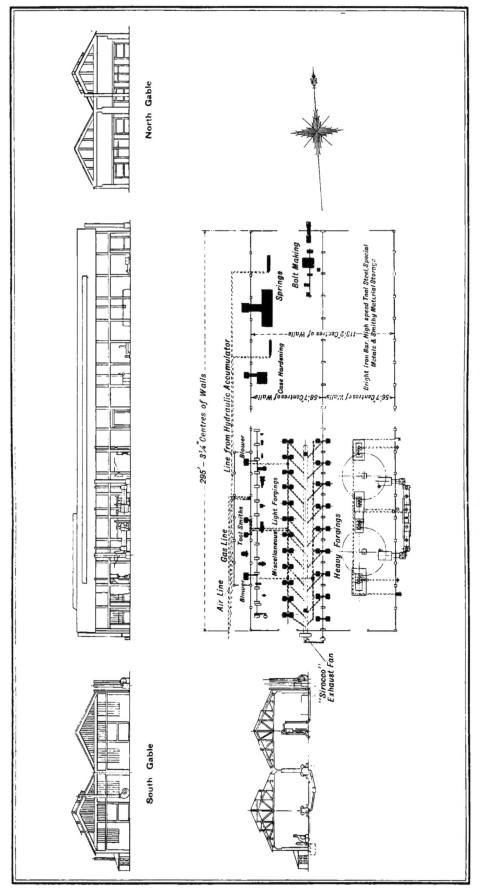

Fig. 14.—Plan showing Lay-out of Smiths' Shops and Forge. The French permanent Buildings shown in elevation were not actually built, but a hastily improvised Shop was run up with Poles, Tarpaulins and (later) Corrugated Iron.

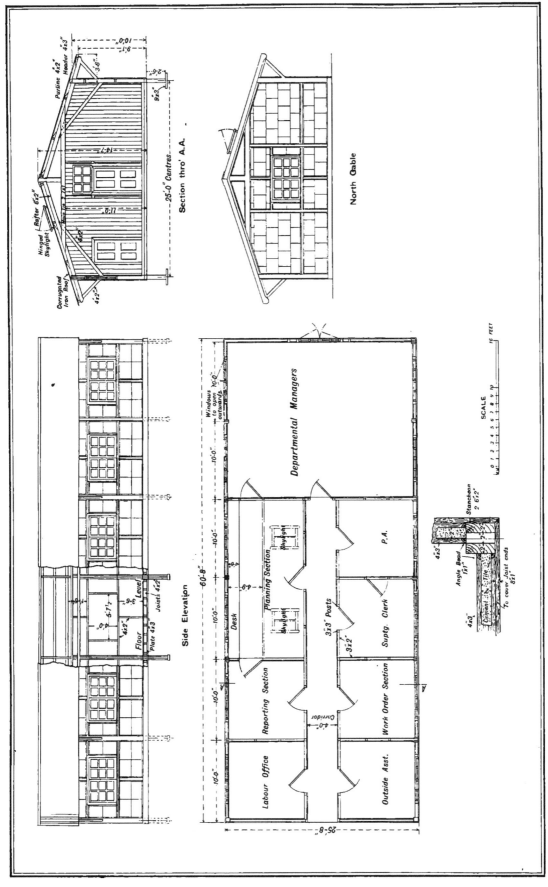

Fig. 15.—Works Control Office, comprising Routing and Labour Sections. The Planning Section takes charge of the Forecast and Planning Boards.

over the equipment while the latter was being transferred and installed on the new site in the north yard. The structure would hardly have satisfied ordinary British building regulations, but sufficed. It consisted of light unsquared timber poles, and, to begin with, tarpaulin roofing. Corrugated iron roofing and sides followed.

The transfer involved two steam boilers, four steam hammers, two light power hammers, shearing machines, bar cutters and benders, the entire spring group, together with 42 forge fires, the spring tempering and annealing and the heavy forge furnaces and other equipment, with, of course, the necessary steam, air and draught pipe lines and connections.

The site, which the lay-out was adapted to suit, was that of a large wheel shop projected by the French on their original plans, but the permanent building itself was never commenced.

Military Organisation and Establishments.

Let it be said at once that so far from a military system of organisation and administration being inefficient or unsuitable for technical results, it has many valuable features to recommend it. "Militarism," misdirected to achieve "frightfulness," was the Devil's Army; but the collective efficiency of a controlled and disciplined body of men, animated throughout all ranks by a common sense of service, is the most powerful weapon possible for success no less in the workshops than in the field.

One of the first lessons that the young officer has to learn is to take care of his men and their welfare at all times, in all places, in all occupations. He must get inside their skins and understand them—their troubles, their hopes, their weakness and their strength. He must work for 24 hours a day to deserve their confidence—for he must be at once their servant, their guide, their leader and their judge, and he must know how to bring out the best in each one of them.

This is precisely wherein a good military organisation finds strength. And it is precisely where the form of organisation imposed on the military railway workshop units was defective, inasmuch as the units chosen—R.E. companies, in each of which a variety of trades was represented—had to be broken up and all officers, N.C.O.'s and men re-shuffled for technical purposes, while remaining for all administrative purposes, camp, discipline and records, in their original form. A new service brings new problems, and this was one. The whole question is understood to be under consideration in the light of experiences gained during the war, and it is no part of this account to anticipate the results, beyond expressing the pious hope that a future generation may reap some benefit.

A more suitable military organisation would have been of very great value. As it was, the difficulties were early recognised (they were only too obvious), and while the technical organisation was framed as far as possible to meet them, much more was due to the common sense of the men and the good team-work of the company officers in reducing or eliminating the vexatious consequences of the establishments.

Technical Organisation.

It was necessary, when passing through successive phases, from the workshop construction period onward, from time to time to change the functions of officers and other ranks and to modify and develop the technical organisation correspondingly. We need not follow this evolution in detail, but from an early stage the framework took a definite form which was adhered to. Working to plans issued to them, the three departmental managers superintended the installation of equipment in their own shops, and thereafter took charge of their operations.

The co-ordinating centre—the planning and routing office—was supervised by the Personal Assistant. The maintenance of equipment and (in 1918) transfers and alterations or additions were under

TECHNICAL ORGANISATION.

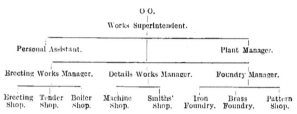

the charge of the Plant Manager. The distribution of labour—a delicate but very important daily problem in the earlier stages—was controlled through the labour branch of the P.A.'s office. A stores officer was attached from the Railway Stores Directorate.

The routing office, whose function it was to forecast the position that each individual engine repair should be in, as far ahead as possible, was handicapped by the lack of any past histories or mileage statements of the engines coming in or likely to come in. Shed

PLANNING, ROUTING AND LABOUR ORGANISATION.

reports, when received in time, were helpful, and on these and a preliminary inspection a rough classification and forecast was based.

Concurrently with stripping, a detailed report, orders and forecast dates were prepared, linking up with work already in hand. The draft engine-programmes thus prepared by the routing office were reviewed at a daily conference between the P.A. and the three departmental managers. This conference practically determined the programme for each incoming engine, and recommended, if necessary, alterations in the priority of engines already in hand, when further defects had been revealed in the course of repairs. After issue, the departmental managers were responsible for the distribution of the approved routing schedules to their respective subordinates and for their execution, or for the prompt reporting of any delays or failures in detail.

The function of the Chief Inspector or Outside Assistant was to keep headquarters (through the P.A.) supplied with every available bit of information regarding incoming engines and their conditions. He was also responsible for their inspection reports being properly filled in.

The duties of the Technical Assistant included the maintenance of all information relating to material or spares, whether required on indent or manufactured locally, and the prompt investigation of all delays. He also had to report on cases of bad work or complaints from running sheds, and was responsible for the proper completion of repair reports. In cases of accident involving courts of inquiry it was the Technical Assistant's office to preside, unless the gravity of a case called for the appointment of a more senior officer.

THE RAILWAY OPERATING DIVISION.—The "R.O.D.," or Railway Operating Division of the Royal Engineers, engaged in France, were responsible for the operation of military trains. Members of the R.O.D. wore either khaki or blue, with the Royal Engineers' cap badge, and, although not nominally combatants, they were constantly under fire, as the railways were pushed close up to the front lines, while sidings and stations, as well as open lines, were, of course, constant targets for enemy bombs. Army railroading was no sinecure, and the number of decorations won by R.O.D. men testifies to the danger of their invaluable work.

General view of one of the Channel Train Ferries.

Rolling-stock on the Channel Ferry for conveyance to the Western Front.

The Connection between the Richborough Railway System and the Ferry.

The Main Line on to the Ferry, which is shown at its berth.

A Train-Load of 12-inch Guns Ready to Run on to the Cross-Channel Ferry.

A general view of the Railway System at Richborough connecting with the Channel Ferry.

Heavy gun mounted on German rolling-stock captured by British 4th Army in August, 1918.

Another view of the captured German gun, brought to Richborough by the Train Ferry.

Back from the Front.   60-cm. Tank Engines returned from France.

Unloading returned empties at the Salvage Dump, Richborough.

Locomotives of 2-8-0 Type, built by the North British Locomotive Company, Limited, awaiting shipment to France.

Barclay, Manning Wardle, and S.E. & C.R. Tank Engines employed at Richborough for shunting and working traffic.

A Bow View of the Ferry Steamer.

The Barge Quay at Richborough and the newly-cut Waterway.

The last of the Guards leaving Cologne for " Blighty."

Naval Guns being Assembled in a French Gun Shop

A special Armoured Railroad Mount- used for Naval Guns.

14-in. Gun being Loaded for Transportation to the Front.

Light Railway Construction through Shell-torn Area, East of Ypres.

Train of R.E. Material for Track-laying.

Construction Troops Grading for Light Railway Construction.

Construction Troops Laying Light Railway Track.

Construction Troops Lining Track, March 7, 1918.

Ballasting and Boxing Track.

Ditching.   German Prisoners were largely used on this Work.

Chinese Labour Battalion Assembling Track.

Trestle Bridge over the Canal at Dunkirk for Doubling of Line between West Side of Docks and the Triage des Dunes.

Engine and Four Wagons (Shells) on Light Railway.

Troop Train drawn by Petrol Electric Locomotive, crossing Trestle Bridge.

" Crewe " Tractor.   Ford Chassis on 60 c.m. Gauge Wheels.

Chaulnes-Peronne Line.   Bridge over Somme Canal as left by the Enemy.   April 3, 1917.

Chaulnes-Peronne Line.   Bridge over River Somme as left by the Enemy.   April 3, 1917.

Chaulnes-Peronne Line.   Somme River Bridge, 35-ton Crane removing debris.   April 19, 1917.

Chaulnes-Peronne Line.   Double Track Pile Bridge on deviation over Somme Canal completed.   May 16, 1917.

Travelling Workshops which were sent into Forward Areas on Repair Work.

Bogie Ambulance Wagon hauled by small Tank Engine.

Peronne–Roisel Line.   Bridge carrying metre gauge (Albert-Ham) over normal gauge at Peronne.   Looking towards
Roisel.   April 3, 1917.

Peronne–Roisel Line.   Bridge carrying Maricourt-Peronne Line (old Albert-Ham metre gauge line) over main line,
re-arranged to allow of latter line being doubled.   May 16, 1917.

Roisel-Cambrai Line. Bridge over Epehy-Velu Line North of Epehy as left by the Enemy.

Peronne-Roisel Line. Bridge over River Cologne at North of Peronne-Flamincourt Station Yard. May 16, 1917.

Armentieres-Comines Line. Bridge over River Lys at Houplines. Repairs by the 8th Railway Company, R.E.,
March, 1915. Repairing Bracings.

Chaulnes-Peronne Line. Peronne Bridge between La Chapelette and Flamincourt. April 3, 1917.

Chaulnes-Peronne Line.   Bridge over Villers Carbonnel-Omniécourt Road.   April 3, 1917.

Chaulnes-Peronne Line.   Bridge over Villers Carbonnel-Omniécourt Road.   April 20, 1917.

Line Cut by Shell Fire.

Chaulnes-Peronne Line.   Trucks rendered useless by the Enemy.

" Walking " Wounded Entraining.

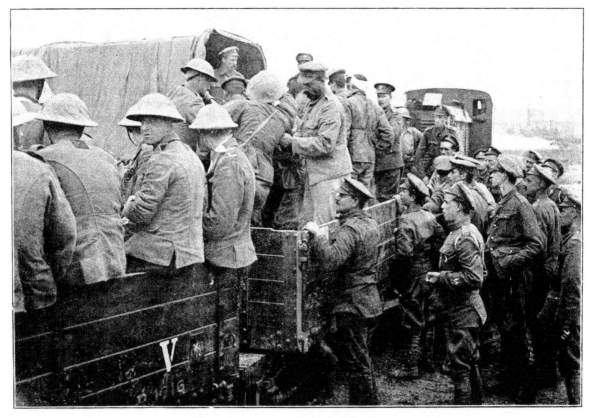

Wounded being transferred from Motor to Railway Vehicles.

Engine on Examination Platform, Westonhock.

Ramp for Off-loading Light Railway Engines from Standard Gauge Wagons.

Engine taking Water from Tank Wagon.

Water Tank and Engine taking Water.

Chaulnes-Peronne Line.   Marchlepot Station Yard, looking towards Chaulnes.   As left by the Enemy.   April 3, 1917.

Dickebusch-Wytschaete Line.   Elzenwalle Loop (looking West) with interlaced 60 c.m. line.

Westonhock Marshalling Yard with loaded Ammunition Trains.

Doullens Exchange Sidings.   Looking North-West.

Armentieres Station.   Looking East.   January 13, 1918.

Armentieres Station.   West End of Station Yard.   Looking West.   January 13, 1918.

" Taking it Easy."

" Where the strange roads go down."

Off the Road.   Breakdown Gang at Work.

Transhipping 15-in. Shells.

Hazebrouck-Armentieres Line.   Merris Marshalling Yard (South Side).   Looking West.   January 13, 1918.

Hazebrouck-Armentieres Line.   Merris Yard—R.O.D. Camp.

A well-loaded Troop Train.

Forward Area Sub-control.

District Control.

Central Control. Vox Vrie. March 7, 1918.

Loading a Tank on Special Railway Vehicle—First Position.

Loading a Tank on Railway Vehicle—Second Position. Note Jacks to take Strain.

Tank Loaded for Transportation. Front View.

Tank in Travelling Position.

Shops in course of Construction—from north end. St. Etienne.—January-February, 1917.

Shops in course of Construction—from south end. St. Etienne.—March, 1917.

General View—from South—of St. Etienne Locomotive Shops.—March, 1918.

South Yard, St. Etienne Locomotive Shops.   Sappers leaving Work.—March, 1918.

" Baldwin " 2-8-0 Engine at St. Etienne Locomotive Shops.

Locomotives in South Yard, St. Etienne.—March, 1918.

First Engine out and Erecting Gang, St. Etienne Locomotive Shops.— July, 1917.

Canadian 2-8-0 Engine, St. Etienne Locomotive Shops.

Engine being Conveyed by Overhead Crane, St. Etienne Locomotive Shops.—March, 1918.

Group of " Baldwin " Saddle-tank Engines, St. Etienne Locomotive Shops.

Engines being Assembled.   Erecting Shop, St. Etienne.—October, 1917.

General View of Machine Shop, St. Etienne.—March, 1918.

Brass Shop, St. Etienne Locomotive Works.—October, 1917.

Machine Shop (at north end of Brass Shop), St. Etienne Locomotive Works.—August, 1917.

Smiths' Shop, St. Etienne Locomotive Works.—August, 1917.

Foundry, St. Etienne Locomotive Works.—December, 1917.

Westinghouse Brake Test Benches, St. Etienne Locomotive Shops.

Power House Main Boilers, St. Etienne Locomotive Shops.

Switchboard, St. Etienne Locomotive Shops.

Power House, Generator and Air Compressors, St. Etienne Locomotive Shops.

Marshalling Yard, Les Flamands, Cherbourg.

Reception Roads and Marshalling Sidings, Taranto.

Wharf and Transit Sheds, Taranto.

Aeroplane Photograph of Rest Camp, Hospital and General Lay-out, Taranto.

SPECIAL TRAIN FOR THE COMMANDER-IN-CHIEF IN FRANCE.

Built at the London & North Western Railway Carriage Works at Wolverton in 1917.

By the courtesy of Mr. A. R. Trevithick, Carriage Superintendent of the London & North Western Railway, we are enabled to reproduce herewith some photographs with particulars of a special train designed and built at the company's works to provide living accommodation for the Commander-in-Chief of the British Army and his staff in France. We also reproduce a diagram showing the arrangement of the vehicles comprising the train, prior to its leaving England. After its arrival in France the train was re-marshalled, but, generally speaking, the diagram represents its make-up fairly accurately.

On April 10, 1917, the London & North Western Railway Company were asked to provide a train of 10 vehicles for the purpose referred to above. Five of them left Wolverton on May 5, and the remaining five on the 12th of the same month, so that the complete train of 10 vehicles was provided in a month from the date of the order. A further request for four additional vehicles was received later, and these were fitted up and sent out on July 20, 1917.

As shown in the diagram, coach No. 1 comprises a dressing room, bedroom and sitting room for the Commander-in-Chief; No. 2

for providing the steam to heat the train when standing, while No. 14 is just an ordinary brake van for stores and other impedimenta.

With the exception of the telephone vehicle and the two brakes, the whole of the cars were converted from 42 ft. by 8 ft. 6 in. bogie picnic saloons, which were taken from stock, and happened to be so arranged so far as lights and doors were concerned that they lent themselves very well to the scheme without a deal of structural alteration.

The train is electrically lighted by a petrol driven lighting set, steam heated by the locomotive when running, and by a boiler fitted in the brake and stores car when standing, and is fitted with the Westinghouse brake.

The telegraph and telephone car was fitted up with the necessary instruments, &c., by the engineering staff of the General Post Office, but the vehicle itself and all furniture, counters, &c., were provided by the railway company. There is a telephone and bell communication throughout the train, and means are provided and cable carried on the telephone car for connecting up to any telegraph and telephone system in proximity to the train.

Special Train for the Commander-in-Chief in France.
Exterior of Telegraph and Telephone Car.

is a bedroom, bathroom and office for the Chief of Staff and his assistants; whilst Nos. 3, 4, 5 and 6 are cars giving sleeping and office accommodation generally. No. 6 has an assembly room, and this is placed next to the Officers' Mess Car No. 7.

No. 8 is the kitchen car, and this also contains the electric lighting set and accumulator room. No. 9 is a car for officers' orderlies, servants, &c. No. 10 provides more sleeping accommodation, chiefly for junior officers. No. 11 gives a large office, and an officers' bed and bathroom. No. 12 is a telegraph and telephone vehicle. No. 13 is a stores van, and in this is fitted a small locomotive boiler

The interior painting is principally white enamel, while the exterior is finished off in lead colour. The ventilation has been studied, and there is an ample supply of fans and roof ventilators, while all the drop lights are fitted with louvres and gauze that can be used in the openings when lights are dropped.

The fitting up and dispatch of a complete train of this description in the short period of time named above was a matter reflecting very considerable credit upon the London & North Western Railway, their Carriage Superintendent, and the works organisation at Wolverton.

Telegraph and Telephone Car Interior.

Lighting Set in Kitchen Car.

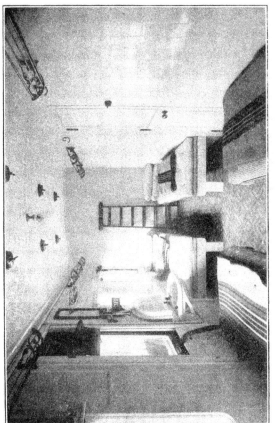

Bedroom Car.

Boiler Room.

SPECIAL TRAIN FOR THE COMMANDER-IN-CHIEF IN FRANCE.

Another Interior View of the Telegraph and Telephone Car.

The Commander-in-Chief's Bedroom.

Large Office in Bedroom Car.

The Commander-in-Chief's Sitting Room.

SPECIAL TRAIN FOR THE COMMANDER-IN-CHIEF IN FRANCE.

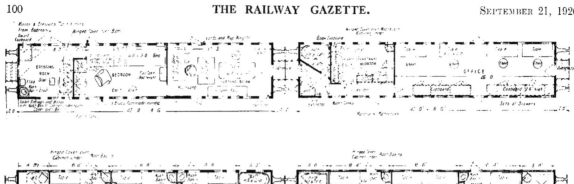

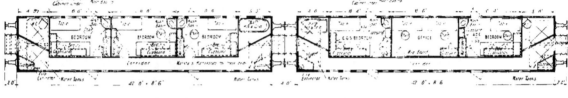

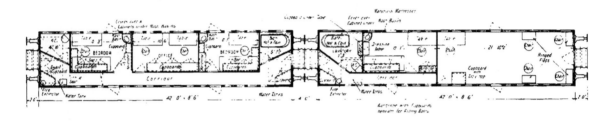

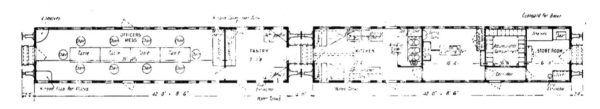

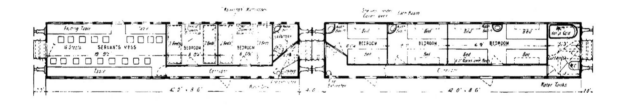

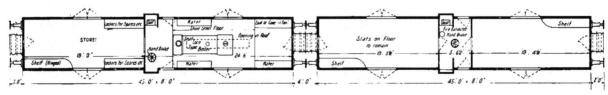

Special Train for the Commander-in Chief in France : Arrangement of Vehicles.

THE MEDITERRANEAN LINE OF COMMUNICATION.

A Description of the Overland Route to the East, with Particulars of the Work Performed.

At the commencement of 1917 the activities of enemy submarines, and the necessity of adopting every expedient to economise in shipping, emphasised the need for an alternative route of supply for our forces in the Near East. Our lines of communication along the Mediterranean were threatened by "U" boats, and it became essential to obtain access to them overland. At a conference held in Rome on January 7, 1917, a scheme was approved in principle for developing an overland route to Taranto in the south of Italy, in order to save tonnage and to minimise shipping risks in the conveyance of supplies and personnel to the Allied Forces in the Near East. Consequently, on January 14, 1917, a mission, headed by the late Sir Guy Calthrop, General Manager of the London & North Western Railway, and including, amongst others, Mr. L. W. Horne, Superintendent of the Line, London & North Western Railway, left London with the object of investigating the possibilities of an overland service for men and material between England and the Mediterranean theatre of war *via* a French port on the English Channel and an Italian port in the south of Italy.

On the 7th of the following month this mission presented its report, which decided in favourable terms as to the practicability of the proposal and put forward three schemes:—The first for a daily service of one passenger and three goods trains, the second for one passenger and five goods, and the third for one passenger and nine goods. In consultation with representatives of the French and Italian Governments, the mission found that the principal difficulty connected with the scheme would be the provision of an adequate supply of locomotives and rolling-stock. To meet the needs, even of the first proposal of four trains per day, the French stated they could only provide engines and rolling-stock on condition that immediately the service started an equivalent of personnel, engines and stock should be handed over to them by the British in France; the Italians, however, stated their readiness to provide engines for four *marches* over their portion of the route, but for any additional *marches* engines would have to be imported. On this basis, for one personnel train, worked by French stock throughout, and by French engines from Cherbourg to Modane and Italian engines from Modane to Taranto, the British would have to hand over to the French railways from 360 to 400 passenger coaches, 22 engines, 22 drivers and 22 firemen; for three goods *marches* worked similarly 2,000 British wagons, 66 engines, 66 drivers and 66 firemen would have to be supplied to the French. For every additional *marche*, 650 wagons, 22 engines, 22 drivers and 22 firemen would be required by the French railways and 25 engines by the Italian railways, the latter being prepared to buy British engines outright.

On March 23 it was decided to proceed with the scheme on the basis of one personnel and five goods trains daily, equivalent to 5,000 personnel weekly and 1,200 tons of stores daily. Surveys and estimates were also to be made for a possible increase of the goods traffic to nine trains daily.

In the meantime survey parties had been collected—with considerable difficulty, be it added, owing to the great demands for engineering experts in those days—and had proceeded to the spot. The constructional work was placed in charge of Lieut.-Colonel Morgan, of the Engineer and Railway Staff Corps, who had just relinquished the position of Chief Engineer of the London, Brighton & South Coast Railway. A tremendous amount of work was involved. It included the construction of a marshalling yard and transit sheds at Cherbourg and a special wharf, transit sheds and sidings adjoining the Mare Piccolo at Taranto. In addition, rest camps for troops had to be erected at Cherbourg, Saint Germain, Faenza and Taranto, with *halte-repas* facilities (*i.e.*, sidings, latrines, wash-houses and cook-houses) at the various places *en route*, as shown on the sketch map at Fig. 16.

The Route.

Leaving Cherbourg, the route passes through Mezidon to Tours and on to St. Germain au Mont d'or (Lyons), where the first rest camp is situated. Here troops can alight and have the benefit of a stop varying from 12 to 24 hours, with rest and hot meals. From Lyons southward trains go through the Mont Cenis Tunnel to Faenza, where there is another admirably-situated rest camp. From Faenza the train follows the Adriatic coast line to Bari and Taranto, the total distance being 2,330 km., or 1,460 miles.

It appears that it was originally the intention that the Italian portion of the journey should be run along the west coast of Italy, but the mission was informed by General Fiastri, the Italian Director of Transportation, that, in view of the heavy traffic down the west coast and the expected increase of French traffic along it, the British route would have to be down the Adriatic coast. The mission pointed out that this appeared more dangerous so far as attack from the sea was concerned, but was assured that the line was amply protected by armoured trains, and that no danger had hitherto been encountered by the large Italian troop movements over the route. Events proved the correctness of the statement. Moreover, the east coast had the advantage in the matter of grades, and was probably in far better order than the west coast route.

From Lyons, it will be seen there is an alternative route *via* Marseilles and the Riviera to Ventimiglia, through the tunnel and up to Voghera: this route lengthens the throughout journey by about 350 km. All goods and passenger trains ran *via* Modane until the services were suspended at the end of October, 1917, on account of the situation in Italy, when, owing to the Austrian advance, French and British troops had to be rushed to the Italian front. On the resumption of the service in the following January, the Ventimiglia route was adopted for all trains, owing to congestion of traffic through Modane, but on March 22, 1918, southward passenger trains were altered to run *via* Modane, the northward trains still running over the alternative route until October 3, 1918, when they also were re-transferred to the Modane route.

It is also interesting to note that, at the southern end of the route, all trains ran originally *via* Brindisi, but in March, 1918, the passenger service was diverted to the direct line from Bari to Taranto, which is 66 km. shorter, though the grades are less favourable.

The following are the distances on the routes taken respectively by passenger and goods traffic:—

	Km.	Miles.
Passenger traffic *via* Modane and Gioia del Colle	2,284	1,419
Goods traffic *via* Ventimiglia and Brindisi	2,701	1,678

The time occupied by personnel trains, including meal and sanitary halts, was estimated by the Commission to occupy roughly 115 hours, excluding 48 hours spent at the rest camps at St. Germain and Faenza. As will be shown later, this was slightly short of the time actually taken in practice.

Constructional Work.

Having regard to the fact that, in addition to personnel, it was intended that the overland route should ultimately cover a matter of 2,000 to 2,500 tons per day of stores and supplies, it is not surprising that considerable special accommodation was needed at the terminals at Cherbourg and Taranto. Through the stress of war, existing accommodation was already fully taxed, and it was necessary to proceed at once with an elaborate system of connecting lines, sidings, sheds and appliances for the handling of the traffic that would be likely to pass.

Extensions at Cherbourg.—The arrangements at Cherbourg were decided upon after several consultations with the French authorities. It was arranged that personnel should be landed at the Gare Maritime, either from transport alongside or by lighter from transport according to the draught of the ship. A rest camp would be erected at Chateau Tour la Ville about 5 km. away, to which the men would be marched, though on occasion it would be possible for troops to transfer direct from ship to train or *vice versa*, the trains running direct from the quay to Taranto. If the men used the rest camp they would, after their stay there, be marched to a point 3 km. from the camp for entrainment.

Bassin du Commerce.—With regard to goods traffic, the

before the transport of stores and munitions on a large scale could begin, siding accommodation should be put in for dealing with the traffic. A site for this adjoining the Port des Flamands and about 3 km. from the Bassin du Commerce was agreed upon; this would involve two new junctions with the Cherbourg-Barfleur line. The French agreed to lay in the new junction points where required, but intimated that all labour and material for the necessary sidings and sheds would have to be provided by the British, a competent French engineer, however, being lent to assist with the work; they agreed that the British should have absolute control of the new yard and sidings and do all the railway operating work there.

The sidings required at Les Flamands would have to be sufficient

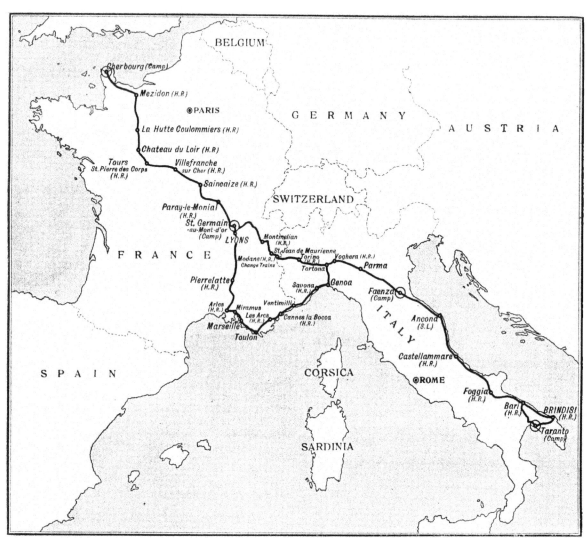

Fig. 16.—Route of the Mediterranean Line of Communication.

French offered to place at our disposal two berths, and, if necessary, three in the Bassin du Commerce, and suggested that, as a commencement, stores and ammunition sent by this route should be limited to the capacity of the basin. This offer was accepted, although the site was not considered ideal and the rail accommodation alongside appeared inadequate. In the first place, it was reached by lock, and vessels could only enter or leave within an hour before and an hour after high tide, and, consequently, working with all berths—day and night, between 1,200 and 1,400 tons only could be put from the ship's side into wagons and despatched. Actually, the tonnage capacity was found to be only 600 per day.

New Yard at Les Flamands.—It was essential, however, that

to hold two days' supply of passenger coaches and of goods wagons; two sidings also were necessary for marshalling trains and a siding alongside the transit sheds for loading and unloading stores. A shunting neck of 40 wagons length would have to be provided with a falling gradient towards the sidings and a connecting line between sidings and main line. It was also decided to put in a *raccordement* connecting the line alongside the Bassin du Commerce with the Cherbourg-Barfleur Line, together with a loop to hold 40 wagons, and shed accommodation also would be necessary to meet A.S.C., Ordnance and R.E. requirements. The Les Flamands yard is shown at Fig. 17.

A survey for the new works at Cherbourg was commenced early

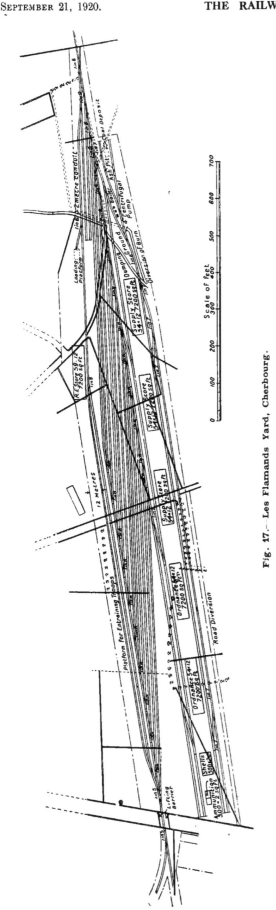

Fig. 17.—Les Flamands Yard, Cherbourg.

in March, 1917, and by the end of the following August, the marshalling yard and six sheds had been finished and four cranes erected and brought into use. The whole of the work was carried out by British civilian labour under the command of R.E. railway construction officers.

New Works at Taranto.

Although the constructional work at Cherbourg was considerable, that at Taranto, the other terminus of the overland route, was on a much larger scale, as shown in Fig. 18.

The site selected was on the south side of the Mare Piccolo, to which it was found possible to construct a branch line from the Italian Marine Arsenal Line : it was considered that a pier, stores and sidings could be built without difficulty and a satisfactory site for a camping ground was found on a bluff overlooking the Gulf of Taranto. To reach the water level very considerable cutting had to be done, but nothing worse than a gradient of 1 in 70 was necessary.

It was originally proposed to provide a pier for ships of medium size, but in view of the shortage in this class of vessel and of the necessary material, there was no choice between a deep-water pier and a lighterage wharf. The former also would have taken a considerable time to construct with consequent delay in starting the goods service ; it was, therefore, decided to provide a wharf, which was afterwards supplemented by the construction of six short jetties. The wharf was finished by the end of November and the jetties by December, 1917.

Constructional work and siding accommodation.—It was necessary also to provide siding accommodation sufficient to hold one personnel and three goods trains at the high level junction with the Arsenal line. Twice as much shed accommodation would be required as at Cherbourg, with a reception road and running round road (to hold 40 wagons) outside the sheds, with two roads to hold 20 wagons each alongside the loading stages of the sheds ; also a shunting neck of 40 wagons length.

The Italian Government acquired the necessary land and placed it at our disposal free of charge. The construction of the wharf wall was carried out on our behalf by the Italian Ministry of Marine, and that of the sidings and sheds partly by the Italian State railways and partly by British staff, the whole under the supervision of Colonel Morgan. In January, 1918, Colonel Rhys Williams reporting on the progress of the work at Taranto stated :—

" The construction of this harbour and port with all its ancillary arrangements in five months is a remarkable achievement. A bare hill-side in July, 1917, has been transformed into the site of a camp capable of containing 15,000 men, most of whom are housed in stone or Nissen huts. One hundred and eighty-eight Nissen huts have already been erected. Hospitals containing 520 beds have been built. A stone-built quay with six wooden jetties, each of sufficient length to load three barges at a time, is in working order. On made ground along the foot of the hill now stand 11 warehouses varying in length from 50 to 100 metres. Alongside the warehouses six sidings each 700 yards in length have been completed, and the warehouses are connected with the quay by a Decauville line. The Triage is in working order with seven lines 1,000 yards long. Work is going on to increase the number of warehouse sidings, and the soil excavated is being used to form a direct approach to each of the six jetties. These approaches should be completed in a month's time. A large stone-built E.F.C. canteen has been built. A stone-built R.E. store adjoins it. A large ammunition shed, 100 metres long, has been commenced at a short distance from the warehouse."

The situation of the camp is ideal. On a low bluff overlooking the Mare Piccolo, covering an area of about 150 acres and situated about 50 ft. above sea level, it is surrounded by olive groves and vineyards. Water has been laid on everywhere and electricity for lighting has been obtained from local sources.

The building of a wharf 1,000 ft. long was the first work to be commenced ; this was constructed of stone as were also the sheds, stone being easily obtainable. Later 10 sheds were constructed, these covering an area of over 2 acres ; the maximum accumulation of stores in the sheds has been as high as 18,000 tons. Most of the loading into lighters has been done by hand, with the assistance of

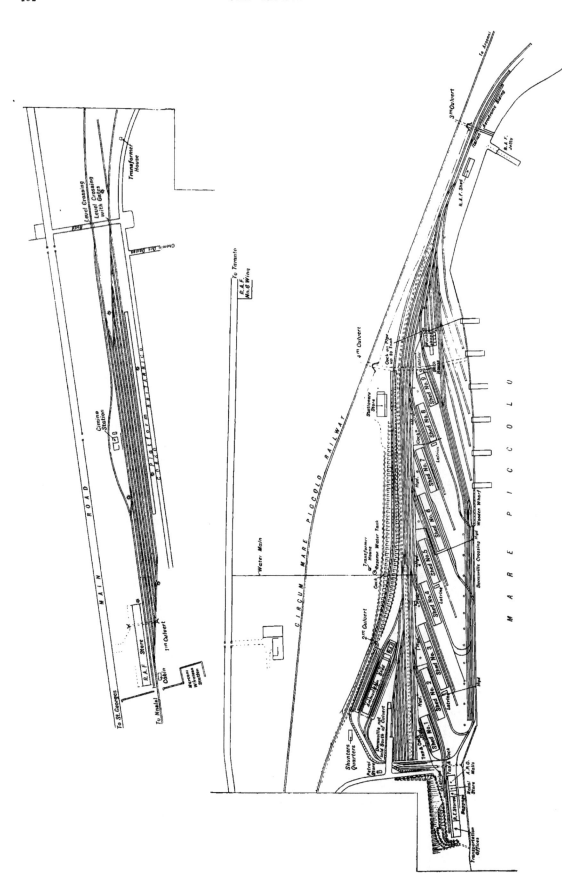

Fig. 18.—Accommodation provided at Taranto, Mediterranean Line of Communication.

gravity runways. The sheds are furnished with 10 cranes and there are 10 also at Cherbourg. Under an agreement entered into with them, the Italians have the option of taking over the port which will, no doubt, be of considerable value to them in the future.

Rest Camps and Haltes-Repas.

In addition to the railway constructional work required at the terminals, special rest camps had to be erected there and also at two intermediate stations, i.e., St. Germain and Faenza. The function of the terminal rest camps was to house the troops whilst awaiting conveyance in either direction, and to provide for accumulations due to shipping delays ; the purpose of the intermediate ones was to afford an interval of rest and recreation to troops in transit on the long journey across Europe. Hospitals were provided at all the rest camps, these being particularly essential for troops proceeding from the malarial regions in the Mediterranean theatre of war. The hospital at Taranto contained 400 beds.

Haltes-repas also were organised and staffed throughout the route to enable trains to stop for an hour or two twice a day, so that the troops could be provided with hot tea and have an opportunity of using latrines and ablution benches ; for this purpose the trains were run into lay-by sidings, along which the necessary accommodation was provided.

Capacity of rest camps.—It was originally proposed to provide accommodation for 2,000 troops in transit at Cherbourg and at the two intermediate camps, and for 5,000 at Taranto. Shipping difficulties, however, and the passage over the route of Egyptian and Indian labour for France necessitated a considerable expansion of the accommodation at Taranto and authority was given to provide for a maximum of 10,000 white, and 5,000 Indian troops in transit, and 4,000 permanent staff and labour. Of the maximum total of 19,000, 6,000 were at first accommodated in huts and the remainder under canvas, though by September, 1918, sufficient huts had been erected to accommodate practically the whole of this number. For the same reasons the camp at Faenza was considerably extended.

Medical arrangements.—The medical arrangements over the route were carried out by Lieut.-Colonel Statham, C.M.G., who accompanied the late Sir Guy Calthrop on his mission. The medical side of the scheme was a very important one in view of the malarial affected districts traversed over a portion of the route and the importation of native labour from the East. The measures taken at Taranto in making huts mosquito proof and providing a segregation camp and disinfecting apparatus were so complete that disease was kept down to a comparatively small percentage. To each train an ambulance coach was attached with medical officers and orderlies in attendance, not only to deal with sickness among the travellers, but to clear hospital cases along the route.

Traffic.

Although the preliminary construction at Taranto was not commenced until May 15, the first passenger train left Cherbourg on June 28 and the first goods train on August 8, 1917.

Negotiations with the French were carried on by the D.G.T., France, and at a conference in Paris on June 19-20, 1917, it was agreed that a personnel service of one train per day (5,000 passengers per week) and a goods service of four trains per day should be instituted, the British carrying out all terminal work with their own staff and shipping coal to Italy in substitution for that consumed by the Italian State railways on the new services. In view of our undertakings in respect of rolling-stock for France, the French agreed to provide all locomotives and passenger vehicles as far as Modane and allow their goods wagons to run through to Taranto.

The passenger service.—On this page the time-table for the journey is given. This shews the distances between stations and a summary of the time occupied ; for personnel trains the period was about 180 hours including 61 hours occupied in stops at two intermediate rest camps and at the *haltes-repas*, the average capacity of each train being 66 officers and 720 other ranks. It should be mentioned that the time-table shown in Fig. 19 is one that was put into operation at the commencement of the service, and subsequent variations were made to meet immediate necessities.

The goods service.—The terminal facilities were not sufficiently advanced to enable the goods service to be started until August 8, 1917 ; even at that date, the works were far from complete, but the increasing demands on shipping rendered it desirable to make an immediate start with a limited service of one train per day, Newhaven being the English port of shipment.

At this time the yard and six sheds had been completed at Cherbourg and four cranes erected, whilst at Taranto the wharf had been completed for a distance of 250 ft. out of the proposed length of 1,000 ft., and two sheds and three sidings had been finished ; 10 lighters also were available for the conveyance of stores from wharf to ship. Between August 8 and August 31, 16 goods trains, average length 29 wagons, were run over the new route, the average net load being 250 tons and running time about 110 hours.

Day.	Arrive.	Depart.				Arrive.	Depart.	Day.
1st		22.39	Cherbourg, 155 km. ..	Camp		1.56		9th
2nd	4.7	5.3	Mezidon, 109 km. ..	H.R. ..		19.43	20.52	
	8.34	9.19	La Hutte Coulomblere, 34 km.	H.R. ..		14.26	15.31	
	10.31	10.54	Le Mans, 100 km. ..	—		12.36	13.15	
	16.43	18.07	St. Pierre des Corps, 200 km.	H.R. ..		5.43	6.57	8th
3rd	1.57	3.22	Saincaize, 115 km. ..	H.R. ..		21.16	21.47	
	7.45	9.12	Paray le Monial, 107 km.	H.R. ..		15.49	17.30	
	13.43		St. Germain au Mont d'or, 174 km.	Camp			11.38	7th
4th		14.54				9.00		
5th	22.12	0.11	Montmelian, 59 km. ..	H.R. ..		0.28	1.50	6th
			St. Jean de Maurienne, 27 km.					
	5.31 F	8.14 I	Modane, 106 km. ..	Change Trains	20.26 I		21.4 F	
	12.47	14.17	Turin, 128 km. ..	H.R. ..		14.47	16.30	
	19.10	20.26	Voghera, 255 km. ..	H.R. ..		6.08	8.27	5th
6th & 7th	8.44	20.54	Faenza, 300 km...	Camp		6.52	19.45	4th & 3rd
8th	7.53	11.48	Castellamare, 177 km. ..	H.R. ..		18.34	20.09	
	18.17	20.16	Foggia, 234 km...	H.R. ..		11.36	12.50	2nd
9th	5.55	9.20	Brindisi, 70 km...	H.R. ..		22.12	22.55	
	12.12		Taranto ..	Camp		17.53		1st

Total distance, 2,350 km.

	Hrs. min.			Hrs. min.
1st day ..	.. 1 21		1st day ..	.. 6 07
7 at 24 ..	.. 168 00		7 at 24 ..	.. 168 00
9th day ..	.. 12 12		9th day ..	.. 1 56
	181 33—180·33*			176 03—177·03*

Including halts at St. Germain	.. 25·11	Including halts at Faenza	.. 36·53
Including halts at Faenza ..	.. 36·10	Including halts at St. Germain	26·38

F = French time.   I = Italian time.
* Italian time is 1 hour in advance of French time.

Fig. 19.—**Timings of Personnel Trains, June, 1917, Mediterranean Line of Communication.**

The traffic consisted of the usual ordnance stores and ammunition, R.E. stores and railway stores, A.S.C. supplies, &c., required for the maintenance of the forces in the Near East, but animals and articles of exceptional weight and bulk were excluded. A considerable number of aeroplanes in cases (maximum dimensions, 28 ft. 6 in. by 8 ft. by 8 ft. 6 in.) were carried, however, and a regular service of letter mails to Salonica passed over the route.

As the terminal facilities at Taranto developed, an endeavour was made to increase the tonnage of stores carried and during the week ending October 27, 1917, two goods trains per day were run regularly, though it was very difficult to obtain the necessary wagons from the French. On October 30 the service had to be stopped altogether on account of the military situation in Italy, and it was not resumed till the beginning of January, 1918.

Conditions retarding development.—During this first period, shortages of wagons in France and of boats at Taranto militated against the development of the route. Except for odd trains, no traffic passed between October, 1917, and January 8, 1918, when a cargo arrived at Cherbourg. The first train load of this cargo arrived at Taranto on January 18; by the end of that month traffic had risen to 11 trains per week and kept at that level until the middle of March, rising to 17 trains, or week ending March 23.

At the end of March the service had again to be suspended owing to the serious military situation in France, the last train leaving Cherbourg on March 28. The goods service was resumed in April, and the passenger service a week later. The goods trains ran at the rate of seven per week until the middle of May, when they reached 13, and gradually increased to 21 per week at the commencement of June; in fact, June, 1918, was the record month, as many as 70 trains being run in 28 days.

Unfortunately, the shortage of shipping led to an accumulation of stores at Taranto, so that during July the service had to be cut down again to one train per day. During August the average rose to 1·6 per day, but from September until the end of 1918 it did not average one per day owing to the continued wagon shortage in France.

Discontinuance of goods service consequent on Armistice. —After the cessation of hostilities in November, 1918, the question of continuing the use of the route was considered and, at a meeting held on December 5 between representatives of the War Office and the Ministry of Shipping, it was decided to recommend the early discontinuance of the goods service. At the same time it was considered that the personnel service should be carried on for use in connection with demobilisation.

The through goods service ceased after arrival at Cherbourg of ss. *Iddo* on December 12, 1918, but on that date there were arrears of 7,530 tons and 2,529 tons at Cherbourg and Taranto respectively. The last through goods train left Cherbourg on January 29, 1919, and the last cargo boats from Taranto were ss. *War Bagpipe* to Salonica and ss. *Tregurno* to Alexandria, which sailed on March 2 and 5 respectively. The contents of a few "cut-off" wagons were subsequently shipped on returning transports. Taking goods trains alone for the whole period from commencement of the service to December 28, 1918, **569 trains were run, an average of 8·5 per week.**

Restrictions on passenger service.—Turning to the passenger service, although it was the intention to run a train daily from Cherbourg to Taranto, there were only three weeks during each of which seven trains were run, although in two other weeks this rate

was exceeded, *i.e.*, 11 trains during week ending Ocotber 13, 1917, and 9 the following week. For the whole period to the end of 1918, an average of 3 south-bound trains ran weekly; the average for the north-bound passenger trains was slightly higher, *i.e.*, 3·1 per week; in fact, during weeks ending June 29 and July 13, 1918, 15 and 16 trains respectively left Taranto in connection with a special troop movement from Egypt and Salonica to France and United Kingdom.

Passenger traffic from Cherbourg to Taranto practically ceased in January, 1919, in which month demobilisation services were initiated to deal with troops returning from the Italian Expeditionary Force, and from the East *via* Taranto. The first demobilisation train from I.E.F. left on December 23, 1918, and the first from Taranto on January 12, 1919. Early in February the demobilisation services were diverted from Cherbourg to Havre, no demobilisation trains being despatched to Cherbourg after the 7th of that month. Subsequent to this date seven ordinary personnel trains ran to Cherbourg; the last of these left Taranto on February 24, and all subsequent traffic from Italy followed the Havre route.

The traffic carried from the commencement of the services till February 8, 1919, was :—

Passengers.		No.
South-bound	..	158,437
North-bound	..	222,118
Total		380,555

Goods.		Tons.
South-bound	..	168,588
North-bound	..	14,962
Total		183,550

The chart at Fig. 20 gives particulars of the traffic passing over the route up to quarter ending December, 1918.

Administration.

The preliminary administration of the Mediterranean line of communication was carried out by Brig.-General Strick under the F.M. C.-in-C. France, but in August 1917, the whole of the Cherbourg and Taranto route was made independent of G.H.Q. France, and placed under the command of Major-General W. H. Grey, C.B., as D.D.G.T.—from October 31, 1917, as D.G.T.—this officer having previously been Director of Inland Water Transport in Mesopotamia. General Grey successfully dealt with a number of questions which had to be solved before the system was perfected. From a military point of view there was a new departure in the carrying of goods on commercial lines, the department concerned in the stores not being responsible for them from the time they were shipped in England to the time of their arrival in Egypt or Salonica, and very careful measures had to be taken by the transport organisation to check, during transit, and investigate losses.

During the period of the Italian reverse, when British troops were

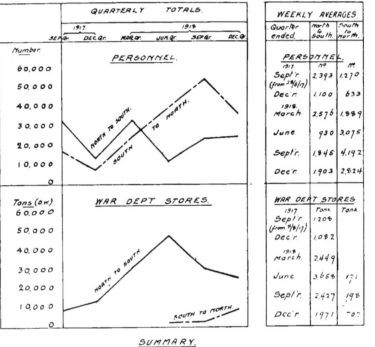

Fig. 20.—Traffic Carried over Mediterranean Line of Communication.

WEEKLY AVERAGES.

Quarter ended.	North to South.	South to North.
PERSONNEL.		
1917.	*No*	*No*
Sept'r (from 29/6/17)	2,393	1,270
Dec'r	1,100	633
1918.		
March	2,576	1,889
June	930	3,075
Sept'r	1,846	4,192
Dec'r	1,903	2,824

WAR DEPT STORES.		
1917.	*Tons.*	*Tons.*
Sept'r (from 4/8/17)	1,208	
Dec'r	1,082	
1918.		
March	2,449	
June	3,668	171
Sept'r	2,427	198
Dec'r	1,971	707

SUMMARY.

	PERSONNEL		WAR DEPT STORES	
	No. of Trains.	Officers and O.R.	No. of Trains.	Tons (D.W.)
NORTH TO SOUTH	205	142,093	552	160,296
SOUTH TO NORTH	236	181,743	47	13,917
	441	323,836	599	174,213

sent to Italy, valuable help was rendered in lending officers who knew Italy to organise new lines of communication for the expeditionary force. A number of personnel were withdrawn from the M.L.C. at Cherbourg and Taranto and the *haltes-repas* stations, to form a new transportation staff for the Italian E.F., and to provide a temporary staff of transportation officers along the route between Paris and Turin *via* Ventimiglia.

On the establishment of a British military command in Italy in October, 1917, the administration of the Mediterranean line of communication was again changed, it being found advisable to separate the control of the route. General Grey's functions as D.G.T. were extended to include the British area in Northern Italy ; the Italian portion of the route was placed under the C.-in-C. Italy, and the French portion under the C.-in-C. France, through the D.G.T. France.

Smoothness characterised all the negotiations connected with the establishment of the Mediterranean Line of Communication, and much assistance was received from the French and Italian authorities. In France the British were indebted to M. Claveille (Minister of Public Works), Colonel Maurier (War Office), and the French authorities at Cherbourg ; in Italy the rapidity with which important structural works were completed and the service commenced, was largely due to the courtesy and willing assistance of General Fiastri (Director-General of Transportation), Commendatore Berrini (Head of the Italian State railways), and Admiral Cerri (Italian Naval C.-in-C. at Taranto).

Freight Checking.

When the scheme of working was being formulated in consultation with the departments concerned, it was suggested that depôts should be provided at Cherbourg and Taranto, at which stores could be received, brought on charge, and subsequently re-despatched by representatives of the services concerned, but it was pointed out by the D.R.R. that this would involve a considerable amount of extra shedding and seriously curtail the carrying capacity of the route. It was decided that Cherbourg and Taranto should be maintained strictly as transit points, a decision which was amply justified by experience. Departmental officers, were, however, attached to Transportation in an advisory capacity and, in the case of the Ordnance Department, to assist in obviating as far as possible the splitting up of consignments, which had caused a certain amount of inconvenience to consignees.

Freight Documents.—Due to consignments breaking bulk at the two transit ports, it was impossible to follow the usual commercial practice of invoicing goods through from English port to destination port, and separate freight documents were made for each section of the route via :—

1. *Newhaven or Southampton to Cherbourg.*—Shipping Note, &c., prepared by department concerned.

2. *Cherbourg to Taranto.*—Wagon invoice prepared by Transportation.

3. *Taranto to Eastern port.*—Lighter Loading sheet, which served also as Bill of Lading, prepared by Transportation.

Reference to cross-channel boat was given on wagon invoice and repeated on Taranto's lighter loading sheet to enable consignee to connect the goods received with the copy of cross-Channel shipping note (or issue voucher) which had been posted to him by the issuing department.

The usual checks were made at transit points and discrepancy reports rendered when necessary. Cherbourg receipted and returned the cross-Channel shipping notes to enable the accounts of issuing departments to be cleared, and similarly Taranto received acknowledgments from Eastern ports.

An enquiry office was formed under the G.O.C., M.L.O.C., when under single control, but was later transferred to the D.R.R.'s Department, which dealt with complaints from Issuing departments as to delays in transit, loss of, and damage to stores, &c., which could not be cleared up locally. Copies of all freight documents were sent to this office by the transit ports.

Due to the conditions under which the traffic had to be worked, certain minor difficulties naturally arose, particularly in getting differences between transit points adjusted, and in regard to the pilferage which took place at various points, and which it seemed impossible entirely to prevent, except at prohibitive expense. Losses arose in consequence of the exceptional amount of handling, combined with the frailty of some of the packing cases, and it was necessary to carry out repair work at the transit points. In view of the difficulties encountered, however, the losses were not excessive, and the general results cannot be considered unsatisfactory.

Summary and Conclusions.

It will be seen that, from one cause or another (shortage of wagons, shipping delays, labour difficulties at Taranto, &c.) the route was not utilised to anything like the extent originally contemplated. The port accommodation placed at our disposal at Cherbourg (three berths in the Bassin du Commerce and the use of the Port des Flamands) was estimated to be sufficient for dealing with 1,200 tons per day, and the authorised scheme was based on this figure. At Taranto the facilities were adequate for the shipment of a similar tonnage as well as the reception of an equal quantity of traffic from the East ; in fact General Grey was of opinion that Taranto could, under favourable conditions, deal with 2,000 tons per day in each direction. The record shipment was 1,300 tons d.w. on September 4, 1918.

The average net load of the Cherbourg-Taranto goods trains was only 290 tons, so that the record traffic in June, 1918 (70 trains in 28 days), did not represent more than 725 tons per day (as compared with the original programme of 1,200 tons). Even with this moderate tonnage the accumulation of stores at Taranto amounted to 18,250 tons at the beginning of July owing to the shortage of ships necessary to clear the traffic. This necessitated a curtailed programme for a time. The accumulation at Cherbourg also amounted to about 8,000 tons. Before the accumulation was finally cleared off, a very serious wagon shortage arose in France. This became more and more acute as military operations on the Western front developed, and was still obtaining when the decision to terminate the goods service was reached.

Leave parties from Salonica.—Whilst naturally the preponderance of goods traffic was in a southerly direction, there was a considerable excess of north-bound passengers over south-bound. The route conferred a great boon on the troops in the Salonica campaign. The great trouble with these troops was always the difficulty of finding the means of transportation for leave in the United Kingdom ; the question of leave became extremely acute by reason of the fact that the percentage of sickness in Macedonia was as great as, if not greater than, in any other theatre of war, and it was realised that a temporary change of climate and surroundings would do much for the health and moral of the troops. On the opening of the overland route, a definite programme of leave parties was made possible, and apart from the interruptions in January and March, 1918, the arrangements worked well and a considerable improvement in the granting of leave resulted.

The service was not only used for the purpose of supplying personnel and stores for the Near East, but in addition it was most valuable for the transport of men and material to and from Italy and France and from the eastern theatres of war to France. Though the road was practically closed down for the ordinary service for some weeks in October, 1917, owing to the critical situation in Italy, and again in March, 1918, on account of the transportation crisis resulting from the German offensive, the route amply justified its existence by the saving of shipping in waters which were infested by enemy submarines. In addition the period spent in transporting troops and supplies was considerably shortened.

Roughly speaking the total tonnage carried amounted to 200,000 d.w. tons, equivalent to 500,000 shipping tons, and a total of 350,000 personnel used the route up to the end of 1918. These figures will show the enormous benefit derived from the Mediterranean Line of Communication.

RAILWAYS AND THE ITALIAN THEATRE OF WAR.

The Allied Assistance to Italy, and the Transportation Problem thus Developed.

It was when the Mediterranean line of communication was getting nicely established that the Italian army met with a disaster which necessitated all the efforts of the French and ourselves being diverted to reinforce the Italian line of defence. Consequently, in October, 1917, the overland route to Egypt and Salonica had to be practically abandoned for the time being, but the forethought in opening out this route was of undoubted advantage in sending relief to the Italian army at the beginning of November, 1917.

During November and December, 1917, no less than 715 trains were despatched from France to Italy, an average of 12 trains per day. made up as follows :—

		442 troop trains
		102 supply trains
		102 ammunition trains
		32 ordnance trains
		28 R.E. stores trains
		9 miscellaneous trains.

Fig. 21 shows average weekly number of trains run during 1918.

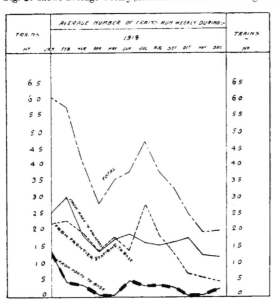

Fig. 21.—Supply Trains Run for B.E.F., Italy.

Although it was understood that we should not be required to provide railway or road material for Italy, it was clear that the Italians were short of rolling-stock and we had to be prepared to receive a demand for anything up to 5,000 wagons. If any large development of light railways took place also, it was evident that we should have to supply material and also standard gauge material for any large quantity of sidings, doublings, &c., as the Italians had no margin of supplies to draw upon. At the outset, however, the question of coal supply for Italy overshadowed everything else, and the large number of coal trains which had to be forwarded from France was one cause which prevented the Cherbourg to Taranto service being resumed on a large scale. It also affected the wagon supply, as it was understood the Italians had to provide the wagons to bring the coal from France. Fig. 22 indicates the coal traffic passing into Italy.

Organisation.

The transportation organisation in Italy, whereby the D.G.T. was responsible for the British transportation and dock services,

including transportation over the Italian portion of the Mediterranean line of communication, was the subject of a good deal of discussion early in 1918. Lieut.-General Lawson, the I.G.C., reported that in his opinion the present organisation tended to lack of co-ordination between the transportation and dock services and at the same time with the existing system there could be no unity of control over these services at the headquarters of the I.G.C. The proposals for the reconstruction of the transportation organisation in Italy were examined by the D.R.R. and alternative proposals were submitted to D.G.M.R. In March the War Office decided that the functions of the I.G.C. Italian portion of the Mediterranean line of communication should be separated from those of I.G.C. to the British forces in Italy, the I.G.C. being responsible directly to the War Office in the former capacity and to the G.O.C.-in-C. Italy in the latter capacity. The D.G.T. was placed under the orders of the I.G.C. with the proviso that D.G.T. should receive orders regarding work in the forward area direct through staff at G.H.Q., the I.G.C. being informed. Under this arrangement the appointment of D.G.T. in Italy was abolished and Brig.-General Colvin was appointed D.D.G.T.

In April, 1918, Major-General Sir Philip Nash, K.C.M.G., C.B., was appointed I.G.T. for the Western Front and British representative on the Inter-Allied Transportation Council, acting, in the former case, in an advisory capacity to the F.M. C.-in-C. France, C.-in-C. Italy, and to I.G.C. Italian portion of the Mediterranean line of communication on all matters of transportation.

Transportation and Personnel.

The working of the British troop and maintenance train services in Italy was carried out by the Italian railway authorities under the co-ordination of the Railway Transport Establishment, and apart from a few officers being required for liaison duties, no broad gauge operating personnel was sent out.

The Italian authorities were unable, however, to provide any operating personnel for light railways and, on January 8, 1918, the G.O.C.-in-C. recommended in view of the situation and probable contingencies that Light Railways Headquarters Staff and one Light Railway Operating Company should be sent out together with a supply of light railway track and a due proportion of rolling-stock, &c. At the same time, it was recommended that a platoon of a transportation store company should be provided to take charge of the light railways and standard gauge equipment. The personnel sent out were eventually utilised for working British traffic over the Thienne-Calveno Light Railway and Ropeways in the Assiago area.

Up to December 28, 1918, a total of 16 locomotives, 15 tractors and 240 wagons, all for 60 c.m. gauge, had been despatched to the Italian Expeditionary Force in addition to 40 miles of 60 c.m. and 40 miles of standard gauge track.

The supplies for the maintenance of the British Expeditionary Force, Italy, originating in the United Kingdom or France were sent to Italy by all rail route. The port of Spezzia was, however, used for coal, commodities such as meat, grain and hay from America being sent by direct shipment to the port of Genoa. The port was used solely as a transit port, whereby all discharging and work in the sheds came under the D.G.T. on the same principle as that adopted at Cherbourg and Taranto. Originally eight sheds at Genoa were allotted to the British forces, with an establishment of 8 officers and 88 other ranks, but with the reduction of the force, and the accumulation of a reserve at the base at Arquata, the accommodation was eventually reduced to some 3,000 tons storage space.

In May, 1918, the I.G.T. reported that, after an inquiry into the general transportation situation in Italy, he was of opinion that the maintenance of a separate establishment to look after the handling of the British Army traffic at Genoa could not be justified, and recommended the adoption of one of the following alternative courses. First, that the traffic should be handed over in wagons to the transportation authorities by the representative of the Ministry of Shipping under the Naval Transport Officer, and way-billed, instead of ex-ship's slings, the checking and invoicing of

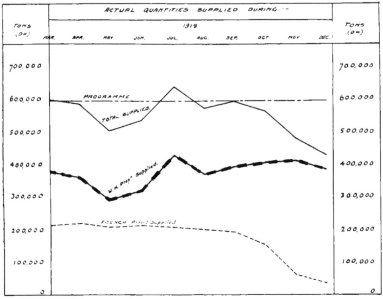

Fig. 22.—Coal Supplied to Italy from United Kingdom and France.

cargoes to be carried out by the existing Cunard Steam Ship Company's organisation under Ministry of Shipping representation. As the second alternative it was proposed to stop direct imports from America to Italy on British Army account, and to buy from the Italians supplies which were already imported on their own account.

These proposals were considered by the Directorate, and it was decided in view of any contingency which would sever or interrupt the railway communication between France and Italy, that it was

essential to maintain a line of communication from the sea to the British Army in Italy, and that this line of communication should have the normal organisation including a military staff at the port. For this reason the retention of sufficient staff to carry out the work actually being done at the port, and to assure timely expansion in case of necessity was deemed advisable. Similarly it was decided to retain such accommodation and railway facilities at the port over and above the normal requirements, as would enable such a contingency as an interruption in the railway communication to be met, or the rapid concentration of a further force in Italy to be carried out. This policy was maintained as a precautionary measure until after the signing of the armistice.

Effect of Armistice.

With the conclusion of the armistice it was possible for the Italian Expeditionary Force to draw largely upon the stores previously accumulated in Italy in view of the possibility of additional British divisions having to be sent there to meet the heavy Austro-German offensive. As a result of this, the tonnage passing through the port of Genoa during the quarter ending December, 1918, was quite small, and amounted to 7,900 tons as compared with 21,700 to s during the preceding quarter, and there was a corresponding reduction in the quantity of stores received by rail from France.

Personnel movements included the despatch by rail of a battalion to Imsk near Innsbruck in the Austrian Tyrol and another one to Fiume. In this connection it is interesting to note that a through train service to Trieste and Fiume was established. On December 23 the first demobilisation train left Italian Expeditionary Force railheads, arrangements being made to run two such trains each week.

During the December quarter the Italians experienced a marked difficulty in the working of their railway traffic, particularly in the south, with the result that the British traffic was affected ; several causes seemed to have brought about the trouble, one being a large and considerable increase in civilian traffic following the armistice ; another, heavy military traffic arising out of leave movements ; dispersal and repatriation of Austrian prisoners, &c., and the return of surplus ammunition ; third, the lack of effective motive power for the large increase of operated mileage resulting from the advance into enemy territory and amounting to about 937 miles. Although 400 locomotives were taken from the Austrians, only 13 per cent. of them were in running order. The situation on the Italian railways, however, quickly improved and no considerable disturbance was made in the general demobilisation movements of our forces.

The chart at Fig. 23 indicates the extent of rail and sea traffic passing to the Italian theatre of war. From the tables it will be observed that the "peak" of traffic was reached in the September quarter of 1918, when well over 100,000 deadweight tons of traffic passed by rail and sea into Italy, the average weekly figure being 6,665 tons. As noted previously, the opening up of the Mediterranean Line of Communication proved of great advantage to Italy during the critical months towards the end of 1917, as it enabled men and material to be rushed through with the greatest expedition, and permitted coal supplies to be hurried forward at a time when the position was very critical.

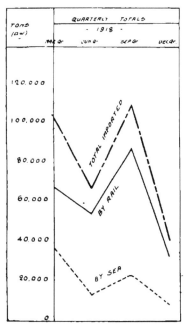

Fig. 23.—W.D. Stores sent to Italy.

AVERAGE	WEEKLY	QUANTITIES	
Quarter ended.	RAIL.	SEA.	TOTAL.
1918	Tons	Tons	Tons
March.	5,132	2,740	7,872
June.	4,138	987	5,125
Sept'r.	6,665	1,780	8,445
Dec'r.	2,505	605	3,110

RAILWAYS AND THE SALONICA CAMPAIGN.

The Railways from Salonica—Dudular, the Main Distributing Centre—Standard Gauge Railway Development—Light Railway Construction—The Overland Service via Bralo and Itea—Practical Working—Locomotives and Rolling-Stock—Labour and Personnel—The Allied Advance and its Effect on Railway Development.

With the object of affording aid to Serbia, which was being invaded by the Austrian and Bulgarian armies, French and British forces in October, 1915, commenced to land at Salonica. The 10th Division of the British Army was brought over from the Dardanelles, its orders being to establish itself for the winter in Salonica and not to cross the Greek frontier unless this was violated.

A decision, however, was reached that the French should push up into Serbia with the object of relieving the Serbs, who were then being hardly pressed by the Austrian and Bulgarian invaders, and General Mahon, commanding the 10th Division, received orders from London to advance as far as Lake Doiran, just across the Greek frontier. Here he relieved the French, who were holding the right wing of the Allied front, and protected the line of communication of the main French force which had advanced and become engaged with the enemy up the Vardar, 80 miles from Salonica. Unfortunately, however, the Allies arrived too late in Salonica to stop the retirement of the Serbian army, who were outnumbered and overwhelmed by the Austrians from the north and the Bulgars from the east.

In consequence, after a bold but ineffective attempt to save at least the southern part of Serbia, the Allied Army had to fall back to a line running along the Greek frontier from Vodena through Doiran and following the River Struma to the Gulf of Orfano in the Aegean Sea. The army was thus thrown solely upon its own resources, and, far from receiving help from the Greeks, had to look upon them as a constant menace from all sides. It had to import from a base thousands of miles away and improvise in a barren country all the requirements needed for the maintenance in proper fettle of an enormous number of men and for the carrying out of modern warfare. Villages were scattered, primitive and thinly populated, the roads were mostly mere tracks, and although three railways were in existence, these ran at divergent angles and necessitated considerable extra construction and improvement. The Allies, therefore, had to build up slowly and laboriously the main part of the system of locomotion necessary for the movement of troops and supplies by the erection of piers and bridges and the construction of miles of road and railway track.

The Railways from Salonica.

There are three main lines radiating from Salonica, as sketched in Fig. 24, which shows the railway position at the end of 1918. Due north runs the Jonction Salonique Constantinople (J.S.C.) line, which, bending sharply eastwards at Doiran, runs through Demir Hissar and Drama to the Bulgarian port of Dedeagatch and thence to Constantinople. Running in a north-westerly direction is the Oriental (C.O.) line which passes through Uskub to Belgrade, whilst going due west is the Salonica-Monastir (S.M.) Railway, from which, at Plati, branches the Athens line to the south of Greece. The last mentioned railway was still under construction when the war began. The last link in the through route, i.e., from Papapouli, near the foot of Mount Olympus, to Plati, was commenced in 1913 and completed in the spring of 1916. The whole of the work was carried out by the Batignolles Company of France.

When operations began in Macedonia, use had immediately to be made of these three main railway systems, as apart from them no means existed for the rapid movement of troops. The roads were mere tracks and several months would necessarily elapse before they could be made even serviceable for heavy military transport. The railways, which are of standard gauge single track, were found to be in fairly good condition, but a shortage of siding and yard accommodation and rolling-stock was soon experienced.

The Allied Railway Commission.—For some months after the landing of the Allies, the railways continued to be worked by the Greek Government, but this proved so unsatisfactory and the charges raised were so excessive, that in June, 1916, General Sarrail compulsorily took them over.

To avoid complications and to secure economy of administration and working as between the French and British forces, the general control of the railways was as from September 10, 1916, vested in a Railway Commission consisting of the "Chef du 4eme Bureau" of the French Commander-in-Chief's Staff and the British Director of Railways (Colonel Hammond, R.E.). For executive purposes there was a sub-Commission, known as the Commission de Reseau, with one French and one English member, the former dealing more particularly with the operation of the C.O. and S.M. lines and the latter with that of the J.S.C. Railway; it may here be mentioned that the British were entirely responsible for the working of the J.S.C. Railway and branches, which will subsequently be referred to, and ran a certain number of trains on the C.O. line originally to Karasuli and subsequently to Gumendgi, and on the Karasuli to Kilindir link.

The organisation for the control of the railways is shown below:—

Joint Railway Commission for General Control.

1 French member.	1 English member.

Joint "Commission de Reseau"—Executive control of all railways.

1 French member.	1 English member.

British Administration (J.S.C. line, Salonica—Kilindir—Karasuli).	French Administration (C.O. line, Salonica—Gumendgi and beyond).	French Administration (S.M. line Salonica—Monastir).

It secured that the three lines should be considered as one system under the "Commission de Reseau" and be worked as such in order to obtain the best results for all the armies concerned. With this object in view the members maintained close touch with one another. The local rolling-stock was divided between the French and British, roughly according to mileage worked, and originally the French provided stores through the Ministry of War in Paris. This arrangement, however, was soon found to be inadequate to meet the increasing demands of traffic and railway development, with the result that each party became responsible for obtaining railway material and stores for the respective lines they operated, but eventually pooling of rolling-stock was arranged. The British imported in all about 30 engines and 1,900 wagons, while the French, Italians and Serbians also contributed between them about 60 engines and 500 wagons.

It is interesting to note that, when the British took over the working of the J.S.C. Railway, they were supplying a front maintained not only by their own but also by Italian troops, but the fluctuations of the campaign soon resulted in the transfer of the Italians to another part of the front, leaving the British in sole possession until the spring of 1918, when the newly trained Greek troops began to arrive and take over a sector of our line.

Limits of Working.—Working over the J.S.C. Railway was only possible as far as Kilindir. The remainder of the line stretching round from Doiran to Demir Hissar and Seres was within range of the enemy's guns. Being in "no man's land," it suffered from considerable depredations, rails and sleepers being torn up by both combatants for use in gun emplacements and dug-outs. The line had severe gradients to Kilindir and, in fact, as far as Demir Hissar. It possessed crossing places of good capacity and lay-out sufficient to cope with maximum train load. Although it was realised that until the troops could force the Rupel Pass, the line from Doiran would be under the enemy's guns, the organisation was such that the service could be carried forward at very short notice, reserves of material being collected with this object.

Before proceeding further, it will be well to consider broadly the difficulties which had to be contended with in the maintenance of the armies in Macedonia. In modern warfare transportation is all-important, and the ease with which reinforcements, guns, material and supplies can be sent to an army in the field is a decisive factor. In this respect, the Allied force in the Balkans had every disadvantage as compared with the enemy. Whereas our home base was some 2,000 miles away by sea and all goods had to be handled several times, the enemy's front was in direct rail communication with his centres of production and he had not to risk the danger of submarines. If necessary he could bring up a division from Germany in about six days, whereas it would take us probably as many weeks. Hence our troops in the Balkans had to do without many things, such as heavy artillery and unlimited ammunition, owing to the long and exposed transport system with frequent breakings of bulk.

Increasing the Capacity of the Port.—Through nearly all the stages of the campaign and until the Taranto-Itea service was inaugurated, everything for the army had to pass over the quays at Salonica, and the first essential was to increase the capacity of the port.

The town of Salonica stretches down to the water's edge and the possibilities of the extension of the port were, therefore, very limited. Nevertheless, the port facilities were gradually extended and the roads leading thereto rearranged, widened and improved. Originally, the quay space at the disposal of the British amounted to two berths on what is known as the "English Quay." Subsequently two shoal-water piers, Gravesend Pier and Marsh Pier, were thrown out to the extreme west of the town. These enabled discharge from ship to lighter in stream and considerably increased the capacity of the port. In fact, it soon became apparent that stores could be discharged more rapidly than they could be moved from the quays and piers.

At the end of 1916, each department of the army was responsible for the discharge of its own stores and material from ships. Thus the English Quay was used for miscellaneous stores (*i.e.*, R.A.F. equipment, M.F.O., Y.M.C.A., and E.F.C. traffic, &c.), *Chantier Anglais*, covering the railway jetty, Malta Pier and New Pier, was used for all classes of stores, particularly ordnance and ammunition, whilst Gravesend Pier dealt with R.E. material, which was conveyed by Decauville railway to the Base Park about 5 km. away. The construction of Marsh Pier was nearing completion and this was subsequently used for the discharge, storage and dispatch of forage.

The responsibility for the discharge of goods from ship to quay and clearance from quay was, therefore, a very divided one, and whilst the quayage space was very confined, the siding accommodation and shunting facilities at the port were limited and the rolling-stock quite insufficient to cope with the traffic. As a consequence, the majority of the incoming supplies and stores were being conveyed from the port to the base depôts 5 or 6 km. away by motor lorry. Owing to the poor state of the roads and their devastating effect on the upkeep of the lorries, to the scarcity of petrol and its comparative cost, and to the large number of personnel required to maintain the service, this was necessarily a most extravagant method of transport, and it speedily became apparent that the facilities must be improved.

Sir Francis Dent's Mission.—In November, 1916, Sir Francis Dent, the General Manager of the South Eastern & Chatham Railway, arrived in Salonica at the head of a Mission with authority from the War Office to investigate the transportation situation. His in-

quiries were mainly instrumental in securing co-ordination and co-operation between the various functions operating at the port.

As a result of these investigations, the discharge and loading of ships subsequently became a function of the Inland Water Transport department, a number of technical officers and men under the command of Lieut.-Colonel J. B. Parkhouse (the Warrington District Goods Manager of the London & North Western Railway), being sent from home for this purpose in June, 1917. Colonel Parkhouse was appointed Director of Docks, with control over discharge from ship to quay, clearance from quay and loading into truck. Traffic dealt with at the port is shown in Fig. 25.

Arrangements were also made for conveying all possible traffic from port to base depôts by rail instead of road. The base depôts were situated at Dudular, about 6 km. from the port, and although the army had already laid a certain number of reception roads and sorting sidings at this place, it was necessary to enlarge the accommodation as speedily as possible. Material for this work was specially ordered from England and an additional Railway Construction Company (No. 267 Company, R.E.) was formed locally from men drawn from the Salonica force.

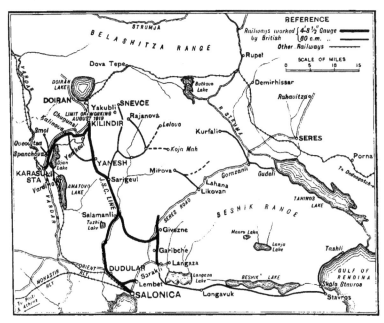

Fig. 24.—Railways in Macedonia.

Supply of D.B. Wagons to Ease Rolling-Stock Shortage.—At the same time the shortage of rolling-stock was alone sufficient to prevent adequate dispatch by rail. An urgent demand was, therefore, made on England for 600 dead-buffered wagons, a large number of which, it was realised must be standing idle at home owing to their expulsion some years ago from the British railways. These wagons, it was considered, would be sufficiently serviceable for maintaining a port to depôt service in Macedonia, and subsequent events showed that they saved the situation, although the local railway authorities had considerable difficulty in maintaining the wagons in proper running order, as most of them, after many years on British railways, were in a very decrepit condition. However, they proved of great value as a substitute at a time when it was practically impossible to provide new wagons owing to the serious rolling-stock shortage in all theatres of war.

The demands on the existing standard gauge rolling-stock in Macedonia had been such that by a gradual process it had been almost confined to work on the main lines between the depôts and railheads. This threw a heavy burden on the motor and horse road transport from the quays and dumps to the main depôts at Dudular and Lembet and naturally interfered with prompt handling and clearance of ships in view of the small capacity of road vehicles as compared with that of railway wagons ; a further point was that the French motor transport service had been overtaxed and this had thrown them back upon rail transit to a greater extent than was anticipated, necessitating a larger proportion of rolling-stock being allotted to them. With the arrival at the end of January, 1917, of the first lot of dead-buffered wagons, it was possible to augment the port to depôt service, but it was not until further wagons had been received and the extensions at Dudular had been completed that the full benefit of rail transport was experienced. Whereas the

railhead, it was the function of the railway to see (1) that incoming wagons were promptly cleared, (2) that the demands for rolling-stock for daily loading were met, and (3) that such wagons were loaded to their full capacity. These duties were carried out by the Chief Traffic Officer at Dudular and his staff, all of whom were experienced railwaymen ; in fact, so far as the accommodation would permit, Dudular was worked in the same way as a marshalling and concentration yard at home. All this was essential as, owing to the very limited amount of rolling-stock available, every possible use had to be got out of it, and the railway department of the Salonica army could justifiably take credit for a most rapid turn-round of wagons.

Method of Working, Port to Depôt.— Trips arriving from the various port stations entered the reception roads. On arrival the trip engine was detached and sent round to the other end of the loops, where it was attached to a rake of empty wagons and sent back again to the port. This "shuttle" arrangement went on throughout the 24 hours. Unfortunately, the accommodation at the port was, generally speaking, insufficient to allow of trips being marshalled in depôt order, so the incoming rakes of loaded wagons arriving rough had each to be sorted out at the northern end of the sidings by one of the Dudular shunt engines. This having been done, the wagons were conveyed to the different depôts and placed on each road exactly where they were required for off-loading by the department. It was, unfortunately, impossible to sort the wagons by gravity, as here again the room for extension was insufficient and moreover the types of wagons were so diversified—varying from an 8-ton D.B. wagon to a 20-ton oil axlebox Continental truck—that this method would not be unattended by danger. However, the best possible was done, and one has only to picture five reception roads each of 100 wagons capacity almost full owing to unavoidable bunching of trips on a day with the temperature at 120° F., to realise the difficulties that confronted the railway staff. Fortunately, most of the latter were trained shunters from home railways, and, despite the oppressive heat, hard work on their part enabled the job to be kept going. No serious delays occurred, and it was rarely, if ever, necessary to resort to the practice of blocking back. This was important, as if once the machinery at Dudular got clogged, the work of discharging at the port would cease, owing to the lack of room there, and ships would be detained—and even one ship might detain the return of a whole convoy !

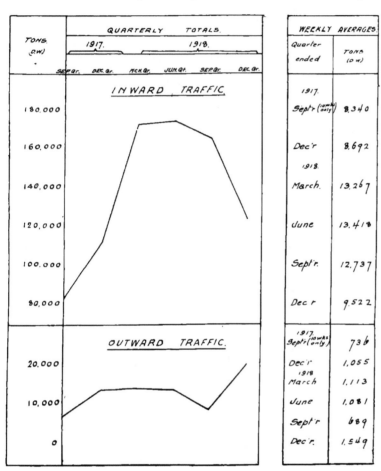

Fig. 25.—Chart showing Traffic dealt with at Salonica.

The Wagon Difficulty.—To maintain the shuttle arrangement and to meet the ever growing demands of the port stations, prompt clearance of wagons was absolutely essential, and it was rarely that more than six hours elapsed between the arrival of a loaded wagon in the reception roads and its departure empty again to the port, although in the meantime the operations of sorting, placing, off-loading and drawing had all to take place. So small became the number of available wagons that it was found necessary to maintain a most comprehensive record, whereby all the movements of a wagon whilst at Dudular, including the times of commencement and completion of off-loading, could be checked. Only in this way was it possible for the traffic officers to keep a tight grip on the off-loading performed in each of the nine depôts.

As already mentioned, 600 D.B. wagons were originally utilised for the port to depôt service, but the wear and tear of these very second-hand wagons in a hot climate was naturally severe, and although every effort was made to doctor them up, it was not

Monastir road had been crowded daily with a constant stream of loaded lorries proceeding to Dudular and empty ones returning to the port, a remarkable transformation took place. All except an insignificant fraction of the traffic was turned over to the railway, and Dudular attained the work and dimensions of an important marshalling yard and distributing centre. Fig. 26 is interesting as indicating the development of railway traffic in Macedonia.

Dudular, the Main Distributing Centre.

At Dudular as many as nine different depôts were instituted to meet the needs of the various services of the British army, viz., North and South Ammunition Depôts, E.F.C., Ordnance, Main Supply, Railway Stores and Ambulance Train Depôts and R.E. Base and Advanced Parks. These depôts were used as concentration points for supplies arriving at the port and transferred therefrom by regular trip workings ; they also acted as distributing centres of stores and supplies regularly despatched to the front by means of the up-country rail services.

Whilst the various departments of the army performed the off-loading of incoming trucks and the loading of those destined for possible to delay for long their departure to the scrap-heap. They performed much useful work, however, and in the spring of 1917 the wagon position was so acute that permission of the War Office had to be obtained for their use on up-country trains, a procedure which soon had to be discontinued owing to their unreliability. Nevertheless, one or two rakes of extra good D.B. wagons were run, ever after that, for the conveyance of hay from port to Salamanli, which acted as a concentration point and distributing centre for this traffic. As the D.B. wagons were marked out of traffic, it became necessary to utilise on the port service more and more of the local spring-buffer wagons, and the situation became increasingly acute until July, 1918, when numbers of new wagons began to arrive from home.

Great care had also to be exercised in fulfilling the requirements of the various depôts for trucks required for loading for up-country. Here again the system generally prevalent in England was followed. Every evening the depôts furnished to the traffic officer particulars of the wagons required for the next day's loading; these requirements were summarised for the information of the night staff. Trains going up-country loaded during the evening would be off-loaded at railhead immediately on arrival, and brought back by the same engines. In this way it was possible to utilise day by day the same wagons for up-country loading, the trucks on their arrival back at Dudular during the night being immediately replaced in the loading roads. On the other hand the situation was somewhat complicated by wagons being received back at Dudular loaded with salvage for the base depôts or for shipment at the port. Again, a certain number of wagons were regularly loaded at port stations for railhead and the requirements in this respect had also to be met.

Standard Gauge Railway Development.

Construction of additional standard and 60 c.m. gauge railways very soon became necessary to meet the requirements of the army and to reduce road transport.

The Lembet Line.—From Dudular Yard there was a short standard gauge line running for a distance of about 10 km. in a north-easterly direction to Lembet. This line with a ruling gradient of 1 in 50 and many sharp curves was constructed by the British in the early part of 1916 to connect with advanced supply, engineering, ammunition and ordnance depôts on the Seres Road. It was a most difficult one to work. All goods trains in the direction of Lembet had to be propelled by an engine in rear and restricted, for a six-wheel coupled engine, to eight vehicles. The line, however, ran through a portion of the French and Italian camps, and owing to the presence of many level crossings, it was not deemed safe to send personnel trains up with the engine in the rear owing to the difficulty experienced by the engineman in sighting obstructions. Personnel trains, therefore, went up " engine first " with vehicles double-coupled and all brakes manned. The line used as a shunting neck at Lembet was on a falling gradient in the direction of Dudular, this necessitating the use of catch points; in fact, it had to be made a rule that any wagons left standing on the main line outside the ordnance dump must be secured by a padlock and chain on the wheels of the last vehicle towards Dudular.

The Seres Road.—At the beginning of 1917 the main line of supply for the British Army was from the end of the Lembet branch along the Seres Road to the River Struma. On the Struma front there were three divisions and a mounted brigade which were all

being supplied by this road through an advanced dump at Likovan. The road was originally of but light construction, with a thin surface of road metal laid on an ill-drained formation. Fit only for the native ox-wagon, when heavy army lorries commenced to pass over it, culverts broke through and the road became almost impassable.

Before the construction of additional railways an enormous traffic passed up the Seres Road: motor lorries and ambulances, staff cars and horse limbers formed a never-ending stream, and the task of maintaining it was a most formidable one, particularly in the winter, when heavy rains made it a quagmire. It stretched for a distance of 45 miles, but from January to March motor transport could not get further than 35 miles. Thence onwards, for a distance of 20 miles

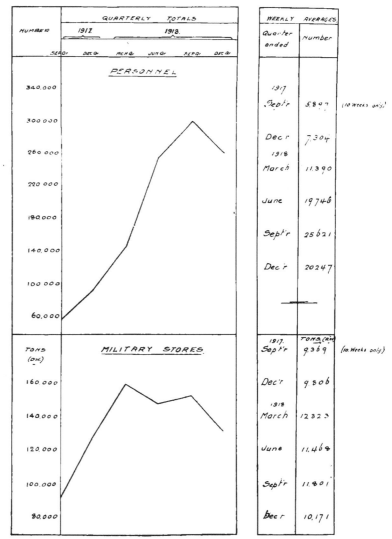

Fig. 26.—Traffic carried over Standard Gauge Railways, Salonica.

to the front line, horse transport had to be utilised. Consequently there was severe congestion and supplies were maintained only with considerable difficulty.

The British undertook the task of repairing and maintaining the road, but some delay was experienced owing to the difficulty of gaining stone in sufficiently large quantities to keep pace with the demands, and the rate of repair could not keep pace with the extraordinary wear and tear.

The Salamanli-Guvesne S.G. Line.—To relieve the pressure of road traffic and to reduce the run of the motor transport on the

Seres Road from 40 to 25 miles, a standard gauge line was constructed by the British from Salamanli, on the main J.S.C. Railway to Guvesne on the Seres Road. Work on this line was commenced at the end of 1916. Apart from the building of a trestle bridge to carry the line over the River Galiko, the work did not present any considerable difficulty, though the ruling gradient with the load was pretty severe, averaging 1 in 60. Construction was retarded somewhat owing to the shortage of labour, but, in January, 1917, it was expedited by the supply of entrenching battalions to assist in formation work. Though bad weather also delayed the work, by the middle of February platelaying had commenced on the branch and in the new yard at Salamanli. Delay was again experienced owing to shortage of material, but at the end of March the line had been opened for restricted traffic, and a month later normal traffic was flowing. A large depôt was constructed at Guvesne supplying A.S.C., Ordnance and R.E. services, which relieved Lembet to a considerable extent.

A branch was also run from the Guvesne line to a quarry at Devi Kran from which stone was obtained and off-loaded at Guvesne for the maintenance of the Seres Road. Another line was run to Arakli, where a large potato farm had been instituted for the supply of the army. The Guvesne line, therefore, thoroughly justified itself, and a large traffic was soon flowing in all directions. It is interesting to note that, owing to the gradients on this line, it was necessary for trains to stop twice in each direction for brakes to be dropped and lifted. In the event of heavy rain, also, careful watch had to be kept for washouts.

At Likovan on the Seres Road, there was an advance depôt. From here a short 60 c.m. line had been run out to Mirova to facilitate supplies to troops in that neighbourhood. This line was re-laid with heavy material in the summer of 1917, but it was soon realised that considerable advantage would accrue by the extension of the Guvesne line up to Mirova and beyond there to Tureka. This, it was estimated, would entirely replace the motor transport on the Seres Road and lead to great economies in time and money. Accordingly, in July, 1917, a preliminary survey was made for a light railway from Guvesne in a north-easterly direction through Lahana, the existing advanced dump, to Tureka, a distance of 35 km. Owing, however, to strategic considerations, this line was not proceeded with, but very soon important works were taken in hand by the extension of the railways to and at Stavros.

Light Railway Developments.

The British front line originally ran along the River Struma, which enters the Gulf of Rendina at Chai Aghizi. The British occupied the ground on the west bank of the mouth of the Struma and a very small piece of ground on the east bank. Supplies were landed by lighters at Tasli, a few kilometres south-west of Chai Aghizi, the lighters being run there from Stavros in the south-west corner of the Gulf. It was frequently impossible to land at Tasli, and the Navy could not allow supply ships to go to this part of the coast. On the other hand, Stavros Bay was protected from attack by submarine, and it was generally possible to land supplies there, a small pier having been constructed.

Originally, there was no rail communication whatever between Salonica and Stavros and, apart from the sea, there were no means of getting there except by a track through the hills ; this route was quite unsuitable for motor lorries, so men and stores had to be sent there by small steamer from Salonica. In January, 1917, consideration was given to the possibility of sending large vessels to Stavros to relieve the congestion at Salonica itself and avoid superfluous handling of goods, and a suggestion for extra piers and lighters was approved.

The Stavros–Tasli Light Railway.—In 1916 the British had constructed a 60 c.m. line for 15 km. from Stavros towards Tasli, and by the end of the year the formation was nearly complete for extending it to that place. It was then proposed to run a double 60 c.m. line from Stavros past Tasli to Chai Aghizi and on a formation suitable for a standard gauge railway, the reasons for not making this a standard gauge line in the first instance being (1) the difficulty of landing S.G. rolling-stock at Stavros ; (2) the doubt as to whether S.G. material and rolling-stock could be supplied; and (3) the necessity

for completing the line in time for operations before the hot weather. If necessary, the provision of a standard gauge line could be commenced at any time without interfering with the use of the 60 c.m. line as soon as material could be supplied, the 60 c.m. track and rolling-stock being then taken up and used for other purposes of the army.

The ultimate aim of the Chai Aghizi line was to enable the concentration of troops on the west bank of the Struma and to follow up the advance, connecting subsequently with the main Seres line. For this, there were two alternatives :—

(1) To cross the Struma near its mouth and join the main J.S.C. line between Borna and Angista ; or

(2) To keep to the west side of the lake of Tahinos, the north-west part of which is dry, and join up probably west of Seres.

The advantage of the first scheme was a shorter railway, the disadvantages steeper gradients, bridging of the Struma and several tunnels and cuttings. From a railway point of view, the second scheme seemed preferable, as from a preliminary survey it was found that the gradients need not exceed 1 in 100. If constructed, it would be a much better means of supplying the forces on the Struma front than by the existing Seres Road, and whether the advance was through the Rupel Pass or towards Drama, it would be distinctly superior to the J.S.C. line through Doiran to Demir Hissar. The extension of the line would mean the supply of 65 miles of track with points and crossings and at least seven additional six-coupled engines and 240 wagons, whilst for operation east of Seres, one locomotive would have to be supplied for each 15 miles operated conditional on the advance. It was realised, however, that the Struma Valley was nothing more nor less than a malarial swamp, and the railway would have to go right through it, causing a heavy drain on personnel.

By the middle of February, 1917, a single 60 c.m. line of 16-lb. material had been laid from Stavros to Chai Aghizi ; in the meantime, a quantity of 2-ft. 6-in. gauge material was being converted in Egypt to 60 c.m., 10 miles of which was on its way to Salonica. In its existing state the capacity of the line was very small, and owing also to lack of engines, the traffic was limited to 150 tons a day.

It was then decided to defer the relaying of the line from Stavros and its extension along Lake Tahinos for consideration only in the event of an advance, though it was pointed out that irrespective of an advance, the proposal had an economic value attached to it, for at the time 500 lorries, excluding ambulances, were being utilised daily to supply three divisions and one mounted brigade on the Struma front. As each of these lorries required two drivers, there were at least 1,000 men engaged on the service in addition to guards and officers and repairing staff. In addition, the constant use of this road involved a very large expenditure on repairs, the weekly percentage of breakages of front springs, for instance, being 24 per cent., and even after the expenditure of considerable time and money, it would not be possible to render the Seres Road suitable for motor transport. Exclusive of ammunition, which varied up to a maximum of 300 tons a day, 750 tons of stores and supplies were being moved daily by the road, and it was estimated that a standard gauge railway from Stavros to the Struma would give much greater efficiency with eight locomotives and not more than 120 men for operation and 100 for maintenance. Sixty-centimetre gauge was not recommended owing to the fact that the line would be about 100 km. in length, and also that standard gauge would only require for the same work about one-sixth of the locomotive staff and one-third of the traffic and maintenance staff, and would be more reliable and easy to maintain.

In March it was found impossible to carry on the work within a distance of 4 km. from the mouth of the Struma, owing to fire from enemy batteries, but the laying of the single track into Tasli was completed by the middle of May after some delay awaiting material. In the meantime the main strength of the British forces had been moved to the western sector of the line for the advance at Doiran, and at the end of the spring campaigning season it was decided to move the British troops back from the malarial Struma Valley to prevent, if possible, the heavy sick list of the previous year. Consequently, the main forces were withdrawn to the hills, outposts only being left at fortified bridgeheads, and the proposed extension of the Tasli line was not proceeded with.

The Guvesne to Stavros Light Railway.—Attention was next drawn to the possibility of connecting Salonica with Stavros by rail. A direct connection in an easterly direction from Salonica was not possible owing to the big range of hills between there and Lake Langaza, and it was deemed advisable to follow the line of least resistance by using, for the commencement, the already existing Arakli Branch of the Guvesne standard gauge line, and running thence along the southern banks of Lakes Langaza and Beshik into Stavros. This and the Tasli line would enable supplies for the army on the Struma to be conveyed by land, and would obviate water transport in a sea infested by enemy submarines, whilst also the Admiralty were anxious that the use of Stavros as a harbour should be discontinued if possible owing to the submarine danger. Accordingly, in October, 1917, a survey was commenced for a 60 c.m. single line from Arakli. By the commencement of the following month, 20 km. had been laid, but the question was then raised as to the advisability of continuing the work owing to the probable small quantity of traffic likely to be dealt with. At that time, however, it was possible in certain circumstances that the army might have to withdraw to a more retired line covering Salonica, in which event a railway such as that proposed would be useful for the feeding of the troops, supplies being taken from railhead by mountain tracks north of Beshik and Langaza Lakes. The railway was, therefore, proceeded with and opened for traffic on April 1, 1918. An R.O.D. Company was formed locally for the operation of the line—93 km. in length.

Fortunately, events did not necessitate the withdrawal of the troops from the forward positions they occupied, but the traffic passing over the line soon justified its construction—in fact, it came to be the most important light railway in the Salonica theatre of war. During the quarter ending December, 1918, out of the 3,000 tons a week carried on the light railways, the Stavros line was responsible for 2,500 and employed much the greater part of the rolling-stock. As a consequence of the opening of the line, traffic by sea into Stavros rapidly declined, and ceased altogether in the middle of September, 1918.

The Sarigol to Snevce Light Railway.—Running in a northerly direction from Sarigol on the J.S.C. Railway is a 60 c.m. line to a place called Snevce, 28 km. away, situated at the foot of the Krusha Balkan Mountains, along which ran our front line. Up to the end of November, 1916, this was worked by the French to supply an Italian division, but about this time a British division took over, and the line and rolling-stock were handed over to us. In the following June a survey was made for the purpose of re-aligning and re-laying the railway with 33-lb. track, and the work was completed by the end of October.

By this time a 60 c.m. line was being constructed from a junction with the Snevce line at Gramatna to Rajanovo *via* Kushova, the object of this line being to facilitate the conveyance of supplies to the troops on the Krusha Range. From Kushova two extensions were to run to Lelovo and Hozo Mah respectively, though these apparently were not proceeded with. The Gramatna-Rajanovo line was commenced on September 24, 1917, and was completed and open for traffic by February 1, 1918. In the meantime, the Snevce Railway was being extended to Karamudli to obviate a certain amount of road transport, sidings being laid and a large depôt opened there. The extension was completed in February, 1918.

The length of the Sarigol-Snevce-Gramatna Railways was about 66 km., and although only single track 60 c.m., they were worked with high capacity wagons and engines. They were the means of supplying the troops on the Krusha Hills and thus saving an enormous amount of road transport over difficult country ; in fact, the troops relied on this railway solely for their existence, as there were no roads between Sarigol and the front line. In the early days, subsequent to our taking over from the French, there were repeated wash-outs, and the situation often became critical, but this trouble ceased as soon as the re-laying and re-alignment of the track had been completed.

Other light railways in Macedonia were the Janesh-Gugunchi, supplying a British brigade and re-laid in the spring of 1918, and the Spancova-Oreovica, which was handed over to us by the French, and another important light railway was the Ekaterini-Dranista line in Greece.

The Ekaterini-Dranista Light Railway.—Ekaterini is situated on the western shore of the Gulf of Salonica, and is one of the principal stations on the northern section of the Plati-Athens Railway. It figures largely in the Salonica operations. In December, 1916, following on trouble in Athens, when a detachment of French sailors were treacherously fired upon, the Allies feared an advance by Greek Royalist troops into Thessaly and to the rear of the French line of communication with Monastir. To stop the advance towards Salonica along the coast, two infantry brigades and some artillery were sent by the British to Ekaterini at the foot of Mount Olympus to bar the passage ; consequently, it became necessary to work supply trains to Ekaterini *via* Plati, but, owing to heavy rains, wash-outs occurred on December 8, 9 and 10, causing 16 breaches in the line over a distance of 30 km. Labour was accordingly withdrawn from other parts of the theatre of war, and the line was repaired through to Ekaterini by December 15, when the working was handed over to the French.

Owing to the shortage of coal for the use of the armies in Salonica, it became necessary to seek fresh supplies of fuel. Lignite mines were known to exist in the hills at Dranista, and in February, 1918, a survey was commenced for a 60 c.m. branch to run from the Plati-Athens line at Ekaterini into the hills at Dranista, 27 km. away, to enable lignite to be readily brought down to the main line and, if necessary, to the seaport for shipment to Egypt, &c. This line was completed and opened for traffic on September 1, 1918.

The Overland Service via Bralo and Itea.

Concurrently with the arrangement of an overland route for troops and stores passing through Europe to the Mediterranean theatres of war, investigations were made with regard to the capacity of the existing lines in Greece, and it was ascertained that on the Athens to Plati line it would be possible to work daily in each direction seven trains of 12 wagons each with the then existing rolling-stock and nine trains if the rolling-stock and personnel were increased. It was estimated that six-wheel coupled engines of the London & South Western type, of which there were a number already in use in Salonica, could haul loads of 130 to 150 tons along the line. The loads were considerably restricted owing to severe grades beyond Skarmitza. From Patras on the Gulf of Corinth, a metre gauge line runs to Athens. Over this it was also considered possible to work seven trains each way daily, or nine if additional rolling-stock and personnel were supplied.

As a matter of fact, five specific routes were considered, namely :—

(1) By sea to Patras, thence by the Peloponnesian Railway along the south side of the Gulf of Corinth to Athens, thence by the Larissa-Salonica Railway.

(2) By sea direct to Piræus through the Gulf of Corinth and the Corinth Canal, thence by Piræus-Larissa-Salonica Railway.

(3) (4) (5) Dealt with the proposals to land at bays on the north side of the Gulf of Corinth, viz., Itea, Aspra, Spitia and Livadostro. The journey in each case would have to be performed by road from these bays to join some point on the Larissa-Salonica Railway, and none of these three roads at that time permitted of the transport of cargo or heavy baggage.

The question of the use of the Port of Volo, which is connected by metre gauge line with the Athens-Plati Railway, was also considered. Owing, however, to the short distance by sea between Volo and Salonica, the expense of extra personnel, &c., was not considered justified.

Investigation was also made as to the possibility of a road route from Santa-Quaranta in southern Albania near Corfu to Salonica, a distance of 480 km., but this route was found only suitable for light motor lorries and touring cars, and the journey would occupy about five days. This idea was, therefore, abandoned, although the road was actually used by the Italians and French between Santa-Quaranta and Florina (on the Monastir Railway) for a distance of 300 km.

With regard to the possibility of shipping troops and supplies *via* Piræus, the Director of Railways reported in July, 1917, that between Bralo and Salonica 2,500 personnel or 430 tons of stores could be conveyed daily, whilst between Piræus and Salonica 1,000 personnel or 150 tons could pass daily. The limiting factor was rolling-stock ; with the addition of 100 wagons and 200 men, the daily capacity between Bralo and Salonica could be raised to 4,000 personnel or 650 tons, and the same capacity could be got between Piræus and Salonica by adding 11 locomotives, 300 wagons, 400 men and additional stores.

The Establishment of the Bralo-Itea Route.—Meanwhile the French were developing road facilities between Itea on the Gulf of Corinth and Bralo, the nearest rail point, the construction of a railway between these places presenting great difficulties. In August, 1917, the suggestion was made that British personnel for Salonica should be sent *via* Itea and Bralo, the troops marching between these two towns, a distance of about 32 miles ; but some time would have to elapse before the route could properly be organised for the movement of troops owing to the necessity of establishing a base and rest camps and improving the water supply. The entire absence of water, however, was a factor which alone prevented the troops from marching between Itea and Bralo, and a service of motor lorries had to be instituted.

In September, 1917, it was definitely arranged to send transports with reinforcements to Itea, commencing the middle of the following month, the troops to join the railway at Bralo and a maximum of 500 men to be conveyed each way daily between there and Salonica. From Itea, where a large rest camp was instituted, troops were conveyed by motor lorry to Bralo, where there was another convenient rest camp for troops proceeding in either direction. The practicability of this route for stores was tested about the middle of 1918 by sending small quantities of cased goods, and during the quarter ending September, 1918, 2,290 tons were discharged at Itea and 1,400 tons loaded on rail at Bralo.

In March, 1918, inquiry was made regarding the possibility and advisability of constructing a railway between Itea and Bralo, whether such a line should be broad or narrow gauge, the various gradients encountered, the possible capacity and the time necessary for completion. A survey was made, but the cost and length of time necessary were estimated to be disproportionate to the advantage likely to be gained.

Alternative schemes for the provision of single and double ropeways between Itea and Bralo were also considered and surveys and estimates made. An investigation of these alternatives resulted in a decision that the cost would be in excess of the advantage gained and that it would be possible to develop the capacity of the road to carry stores as well as troops sufficient to meet all requirements of the armies. The estimated maximum capacity of the road was 300 tons daily.

In August, 1918, British, French and Greek railway construction troops were employed on the lengthening of loops, &c., and general improvement of the Piræus-Salonica main line, to facilitate the working of traffic to Bralo.

Advantages of Bralo-Itea Route.—The route *via* Bralo and Itea was invaluable as an extension of the M. L. of C. route through Italy in connection with leave parties proceeding from Salonica, as many as three leave trains, each consisting of 60 officers and 700 men, being run weekly during the summer. The difficulties in the matter of leave had become acute owing to the shortage in shipping, and the opening of the route did much to relieve the situation.

Practical Working.

As previously mentioned, the general system of working was for the major portion of stores, material and supplies discharged at the port to be worked to Dudular Yard from the port stations by shuttle service. Dudular was, therefore, the concentration point whence supply and personnel trains were despatched up-country.

Trains working over the main lines were run on a line clear block system, only one train being allowed in the same section at the same time, and line clear being obtained by means of telegraph or telephone. No train staff or tablet system existed, and the fact that this primitive method of working was carried on with ease and comparative immunity from accident is evidence of the constant and careful attention of the railway personnel. The Greeks used a telegraph instrument which was in operation before the war, but for stations at which British personnel did the signalling an ordinary telephone circuit was installed.

For the working of the railways a special rule book was compiled for the use of R.O.D. personnel.

Signalling.—Fixed signals were only used at junctions in the base area where they were essential owing to the comprehensive network of railways.

Point indicators were in general use on the main lines. The point indicators worked with the points on the point lever ; when in normal position they showed an oblong green glass or light in the facing direction, and a square white glass or light in the trailing direction (vide diagrams A and B, Fig. 27). When the points were set for a loop or siding in the facing direction a white double-headed arrow was shown on the indicator. This arrow ran diagonally across the disc and the direction of the top pointer indicated the direction for which the road was set (see diagram C, Fig. 27). When the points were set for a loop or siding in the trailing direction a round white light was shown (see diagram D, Fig. 27).

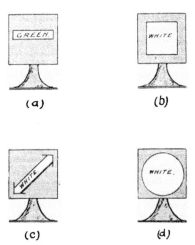

Fig. 27.—**Point Indicators on Macedonian Railways.**

The signals at junctions were worked by wires connected to a ground frame, but the points had each to be set by means of the switch lever. Fixed semaphore disc signals were placed on the right hand side of the line to which they applied, the various position of such signals being indicated in Fig. 28.

The Service.—The time-table that existed in pre-war days provided for an elaborate system of " marches," which, generally speaking, were adopted for running the military trains, though various improvements were made with the object of speeding up. Most of the supply trains were run from Dudular during the late afternoon and evening, being off-loaded by fatigue parties immediately on arrival at the railheads, and returned empty in the early hours of the morning. In this way the fullest possible use was got out of the wagons. As a rule the earlier trains conveyed perishable supplies and ammunition, the later ones taking the less important supplies, such as hay and fodder, ordnance stores and R.E. material.

Every morning by 12 noon the departments had to commence sending in to the Traffic Officer, Dudular, particulars of the wagons they were loading, showing wagon number, contents, weight, destination and road in which being loaded. The port stations also furnished similar particulars of railhead wagons being loaded by them. These particulars were transferred by train clerks to marshalling lists for the particular trains, and passed to the head.

shunter in charge of the marshalling. Meanwhile an engine would be engaged drawing the loaded wagons from the various depôts and transferring them to the sorting sidings. The work of marshalling them proceeded throughout the afternoon and evening, trains on completion being brought up to the station if possible fully half an hour before departure time. Train engines ran from Salonica on a booked timing, and on its arrival the guard and under-guard examined the train and checked the wagon numbers, &c. A very elaborate checking system had to be introduced to stop pilferages, whilst the shortage of wagons and sheets rendered it essential for their movements carefully to be controlled.

Traffic Control.—A system of traffic control was inaugurated, with most satisfactory results to the working of the lines under British administration. The central control was instituted in the Traffic Superintendent's Department at the J.S.C. station, Salonica, and telephone circuits connected it with all the port stations, with Dudular yard and station, and with all stations along the main line up to railheads. All lines were diagrammatically shown in the central control office, discs being used to indicate the passage of trains in the manner followed at control offices in England.

Not only did the control system enable headquarters to keep in touch with trains throughout their journeys, but it also led to the quick turnover of rolling-stock and economy of engine power. At 18.00 hours (6 p.m.) daily, each station would advise Control the number of wagons it would require for the next day's loading either for port to depôt traffic or railhead. In this way wagon requirements for the whole of the line could be summarised and the best distribution made. The necessary particulars having been obtained, it was easy to advise Dudular the number of empties that were to be sent by each trip during the night and the following day. If wagon demands were excessive, as they generally were, the Traffic Officer at Dudular could take steps to warn the depôts to unload by night to ensure the quicker release of the wagons. Every six hours Dudular and the port depôts would telephone to central control the state of their yards, giving for each siding the number of covered and open empties and loaded. This enabled the controller to check his board and to take up at once with the department concerned in cases of empties lying idle, or of loaded wagons awaiting clearance. In the event of unexpected and heavy demands for rolling-stock for ammunition or other special trains, it was always possible to get in touch with control, who would arrange for the supply under the best possible circumstances.

It is interesting to note that each station was known by a code letter, "E" stood for Sarigol, "L" for Janesh, &c., &c., and all train lists and wagon labels merely contained these letters and not the names. A specimen label would read:—"Supplies for R.S.O. at L," meaning that the wagon conveyed supplies for the railhead supply officer at Janesh. This arrangement was not only useful in maintaining secrecy, but also saved considerable time in the making out of documents and in the wiring of trains forward—and incidentally all trains were wired forward to railhead in order that the R.T.O. there could arrange with the departments for the supply of the necessary labour for prompt off-loading.

Locomotives and Rolling-Stock.

Reference has already been made to the shortage of wagon stock. There was no less a shortage of locomotives, though every effort was made to keep them in running order.

In October, 1916, when the standard gauge rolling-stock position was reviewed, it was found that for the purposes of the Allied armies the following rolling-stock only was available :—

	In service.	Awaiting parts.	Total.
Locomotives..	103	18	121
Wagons	1,100	130	1,230

The locomotive figures, moreover, included 10 engines which were expected from the Midi Railway and 21 which were due to

arrive from New York for the Serbian Government. The number actually in service, therefore, was only 72. However, the locomotive power at that time was considered sufficient so far as could be foreseen under the existing conditions.

With regard to the wagons, the 1,100 in use were barely sufficient to enable the demands of the troops then based on the railways to be fulfilled, and consequently none was available for the heavy traffic from the port and quays to the depôts, which had then to be carried by road, nor to meet any increased demands which might arise for traffic to railheads. It was estimated that at least 950 additional wagons would be necessary to meet requirements.

The following figures giving the position for the whole of Greece at December, 1917, will show the year's growth in rolling-stock :—

	In service.	Under repair.	Total.
Locomotives..	124	48	172
Wagons ..	2,614	192	2,806
Carriages ..	216	16	232

Ninety-four locomotives were in the country at the time of the occupation, 78 having been imported, 19 of these from England. Of the wagons 1,505 belonged to various Greek railways and 1,301 had been imported, 781 (including D.B. wagons) from England; all but 15 of the coaches, which had come from France, were found in the country.

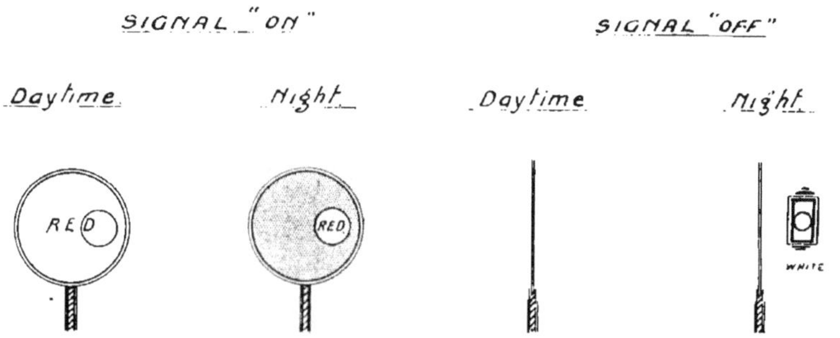

Fig. 28.—Signals on Macedonian Railways.

By December, 1918, the quantity of rolling-stock on the charge of the British alone was approximately as follows :—

	In working.	Under repair.	Loaned to French.	Total.
Locomotives.. ..	41	13	16	70
Wagons	1,344	280	189	1,813
Coaches	54	6	—	60

Engine Types and Capacity.—The following were the types of engines in use on the British-worked railways :—

Engine type.	Nos.	Wheel arrangement.	Known as.
J.S.C.	1—16	0-8-0	"B" class
Serbian (American) ..	01—07	2-6-2	"B" ,,
J.S.C.	101—110	4-6-0	"A" ,,
G.W.R.	25—39	0-6-0	"A" ,,
L. & S.W.R.	—	0-6-0	Shunting
American tank	—	0-6-0	,,

Generally speaking, the "B" class engines could haul a load of 800 tons and the "A" class one of 600 tons on a level road, though these maximum loads were much reduced over certain sections of the line where heavy grades were encountered. The weight of trains was calculated on the tonnage basis, empty vehicles being counted according to tare weight, and loaded vehicles having two, three or more tons added to the tare weight according to contents.

There were no continuous brakes on the trains, but a rule was made that screw-brake vehicles should evenly be distributed through the trains, their proportion varying according to the gradient of the line to be traversed. On the level, a minimum of one screw-brake vehicle to every 15 loaded vehicles was necessary, whilst on a gradient of 1 in 50-60 it was as low as one screw-brake to every five loaded. The screw-braked vehicles were of the Continental type and manned by native Greek brakesmen seated in a caboose on top of the wagon. The engines were fitted with a steam brake.

The locomotive position was considerably eased at the beginning of 1917 by the arrival from New York of 21 engines, 2-6-2 type, built for the Serbian railways by the American Locomotive Company. These locomotives were shipped in parts, with all the motion, &c., disconnected and in cases. Though several of the engines were subsequently handed over to the French, the erection of all of them was performed by the British in an ill-equipped locomotive shop. In addition, six 0-6-0 side tank shunting engines were received from the Vulcan Ironworks Company, U.S.A. These did good work in Dudular yard, as did also a number of London & South Western six-wheeled coupled engines, which were also used for shunting purposes. The 0-6-0 Great Western engines performed some very useful work on the main line and proved capable of hauling 600 tons on the level.

With regard to the 60 c.m. lines, the principal locomotives used were the Hudson 0-6-0 type and Baldwin 4-6-0, as well as petrol tractors, and the rolling-stock was of high capacity, the trucks being capable of taking 10 tons. The Baldwin locomotives had a haulage power of 45 tons over a 3 per cent. gradient, and under normal conditions could haul a gross load of 100 tons on a 1 per cent. gradient. In December, 1918, rolling-stock on charge with the Salonica light railways amounted to 54 locomotives and 469 wagons.

Labour and Personnel.

For constructional work on the railways various types of labour were employed in addition to the railway construction companies. Large numbers of Greek civilians were utilised, as also Egyptians, and Turkish prisoners. Egyptians were sent over in companies for plate-laying under six-monthly contracts.

For the loading and off-loading of wagons at the port depôts and railheads there was a fair supply of local labour, and, given sufficient inducement, the men were physically capable of handling heavy goods in an expeditious manner. Failing such inducement, they could hardly have worked more slowly or more unsatisfactorily. The rate of pay for day work was 4 drs. (or 3s. 4d.) per man, and it was quite apparent that very few of the men really earned even this wage. A system of piecework was, therefore, instituted, with most satisfactory results, under the guidance of officers and N.C.Os. experienced in loading. Much was also done to improve the loading of wagons; in fact, the improvement was so great that one wagon was made to accommodate the quantity of supplies which had formerly occupied 2·75 wagons under the old methods. Considerable economies in rolling-stock resulted from these arrangements.

The Railway Staff.—The organisation of the railway department was quite simple. There was a Director of Railways (formerly Colonel Hammond, R.E., latterly Colonel Rhodes, R.E.) with two assistants, one for traffic (Lieut.-Colonel Kirkness) and another for construction (Lieut.-Colonel Douglas). Under the A.D.R.(T.) were the Traffic Superintendent, responsible for traffic working; the Superintendent of Works, responsible for permanent way and works maintenance, also for new structures; the Locomotive Superintendent, responsible for the maintenance and working of locomotives; and the Superintendent of Light Railways, responsible for the operation of all lines other than standard gauge. The A.D.R.(C.) was responsible for all construction both of standard gauge and 60 c.m. lines, and, therefore, supervised the work of the railway construction companies.

A rough chart of the organisation is shown below:—

Director of Railways.

A.D.R. (T.).		A.D.R. (C.). Railway Construction Companies.
Traffic Superintendent. Railway Traffic Officers. R.O.D.	Superintendent Works. Maintenance. Personnel.	Locomotive Superintendent. Locomotive Officers. R.O.D.	Superintendent L.R. L.R. Officers and personnel.

The British operating staff worked particularly hard and their duties were rendered more arduous owing to the establishment being invariably below strength owing to sickness. The unhealthiness of the country was a great difficulty. During the summer all units were from 30 to 35 per cent. and some as much as 50 per cent. below strength; in fact, it was stated by one of the local railway authorities that in peace time the normal estimate of sick for local requirements was 25 per cent., and the climate was considered worse than the west coast of Africa.

The Allied Advance and its Effect on Railway Development.

In September, 1918, an advance was carried out on the whole of the British front, and a complete capitulation of the Bulgarian armies took place on September 30. This necessarily added greatly to the length both of the light and standard gauge railways under the control of our forces. At the same time, however, it was found possible to close the Likovan, Spancova and Janesh Light Railways, as, owing to the onward sweep of our troops, these lines were rendered useless. The traffic over the railways was also somewhat eased by the use of the Bulgarian port of Dedeagatch on the Ægean Sea for the reception of supplies for the British division which had moved up into northern Bulgaria.

With the withdrawal of the Bulgarians, a further section of the J.S.C. line was occupied and the length operated by the B.E.F. increased from 78½ to 107 miles. Reconstruction also was carried on between Vetrina and Seres on this line, and by the end of January, 1919, through rail communication was instituted between Salonica and Constantinople. At Demir Hissar, the bridge carrying the railway over the Struma had been destroyed by the British in January, 1916. Reconstruction was at once put in hand; pending completion, a line of 60 c.m. gauge was run from the railway and carried over a road bridge.

On November 30 the light railway was completed from Vetrina on the J.S.C. line, a little to the west of the River Struma, to Rupel, a few miles north, crossing the River Struma by a road bridge near Rupel, where it connected with the Bulgarian 60 c.m. line to Radomir, from which place Sofia is reached by standard gauge railway. In this way through communication was instituted between Salonica and the whole of Bulgaria.

An important piece of construction was also carried out with the help of Greek troops in the extension of the Stavros Railway from Tasli (north of Stavros), crossing the Struma River at Neohori to near Angista, where it joined up with the main J.S.C. Railway. This, it will be remembered, was one of the alternative schemes originally put forward for the extension of the Stavros Railway, when an advance from the Struma was in contemplation at the beginning of 1917.

The general railway situation in the Salonica theatre was rendered much more complicated as a result of the cessation of hostilities. To ensure compliance with the terms of the armistices with Bulgaria and Turkey, it became necessary to assume a certain amount of control of the railways of both countries. A problem at once presented itself in the shape of German railway personnel, whom it was difficult to replace by reason of the lack of sufficient railway troops of our own. A further serious difficulty arose from the shortage of coal for locomotive working. Even when operating at full pressure, the Bulgarian and Turkish railways had not been able to meet military and civilian transportation requirements, and during the war very large supplies of coal had been imported from Germany. These difficulties manifested themselves not only in Turkey in Europe, but to an even greater extent in connection with the Anatolian railways and the Baghdad Railway in Asia Minor. On the reversion of the lines to Allied control, steps were immediately taken to adjust the matter.

During the December quarter Major-General de Candolle was transferred from Mesopotamia to act as expert adviser to General Milne, G.O.C., Salonica Army, in all transport matters concerning our interests in the Balkans, Turkey, Southern Russia and the Caucasus and Western Asia Minor. General headquarters were moved to Constantinople whence, so far as Asia Minor was concerned, authority was exercised as far as Konia, the junction of the Anatolian and Baghdad Railways.

After the armistice the headquarters of the Allied Railway Commission moved to Constantinople. Its function was then extended to cover the control of the Turkish and Bulgarian railways in Europe and the Turkish railways in Asia Minor.

THE PALESTINE CAMPAIGN.

Co-ordination of Requirements—The Main Line East of Kantara—Constructional Details—Bridging—Locomotives and Rolling-Stock—Workshops and Running Sheds—Traffic and Capacity—Organisation and Personnel.

The development of military railways in Palestine began in the early part of 1916. Up to that time the British Forces had merely maintained a defensive position along the Suez Canal, but towards the end of 1915 the situation on this front was considered to present several features favourable to an offensive campaign. The system of railways then inaugurated and subsequently developed according to the exigencies of the campaign is shown on a map at Fig. 29.

Doubling of the line from Zagazig on the Nile Delta to Ismailia on the Suez Canal was of obvious urgency, but, in addition, it appeared necessary to construct at least three standard gauge lines and water-pipe lines to meet the enemy's advance, connecting these lines if possible by a cross line east of the canal. It was also considered desirable to provide ferries for taking loaded trucks of material, supplies, &c., across the canal to avoid the necessity for transhipment. It was important that the proposed railways east of the canal should be of the standard gauge, in order to minimise transhipment and simplify the provision of rolling-stock and repair shops, &c.

Following on the decision of this forward policy, Sir George Macaulay (late R.E.), Director of the Egyptian State Railways, was appointed Director of Railways to the Egyptian Expeditionary Force, with the temporary rank of Colonel, being assisted by Lieut.-Col. Blankeney, Deputy Director, and Lieut.-Cols. Hall and Sowerby, Assistant Directors, all officers with extended experience on the Egyptian and Sudan railways. Lieut.-Col. Lubbock was appointed Deputy Director of Railway Construction, but was subsequently ordered to Mesopotamia as Director of Railways.

Assistance from Egyptian State Railways.

The Egyptian State Railways undertook to act as agents for new military lines along the Mediterranean and to supply them with stores as far as possible. At the same time it was pointed out that a good deal of new railway work for the army had already been done in Egypt, and that, as the railways there had been working on war conditions for some time, their resources were depleted, and it would not be possible to do a very great deal in the way of supply for new railways. In addition to having built a large number of wagons, pontoons, &c., for the Australians, the administration had also supplied practically all its spare pile drivers, plate-boring plant, &c., and many stores to Mudros for use there and at Gallipoli. Considerable quantities of bombs and grenades were made in the railway shops and extensive repairs to guns and machine guns were carried out there. Several new stations for camps had been opened and many new crossing stations put in to enable an increased traffic to be dealt with. And all this time the traffic on the State lines had been much increased by the movement of considerable numbers of troops and the collection of supplies for them.

The doubling of the line from Zagazig to Ismailia was undertaken by the State Railways, which also laid out large stations for camps in the Delta and on the Suez Canal, and new sidings from the main line to the Suez Canal bank. This work alone used up 150 km. of standard gauge track and left nothing for maintenance; it also took a large number of platelayers away from the work of the Egyptian State Administration, with the result that the maintenance of the State lines got into arrear when the traffic over them was increasingly heavy. Many small bridges also had to be built, some of them with opening spans to enable boats to pass, and one or two bridges had to be doubled in width. Local resources were, therefore, considerably taxed, particularly in view of the fact that the merchants did not import a single cargo of timber during the first 18 months of the war, and very little afterwards.

The State Railways also undertook to lay eight short 2 ft. 6 in.

gauge lines on the east bank of the canal, all of which, including the Zagazig-Ismailia widening, had to be finished by the middle of January, 1916. For the light lines the State Railways provided 40 km., which had been pulled up, the balance coming from a stock of 2 ft. 6 in. gauge railway material which had been sent to Alexandria for use at Gallipoli, but not wanted there. Most of the labour for these works was provided by the State Railways, but valuable assistance was received from two R.E. construction companies, although the men from military sources numbered only about 500 out of a total of 18,000 employed by the railway on all works for the Army.

The railway administration then proceeded to lay 2 ft. 6 in. gauge lines towards the oasis of Baharia and from the Nile to Kharga oasis, the distances amounting to about 170 km., the material being provided by pulling up existing 2 ft. 6 in. gauge lines belonging to private companies, as the State Railways had no more. In addition, a line of standard gauge material was being constructed to follow up the troops from Kantara as far as Romani and Mohamedieh with materials supplied by the War Office, the earthwork being done by Egyptians and the track laid by R.E. companies. This will be dealt with later.

Co-ordination of Requirements.

By the end of 1916 the condition of affairs on the Egyptian State Railways had become serious. It had not been possible during the war to obtain rolling-stock or permanent way materials to replace ordinary wear and tear on the main lines, and this despite a greatly enhanced traffic, and the limit of resources for outside supply had practically been reached.

Sir Francis Dent's Mission.—In order, therefore, to avoid throwing additional work on the local staff and to enable local conditions to be given weight, the War Office decided to send a special officer in the person of Sir Francis Dent to collate all necessary information regarding ports, railways and inland water transport.

Sir Francis Dent reported in January, 1917, that the Kantara line was well constructed, of easy gradients, and was capable of supplying the three divisions and mounted troops then forming the force, and, in addition, at least three other divisions. The rolling-stock position was not acute, and, provided greater use was made of water rather than rail communications in Egypt itself, the State Railway rolling-stock might be considered sufficient for the time being. It would, however, be necessary later to supply additional stock, but this question could be considered when the full effect of the transferred military traffic from the State Railways to water had been appreciated.

Measures for Economising Rolling-Stock.—In order that the State Railways should be in a position to loan the necessary rolling-stock it was deemed essential that the Army should restrict its use of the Egyptian State Railways as much as possible until the loan of the extra rolling-stock had been repaid, and that it should study the economical use of rolling stock, not only on the military lines, but also on the State Railways.

It was therefore proposed that traffic which was passing by rail from Alexandria to Kantara and other points on the canal should be sent to Port Said for transhipment to lighters or go direct by sea to the point required, and that stores and material purchased in Egypt or the Sudan and sent by rail to Alexandria or other depôts should be conveyed by water where there was a water route available. It was also considered that traffic from Suez to Alexandria, instead of being sent by rail, should go through the canal, although it was realised this would involve the payment of canal dues on traffic for Salonica, which would probably be more costly than the extra transhipment plus the rail charges.

With regard to the more economical use of rolling-stock, it was considered that a great deal could be done by more careful loading of wagons, and the services of skilled British loaders or loading checkers was recommended for the purpose of educating the military or native loaders. The adoption of a train control system, also, was deemed expedient to ensure fullest use of trucks.

Brig.-General Stewart's Commission.—In June, 1917, a Commission headed by Brig.-General J. W. Stewart, C.M.G., reported on the railway situation as affecting the operations of the Egyptian Expeditionary Force.

With regard to supplies for the force, the Commission found that these were derived from three main sources (England, Egypt and India), and the arrangements made for the reception and handling of these supplies aimed at a co-ordination of rail and water transport. In pursuance of the policy of using all possible water transport, goods from England were sent to Port Said whenever practicable and lightered from there to Kantara (East) on the Suez Canal, 30 miles south of Port Said, and there transferred to the railway serving the army in Southern Palestine.

Goods originating in Egypt, and consisting chiefly of fodder and wood fuel for cooking, reached Kantara (West) *via* the Egyptian State Railways, whence they were conveyed by lighter to the east bank of the canal. A small proportion of these goods, however, was transported to the east side of the canal, without breaking bulk, in an improvised truck ferry. Stores from India, consisting chiefly of rails and sleepers, were discharged at Kantara (East) by mooring the ship alongside a wharf of lighters. For the passage of troops and heavy road traffic a barge pontoon bridge had been constructed across the canal.

Methods of Crossing Suez Canal.—In these circumstances there were three methods by which goods could be transferred from the west to the east bank of the canal :—

(a) By breaking bulk and lightering ;

(b) By conveying the truck across complete on the improvised truck ferry referred to ; and

(c) By the pontoon bridge.

The great proportion of goods crossed by the first method, the last being used primarily for troops and incidental road vehicular traffic. The goods lightered across broke truck bulk twice—at the west side of the canal from truck to lighter ; at the east side from lighter to truck.

The traffic crossing the canal at Kantara amounted to between 4,000 and 5,000 tons per week, and the Commission recommended that if the force were to be largely supplemented a more elaborate form of train ferry or a pontoon train bridge was worthy of consideration. The latter was considered feasible and probably preferable.

The Main Line East of Kantara.

Following on the decision to advance in Palestine, a line from Kantara on the east bank of the canal running along the coast towards Romani and El Arish in rear of the troops was an obvious necessity to maintain efficient communication with the base.

It was decided to construct this as a single line of standard gauge material, the question of doubling being deferred pending developments in the campaign. Consequently, in the spring of 1916, a commencement was made with a quantity of material supplied by the War Office. Egyptian labour was utilised on the formation, but R.E. construction companies were responsible for the laying of the track. By the summer the line had reached Romani (41 km. from Kantara) in the rear of the British position. On August 4 the Turks carried out an attack on the British forces near Romani, but had to retreat with heavy losses. The British then advanced, and, after meeting with some resistance from the enemy, entered

El Arish on December 21. Meanwhile the railway was being pushed forward, and on January 20, 1917, *i.e.*, one month after the town had been occupied, a new station was opened for traffic at El Arish (155 km. from Kantara).

The troops followed up their success at El Arish by a further advance, and on January 9 the strong enemy position at Rafa was taken by Anzac mounted troops and the Imperial Camel Corps. It therefore became necessary to progress with the railway to Rafa, and arrangements were made by the War Office to supply further material. By the middle of March, 1917, the railway had reached Rafa, a distance of 200 km. from Kantara, the base.

So rapidly did the British advance that on March 27 General Sir A. Murray reached the outskirts of Gaza and there defeated 20,000 Turks, taking 900 prisoners, including the General and Divisional Staff of the 53rd Turkish Division.

At the time of General Stewart's visit—June, 1917—the railway, which followed closely the Mediterranean coast line, and had no gradient exceeding 1 per cent., had been constructed for a distance

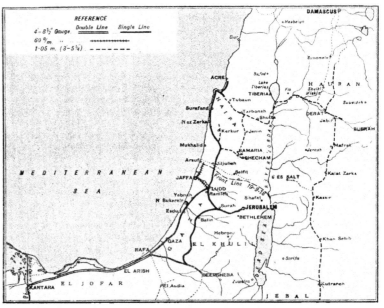

Fig. 29.—Map of Palestine, showing Railways Constructed and Converted during War.

of about 219 km. to El Belah, a point about 13 km. south-west of Gaza, where our advance at that time was halted. In order also to widen the front served by the railway and possibly to connect with the trace of the Turkish line at Beersheba, a branch line was being constructed from Rafa running due east for about 24 km. past Shellal and over the Wadi-el-Ghuzzee, where an embankment and bridge were being constructed.

The Question of Doubling, Kantara to Rafa.—On June 29, 1917, General Allenby took over the Palestine Command, and plans for a further advance were prepared. To meet the increasing needs of the force, consideration was given as to the necessity or otherwise of doubling the Kantara line. The requirements of the army were then being met by running 11 trains a day in each direction, the traffic along the railway being operated by a train control telephone system, whilst a signalling equipment was being erected to supplement it. Additional passing places also were being inserted which would permit of an average of 16 trains each way being run daily.

In considering the ultimate capacity of the line if left as a single track, it had to be borne in mind that the sleepers were laid directly on the sand without any other form of ballast. The track when laid was liable in parts to be covered by drifting sand in a storm.

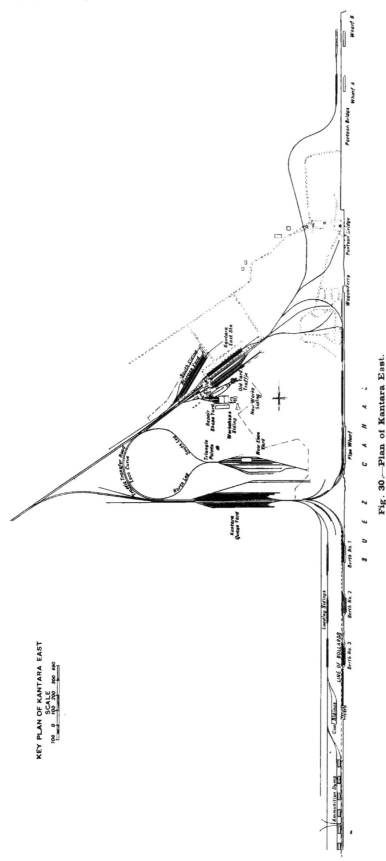

Fig. 30.—Plan of Kantara East.

KEY PLAN OF KANTARA EAST

SCALE

During a sand storm traffic was considerably delayed. Efforts had been made to push trains through, but this only led to a number of derailments, so that, in the event of a storm lasting five days, there were heavy arrears to be made up. Sand fences to guard against drifting were being erected as rapidly as possible, but the standard speed for normal operation had always to be kept below that possible on a well-ballasted stone formation. Some trouble was experienced by sand blowing into the axle-boxes and working parts of locomotives and rolling-stock. This was accentuated whenever the weather was windy.

It was estimated, however, that the 16 trains a day referred to could be operated over a single line between Kantara and Jaffa with the staff then existing and available from the Egyptian State Railways, and this number was ample for the reinforcements which were expected. It therefore appeared that if the objective of the army was Jaffa, and if the forces, for which arrangements had been made were not largely increased, it was unnecessary to double the track of the Kantara line or to send out additional rolling-stock from England.

On the other hand, if an advance beyond Jaffa were probable, the line would have to be doubled at least as far as Rafa, in which case two companies of platelayers would be required as an addition to the skilled railway troops then in Egypt. The Commission recommended in any event the collection at some suitable point on the Kantara line of 100 miles of track material, with a considerable supply of bridge timber, to provide for sudden developments or unforeseen eventualities.

The whole question was considered in conjunction with the possibilities of an adequate supply of water (which will be referred to later), and in July, 1917, the doubling of the railway between Kantara and Rafa was approved, and it was anticipated that when the doubling was completed (probably in six months) 28 trains could be run daily between Kantara and Rafa, 16 trains between Rafa and Gaza and 12 between Rafa and Beersheba.

It was suggested that, to provide material for the doubling, a line west of Alexandria, running for 175 km. along the coast to Darbaa, might be pulled up, although this step was not recommended unless absolutely necessary. The line was found to be capable of yielding 85 miles of track, but 30,000 additional sleepers and also fish-plates, fish-bolts and dog-spikes in proportion would be required. By the end of July a commencement had been made with the doubling of the line to Rafa. Some difficulty having been experienced on the severe gradient east of Rafa Station, a deviation of about 10 km. in length was made to do away with the necessity of reducing the weight of trains east of El Arish. A similar deviation was made between kilometre 191 and 194, making it unnecessary to reduce engine loads beyond El Arish.

Extensions beyond Gaza.—In the contemplation of a further advance it was thought that if sufficient water for the railway and for the use of the troops were available, divisions could be maintained as follows :—

	Infantry divisions.	Mounted divisions.
(a) With a single line between Rafa and Jaffa ..	7	3
(b) With a double line between Rafa and Jaffa ..	14	3
(c) With a single line between Rafa and Jaffa, plus a single line from Jaffa to Shellal, thence using Turkish Beersheba Railway	12	3

Although it was necessary to proceed speedily with the doubling to Rafa, it was also essential to push on with the extension of the main line beyond Gaza to Jaffa. For this reason 199 more miles of rails were required from India before the end of the year, in addition to what were still due from an order of 51 miles already placed : 27 more engines also would be required, and inquiries were made as to the possibility of supplying these from the Egyptian State Railways. If, in addition, all the heavy artillery asked for were supplied, 3 more engines and 50 more wagons would probably be

and 35 respectively, and the 1,200 wagons were already being met out of existing orders.

Jaffa and Wadi Surar Extensions.—By September, 1917, further developments were being planned in the Palestine Campaign, and the question of Egypt's rail requirements in connection with a contemplated advance were given further consideration. General Allenby intimated that in order to satisfy his tactical requirements, and to maintain the right and left flanks of his force as it advanced, he would require one single line from Rafa to Jaffa along the coast, and another single line from Rafa by Shellal and Ifteis, and thence following the Turkish track to Wadi Surar and on to Jerusalem, with a connecting single line from Jaffa via Ramleh to Wadi Surar. The first line would have to leave the coast in the neighbourhood of Yebna, reaching Jaffa via Ramleh, and it was hoped that no severer gradient than 1 in 100 would be encountered. This line would enable 7 infantry and 3 cavalry divisions to be maintained, and the second line to Wadi Surar 5 divisions. Arrangements were

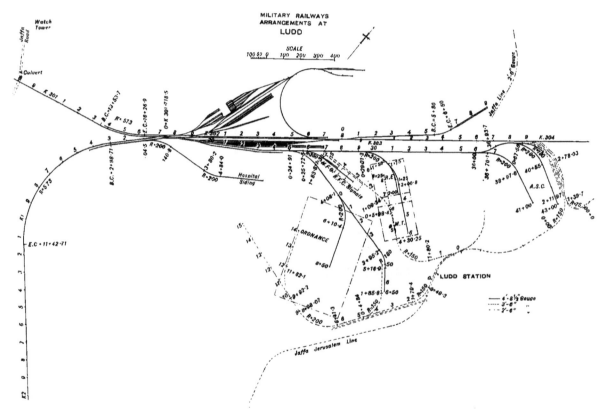

Fig. 31.—Lay-out of Ludd Station and Yard.

required. For the maintenance of any additional divisions, the line beyond Rafa would need to be doubled, and each additional division would necessitate 12 engines and 235 wagons, this being on the assumption that no water was carried by rail.

An extension of the Rafa to Shellal line towards Ifteis, 8 miles north-east, was then sanctioned, and schemes for a single line from El Belah to Jaffa and alternatively a double line from Rafa to Jaffa, were being prepared. The former, it was estimated, would require 112 miles and the latter 220 miles of track. In addition a large quantity of tools would be required, and 230 2,000-gallon tanks to be carried on 12-ton wagon frames, also the following additional engines and rolling-stock :—70 main line engines, 3 shunting engines, 1,200 wagons and 48 brake vans, these figures being based on the possibility of seven additional divisions, necessitating the running of a total of 28 trains per day. It was found possible, however, to reduce the estimate of 70 main line engines and 48 brake vans to 41

also being made to use motor transport to a modified extent if suitable roads became available, but it was realised that this form of transport could not be relied upon except as a means of distribution from the railways.

The construction of a line from Rafa towards Jaffa was not considered to present any considerable difficulties, but the question arose as to the line required from Shellal via Ifteis through Sheria and El Tineh up to Wadi Surar. An alternative for the latter line was suggested from Beit Hanum, a few miles north-east of Gaza along the old Turkish formation to El Tineh, as it was understood that the gradients were less severe than those between Tel-es-Sheria and El Tineh, and that the Beit Hanum to Tineh line could be more easily converted to standard gauge. It was, however, pointed out that the tactical position was such that, if the Gaza-Beersheba position were evacuated by the Turks, it did not follow that they would fall back on the Jaffa-Jerusalem position, but might accept battle at an intermediate point—for example, Wadi Heri ; and consequently an alternative railway line was needed to supply the right flank and the Ifteis-Sheria-El Tineh line was, therefore, necessary.

Attention was then drawn to the fact that there were 13 bridges between Sheria and El Tineh, two of which were over 100 ft. long, whereas the Beit Hanum-El Tineh line crossed all valleys by embankments instead of bridges, and there seemed distinct advantages in this route from a railway point of view. The right flank of the army might be fed by a light railway extended from the standard gauge line. After further consultation, however, it was decided that the separate Tel-es-Sheria-Wadi Surar line was necessary, and it was arranged that the standard gauge should be continued as far as Um Dalkal Station, the gauge of the railway beyond that point depending on the course of military operations and the number of troops to be maintained on the right flank.

The contemplated advance on the whole of the British front was successfully carried out and, on October 31, General Allenby took Beersheba, capturing 1,800 Turks and 9 guns. The fall of Gaza took place on the 7th of the following month, and on the 9th the Turks were in full retreat from Wadi Hesi and Ascalon on Hebron and Jerusalem, suffering a loss of 70 guns and 10,000 casualties. The rout of the Turks was so complete that by the 17th of the month Jaffa was entered by Australian and New Zealand troops, and December 9 witnessed the fall of Jerusalem. On the 11th General Allenby entered Jerusalem accompanied by the military *attachés* of France, Italy and the United States, and received a message of congratulation from the King. The result of this extensive advance was to necessitate still further railway construction and working, and steps were at once taken to push the work forward.

The Position on the Egyptian State Railways.—Owing to the increasing demands of the theatre of war, the position on the Egyptian State Railways became more and more difficult, and in October, 1917, it was reported that some branch lines would have to be closed to passenger traffic if the State Railways had to provide more passenger stock for army use. The position of wagon stock in Egypt was also precarious ; it was stated that out of 9,000 wagons belonging to the Egyptian State Railways 4,200 had been allocated for army purposes and 1,200 had been transferred to the Kantara Railway, leaving only 3,600 for civilian traffic, and it was represented that, if any increase were made to the existing force, supplies to feed additional men would have to be imported into the country and moved in Egypt by means of inland water transport.

The Beit Hanum-Wadi Surar Line Captured from the Turks.—The Turkish Beit Hanum-Wadi Surar line, which was captured in the advance, was found to be practically undamaged, and by the end of November, when the main line had been extended as far as Beit Hanum, the Turkish line was being used for carrying supplies. Arrangements were made for continuing the construction of the main line from Beit Hanum within easy distance of the coast as far as Yebna and thence to Ludd.

By the middle of December the Turkish line from Beit Hanum to Wadi Surar (1·05 m. gauge) was being regularly used. From Deir Sineid, the transhipping point on the standard gauge line, to Wadi Surar, the number of trains per day averaged 7 of a capacity of from 45 to 85 tons of useful load according to engine. One ammunition train was being run each day along the branch to Jerusalem as far as we could get to feed the advancing troops. An interesting fact was that the Turkish line had 11 sleepers to a rail length, of which four or five were steel and the remainder wood. In the wood sleepers there were no fastenings, and they relied on the steel to keep the gauge of the line, which seemed to answer the purpose quite well. The line also was roughly ballasted.

With the capture of Jerusalem on December 9, 1917, the branch from Wadi Surar to that point, a line of 1·05 m. gauge, fell into our hands. On this line all bridges were thoroughly destroyed by the enemy, but on January 6 they had been repaired, and the line would have been opened on that date had not heavy rains caused wash-outs.

It was estimated that when the broad-gauge track had reached

Wadi Surar, the rolling-stock which had been captured and a certain amount borrowed from Egypt and Sudan would suffice for 600 tons of supplies or stores daily from Wadi Surar to Jerusalem on the 1·05 m. gauge. This, apparently, would meet military needs. If, however, food had also to be transported for the civil population, it would probably be necessary to carry the standard gauge as far as Jerusalem. The line was made fit for traffic for a distance of 43 km. by December 14, and during the following week an average of 364 tons were carried per day, there being a short ruling gradient of 1 in 50, with curves of 140 m. radius. The total distance from Ludd to Jerusalem was 60 km. The fact that several of the engines were too heavy for the rails and that all the stock from Egypt and the Sudan (3 ft. 6 in. gauge) was ½ in. too wide for the Turkish gauge (1·05 m. or 3 ft. 5½ in.), necessitated very careful working ; the speed was kept down and everything possible done to make the line last until such time as it was possible to relay it with standard gauge.

Whilst the British were working the Turkish lines, the question of rolling stock for the 1·05 m. gauge was a difficult problem. The Sudan Government agreed to let us have the following 3 ft. 6 in. rolling-stock :—

3 engines with tenders, weight about 45 tons each.
10 covered wagons (15 tons).
15 open wagons (15 tons).
25 bogie wagons (25 tons).

In addition there were 5 engines in a very bad condition and 60 trucks which had been captured from the Turks. There were also 3 heavy engines from the Hedjaz railways and 2 Hedjaz tank engines sent from England. Six locomotives from the Luxor-Assouan section of the Egyptian State Railways had also been sent over with 28 open wagons.

The Jerusalem branch was gradually converted to standard gauge, and by April 5, 1918, the standard gauge had reached Artuf (53 km. from Jerusalem). To avoid interference with traffic during the conversion, the method followed was to provide a third rail to the 1·05 m. gauge. The extension of the standard gauge from Artuf to Jerusalem then became necessary, as the 35-lb. rails on the Turkish lines would not stand the heavy engines and axle loads, nor was it possible to deliver sufficient tonnage daily into Jerusalem. The necessary work was, therefore, put in hand.

Further Railway Developments.—The year 1918 marked a considerable extension of the main line from Kantara coincident with the rapid advance of General Allenby's troops. In February the Turks retreated north of Jericho beyond the Jordan. In the following month the Jordan was crossed by General Allenby, an advance being made towards the Hedjaz Railway. Es Salt, situated midway between the Jordan and the Hedjaz Railway, was occupied by Australian troops on May 1, but in order to consolidate the front line, troops withdrew from Es Salt behind the Jordan on the 3rd of the month, capturing 900 Turks. At this time the front occupied by the British stretched from a point on the coast about 10 miles north of Jaffa across to the River Jordan, and thence down to the Dead Sea.

By March 30 the construction of the main line had reached kilometre 315, i.e., about 8 km. north of Ludd. By the end of June the branch line from Rafa to Beersheba had been completed and the branch line from Ludd to Jerusalem had been converted from the Turkish 1·05 m. gauge to 4 ft. 8½ in. gauge. The Turkish line running northward from the Beersheba branch at Irgeig up to Wadi Surar on the Jerusalem line was being converted to standard gauge, the intention being that when this line was complete it would serve as an alternative route to the single track main line from Rafa to Ludd. By July 15, 1918, the conversion to standard gauge of the Turkish line from Irgeig to Wadi Surar Junction on the Jerusalem branch had been completed, but owing to the rapid advance of the troops, it was decided to pull up the line, as the track was urgently required for other theatres of war. This line was therefore closed to traffic on October 18, 1918.

Coincident with a further general advance during the summer campaign, there was great constructional activity on the main line of the Kantara Railway, which by the end of September had reached kilometre 323. The progress of the troops was very rapid and by

September 20 Nazareth was occupied, and on the 22nd the 7th and 8th Turkish armies were rendered *hors de combat*. The army on the left flank forged ahead, and on the 23rd Haifa and Acre had been captured, thus rendering necessary an extension of the Kantara main line up to these points. The armies on the right flank had also been active, and on the same date Colonial and Jewish troops in pursuit of the 4th Turkish army reached Es Salt, and Maan was occupied by King Hussein's Arabs. On the 25th, Tiberius, on the Sea of Galilee, and Annam on the Hedjaz Railway, were both occupied by General Allenby, who, up to that date, had captured 45,000 prisoners and 265 guns.

Consequent on the advance, there was an appreciable increase in the personnel and goods carried, the former amounting to 44,000 per week for the September quarter, as compared with 36,270 per week during the quarter ended June 30, and the latter 30,800 tons per week as compared with 28,800. Additional locomotives had also been supplied, as many as 164 then being on charge with 2,035 wagons. There were also 127 narrow gauge locomotives and tractors and 845 wagons and coaches.

The advance was continued in October, and on the 1st of that month Damascus was entered by the British, 7,000 prisoners being captured. From Damascus the troops pushed forward rapidly, and on the 7th of the month General Allenby reported that he, with the King of the Hedjaz, had, since September 18, taken 79,000 prisoners. Sidon was occupied by the British and Beirut by the French. On the 26th of the month Aleppo was taken, thus completing the conquest of Syria, and cutting the Turkish communications over the Baghdad Railway.

Meanwhile, the main railway in the rear of the troops was being very rapidly laid, and the quarter ending December, 1918, witnessed an extension of nearly 100 km. In September the line reached only as far as kilometre 323, but by the end of the quarter it had been extended to Haifa at kilometre 412, where a station was opened, and 12 new stations had been opened *en route*.

Following on the conquest of Syria, the Turkish army on the Tigris was defeated on October 30 by the Mesopotamian Expeditionary Force, advancing north-west towards Mosul. The enemy sued for an armistice, which was granted from 12 noon on the following day.

Constructional Details.

From Kantara as far as Rafa the country traversed by the railway was a waterless desert, the line winding its way through shifting sand hills which were a frequent source of trouble, constantly silting up the track when the wind blew strongly. A quantity of special grass seed had been ordered from Australia, as it was considered the sowing of it might reduce the trouble. Northward from Rafa and along the Beersheba branch, the railway entered a fertile plain where there was only occasional interference from sand. Beyond Gaza, when marshy ground was met with, frequent trouble was experienced from the cotton soil. As Ludd was approached the railway entered hilly country and heavy earthwork was involved.

Difficulties owing to Sand and Soil.—The chief difficulty met with at the beginning of the railway was the shifting nature of the sand, necessitating constant clearing in order to avoid the line being blocked altogether. In the early days derailments were very common on this account, but as quickly as possible the banks were covered with brushwood and thorn, so arranged as to offer resistance to the wind from whatever quarter it might come, and this proved most effective. This sand nuisance necessitated the provision of wider cuttings and banks than would otherwise have been necessary, but once the line became well established on the sand formation, it assumed a permanent condition, the hard packed sand making an excellent substitute for ballast; indeed, the military railway was not ballasted at all, except where the old Turkish or French formation was adopted and the ballast already in existence used.

Once the desert was left, and the soft cotton soil of the more northern plain was reached, further trouble was experienced, the soil being so spongy as to make it almost impossible during wet weather to build banks at all. In many places it was necessary, in order to provide a bed for the track, to transport sand and lay it on the top of the cotton soil, but this did not eliminate the

effects of rain on the soil; in fact, only a most extensive system of drainage could be hoped to produce the proper results, but as this would have the effect of rendering sterile large areas of land which were fertile, it was a step which required careful consideration. The nuisance was considerably reduced, however, by putting in many culverts and drains under the track. Over the more northerly portion of the line, the soil met with was similar to the fine clay of Mesopotamia and rendered earthwork on banks a difficult undertaking during rainy weather, a fact which greatly hindered construction. The effect of rain on the track was generally felt between November and March, and that of wind between December and May. During the other months of the year, no unusual difficulties were encountered except the great heat, which generally caused the stoppage of all heavy work between 11 a.m. and 3 p.m. This was counteracted during moonlight periods by starting labour on railway work at 2 or 3 in the morning, but as the railway was pushed further northwards the extent of the interference of the heat on construction work diminished considerably. Another nuisance in the fertile districts was the heavy growth of grass and corn on the tracks which necessitated large maintenance parties to keep them clear.

The construction of the line was carried out with such speed that it was not possible to spend all the time necessary for the preliminary survey and in many cases the proximity of the enemy made it impossible to keep the survey sufficiently far ahead of railhead. In the early stages also the time available did not admit of sufficient earthwork being undertaken, with the result that there were several long gradients (1 in 100 being the ruling gradient) and long stretches of sharp curves; the effect of these singly or in combination, more particularly when a heavy wind was blowing, reduced not only the weight, but also the length of trains which could be run and was a limiting factor in the capacity of the line. By the spring of 1918 the doubling of the Kantara line had reached kilometre 170, and was being pushed on as rapidly as material could be transported and labour made available, the labour in question being largely civilian. At the same time the doubling of the line was carried out on a better alignment than the original single line and in many cases awkward curves and gradients were eliminated. As the new line was used as a down line (*i.e.*, for loaded trains), the improved location had a very beneficial effect on train running.

Permanent Way.—The permanent way employed was almost entirely 75-lb. British standard flat-footed rail, spiked with bearing plates on to wooden sleepers—2,060 being used to the mile. All sleepers were adzed and bored before being put into the track: this was done by contract labour at Kantara. Rails were laid with staggered joints, and where clay soil was met with north of Ludd, an outward slope was given to the boxing in order to run water off the track—very similar to that adopted in Mesopotamia. In certain sections 37 km. rails were used owing to shortage of 75-lb. material.

The Jaffa-Jerusalem Line.—This line presents some interesting features. It was built in 1892 and took six years to complete from Jaffa to Jerusalem. On the section Jaffa-Ludd (which was dismantled by the Turks) there were no serious obstacles, curves or gradients, and generally speaking the line, which was ballasted throughout, ran on a bank to keep it above the level of the floods which rendered the ground treacherous.

From Ludd to Jerusalem, the first part of the line had a succession of gradients and curves and considerable earthwork, as the formation climbs towards the limestone areas of the centre of Palestine. On this section, pending its conversion from 1·05 m. to 4 ft. 8½ in. gauge, rolling-stock of 3 ft. 6 in. gauge was successfully run. The light material displaced by the standard gauge was taken up for use elsewhere. It consisted of 36-lb. rails laid with two steel sleepers per rail length, and the rest wooden, and throughout a large portion of its length there were no fastenings to the wooden sleepers. The rail was of a bad section and owing to its excessive height frequently turned over during the passage of a heavy Decapod locomotive, causing many derailments.

As the line proceeds towards Jerusalem from Artuf, curves become sharper and gradients steeper. Long sections of rock cuttings and stone-pitched embankments are involved as the line threads its way up rocky ravines and through narrow gorges—the beds of torrents in wet weather. The initial cost of construction must have been considerable, and there can be little doubt that the line was laid for political and strategic reasons. It may be mentioned that the narrow rock cuttings caused difficulties in altering the gauge to 4 ft. 8½ in.

Water Supply.—When consideration was being given to the question of doubling the Kantara main line as far as Rafa, the means of obtaining water for locomotives, without which it would be

drew all their supply from the pipe line, but beyond this the capacity of the pipe line was reduced and a certain amount of water was carried forward on railway tank trucks. The water used was excellent for boiler purposes, so that no limitation of the locomotive mileage arose through the use of bad water.

The water supply was investigated by Brig.-General Stewart's mission. The pipe line system was found to consist essentially of a filtration plant at Kantara, drawing its supply from the sweet water canal which runs parallel with and immediately to the west of the Suez Canal; of syphon pipes under the Suez Canal; of steel

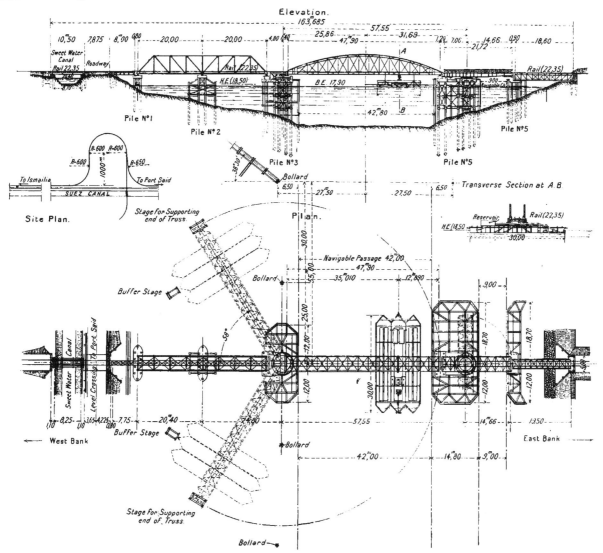

Fig. 32.—Elevation and Plan of Swing Bridge over the Suez Canal at Kantara.

useless to double the track, came up for examination. Experiments were being made at the time to see whether any large quantity of suitable water could be found by means of deep wells at El Arish, water produced from the shallow wells there being too brackish for efficient use in locomotive boilers, but sufficiently good for watering camels, for which purpose it was largely used.

The route traversed was an old caravan trade route, but although water was found at stages along the route, it was brackish and up to then had not been used by the railway for locomotive requirements. Locomotives were watered from the new pipe line which was laid generally along the same route as the railway to supply the needs of the army. Between Kantara and El Arish locomotives

water pipes with screwed socket joints laid along the railway; and of pumping stations at intervals of 25 miles with two covered ferro-concrete tanks each capable of holding 250,000 gallons alongside each pumping station.

The whole system between Kantara and El Arish, which formed the limit originally contemplated for the line, was designed to deliver 600,000 gallons of water per 24 hours. This it accomplished in spite of the fact that owing to the impossibility of getting sufficiently prompt delivery, the original idea of making the pipe line 12 in. internal diameter throughout had to be abandoned and a mixed system of 12 in., 10 in. and 8 in. diameter used as far as El Arish (97 miles) with two smaller diameter pipes beyond to Rafa, a further 31 miles.

To cope with extensive development of the railway traffic the Mission recommended the increase of the capacity of the piping system by (1) Providing intermediate pumping stations and so increasing the velocity of the water in each stage ; and (2) Ordering sufficient 12-in. piping to extend the line at the full diameter to Rafa and to permit of the replacement of all the 8-in. section between Kantara and El Arish. It was also considered important to have in stock sufficient piping of 6 in. or 8 in. diameter to lay down branches at right angles to the railway and so extend the front over which it was possible for the forces to operate.

By March, 1918, the consumption from the pipe line was approximately 400,000 gallons daily, of which only 25,000 gallons were used by the troops. By that time extensive new installations of engines and pumps were being put in at a cost of £376,000, enabling nearly double the quantity of water to be supplied. It was understood that one of the reasons for this excess capacity was the fact that should the army at any time be forced to retire across the desert its position would be serious without this additional water supply. There was storage accommodation of half-a-million gallons each at Kantara, Romani, El Abd and Mazar ; and of three-quarters of a million gallons at El Arish and 1½ million gallons at Rafa, or sufficient for three days' supply at full load. There was also a separate water supply system for Kantara yard, where 200,000 gallons a day were consumed largely in washing out engine boilers. The furthest point from Kantara at which water was drawn for locomotives was at kilometre 194 on the main line and Karm on the Beersheba branch. Beyond kilometre 194 water was obtained from wells.

Bridging.

In the early stages of railway construction, i.e., as far as El Arish, no bridges were necessary, but from there northwards a number of Wadys were encountered of varying dimensions and depth, which became more and more frequent as the line proceeded northwards, perpetual streams also being met with. It was fortunately possible to begin the building of most of the bridges in dry weather, with the advantage that foundations of concrete or masonry were put in in the dry. Pile bridges were the exception, the general types being trestle bridges on masonry footings with timber or steel road bearers, or, in the case of the shorter gaps, sleeper cribs filled in with concrete to form the abutments spanned over by timber or girders.

Owing to the very soft nature of the soil in which these Wadys occur, extensive precautions were necessary to prevent scouring round the foundations and also behind the abutments. To avoid this as far as possible, a concrete floor strengthened with rails was laid across the Wady tieing together the foundations, and aprons or wing walls were carried back a long way on either side of the main abutments. The waterway in the Wadys was artificially restricted by making banks for a large portion of the section, and only bridging the centre gap ; this, of course, accentuated the effect of scour.

Even with these precautions, scour action round the abutments was not uncommon. At one bridge during the night of March 25-26, 1918, a hole 18 ft. deep was scoured out, stopping traffic altogether. Rises in the streams are very sudden ; in fact, it is not uncommon for a Wady which is practically dry to rise 5 ft. in half an hour. In a country of this nature wash-outs on the line were bound to be frequent, although numerous culverts and drains were put in. In order to avoid scour action on the latter a special type of concrete mouth was introduced with each culvert.

The El Arish Bridge.—In two cases at El Arish and Gaza the bridging department of the Egyptian State Railways built permanent bridges. In the former case the bridge was at first only a single line bridge, but subsequently doubled as rapidly as possible, as following the Kantara-Rafa widening it became a very serious restriction on traffic. As regards the Wady Ghuzzee bridge at Gaza, the Wady is very ill-defined and quite shallow, the bridge consisting of eight spans of steel lattice girders each 15 metres in the clear, composing one continuous span on roller bearings carried on cast-iron caissons filled with concrete.

The Suez Canal Bridge.—One other bridge of special interest is that constructed across the Suez Canal by the Egyptian State Railways in order to accommodate the additional traffic from the Egyptian side of the Canal after May 1, 1918, consisting of a large

quantity of supplies grown in Upper Egypt and the Sudan for the troops in Palestine. The bridge consists of two fixed shore spans, one short swing span on a central pivot next the shore span on the eastern side, and one large swing span in the centre with a 42 m. opening. The latter span rests on solid footings during the passage of trains, and is jacked up (the weight being taken by a pontoon) and towed clear for the passage of ships, as shown in the drawings at Fig. 32.

To ensure minimum hindrance to the traffic on the canal the bridge was made capable of being opened in 10 minutes or so. The Suez Canal Company, however, insisted that no fixed times could be made for opening or closing the bridge, but that it should be opened whenever required for the passage of ships. This limitation necessitated the introduction of groups of sidings on either side of the canal in which trains could be stabled and thence taken over quickly whenever the bridge was available. In order to avoid a right-angled crossing extensive remodelling of the Cairo-Port Said Line in the neighbourhood of the bridge was also necessary.

Locomotives and Rolling-Stock.

In March, 1918, representations were made by an officer who had been deputed by the D.G.M.R. to report on the military railways in Palestine, as to the grave shortage of locomotives, this being rendered all the more serious owing to the extremely heavy number under repair, and arrangements were made to supply 30 locomotives still due from the United Kingdom to complete the demand made for working the railway to Ludd. This officer made a most comprehensive report from which information has been drawn for much of the matter in this narrative relating to the working of the railways.

Many of the engines in use on the railways were hardly suitable for the work they had to do ; they were not in the best of condition and as the traffic grew, heavier types, such as the Baldwin (4-6-0) as supplied to France, became necessary. The following is a list showing the various engines in traffic in March, 1918 :—

Description.		Steam.					Petrol.
		0-6-0	2-6-0	4-4-0	2-4-0	Total.	0-4-0
Stevenson (E.S.R.)	..	25	—	—	—	25	—
L.S.W. (W.O.)	..	26	—	—	—	26	—
L.N.W. (W.O.)	..	15	—	—	—	15	—
Franco Belge (E.S.R.)	..	8	—	—	—	8	—
Tank (E.S.R.)	..	3	—	—	—	3	—
Tank (W.O.)	..	2	—	—	—	2	—
Baldwin (E.S.R.)	..	—	20	—	—	20	—
Baldwin (E.S.R.)	..	—	—	10	—	10	—
Franco-Belge (E.S.R.)	..	—	—	—	4	4	—
Manning-Wardle							3
Totals	..	79	20	10	4	113	3

Their capacity on a level road ranged from 360 to 500 tons.

The goods work on the Kantara line was comparatively fast, the bulk of the traffic being in through loads. With the extension of the line came longer hauls and a growing necessity for sound and more powerful engines. As to the most suitable type of engine for the work, the Locomotive Superintendent considered that it should be a powerful mixed traffic engine, with a leading bogie to take the curves easily and a trailing axle to enable the three coupled axles all to be got close together in front of the firebox, with the object of reducing the coupled wheelbase to a minimum and saving flange wear and grinding round the sharp curves. It would also enable a wide short firebox to be used instead of a long narrow one, the former being much easier to fire for inexperienced firemen than the latter. A trailing pony axle would also be an advantage when running tender first.

The following outline specification was suggested :—

Wheel arrangement, 4-6-2.
Boiler to be as large as possible without producing too excessive an axle load ; say, about 50 tons on the six wheels.
Superheater and mechanical lubricator : (The saving effect of the superheater on both water and coal consumption is a very vital factor where the capacity of the line, as in this case, is taxed to the utmost).
Steam brake on engine and tender : The lack of good brakes on existing engines reduces the speed at which the trains can run, and hence the line capacity.
Vacuum ejector fitted for use on train only.
Diameter of coupled wheels about 5 ft. 3 in. to 5 ft. 6 in.
Springs to be interconnected with compensating beam.
Bogie tender with about 6,000 to 8,000 gallons water capacity and 8-ton coal capacity.

The average life of a goods engine between general repairs was approximately 14,000 miles, except in the case of some of the Stephenson engines, whose tyres had to be turned every 6,000 miles. Some of the London & South Western engines ran up to 20,000 miles before going into shops.

In March, 1918, the locomotive mileage averaged 57,000 miles per week, the number of engines in service being 81. The average mileage per engine in service was 700 per week, but this figure excluded all shunting, pilot, ballast and passenger engines, with the result that the average goods engine ran at least 1,000 miles and sometimes as many as 1,400 miles a week. The total average coal consumption (including engines standing in steam, raising and dropping fires) worked out at about 57 lb. per mile. The total consumption on military railways in March, 1918, was 8,000 tons per month, and rose to about 13,000 tons per month by the time Haifa was reached.

Rolling-Stock.—On the whole the rolling-stock was good and the W.D. wagons supplied from home were particularly well built, the only disadvantage being that the timber under-frame was liable to suffer in the Palestine climate, and in the case of fire (which was not uncommon) the whole wagon was destroyed. A steel under-frame such as on the G.W. wagons was therefore considered the most suitable.

The life of a wagon tyre in Palestine averaged from eight to nine months between turnings. The utmost capacity was got out of all the wagons supplied; in fact, wagons delivered with a marked 10-ton capacity were marked as 12 tons, and those marked 12 as 15 tons wherever the size of the journal, in comparison with other wagons, made this possible. The result was that an average wagon load in an equivalent 10-ton truck for all classes of goods carried was just 7 tons, which, seeing that a large quantity of the material carried was hay and tibben (which only gives a 5-ton load), was a particularly good average.

The method of calculating rolling-stock requirements was identical with that on which locomotives were demanded, i.e., on a proportionate train-mile basis; and, roughly speaking, it was found that an extra truck was required for every 2 additional train-kilometres per day. The average turn-round of trucks was about 72 hours, and with a total daily requirement of about 800 trucks, an equipment of 2,400 left no margin for extension.

Workshops and Running Sheds.

The main railway workshops for the 4 ft. 8½ in. gauge lines were situated at Kantara. In March, 1918, the only class of work which the shops could not then undertake was re-tyreing, re-axleing, heavy boiler repairs, repairs and tempering of springs, and repairs to pressure gauges. The shops were very well equipped and were extremely well managed and run. Two 8-hour shifts a day were then worked, and if sufficient skilled labour were available work could be carried on throughout the 24 hours. The shop machines were driven by electrical power.

The wagon repair yard was situated round a turntable, and the repair roads measured approximately 435 m. The carriage shed itself had two roads and a dead-end giving a further 260 m. of space.

There were three pits—one outside and two inside the carriage shed (which was originally the locomotive shed). In this shed all carriage and brake van repairs were carried out. Some 600 wagons were repaired each month in the wagon shops, and about 3 per cent. of the total wagons on the line could be taken as out of service at any one time. In February, 1917, 538 brasses were re-metalled and 44 pairs of wagon wheels turned up. About 40 pairs of wheels were sent per month to Cairo for turning up and re-tyreing owing to the shortage at Kantara of wheel lathes at that time.

Running sheds for No. 1 district (i.e., Kantara to El Arish exclusive) were situated at Kantara. Here there was a run-through shed with four roads, each with a 60-m. pit, and all running repairs were executed, the necessary machine work being carried out in the main workshops. The number of engines allotted to this district, including those under heavy repairs and those standing with broken axles, was 54. This figure included two little pug engines which were only suitable for coal shunting. The engines consisted chiefly of the very old Stephenson and Baldwin locomotives,

thus releasing the better London & North Western and London & South Western locomotives for the district further up country and more distant from the main shops. The number of these locomotives usually available for main line service was only 20. In addition, there were 4 yard shunting engines, 1 rail train engine, 1 ballast train engine, and 2 emergency pilot engines working through the 24 hours. With the number of trains per day then working out of Kantara, it was stated that there should be at least 28 engines in that district on the main line service, otherwise sufficient attention could not be given to repairs and avoidable failures would be likely to occur. The engine run was from Kantara to El Arish—155 km.—with water stops for goods trains at Romani, El Abd and Mazar; and at El Abd only for passenger and hospital trains. Engine crews worked through to El Arish and were relieved there.

No. 2 District was from El Arish to Ludd exclusive. All minor repairs to engines in this district were carried out in the locomotive shed and shops at El Arish. Any engines requiring heavy repairs or wheel turning were sent to Kantara. The number of engines allotted to this district was 50. These consisted, with the exception of shunting engines, entirely of London & North Western, London & South Western, and Franco-Belgian engines. The number of locomotives then available for main line work was generally about 32, in addition to which shunting and pilot engines were required at El Arish, Rafa, Gaza and Deir Sineid. It was estimated that in order to place this district on a satisfactory basis, a further eight engines would be required. The engine run was from El Arish to Ludd (147 km.).

At Jerusalem there was a small running shed with two roads and pits, capable of accommodating four small tank or two tender engines, and also a machine shop which was equipped with tools purchased in Alexandria, as the Turks badly damaged or dismantled the tools originally in the shop. Many parts of dismantled machines were found buried near by, by the simple expedient of re-employing the labour which had been used by the Turks. This shop was used to carry out all repairs for the Jerusalem line other than exceptionally heavy ones, which were done at Kantara.

Traffic and Capacity.

Conditions affecting traffic capacity have already been outlined in preceding paragraphs. There are certain other points in connection with traffic working which do not readily fall under any of the headings given. These are set out below.

In March, 1918, traffic was worked on a central control system, there being two controls at that time, one at El Arish, which worked the traffic between Kantara and Gaza, and the second at Ludd, which worked the traffic from Gaza to Ludd, and was found capable of controlling the traffic northwards when the line was extended. A direct wire from the control office was carried to every third station, so that by only one repetition the controllers could despatch messages to every station on the line. Two pairs of control wires on either side of the control office proved sufficient for the purpose. The controllers in the various offices, instead of keeping the ordinary tabular records of train and engine movements, kept them instead in a graphic form somewhat similar to the graphic time-tables used on any civil railway. If necessary they made notes on these sheets explaining any special delays, &c., but the whole of the information likely to be required by the Traffic Manager was contained in these graphic charts, and their introduction proved an unqualified success. There were 32 theoretical "marches" per day, but practically speaking 22 trains a day proved to be the limit on the single line, although as many as 27 each way had been reached.

The Director of Railways definitely undertook to work 22 trains each way per day on the single line and no more. On the Karm and Sukeria branches, owing to the steeper gradients (1 in 75) and longer sections, only 14 or 15 trains a day could be worked as a maximum, but nothing like this number was actually necessary. To facilitate the feeding of the growing force in Palestine, considerable use was made of locally grown corn, and much assistance was provided by water transport, so as to reduce railway transport to a minimum.

Trucks were loaded and unloaded departmentally, and all demands for truck allocations for the following day had to reach the A.D.R.T.

at Kantara not later than 6 p.m. the night before. Traffic and marshalling yards existed at Kantara, El Arish, Rafa and Ludd, besides minor yards at Junction Station (Wadi Surar) and Jerusalem on the 3 ft. 6 in. line.

Signalling.

A system of outer and inner homes, starters, and in some cases, advance starters, was installed on the whole line to eliminate flag signalling, which was originally employed, but which necessitated all trains slowing up so much that their average speed was very much reduced. Nowhere were the signals interlocked with points except at Kantara Junction and at either end of the single line running over the bridge at El Arish.

On the double line traffic was operated with single needle block instruments, while on the single line electrical staff was either in operation or being installed. On the double line, where block

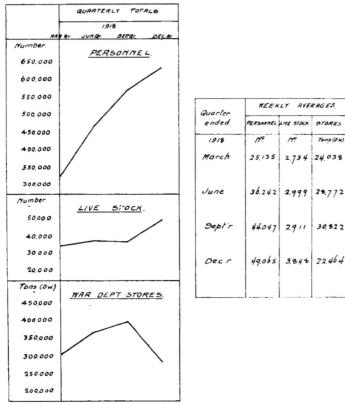

Fig. 33.—Traffic Carried during 1918 on Military Railways in Palestine.

Quarter ended	WEEKLY AVERAGES		
	PERSONNEL	LIVE STOCK	STORES
1918	N°.	N°.	Tons (cwt)
March	25,135	2,734	24,038
June	36,242	2,999	24,772
Sept'r	44,047	2,911	30,822
Dec'r	49,065	3,848	22,464

instruments had not yet been installed, traffic was operated on the telephone line-clear system, while plugs were inserted in dummy instruments to indicate the correct needle positions. Further, a central control had been instituted, whilst ample lines and telephones, all in capital order, existed both for this and for the railway signals and telegraph service. All stations were well fitted, each single line loop having the two ends connected by telephone, and the double-line stations being equipped proportionately. Along the whole railway there was a box-to-box block line, either for staff or block instruments, and two pairs of 100 lb. telephone line for the control circuits.

Organisation and Personnel.

The chart indicates the organisation of the Railway Directorate. The Director was responsible to the D.Q.M.G., and although spending the bulk of his time in Cairo, kept personally or through his D.D.R.T. in the closest possible touch with the D.Q.M.G. at G.H.Q. :—

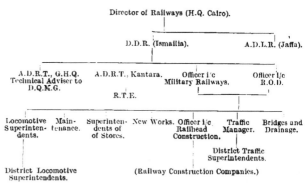

Personnel.—The personnel on the Palestine railways included about 15 operating sections (each of 267 men), four construction companies (each of 250 men) and a large amount of native labour. It was found, as the result of experience, that, broadly speaking, on a basis of 16 trains a day, one operating section (as far as numbers go) was required for every 22 to 25 miles. It was not possible to employ the men in sections as on most other military railways, as there existed only a comparatively long main line of railway, with central workshops, running sheds, traffic control arrangements, &c. Actual construction, and first and second lifts of the line were carried out by construction companies, but the maintenance was performed by the R.O.D. The maintenance gangs were not responsible for clearing the track of sand, special sand gangs being employed for this purpose and allocated from place to place as required.

Conclusion.

By far the greatest achievement in connection with railway transport in the Palestine Campaign was the construction of a standard gauge line from the Suez Canal for 412 km. to Haifa. As has been indicated, the line was rapidly constructed in stages over all manner of difficult country, from the desert in the early stages to hilly regions in the latter part of the campaign, while a sea wall had to be built for a considerable distance south of Haifa. The water difficulty was successfully overcome, and, despite the oppressive climate, a regular service of trains was maintained up to the front some 300 to 400 km. from the base.

As lateral communications, the two branches running eastwards, one to Beersheba and the other to Jerusalem, were exceptionally useful. In the latter case many constructional difficulties had to be contended with, as from Artuf to Jerusalem the line runs through a hilly region, and the sharp curves and exceptionally steep gradients rendered traffic working a matter of considerable difficulty.

The essential characteristic of this campaign was the fact that the railway had almost entirely to be relied on for the feeding of the troops. In the initial stages there were no existing lines which could be used, and the line of communication had to be steadily built up under the supervision of the Railway Directorate. Even when Turkish lines were captured they were, owing to the narrow gauge, of little use as a means of supply on a large scale, and reconstruction and conversion to standard gauge had to be performed.

The quantity of traffic carried over the Palestine railways during the year 1918 is shown in Fig. 33. From this it will be seen that personnel carried increased during the year from 325,000 to nearly 650,000, whilst during the September quarter 400,000 tons of stores were conveyed. A large amount of traffic was also carried by Inland Water Transport, which served to a considerable extent to relieve the pressure on the railways, which at all times suffered from a shortage of rolling-stock.

THE RAILWAYS OF MESOPOTAMIA.

Transportation Control—The First Railways—Railways in the Baghdad Area—Extension to Persian Frontier—Locomotives, Rolling-Stock and Traffic—Control and Working—The Baghdad to Basra through Route—General Survey.

Operations against the Turks in Mesopotamia began in November, 1914, when a force from India captured the Fao fort at the mouth of the Shatt-el-Arab and subsequently occupied Basra, 67 miles above the head of the Persian Gulf. The Turkish forces retired inland, and during the following month British and Indian troops, assisted by the Euphrates Blockade Flotilla, captured Kurna at the junction of the Tigris and Euphrates, and thus obtained a firm footing in the country.

In its initial stages. the Mesopotamian campaign was undertaken primarily for defensive purposes, and especially for the maintenance of British interests and prestige on the Persian Gulf and in South-Western Persia. For some few months, therefore, no extensive developments matured, but it eventually became of importance to consolidate the area in our possession, and in June, 1915, Amara on the Tigris was taken, whilst Nasiriyeh on the Euphrates was occupied during the following month. The British forces were then concentrated within a triangle of which Amara was the apex and Ahwaz (in South-Western Persia) and Nasiriyeh the base corners, but very shortly an advance was made along the Tigris. The troops made such speedy progress that, in November, 1915, issue was joined with the enemy at Ctesiphon, a point only 18 miles from Baghdad, and whilst the actual battle went in our favour the subsequent arrival of heavy Turkish reinforcements compelled a retirement. General Townshend held on to Kut, and the remainder of the forces retired beyond that town to await reinforcements then *en route.*

The control of military operations in Mesopotamia was taken over by the Army Council from the Indian Government in February, 1916, and at that time Kut was closely invested, whilst the Turks were in strong force in the neighbourhood of Ess Sinn, some 23 miles nearer Basra. It is now a matter of history that the relief force, headed by General Gorringe (who succeeded General Aylmer in command) made a gallant but unavailing effort to relieve the hard-pressed garrison, and that, after a dashing, but unsuccessful, attempt by rivercraft to carry much-needed supplies to the besieged garrison, General Townshend, with 2,970 British and 6,000 Indian troops, was compelled to surrender at the end of March, 1916, owing to the total exhaustion of supplies.

Transfer of Transportation Control.

There was a lull in hostilities following the fall of Kut-el-Amara, and, during the re-organisation of the British Forces that ensued, it was found desirable to transfer the administrative responsibility from the Indian Government to the Army Council. In September, 1916, therefore, the direction of transportation and the maintenance of all communications became vested in the War Office, and Colonel Lubbock, R.E., was transferred from Egypt, and appointed Director of Railways in Mesopotamia.

During this period, communications were comparatively short, and were mainly confined to river transport, the total weekly tonnage conveyed on the Tigris being no more than 6,000 tons. No railways were then open, but the construction of lines from Basra to Nasiriyeh on the Euphrates and Kurna to Amara along the Tigris was proceeding, these having been authorised in May to meet the necessity for additional transportation facilities to supply the requirements of the augmented Force.

Preparations for a sustained offensive were at this time in full swing and, as it became of increasing importance to develop the means of communication to the greatest possible extent, the question of expediting the completion of the railways was energetically taken in hand. At the outset, the general idea was that the rivers should form the main communication link and that the railways, then under construction, should supplement river transport. The development of river traffic by the supply of additional craft was, obviously, of primary importance, as this was a relatively speedy matter, and the construction of a railway, even of the most temporary character, was a matter of time.

Whilst, therefore, it may definitely be stated that the River Tigris remained the principal line of communication throughout the campaign, it might be well to remark that the rivers, unassisted by the railways, could not have met the transportation demands. Indeed, after the capture of Baghdad and the subsequent advance on a wide front, river transport was solely confined to through and sectional working between Basra and Baghdad. Troops were stationed at points far distant from the rivers, and it was solely the rapid development of railways that enabled them to pursue the campaign to a victorious conclusion. A map is given in Fig. 34, showing railways in Mesopotamia at the end of 1918.

Transportation Difficulties.

It is probable that the difficulties in the way of developing communications in Mesopotamia were more pronounced than in any other theatre of war, for the severe extremes of climate and other elements peculiar to the country rendered both water and rail transport very precarious at certain periods of the year.

The rivers are subject to violent floods due to snow melting in the mountains, and, throughout the high-water season in a normal year, the volume of water is too great to be contained in the channels of the rivers themselves. This is aggravated by the fact that they carry a very high proportion of silt, which they deposit, and as this process has been going on for centuries, the beds have not only become constricted, but their levels are actually above that of the surrounding country a short distance away from their banks. The results of this are seen in the enormous floods which occur practically every year, when hundreds of square miles of this "Noah's domain" are inundated to a depth of 3 or 4 ft. To guard against these floods, earth protection banks or bunds have been built by the inhabitants for many miles along the course of both rivers, but even with proper maintenance these are not sufficiently strong to hold the huge volume of water.

A chart illustrating the effect of rainfall, floods and climatic conditions on transport is given in Fig. 36. This was furnished by Major-General Freeland, R.E., who investigated the transportation situation in Mesopotamia at the end of 1917, and submitted a very comprehensive report on the subject. The chart indicates that railway working was endangered during the early months of the year, whilst low water in the rivers between July and January reduced the efficiency of the Fleet and imposed a great strain on the railways. In addition to these troubles, the great heat experienced in Mesopotamia during June, July and August, necessitates the cessation of loading and other work at depôts for several hours in the middle of the day, and also reduces the output per labour-unit during working hours. Basra and Kurna are particularly bad places for heat, and the latter place proved so unhealthy that it was eventually evacuated. On the other hand, the mornings and evenings during January, February and December are so cold that the output of Eastern labour is greatly depreciated during those months.

It will, therefore, be appreciated that there were exceeding difficulties in the way of conducting transportation in this inhospitable region. On the general question of traffic capacity, for example, it is obvious that this is limited by the work at terminals (either docks or handling stations *en route*) and that, in the absence of their proper functioning, the most effective working of the communication links will be rendered of little avail. On the other hand, the effect of rain on the finely-divided marl soil in the Mesopotamian plain

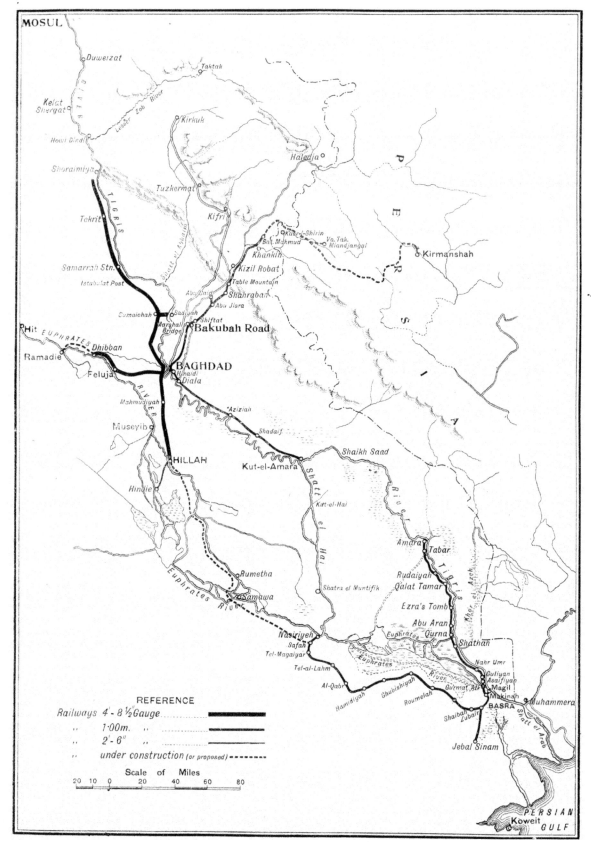

Fig. 34.—Railways Constructed in Mesopotamia during the War.

had a very serious effect on the railway tracks, which being unballasted, were quickly turned into a sea of mud. In a very short time, therefore, a purely surface line became unworkable, and during the campaign several severe interruptions to railway traffic occurred from this cause.

The First Railways.

Railway construction in Mesopotamia commenced in the middle of 1916. Two railways were authorised, one between Basra and Nasiriyeh on the Euphrates, 140 miles in length, and the second from Kurna to Amara, both on the Tigris, 70 miles in length.

The projected use of the Basra-Nasiriyeh link was to facilitate the transport of supplies for the troops stationed at Nasiriyeh, which had always to be strongly held to prevent the Turks from attacking Basra from that direction ; the principal object of the Kurna-Amara line was to assist navigation on the difficult section of the Tigris River between those places. The difficulty of obtaining material and rolling stock impelled much controversy as to the gauge to be adopted, but it was eventually decided that the Basra-Nasiriyeh line should be built on the metre gauge, and the Kurna-Amara line on the 2 ft. 6 in. gauge.

The Gauge Question.—The controversial gauge question cropped up again in the autumn of 1916 and raised the problem of future

Sheikh Saad-Ess Sinn Line.—Railway communication between the Advanced Base and the fighting front was opened in the middle of October, 1916, and comprised 24 miles of 2 ft. 6 in. gauge track, built up of 21-lb. section rails. It was constructed and operated by British and Indian railway troops and proved of great utility, as it enabled the troops stationed in the vicinity of Twin Canals and Ess Sinn to be maintained with facility. Being close to the front, the line was protected by blockhouses and barbed wire and held by L. of C. defence troops. During January, 1917, activities in connection with the renewal of the offensive increased traffic on this line to such an extent that additional locomotives had to be obtained from the Kurna-Amara line to keep things going, the monthly traffic then amounting to nearly 8,000 tons, together with a heavy personnel movement.

Kurna-Amara Line.—A second 2 ft. 6 in. gauge line was completed and opened for traffic on November 28, 1916, by which time it had been decided to convert the line to metre gauge as soon as sufficient material was available. The track was composed of 21-lb. F.F. rails and was 70 miles in length, 35 miles being laid on steel sleepers and the remainder on wooden sleepers, 2,200 to the mile. Earthwork was very heavy, and many bridges were required to span spills and creeks, the principal of which were the Majar Kebir and

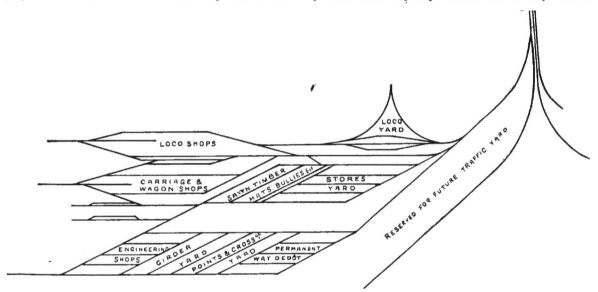

Fig. 35.—General Arrangement of Yard at Makina.

railway policy. Further railroad projects were than being contemplated, and it was recognised that a break of gauge would prove a tremendous handicap to the efficiency of the communications owing to the great restriction of stock mobility thus entailed. The problem was further complicated by the terrible shortage of railway material.

The question was considered by the War Office in conjunction with the India Office and Foreign Office, and, as it was pointed out that the whole question of railway construction in the Middle East was about to be discussed by an Inter-Departmental Committee in connection with the revision of the Anglo-Russian Convention of 1907, it was decided to postpone a decision on the gauge question until the Committee's recommendations were received. Owing, however, to the altered situation in Russia, this Committee never met, and no definite gauge policy was officially decided upon.

In general, the gauge of each railway was fixed by the necessity of urgency in construction and the facilities offering for the supply of material and rolling-stock, but it is probable that the decision to convert the Kurna-Amara line to metre gauge—owing partially to the fact that the capacity of the 2 ft. 6 in. track was insufficient—virtually settled the gauge question in Mesopotamia during the war period, and committed all new constructions south-east of Baghdad to the metre gauge.

Tabar spills, 200 ft. and 120 ft. wide respectively. Practically the whole of the country on this route is under water during high flood season, and to avoid washouts the line had to be carried on high banks. These were riveted by means of reeds and brushwood, according to Arab methods, and were expected to enable the banks to resist the wash of the floods.

The traffic capacity of the line was very restricted owing to the shortage of rolling-stock, India having found it impossible to provide sufficient light locomotives and wagons, whilst the great urgency of free traffic circulation on the Sheikh Saad line early in 1917 necessitated the transfer of some of the few locomotives in use. The importance of completing the metre gauge conversion was keenly appreciated, and this work was urged in such a satisfactory manner that the whole of the metre gauge line was opened for traffic during April, 1917.

Basra-Nasiriyeh Line.—The first metre gauge line to be opened in Mesopotamia was a railway running along the Euphrates from Basra to Nasiriyeh. It was 140 miles in length and was built of 75-lb. section F.B. rails spiked direct to sleepers, of which there were 1,600 to the mile. The sleepers used were mostly Indian broad gauge type, and the rails were so laid on the sleepers that, by shifting one rail, the line could be converted to a standard gauge track placed centrally on the formation. The ruling grades were 1 in 400 for up traffic and 1 in 300 for down traffic, the only rise of any importance being from Zubair on to the Shaiba plateau. For quite a long length, the line traverses ground normally below high flood level and properly reveted banks had to be built. Crossing facilities were located at 25 "stations," the average distance apart being 5 miles, whilst shops were temporarily situated at Magil, though they were subsequently transferred to Shaiba, 2 miles north-west of Zubair.

Other Railway Projects.—The railways open for traffic at the end of 1916 totalled 234 miles in length. They comprised disconnected lines, one running south-west from a point on the right bank of the Tigris, the second running along the right bank of the Tigris from Kurna, and the third following the Euphrates from Basra.

The construction of a further 126 miles of railway had also been authorised for the purpose of effecting through communication by rail between Basra and Sheikh Saad. This required the linking-up of Basra with Kurna and of Amara with Sheikh Saad and, at that time, the completion of such lines would have been of great utility to the communications, as the river could have been relieved of a considerable quantity of through traffic from Basra to Advanced Base. As, however, certain difficulties hindered the development of this project, it eventually happened that whilst the Basra-Kurna link was completed, the other construction was postponed. The Amara-Sheikh Saad line would have been about 86 miles in length, and was to be built of 50-lb. rails, with crossing stations at 10-mile intervals. As originally proposed, it was intended to commence the construction as soon as the Kurna-Amara conversion to metre gauge was completed, but the rapid advance of the British Forces in pursuit of the retreating Turks urgently demanded a line between Kut and Baghdad, so the material earmarked for the Amara-Sheikh Saad line was utilised for this purpose.

Basra-Kurna Line.—A line from Basra to Kurna was projected for the purpose of giving through communication to Amara and, ultimately to Sheikh Saad and, possibly, Baghdad.

The principal difficulty in the construction of this line was the crossing of the new channel of the Euphrates at Gurmat Ali. The river at this point is between 60 and 70 ft. deep and an ordinary pile bridge was out of the question. Arrangements were made to meet this problem by the transfer of a floating bridge, 420 ft. long and designed for metre gauge loads, from the Rohilkhand and Kumaon Railway of India. The old channel of the Euphrates at Kurna was crossed by a pile bridge 900 ft. long, a swing span giving a clear opening of 21 ft. and a movable span a clear opening of 60 ft.

Earthwork on the line commenced early in February, 1917, but work was practically suspended during the flood months, i.e., April to August. By September the track was laid in between Basra and Gurmat Ali, and during the following month the newly-established river port of Nahrumar was linked with Kurna. The placing in position of the pontoon bridge at Gurmat Ali was not completed until December 26, and, whilst the first train crossed on that day, further work in connection with the raising and lowering gear of the bridge delayed the commencement of regular through working until January 1, 1918. The Gurmat Ali bridge proved a weak spot, and considerably reduced the capacity of the line. Owing to the rise and fall of the tide, it was found impracticable to use the bridge for more than 16 hours daily, that is to say, four hours on each side of high water.

With the completion of the Kurna-Amara conversion it was expected that the capacity of the railway would be eight trains per day, say, equal to 1,300 tons of traffic, averaging 9,000 tons per week. Much needed relief would thereby be given to the heavily worked I.W.T. service between Basra and Amara, and as the line settled and permitted heavier train loads to be run, it was anticipated that the weekly traffic capacity would be 10,500 tons. Crossing stations were planned at 21 locations between Basra and Amara, the average distance apart being about 5 miles.

Railways in the Baghdad Area.

Renewed operations against the Turks in Mesopotamia began in December, 1916, when British troops, under the command of the late General Maude, resumed the offensive towards Kut. Issue was joined at Sanna-i-Yat and after some heavy fighting extending over a period of two months, the Turkish trenches west of Kut were stormed and the celebrated "Liquorice Factory" captured. The second occupation of Kut took place on February 24, 1917, and the enemy thereupon hurriedly evacuated Sanna-i-Yat, and retired in disorder towards Baghdad, leaving 1,650 prisoners in British hands. Cavalry, infantry and gunboats took part in the pursuit of the routed enemy, whose discomfiture was so complete that, after some little resistance on the Dahra bend of the Tigris had been overcome, the retirement continued beyond Baghdad.

Dismantling of Sheikh Saad-Ess Sinn Line.—With the pushing forward of our troops in pursuit of the retreating Turks, the line connecting the Tigris advanced base with the Kut front became redundant. Accordingly, after being used for the evacuation of the Divisional Artillery and supply dumps, the line was dismantled, and the material transferred to Baghdad for use in that area. This short line was extremely useful and, apart from the weight moved during the evacuation, 22,000 tons of ammunition and supplies and 11,380 passengers were carried between January and March, 1917.

Baghdad-Samarra Railway.—In the course of the operations around Baghdad during March, 1917, the first 10 miles of the Baghdad-Samarra standard gauge line fell into British hands, whilst full control of the line, which is 74 miles in length, was obtained during the following month, when our troops captured Samarra Station after clearing the enemy out of Deltawa and Sindia and defeating the 18th Turkish Army Corps at Istabulat. This line was built by the Germans during 1915 and follows the route of the Berlin-Baghdad Railway. It is a well-ballasted track with easy grades laid on banks above flood level.

The line was considerably damaged by the Turks in their retreat. Bridges were blown up, and station buildings were destroyed, but no attempt was made to demolish the track. As far as was possible in their hurried flight, the Turks removed both locomotives and rolling-stock and did what they could to render unserviceable all the plant that was left behind. The captured material included 15 locomotives, 200 wagons and 10 coaches for standard gauge track, together with 1 engine, 50 wagons and 2 miles of track for the 60 c.m. gauge.

Efforts were immediately concentrated on the standard gauge line and rolling-stock, and, within a fortnight, the line was sufficiently restored to permit of traffic working. Meanwhile, two locomotives and several wagons had been repaired, and on May 6, 1917, the first train ran through from Baghdad to Samarra, this materially easing the supply situation beyond Baghdad. All the locomotives were damaged by the bursting of the boilers and fireboxes by explosives and the destruction of the cylinders and motion, but repairs were so actively pushed on at Baghdad, where there was a fairly well-equipped workshop and a roundhouse accommodating 10 engines, that several locomotives were soon in running order. As a matter of fact, with the exception of four light tank engines sent to India for heavy repairs, all the captured rolling-stock was repaired by the military personnel at Baghdad, and great credit must be accorded to the authorities for the ingenious manner in which, by "ringing the changes" on several locomotives and other vehicles, they speedily turned out sufficient serviceable stock to maintain a service.

The provision of additional locomotive power to work over the captured line was essential, and as four large engines belonging to this line—captured in transit at the beginning of the campaign—had been sent to Egypt, steps were taken to arrange for the return of these locomotives which, although very heavy, were considered likely to be of utility. The railway authorities in Egypt, however, were indisposed to return these large engines, which were then doing excellent work on the Kantara main line, and offered six English goods engines of the 0-6-0 type, with axle weights of $13\frac{1}{2}$ tons and 15,000 lb. tractive force, conditionally on the power still being required. The locomotive position in Egypt being also serious, the railway authorities there were averse to the supply of any locomotives unless they were absolutely essential, and as it was found that the repair of the captured engines somewhat eased the situation in Mesopotamia, Egypt was eventually relieved of the necessity of provision.

Development of the Baghdad System.—By July, 1917, the British force was spread out fan-wise ahead of Baghdad. The left flank held a position in front of Feluja, on the Euphrates, which was captured late in March ; the centre occupied both banks of the Tigris between Samarra and Tekrit, and the right flank, having defeated the Turks with heavy loss at Deltawa during April, was working forward in a northerly direction to frustrate any enemy thrust towards Kasvin and Teheran.

Early in August it was found that the lack of railways in advance of and around Baghdad restricted the offensive power of the army, and the construction of additional railways radiating from Baghdad became, therefore, of increasing importance, as also the completion

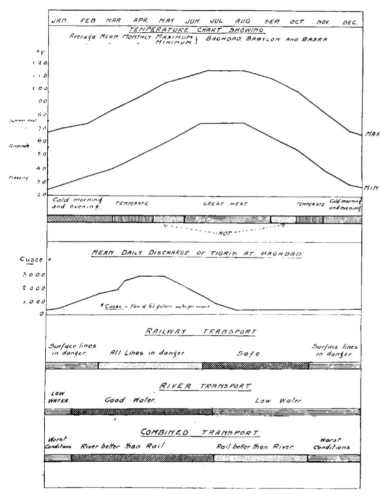

Fig. 36.—Chart Illustrating effect of Rainfall, Floods and Heat on Transport in Mesopotamia.

of the Kut-Baghdad line then in course of construction. Further operations were being planned, and it was highly essential that the traffic capacity of the lines of communication should be expanded to the highest degree. With the fall of Baghdad, there also fell into British hands a 60 c.m. tramroad, about 25 miles in length, running from Baghdad to the junction of the Mahmudiyah Canal and the Euphrates, below Feluja. Though of limited capacity, this line proved very useful for supplying the troops on the Euphrates front. It was dismantled during December, 1917 (on the completion of a line to Feluja), and up to that date carried traffic equivalent to 7,000 passenger-miles and 70,000 freight ton-miles.

For the support of the troops on the Diala front, the construction of a 2 ft. 6 in. gauge line to connect Baghdad and Baquba was com-

menced during May, 1917, and although this line did not reach Baquba until July 13, 1917, the widening of the Diala front impelled a decision to extend the line towards Table Mountain for the effective maintenance of the right flank. The improvement of the supply situation on the Euphrates, moreover, prompted the development of further railway facilities, and additional standard gauge lines were promoted from Baghdad to Feluja and Museyib respectively. These lines were also expected to be of great utility for the rapid transference of troops from one front to another.

It will therefore be seen that the development of railways in the Baghdad area was of a very hybrid character. Apart from the existing standard gauge line between Baghdad and Samarra, subsequently extended towards Tekrit, two additional lines on this gauge were projected, whilst a metre gauge line was making good progress from Kut to Baghdad, and a 2 ft. 6 in. gauge line between Baghdad and Baquba was in hand.

Kut-Baghdad Railway.—The metre gauge line connecting Kut with Hinaidi, 4 miles south of Baghdad, was completed on July 24, 1917, the first through train arriving at Hinaidi the following day. Platelaying started on May 20, and the average rate of progress works out at about 1½ miles per day, exclusive of sidings. The rate of 14 miles per week was, however, kept up for several weeks in succession, and this maximum effort would have been maintained if the supply of material had been equal to the demand. Hinaidi remained the centre of terminal activity, but the line was soon extended to Baghdad East, in order to supply the depôts in that city. The line is 109 miles in length, and crossing stations were located at 13 points, the average distance between crossings being about 8 miles. A repair shop was provided at Kut, whilst sheds were built at Kut and Hinaidi with accommodation for 24 and 6 engines respectively.

The length of the Kut-Baghdad line was about half the distance by river, and whereas the up-stream journey occupied two days Baghdad could be reached from Kut in about eight hours by railway. The route followed the left bank of the river in preference to the right bank, which presented certain constructional difficulties, and as the river bunds were in a good state of repair it was possible to lay a surface line all the way. The original intention was to use 50-lb. section rails throughout, but as the output of these rails was stopped by Tata's works in India in favour of an urgent demand for 75-lb. rails from Egypt for the doubling and extension of the Kantara line, the track on the Kut-Baghdad line was completed with 41¼-lb. rails.

The Kut-Baghdad line soon afforded considerable relief to the river communications, and Kut became an important transhipping point at which traffic was exchanged between river and rail. At least five, and sometimes six, trains were run daily between the terminals, the average weekly tonnage during November, 1917, being equal to 1,000,000 ton-miles. Nothing transpired to interfere with free movement during 1917, but during the early part of 1918 portions of the line were badly damaged by rain. In April, moreover, heavy floods swept over the railway and breached the track in several places, the line being under water to a depth of 2 ft. for a distance of 5 miles. Strenuous efforts were made to renew through working, but this was not effected until the 7th of the following month.

In due course the flooding difficulty was overcome to some

extent by ditching on either side of the formation and building bunds alongside with the excavated material.

Baghdad to Table Mountain Railway.—Coincident with the advance of our troops north-east of Baghdad during May, 1917, earth-work was commenced on a line to the Diala front. It was desired that the line should be on the metre gauge in order to connect with the Kut-Baghdad line, but the necessity of rapid completion occasioned by the military position forced the railway authorities to construct a track on the 2 ft. 6 in. gauge, and the material taken out of the Sheikh Saad-Ess Sinn and Kurna-Amara lines was utilised for this purpose. The line follows the right bank of the Diala River to Baquba, which place was reached and the line opened for traffic on July 13, 1917. As mentioned previously, the extension of the Diala front had led to a reconnaissance in advance of Baquba through Shahroban and upwards to Table Mountain, situated at the foot of the Jebel Hamrin range and some 65 miles from Baghdad. The extension of the Baquba line became of increasing urgency, as the Russian forces had evacuated the Persian towns of Khanikin and Kasr-i-Shirin which they captured from the Turks in March, 1917, and this necessitated the early development of communications to meet any possible Turkish advance in that direction. The Baquba line was therefore pushed on to Table Mountain, from which place there was a service-able road to Khanikin for the working of motor transport.

About a month before the 2 ft. 6 in. gauge line reached Table Mountain, a commencement was made on the conversion to metre gauge. This was really the laying of a new line, rather than a conversion, as the metre gauge track, which was built up of 41¼-lb. rails, was located alongside the existing railway. The line was opened for traffic as far as Baquba on November 28, 1917, but, owing to the shortage of material, it was not until June 4, 1918, that the section between Baquba and Table Mountain was finished. The railway was carried over the Diala River at Baquba by a high level pile and trestle bridge (Marshall's) and, early in 1918, owing to the rush of the early flood waters, two piers of the bridge were undercut and rendered unsafe. Repairs were immediately taken in hand, and, until through communication by train was restored about a fortnight later, through traffic was handled by the troublesome expedient of manhandling narrow gauge trucks across the bridge. The vital importance of this bridge on the line of communication with Persia subsequently impelled a decision to replace the pile bridge by a permanent bridge, consisting of four spans of 100 ft. and two spans of 75 ft. on well piers. This work was commenced in May, 1918, and was almost completed by the end of the year.

Abu Jisra-Abu Saida Branch.—While the first section of the Baghdad-Table Mountain line runs along the right bank of the Diala River, the second section is some distance away from the left bank at various points, and it was decided to put in a branch to connect the railway and river. Light gauge material was available on the spot, owing to the conversion of the Baghdad-Baquba line to metre gauge, and this was used for the construction of the branch, which is 4 miles in length. The line was opened towards the end of 1917, and connects Abu Jisra (about half-way between Baquba and Table Mountain) and Abu Saida on the Diala River. It was converted to metre gauge following the completion of the metre-gauge line to Table Mountain.

Sumaichah-Sadiyah Branch.—A railway between Sadiyah and Kifri was in process of construction by the enemy prior to the retreat beyond Samarra, and a considerable quantity of German standard gauge track material was found near Sadiyah on the British occupation of that district. This material was utilised to build a branch from the Tigris at Sadiyah to Sumaichah on the Baghdad-Samarra Railway. The construction was hastened in order to facilitate communication with a force on the Tigris at the gorge of the Shatt-el-Adhaim, but, before the line could be completed, the 13th Turkish Army Corps had been heavily defeated and had consequently retreated. The line was opened for traffic in July, 1917, and during the period July to September, when traffic figures for the branch were recorded separately, the work done was equal to 442,714 passenger-miles, 2,021 (livestock) vehicle miles, and 543,222 freight ton-miles. The traffic figures from

October, 1918, were included in the return for the Baghdad-Samarra line and branches.

Baghdad-Feluja-Dhibban Line.—Towards the end of August, 1917, a standard gauge line was commenced from Baghdad by a route running westward towards Feluja, its projected utility being to connect the Euphrates front with Baghdad and relieve the motor transport then conveying supplies to the troops. The construction proceeded very slowly owing to shortage of material, and railhead did not reach Feluja until December 21, 1917. No serious constructional difficulties were encountered, the railway being laid as surface track and depending for its safety on the maintenance of the Saklawiyah Bund, which holds up the flood waters of the Euphrates. Only one bridge had to be built, but this was 290 ft. in length, and comprised a pile bridge with ten 21 ft. girder spans, two 8 ft. shore spans, and nine 7 ft. trestle spans. The bridge is located just outside Baghdad.

Meanwhile the British forces, after pushing back the Turkish Army along the Euphrates, arrived in front of Ramadie, where a furious battle was fought. The Turks were heavily defeated, and retired in the direction of Hit; 13 guns and 3,435 prisoners were taken, including General Ahmed Bey and his staff, and Ramadie was occupied at the end of September. For the more effective support of the troops on this front the Feluja line was thereupon extended and reached Dhibban, 48½ miles from Baghdad, on February 18, 1918. A reconnaissance was subsequently made for the extension of the line to Ramadie, but no detailed survey was conducted. In March, 1918, a detachment of the British force advanced from Ramadie, and, after several skirmishes with the enemy along the Euphrates, attacked and routed the small Turkish army left in this area. The town of Hit was consequently occupied, and whilst small disorganised sections of the enemy were in the neighbourhood until the conclusion of hostilities, this put an end to the fighting west of Baghdad.

Baghdad-Hillah Line.—The necessity for developing more fully the supply situation on the Euphrates, and the planning of certain operations for the pacification of the country south-east of Baghdad, prompted consideration of a line from Baghdad to Museyib. This line was to branch from the existing standard gauge line to Dhibban at a point west of the Khirr bridge, 3 miles from Baghdad. The expected strategical value of this line caused the project to be given priority, and, in order to ensure the rapid supply of material, 100 miles of the Sutlej Valley section of the Southern Punjab Railway in India was speedily dismantled and shipped to Mesopotamia.

Certain changes in the strategical position, occasioned by the capture of Hillah, Kifl and Samawa, a point some 57 miles north-west of Nasiriyeh, during December, 1917, ultimately impelled a decision to abandon the line to Museyib and, in lieu thereof, to build a line direct to Hillah, which was a more important centre. An additional reason was the fact that a large scheme for the local production of supplies was then being planned in the area south-east of Hillah. The survey was completed in March, 1918, the advanced railhead established at a point 18 miles distant from Baghdad in April, and the whole of the line, which is 58 miles long and built of 75-lb. rails on broad gauge sleepers, completed and open for traffic during May, 1918.

Hillah-Kifl Line.—As the agricultural scheme on the Hindieh branch of the Euphrates River developed, it was found desirable to provide means for the expeditious conveyance of the harvest to Baghdad, and a 2 ft. 6 in. line was therefore constructed from Hillah to Kifl. The permanent way material and rolling-stock for the line were obtained from the Hinaidi-Baquba light gauge line after the conversion to metre gauge. Construction commenced on July 8, 1918, and the line, which is 21 miles long, was opened for traffic on August 4. Considerable relief was afforded to the motor transport, which previously carried the traffic to Hillah, as, during the harvest season of 1918, a rich harvest of barley and wheat was obtained in this district.

Extension of the Baghdad-Samarra Line.—The British advance continued after the defeat of the Turks on the Tigris before Tekrit in November, 1917, and early in May, 1918, the British Force under the command of General Marshall occupied Kirkuk, a point situated 110 miles south-east of Mosul.

The desirability of pushing forward the Baghdad-Samarra line was therefore apparent, and the extension was commenced in June, 1918. The extension to Tekrit was completed on the first day of September, and as by this time General Marshall's army was impelling the retirement of the Turks along the Tigris towards Kalat Shergat, a point 50 miles south of Mosul, it was decided further to extend the Baghdad-Samarra-Tekrit line. Construction commenced early in October, and was intended to proceed for 30 miles to Shoreimiyeh, but, by the time the line had reached Baiji, 26 miles beyond Tekrit, the Turks had been engaged in the final battle of the campaign, 5 miles north of Kalat Shergat.

The British victory was so complete that 7,000 prisoners were taken, and the Turkish Commander, General Ismail Hakki, and the remnant of his army surrendered. The Turks thereupon sued for an armistice, and this was signed to take effect from noon on the first day of November, 1918. This Turkish general was the same officer who, in the early spring of 1917, commanded the Turkish forces on the right bank of the Tigris opposite Kut, and was one of the last to escape across the river when the remainder of his army was captured in the Dahra bend. The British cavalry forces were subsequently engaged in rounding up isolated Turkish detachments between Kalat Shergat and Mosul, and, as the victorious conclusion of hostilities rendered unnecessary any great haste in the further construction of the Baghdad-Samarra-Tekrit line, and there was a very great shortage of standard gauge material, this railway was not continued beyond Baiji.

It might further be added that the Turkish Commander who negotiated the armistice endeavoured to evade its terms, and energetic measures had to be taken to clear the Mosul Vilayet of the remainder of the Turkish troops. They retired in a north-westerly direction to Nisibin, then the terminus of the Constantinople-Baghdad Railway, about 100 miles from Mosul. This led to the building of a 2 ft. 6 in. gauge line from Baiji towards Mosul for conveyance of supplies, &c., and it is understood that this line has materially assisted in the work of pacifying the disaffected area in the Mosul district.

Railway Extension to the Persian Frontier.

The despatch of a detachment to the Caspian Sea, and the consequent maintenance of a gradually lengthening line of communication through Persia, prompted the development of surveys during the middle of 1918 for an extension of the Baghdad-Table Mountain line to Khanikin on the Persian frontier. Construction soon commenced, but as the first 10 miles included heavy earthworks, in addition to two tunnels and considerable bridge work, it was not until November 25, 1918, that railhead was established 11 miles beyond Table Mountain. Forward construction, however, was somewhat easier, and the last section of the line was in course of completion at the end of 1918.

Meanwhile the British force had advanced through Persia, and arrived at Enzeli, on the Caspian Sea, during July, 1918, a detachment being sent forward to Baku in the following month. The establishment of this force effectively put an end to the possibility of any enemy thrust towards Persia, but the maintenance of the expedition was a matter of considerable anxiety by reason of the long and vulnerable line of communication to the Caspian Sea. The force was supplied from Baghdad, and as at that time the railway was not completed beyond Table Mountain, supplies had to leave the railway at that point and be carried by light motors along the Khanikin-Hamadan road to Enzeli. From railhead to Hamadan, a matter of 340 miles, a lightly-metalled road was constructed, whilst an existing metalled road, which extended for 300 miles between Hamadan and Enzeli, had to be kept in constant repair.

The conveyance of supplies over such a long line of communication imposed a heavy strain on the heavily-taxed transport resources of the expeditionary force, and it became desirable to relieve this as far as possible by extending the railway in the direction of Kermanshah, in Persia. During October, 1918, therefore, the necessary surveys were undertaken, and whilst at first the intention was to extend

only as far as Pai Tak Pass, where the mountainous section commenced, a practicable route appeared feasible for a railway to Khermanshah, and it was decided to make definite surveys for a line through to that place. Towards the end of the year a goodly proportion of the earthworks on the Khanikin-Kasrishirin section had been completed, bridgework was well in hand, whilst the survey of the Saripul-Khermanshah section was proceeding satisfactorily. The progress of the railway towards Khanikin, moreover, had immensely relieved the road transport, which had been severely tested following the conclusion of hostilities and the reoccupation of Baku by the 39th British Infantry Brigade, in co-operation with Allied forces.

The line was subsequently completed to Quaritu, on the Persian frontier, owing to Khanikin proving inconvenient as a terminal station, the distance from Baghdad being about 130 miles. Whilst the general contour of the country in south-west Persia does not lend itself easily to railway construction, there seems little doubt that sooner or later Baghdad will be connected to Teheran, the Persian capital. The centre of Persia comprises a main plateau, to which the railways would necessarily have to rise, although it would be difficult to follow the watercourses owing to the distribution of the mountains and the nature of the rock, through which the rivers have eroded deep gorges very badly adapted for railway construction. This question of railway development in Persia was studied by General De Candolle (D.G.T.) during his visit to Mesopotamia, and he came to the conclusion that the only practicable route for a railway up to Teheran was one climbing the main plateau other than by a watercourse.

Locomotives, Rolling-Stock and Traffic.

The Mesopotamian railways first commenced to carry traffic during December, 1916, and whilst, of course, the one line then open could not carry any great weight of traffic, a very respectable start was made during the first week by the transport of 3,300 tons of freight. By the last week in December, 1916, the weekly tonnage carried by rail had increased to 10,000 tons, the transfer of this traffic from river to railway giving valuable relief to the waterways on difficult sections of the river.

Metre Gauge Lines.—At the beginning of 1917 only 19 locomotives and 471 coaching and goods vehicles were in service, but demands had been placed for 24 locomotives and 616 vehicles for the Kurna-Amara line, then about to be completed to metre gauge, and 24 locomotives and 676 wagons for the Amara-Sheik Saad line, which was at that time projected. Further rolling-stock to form four ballast trains, three ambulance trains and two armoured trains was also on demand.

The locomotives were of a light type and known in India as " F class." In full working order they weighed 40 tons, including tender, and were credited with a hauling capacity of 40 vehicles on a moderate grade. These locomotives, which were all second-hand, were not in the best condition when received, and as the use of muddy water from the rivers and the lack of adequate repair facilities in Mesopotamia still further impaired their efficiency, traffic working was handicapped. It was found expedient to limit the train load to 35 vehicles on the Basra-Nasiriyeh line, whilst this had further to be reduced on the other two lines, where the banks were soft, to 31 wagons, though the load was greatly increased as the banks settled. The wagons were mainly of 8 tons capacity, about 20 per cent. being 10 tons, and the wagon load was taken at the general average of 6 tons. The rolling-stock requirements were based on an estimated weekly up traffic of 1,000 tons, on the Basra-Nasiriyeh line, 7,000 tons on the Kurna-Amara line, and 6,000 tons on the Amara-Sheikh Saad line, together with a small amount of passenger traffic, which, however, on the Tigris lines of communication would normally travel by water. Difficulty arose in supplying the necessary stock, and in April, 1917, it was found impossible to satisfy the full traffic requirements. In September, 1917, however, the whole of the rolling-stock previously mentioned was in service, and the carrying capacity of the Basra-Kurna-Amara and Kut-Baghdad lines was then estimated at 7,000 tons weekly, whilst the Baghdad-Baquba line was given as 2,400 tons weekly.

Ton-miles and Passenger-miles.—During April, 1917,

arrangements were made for railway traffic returns to follow the lines adopted in connection with river traffic, which returns were forwarded by the respective Directors through the Inspector-General of Communications to the Director-General of Movements and Railways at the War Office. Accordingly, railway traffic reports from that date gave ton-mileage, passenger-mileage and (for animals) vehicle-mileage figures separately for each railway. In the first week for which such figures were available, railway work was measured by 250,000 ton-miles, whilst river traffic movement exceeded 4,000,000 ton-miles.

Though the railway contribution to the total transportation effort, viewed from the ton-mile figures quoted, was not very great, it must always be remembered that the military situation had developed in such a favourable manner that the principal line then open (Basra-Nasiriyeh) had lost much of its importance, and that the newly-converted line from Kurna-Amara had only just been opened for traffic. Additionally, the shortage of rolling-stock naturally limited the traffic capacity of the railways, whilst river traffic figures, measured in ton-miles, were unduly inflated in relation to the effective transportation performed owing to the inordinate length of haul. It should also be noticed that the necessity of transhipping intended rail traffic into lighters some distance from Kurna, and the further transhipment at Kurna, would unfavourably react on railway tonnage. When sufficient river-craft offered, it was probably more convenient to forward throughout by the river route; more especially was this the case after the transfer of the Advanced Base to Baghdad, for the carrying of any of the through traffic over the railway section required transhipments both at Kurna and Amara.

Assistance to River Transport.—During the last quarter of 1917, when the railway system had been considerably extended and consolidated, the freight carried by railway totalled 523,145 tons, this representing an increase of 84 per cent. over the preceding quarterly period. Personnel and livestock traffic increased by about 50 per cent., whilst the freight ton mileage more than doubled, the figure for the December quarter being nearly 30,000,000. The great assistance rendered to river transport will be appreciated from the fact that during this quarter the Tigris Valley railways, Basra-Kurna-Amara and Kut-Baghdad lines, carried freight traffic equivalent to 28,000,000 river ton-miles, after making allowance for the greater length of the journey on account of the windings of the river. This compares with 10,000,000 river ton-miles in the previous quarter and shows how very effective the assistance given by the railway to river transport had become.

Standard Gauge Lines.—In July, 1917, the standard gauge plant in Mesopotamia comprised 20 locomotives and 323 wagons, whilst the line operated was 75 miles in length and was estimated to have a weekly traffic capacity of 7,000 tons. To supplement the tractive possibilities, four Peerless motor lorries were adapted to run on standard gauge track, and were able to haul four wagons. The necessity for the supply of additional wagons was urgent, and in the middle of 1917 the Indian railways converted 150 5 ft. 6 in. gauge wagons to the standard gauge and shipped them for use on the Baghdad-Samarra Railway.

The operation of the extended standard gauge lines beyond Samarra and the newly constructed lines between Baghdad-Feluja-Dhibban and Baghdad-Hillah required the provision of additional rolling-stock and by March, 1918, 29 locomotives and 371 wagons were in service, this representing an increase over the previous figures of 9 locomotives and 50 wagons. By July, 1918, 38 locomotives were in service, the "stud" having been added to by 9 London &

South Western 0-6-0 type engines which later performed most useful work. Wagons had also increased to 431, whilst they went up to 562 in September, 1918. Further wagons were then on demand, and it is probable that the number of standard gauge wagons in the country is now between 800 and 900 units.

Additions to Metre Gauge Stock.—The metre gauge stock was increased considerably during 1918. The number of trains required, especially on the Tigris sections, necessitated the provision of additional plant, and, whilst in July, 1917, there were only 57 locomotives and 979 wagons, these figures had increased to 92 (majority "F class") and 2,704 respectively by March, 1918. This extensive provision of stock had proved necessary owing to the great demands on the new lines from Basra to Amara, Kut to Baghdad and Baghdad-Baquba-Table Mountain which were required to handle a weekly traffic of 7,000 to 8,000 tons.

The enormous extent to which the traffic had grown is reflected by the fact that, by the end of 1917 the traffic conveyed by railway exceeded 40,000 tons weekly. The railways continued to perform

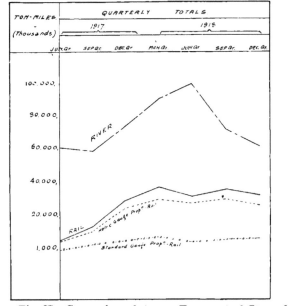

Quarter ended.	% Proportions of total ton-miles (River and Rail)	
	RIVER	RAIL.
1917.	%	%
June	93	7
Sept'r	81	19
Dec'r	72	28
1918		
March	71	29
June	76	24
Sept'r	67	33
Dec'r.	65	35

Fig. 37.—**Comparison between Transport of Stores by River and Rail, expressed in Ton-Miles.**

magnificent work under conditions militating against good results, and in the first week of March, 1918, transported 16,000 passengers and 60,000 tons of traffic, this being 6,000 tons in excess of the previous "record." By September, 1918, the wagon stock had increased to 4,158, an addition of roughly 600 since June, and this assisted materially to improve the position. The fact that, as the lines settled down properly, it was possible to increase train loads also had its effect on stock questions, as each train was gradually lengthened until it comprised between 35 and 40 vehicles.

When Major-General Freeland visited Mesopotamia, he observed that metre gauge stock estimates were being based on the necessity of carrying 1,200 tons (approximately seven trains) per day on the Basra (Makina)-Amara and Kut-Baghdad lines, and as it was at that time considered that the prospective increase in the forces and the necessity for transporting material for certain new lines would increase traffic demands, revised estimates of rolling-stock requirements were drawn up, based on 18 pairs of trains per day on the Tigris lines and a lighter service on the other metre gauge lines. The additional stock required comprised 30 locomotives and 1,000 wagons, and whilst it was eventually decided that the force would not be increased and the 18 pairs of trains were reduced to 14 pairs, 26 Baldwin "Mallet" locomotives were shipped from America and about 650 wagons from India before the conclusion of hostilities.

The general improvement in the rolling-stock position is indicated in the following statement :—

	Standard gauge.		Metre gauge.	
	Engines.	Wagons.	Engines.	Wagons.
July, 1917	20	323	57	979
March, 1918	31	371	92	2,704
September, 1918	38	562	145	4,158

whilst about 23 locomotives and 243 wagons were available for 2 ft. 6 in. gauge. It should, however, be pointed out that a large percentage of locomotives and wagon stock was out of service for repairs during each period.

Traffic Development.— The following table indicates the general trend of freight traffic development on the Mesopotamian railways, and it should be said in this connection that a considerable weight of traffic from local points developed in the course of time.

STATEMENT SHOWING WAR DEPARTMENT STORES (D.W. TONS) CARRIED ON THE PRINCIPAL RAILWAYS DURING EACH HALF-YEAR, YEARS 1917 AND 1918.

Line.	Half year ended—				
	June, 1917.	December, 1917.	June, 1918.	December, 1918.	Total.
Metre gauge— Basra-Nasiriyeh ..	202,747	153,488	96,402	89,770	542,407
Basra-Amara ..	36,390	148,750	256,581	257,805	699,526
Kut-Baghdad ..	—	159,869	216,019	196,808	572,696
Baghdad-Bakuba-Table Mountain and Kizil Robat ..	—	54,685	191,792	156,610	403,087
Standard gauge— Baghdad-Samarra-Tekrit and Baiji ..	12,161	125,020	138,516	113,237	388,934
Baghdad-Fellujah-Dhibban ..	—	6,475	64,062	51,464	122,001
Baghdad Hillah ..	—	—	1,030	36,521	37,551
	251,298	648,287	964,402	902,215	2,766,202

The diagram in Fig. 37 shows the proportions of traffic, measured in ton-miles, carried by the standard gauge and metre gauge lines in comparison with the river transport.

Utilisation of Oil Fuel.—In this section reference might fittingly be made to the use of oil fuel both by locomotives and river steamers. The suggestion was first mooted in 1917 owing to :—

(1) Difficulties of coal supply.

(2) Saving to be effected in shipping freight and unloading at Basra.

(3) Financial saving,

and whilst, of course, it was a gradual process to convert the engines for the employment of oil fuel, it was decided to do this as expeditiously as possible. By the end of 1917 considerable progress was effected, and it was anticipated that the complete conversion would decrease coal imports by some 200,000 tons per annum, and thus economise shipping tonnage. The oil was obtained locally from the Anglo-Persian Oil Company at Abadan.

Control and Working.

Originally, the Director of Railways, Brig.-General Lubbock, had his headquarters at Basra, but, following the advance beyond Baghdad and the consequent extension of the railway system, it became important for him to move to General Headquarters, which were established at Baghdad. In due course, therefore, Colonel Oakes, with the rank of Deputy Director of Railways, was sent to Mesopotamia and stationed at Basra, with full control under the Director of Railways of all railway transportation in the Basra area. The further development of transportation rendered necessary the extension of the organisation, and an Assistant Director of Railways was appointed at Kut, and subsequently at Baghdad. Following Major-General Freeland's report on the communications in Mesopotamia, Major-General De Candolle was appointed D.G.T. in this theatre of war, but, owing to the conclusion of an armistice with the Turks, almost immediately following his arrival in the country, no change was made in the railway organisation.

Train Operation.—The whole of the system was comprised of single lines more or less unballasted, and this necessarily prohibited any rapid movement of trains. The relatively long distance between the crossing " stations " generally averaging between 6 and 7 miles, also imposed a distinct limitation on the traffic capacity of the railways, and it was found to be impracticable to run more than eight trains daily in addition to occasional troop and ambulance trains. Other limiting factors were the shortage of locomotives and rolling-stock and the absence of a through line between Basra and Baghdad. There was a fairly comprehensive telegraph and telephone equipment along the railways, and, as will be noted from subsequent remarks, every effort was made to accelerate the working. It is interesting to record that, in the week ending October 4, 1917, when the total length of line operated was 500 miles, 334 loaded trains were run, with an aggregate of 22,690 train-miles, the average train load in the up direction being about 150 tons. It might also be explained that considerable yard accommodation was provided both at Baghdad and Basra, whilst smaller terminals were built at other places. At the Basra end the yard was established at Makina and a considerable mileage of sidings laid down to the wharves at Magil, whilst separate lines were constructed to the Ordnance, Supply and Transport and R.E. Depots. All traffic arising in the Basra area was worked to this yard, there marshalled in proper order, and despatched as required.

A complete remodelling of the railway system serving the wharves and port area was also taken in hand during 1918, following the adoption of General Freeland's recommendations with regard to future developments, and by the end of the year some 50 miles of track had been laid in to connect with the various depôts. The lay-out of the yard was designed on an up-to-date plan and offered suitable facilities for rapid working.

Workshops and Stores.—Whilst the stores were originally located at Magil, they were subsequently removed to Shaiba, 14 miles from Basra, on the Nasiriyeh line. The stores were eventually transferred to Makina, as this was found to be a far more convenient location for the two lines. Magil, Abu Aran, Kut and Baghdad were subsidiary depôts, whilst the permanent way stores was established at Nahumar. The running shed for the Basra area was at Makina, where accommodation was provided for 40 engines, whilst all repairs to locomotives and rolling-stock were performed at Shaiba. The shops at this place consisted of a machine shop and foundry, 200 ft. by 50 ft., and an erection shop of the same dimensions, with an annexe 200 ft. by 30 ft. A carriage shop, consisting of two bays 40 ft. by 50 ft. each, was also built, but this was subsequently converted for use as a smithy and boiler shop. A round house, with accommodation for 10 standard gauge engines, was captured at Baghdad, whilst workshops situated in close proximity were extended and re-equipped. Additionally, a locomotive shed and shops were established at Kut, to deal with the engines working on the metre gauge lines connected with Baghdad.

Watering Facilities for Locomotives.—In the early days of the railways the watering facilities for locomotives in the Basra area were not by any means as complete as could have been desired. On the Tigris lines, and at Basra and Nasiriyeh, river water was used, but at intermediate stations on the Nasiriyeh line the only supply available was drawn from wells, and this usually proved too salty and always too hard for locomotives. To meet this difficulty it became essential to draw water from the Euphrates, and a pipe line was laid in from the Euphrates to Ghubashiyeh, 2 miles from the river. The water supply for the Shaiba shops was supplied from Magil through a 6-in. pipe. Subsequently settling tanks were introduced all over the line, and this much improved the position.

Rules and Regulations.—The necessity for rules and regulations in regard to the working of traffic was met by the publication of a special book (" General Rules for Working Railways "), based on the rules and regulations in vogue on the North Western Railway in India. With suitable qualifications to meet local conditions and due regard to military requirements, these were put into operation as from June 1, 1917, and were afterwards followed in the working of the railways.

Until the middle of 1918 there was no signalling of any description. Even after that date only the most important stations were signalled, the equipment comprising a distant board at each end of the "station," which boards were operated from a winch placed midway between them. All traffic was worked on the telegraphic line-clear system and adequate precautions were taken to guard against conflicting movements. A special code was given to each station for use in connection with "line clear" messages, and authority for a train to approach had to be given with this code. A record was maintained, separately for up and down traffic, of all messages sent and received, and special regulations were in vogue to govern the working of traffic on the "train following" system. Trains were given "line clear" either conditionally or unconditionally, and special forms, clearly distinguished by certain markings, were used as authority for the drivers.

The Baghdad to Basra Through Route.

Whilst the Baghdad-Basra through railway is to-day a completed line, *via* the Euphrates route, it is probable that a more abundant supply of personnel and material during 1917 would have resulted in this connecting link being first completed down the Tigris Valley. From the time that the occupation of Baghdad rendered the project possible of fulfilment, there was much difference of expert opinion as to the military and, subsequently, commercial advantages that would accrue from the completion of such a line. It is of some interest to note that, whilst the potential commercial value of the line was fully appreciated, it was at that time considered that military reasons were not sufficiently cogent to justify the use of material (much needed in other places) for the Amara-Sheikh Saad-Kut Railway, which would have completed the through line *via* the Tigris route by connecting the Basra-Amara and the Kut-Baghdad lines.

Euphrates or Tigris Route.—General consideration of the proposed through route, first *via* the Tigris and secondly *via* the Hai, was accorded from an early date in 1917, as it was recognised that the completion of such a line would permit of the expansion of railway traffic capacity and add to the relief given to the waterways. The many difficulties inseparable from construction down the Tigris and the further suggestions that the Hai or Euphrates routes might be more suitable impelled a decision to defer the project, but in May, 1917, it was reported that the constant process of supplementing river transport by the supply of additional craft was a severe strain on India's resources. It was thereupon suggested that the lines of communication would be much more effective if the missing railway link were completed, and the railway thus enabled to relieve river transport of some of the through traffic ; this also would obviate the labour and delay involved in transhipments. The crucial factor of time came into the question at this point, as it was certain that such a railway could not be completed in sufficient time to enable it to be used for military purposes to meet an expected Turkish advance during August and September, 1917. Owing to these considerations, the military authorities at home deemed it a wiser policy to concentrate on improving river transport and leave the question of a through railway route in abeyance.

It was fully recognised that increased railway facilities were very desirable, but the exigencies of the situation demanded that all available material should be utilised for constructions in forward areas, as it was in the Baghdad vilayet that railroad communications were most vital. It was impossible, owing to limitations of personnel and material, to proceed with the construction of the Amara-Kut line at the same time as railways were being developed round Baghdad, and in September, 1917, it was decided that the Amara-Kut line, owing to constructional difficulties, probable absence of post-war value, and disadvantages as compared with alternative routes, should be deferred. There was also the further point that, on the possible completion of a through line by an alternative route, suggestions had been made to take up the existing Kut-Baghdad line and utilise it for developing additional communications in the Baghdad area.

In the programme of railway construction to meet the military requirements of 1918, the question of a through route, *via* either Tigris, Hai or Euphrates, was further raised, but as a special Mission from England had been sent out to review the whole question of transportation in Mesopotamia, the question was deferred, pending Major-General Freeland's report on the subject. The subject was very thoroughly considered by Major-General Freeland, whose recommendations agreed with those of a Government of India Commission. holding an investigation at the same time, that the through line should be built by the Euphrates route, the alignment generally considered to have the greatest scope for commercial development.

Alternative Through Routes.—There were three practicable routes for a through railway, viz. :—

(*a*) The *Tigris* route. From Basra (Makina) along the right bank of the Tigris to Amara, thence across the river to the left bank, which would be followed through Kut into Baghdad (Hinaidi), distance about 344 miles.

(*b*) The *Hai* route. From Basra (Makina) to Nasiriyeh, thence across the Euphrates and in a northerly direction along the right bank of the Hai River to Kut, across the Tigris there and by the Kut-Baghdad line into Hinaidi or along the right bank of the Tigris from Kut. Distance about 375 miles.

(*c*) The *Euphrates* route. From Basra (Makina) to Nasiriyeh and along the Euphrates to Samawa, thence crossing the Euphrates and passing through the centre of the cultivated areas *via* Hillah to Baghdad. Distance about 335 miles.

There were certain advantages and disadvantages attached to each of the proposed routes. Whilst the Tigris route already possessed 214 miles of track against the 126 miles of the other routes, it had the disadvantage of requiring much more difficult construction than the Hai or Euphrates links, whilst it was not anticipated that the requirements of future peace railway policy would be met by this line which runs, for the most part, through barren or marshy country, far removed from the more thickly populated agricultural areas. The Tigris route was, therefore, ruled out. Between the Hai and Euphrates routes there appeared to be a pretty even balance. Both would pass through areas eminently suitable for the development of the agricultural resources of the Mesopotamian plain, though in this connection it might be remarked that, on the Euphrates route, large areas were already under cultivation for the supply of the troops, whereas, in the case of the Hai route, agricultural development had perforce to await the completion of large protection works projected by Sir William Willcocks.

Euphrates Route Adopted.—After taking all the circumstances into consideration, the War Office (on the advice of the D.G.M.R.) decided that the through line should follow the Euphrates route, this being also favoured by India and Mesopotamia. For part of its length, this had the alignment selected by the Germans for a through continental route, whilst it promised the minimum of engineering difficulties and, consequently, the smallest expenditure of time and material before it could be opened as a reliable through line. This construction, it was further recommended, should be of the metre gauge throughout, owing to the existing difficulty of obtaining standard gauge locomotives and rolling-stock. The track was to be laid with 75-lb. rails and standard gauge sleepers in order that any subsequent conversion to the standard gauge might be effected with facility.

The matter was very carefully considered at the War Office, and after it had been decided in February, 1918, not to increase the Forces in Mesopotamia, it was considered that there no longer existed any urgent necessity for a through line, and the question was deferred. The railway authorities in Mesopotamia were duly instructed to this effect and informed that efforts were to be concentrated in improving the existing lines on the 18 trains a day basis, this being subsequently reduced to a basis of 14 trains a day.

Advantages of Through Route.—In June, 1918, the subject was again brought forward, and it was pointed out that the construction of the proposed line would require no additional personnel, whilst there would be considerable economy in the fact that the Tigris fleet could be greatly reduced, and the proposed line would serve to collect the harvest in the Euphrates Valley. It was also stated that, if the metre gauge were adopted, standard gauge stock which was very badly required would be released from the Hillah branch for use on the other standard gauge lines around Baghdad, whilst the great expenditure of labour involved in transhipment at Amara and Kut would naturally be avoided. Certain objections were again raised to the proposal, one being that the existing lines of communication were sufficient to supply a force 50 per cent. more than that in Mesopotamia and, also, that the enemy showed no signs of improving his communications, but it was eventually decided that the through railway between Nasiriyeh and Hillah should be constructed. It was, however, laid down that the extension of the Baghdad-Khanikin line into Persia should precede the linking-up of the Hillah-Nasiriyeh section of the Euphrates line.

Commencement of Work.—A start was made on the earthworks at both ends of the link in the middle of August, 1918, the construction of bridges was in hand, and about 1½ miles of track had been laid in, when rail laying was discontinued. The earthworks were proceeded with, and by March 19, 1919, 74 miles of earthwork were constructed, the bridge work was well advanced, and 21 miles of track laid in from the Nasiriyeh end. The question of rail supply became important about this time, as there were not sufficient rails on hand to complete the track, and it was finally decided that the Kut-Baghdad line should be dismantled to supply the material necessary to complete the through line.

Transcontinental Railway.—Thus the through railway from Basra to Baghdad, albeit on the metre gauge, is now an accomplished fact, and with the extension of the Baghdad-Samarra line to Baiji, this being within 200 miles of Nisibin, to which point the Germans have extended the Baghdad line, it would seem that we are within measurable distance of completing a transcontinental railroad between Europe and the Far East. The metre gauge line from Basra to Baghdad will undoubtedly be converted to the standard gauge in due course and probably extended to Koweit. On the completion of the Nisibin-Mosul-Baiji section, a very valuable line of communication will result and transit to India will immeasurably be improved by means of a land journey from Europe to Basra or Koweit, thence by sea to Bombay.

General Survey.

Whilst it must be admitted that the rivers formed the first line of communication in the Mesopotamian theatre of war, it is singularly interesting to note that the commencement of the sustained offensive, which culminated in the conquest of some 114,000 square miles of the Turkish Empire in Mesopotamia, coincided with the development of railways. The first railway opened for traffic in this vast country, at least east of Baghdad, was the Sheikh Saad-Ess Sinn narrow gauge line, and whilst, as narrated in these pages, this short line was speedily dismantled on the advance of the British force beyond Kut, it must be regarded as the pioneer line of the Mesopotamian railway system of to-day. True it is that the Baghdad-Samarra line was then in existence, built by the Germans as part of their scheme of Middle East penetration, but this was an isolated length of line which only evolved into a compact system on the capture of the country in advance of Baghdad by the British Force.

The railways of Mesopotamia have been developed in a wonderful manner, considering the many difficulties experienced both in regard to the supply of permanent way material, locomotives and rolling-stock. Their construction and equipment has been a very severe tax on the resources of India; in fact, the great drain on India for both personnel and material became so serious that, in September, 1917, when the heavy demands necessitated by the development of railways in the Baghdad area were put forward, the Viceroy of India was compelled to represent to the War Office that the position on the Indian railways was extremely serious. It was further pointed out, that including 225 miles lifted from working lines, India had supplied over 1,350 miles of track to various theatres of war up to that date. Of this, Mesopotamia received 735 miles, Egypt 422, and East Africa 185 miles, whilst Mesopotamia was also supplied with the equipment and personnel to operate the railways.

Extent of Railway Network.—At the beginning of 1919, or within 27 months after the opening of the first railway, the whole of the system comprised about 1,000 track miles of line, 800 miles being main line and 200 miles in port areas, termini, crossing loops and sidings. This 25 per cent. proportion of secondary lines appears

somewhat high, but is should be remembered that the railways were all single lines and that long crossing "stations" at suitable intervals had to be introduced to facilitate traffic working. Such crossing loops are included in the siding mileage, which also takes in the 50 miles comprised in the Basra local system which serves the Magil wharves and the Makina Yard, together with the Port of Nahrumar.

Basra Light Railway.—It might be mentioned that, in addition to the Basra local system which consisted of metre gauge track connected with the Basra-Amara and Basra-Nasiriyeh lines, there was some 30 miles of decauville track in this area. This was called the Basra Light Railway (B.L.R.) and was akin to a tram road. It served all the depôts in the district, and also carried a passenger traffic, the trains being hauled both by steam and petrol driven locomotives. In fact the Basra Light Railway was a very comprehensive self-contained system, and was worked as a separate entity. Military requirements were of course given priority, but in general it might be said that it was run on a commercial basis, fares being in operation and ordinary passengers carried in addition to military stores.

Track Mileage.—Apart from the 2 ft. 6 in. gauge feeder line of 21 miles in length running from Hillah to Kifl, the whole of the railways were composed of standard gauge and metre gauge track. Seven distinct lines were in operation and the mileage of each is indicated below:—

	Length (in route miles).
Standard gauge lines—	
Baghdad-Samarra-Tekrit-Baiji line and branches ..	144
Baghdad-Feluja-Dhibban line	48
Baghdad-Hillah line	58
	250
Metre gauge lines—	
Basra-Nasiriyeh line and branches	180
Basra-Kurna-Amara line	109
Baghdad East-Kut line	109
Baghdad East-Baquba-Table Mountain-Quaritu line	130
	528
Total length (route-miles), including 21 miles 2 ft. 6 in. gauge	799

The map in Fig. 34, which shows the various railway routes, also indicates the projected extension of the Baghdad-Quaritu line through South-West Persia to Kermanshah, together with the route of the newly constructed link which completed the Basra-Baghdad through line. With the completion of these projects, and bearing in mind (1) the Kut-Baghdad line is to be dismantled, and (2) the Baghdad-Hillah line is to be converted to metre gauge on the linking-up of the track from Hillah through Samawa to Nasiriyeh, the Mesopotamian railways will comprise some 200 miles of standard gauge line (route-miles) and more than 800 route-miles of metre gauge track. A very respectable system of railway communications has therefore been built up in this Eastern theatre of war. When it is recalled that, in addition to all the other difficulties, this work has been achieved in a country of tremendous heat during the summer, and despite the hindrance caused by enormous floods, the railways of Mesopotamia must be held to form an enduring tribute to the courage and devotion to duty of those British and Indian officers and men whose untiring energy contributed so largely to the successful outcome of the operations in this area.

Conclusion.

The importance and extent of the development of communications in Mesopotamia will be appreciated from the fact that whilst, at the end of 1914, the ration strength of the expeditionary force was less than 4,000, this increased until, at the time Mosul was occupied, the total was 420,000 men. In meeting the requirements of this large force and furnishing the transportation necessary to pursue to a successful conclusion the operations in this theatre of war, the Mesopotamian railways played a great part. If the sole motive for their initiation was the desire to supplement river communications, it must be held that they more than satisfactorily performed such a function; indeed, in the offensive beyond Baghdad, and in the work of pacifying turbulent areas, it was solely by means of railway communications that operations were successfully conducted. If railways had been introduced at the very beginning of the campaign it is certain that they would have done still more; but, as explained, the exigencies of the situation and the existence of navigable rivers influenced the decision—unavoidable in the circumstances—to improve the capacity of inland water transport to the utmost. Without railways it is certain that the rapid carrying on of the offensive would have been beyond the capacity of the other lines of communications, for the advance beyond Baghdad extended the communications far more than was expected, and it was mainly on the railways that the Army depended for its maintenance.

Whilst it might seem that the through line between Basra and Baghdad should have been completed earlier, it is hoped that the section dealing with that subject will have indicated the impracticability of this under the conditions prevailing at the time. Not only was there a grave shortage of material in *all* theatres of war, and the existing through line of communication served all requirements, but the possibility of constructing the through line by the most advantageous route was out of the question until the country north-west of Nasiriyeh and south-west of Baghdad was thoroughly pacified. The decision to complete the projected Basra-Baghdad through route, it might be stated, was mainly because this would

prove of post-war value rather than the absolute necessity of such a line for the maintenance of the forces.

This survey of railway construction and development in the Far Eastern theatre of war might well be concluded by reference to General Marshall's final despatch on the operations in Mesopotamia. In the eulogy of his Army he pays full testimony to the real hard work, indomitable energy, and splendid judgment of the railway administration and to the railway personnel, who, equally with the fighting forces, worked " uncomplainingly in spite of heat, thirst, rain and discomfort " in the maintenance of the communications on which everything depends.

The railwaymen have left behind them a rich heritage in Mesopotamia. While military requirements naturally governed priority of construction and decision as to routes, the future development of the country was at all times borne in mind in concerting plans for new railways. Despite international complications, which might hinder the completion of various schemes, the result has been to leave a railway system that will prove of the greatest possible utility in the future.

RAILWAYS IN EAST AFRICA.

The success of the British Forces in this campaign during 1915 resulted in the capture of the German Central Military Railway, a metre gauge line, 712 miles long, running from Dar-es-Salaam to Ujiji, on Lake Tanganyika, and also the Usambara Railway, 220 miles in length, which was occupied and repaired as far as Tanga between May and August, 1915. To connect the latter line with the Uganda, the Voi Lake Railway, 92 miles long, was built during 1915. In addition, 48 miles of branch lines were constructed in 1916 and 1917, but were afterwards picked up. Between November, 1915, and December, 1916, the Uganda Railway in British East Africa was also under military control.

Rolling-stock captured from the Germans included 41 engines and 164 vehicles (metre gauge), and 7 engines, 1 tractor and 728 trucks (60 c.m. gauge). Rolling-stock imported by us comprised 62 engines and 674 vehicles (metre gauge), and 2 engines, 5 heavy tractors, 160 light tractors and 280 trucks (60 c.m. gauge).

From 1916 a considerable mileage of tramway lines (mostly 60 c.m.) was either repaired by us (after being taken from the enemy) or constructed. A good deal of this track has been lifted, and there are now but two lines remaining—the Lindi tramway, originally 18 miles long, which was repaired and extended by the construction of a further 67 miles, and the Mbagathi tramway, 12 miles long, constructed in 1918.

The following is a brief description of the railways in existence during 1918 :—

Voi-Tanga Military Railway.—The first is a metre gauge line running from Tanga on the coast to Moshi, and thence to Voi on

the Uganda Railway. Including two short branches, the railway is 332 miles in length, with a ruling gradient of 1 in 40. There is enough rolling-stock for one train of 10 vehicles each way daily, and for a second train between Tanga and Buiko.

Central Military Railway.—The second important line captured was the metre gauge German line running from Dar-es-Salaam to Ujiji, on Lake Tanganyika. This railway is 712 miles in length, including one short branch. The ruling gradient is 1 in 40 and the sharpest curve 5 chains in radius. Rolling-stock suffices for three trains of 15 vehicles each way daily between Dar-es-Salaam and Tabora, with an occasional train between Tabora and Kaliuwa, 70 miles to the west, on the Belgian frontier. During 1917 surveys were made for a branch to run from this line from Dodoma due south to Neu Iringa, and by the end of October, 1917, the first 26 miles had been completed, constructional difficulties then being encountered owing to serious floods.

60 c.m. Lines.—For the purpose of facilitating the transport of supplies to the British frontier and to evacuate the wounded, two 60 c.m. lines were built during 1917. The first ran from Kaliuwa to railhead, 77 miles in length, in the early part of 1918, and was being increased at the rate of 3 miles per week. The other line started 10 miles up the Lindi Creek, and in the early part of 1918 was 20 miles in length and advancing at the rate of 2 miles per week. The ruling gradient was 1 in 50. These two lines delivered 160 tons daily at railhead, and were useful for the evacuation of the sick and wounded, who were returned to the base points in the wagons.

CAPTURED RAILWAY WAGONS.

During the war the Germans utilised a large quantity of railway rolling-stock belonging to the lines of Belgium and the occupied districts of France, and it will be of interest to indicate the system under which these captured vehicles were operated. To begin with, it was part of the German policy to remove all indications of ownership from the vehicles, which were accordingly endorsed in large white letters with the inscription " Mil. Gen. Direktion, Brussel " (General Military Administration, Brussels). But for some reason, whether Teutonic thoroughness or the idea that eventually it would be necessary to restore the stock to its real owners, a large capital letter was placed beneath this inscription to

indicate the original ownership. These letters ran, for example, from " A " to " R." " A " indicated the Belgian State Railways, and from " B " to " K " various private Belgian lines, including the Nord-Belge offshoot of the Northern of France, which was indicated by " D." The French stock was lettered from " L " to " R " in the following order : Northern, Eastern, Orleans, Midi, Old State System, and Western State. Private wagons retained the name of the owners, but any inscription showing the railways on which they normally run was removed. Individual indications on coaches or wagons, such as numbers, series numbers, indications regarding the nature or use of stock, weight, loading, capacity, &c., were retained.

THE DIRECTORATE OF INLAND WATERWAYS AND DOCKS.

A description of the Organisation of the Inland Waterways and Docks Directorate, the Development of Richborough and the inauguration of the Cross-Channel Ferry and Barge Services, Dock Work at Salonica and East African Ports.

The Inland Water Transport Section of the Royal Engineers was orginally formed in December, 1914, to deal with and develop transport on the canals and waterways of northern France and Belgium. The section operated as a branch of the Directorate of Movements under the administration of the Quartermaster-General. The late Brigadier-General Holland—who, in pre-war days, was the Marine Superintendent at Holyhead (London & North Western)—was appointed Deputy Director of Inland Water Transport in France, under the general control of the Director of Railways. The rapid development of work in France, however, soon rendered it desirable for the Inland Water Transport section to be separated from the railway establishment. In October, 1915, therefore, the organisation was formed into a separate Directorate overseas.

The first recruits of the Inland Water Transport received their training at the depôt of the railway troops at Longmoor, Hants, whilst the first base from which craft were despatched to France was situated at Dover. Owing, however, to the importance of Dover as a Naval Base, it was not an ideal port for Inland Water Transport services, whilst the store formed at Ashford proved very inconvenient from a transport point of view. It was, therefore, decided that investigations should be made along the south coast for the purpose of locating a suitable port from which craft could proceed to France without touching Dover, and for the establishment of a stores depôt.

A suitable place was found at Richborough, a stretch of land between Ramsgate and Sandwich, east of the South Eastern & Chatham Railway. This site had the advantage of being on the banks of the River Stour, a tidal water of very slight fall and eminently suitable for barge traffic. Its proximity to the South Eastern & Chatham Railway also rendered it adaptable from a shipping point of view. Accordingly, the headquarters of the Inland Water Transport section were gradually transferred from Dover to Richborough, whilst the depôt for personnel was eventually located at Sandwich.

Stores Depôt.

The Inland Water Transport stores depôt at Richborough was situated in a yard originally occupied by a contractor who was engaged in making concrete blocks for Dover Harbour. The lay-out of the yard was completely remodelled, and the existing wharf extended to accommodate four barges. This wharf and yard were exclusively provided for Inland Water Transport stores and the repair, upkeep and fitting out of Inland Water Transport craft. Twenty stores buildings, each 100 by 25 ft., were erected, and so designed and situated that traffic could be unloaded direct from railway wagons and at the same time be convenient to the stores wharf for dealing with inwards or outwards barge traffic. The stores were constructed of concrete blocks with steel trusses and roofing of asbestos fibre-cement slating.

Evolution of Separate Directorate.

As previously described, a new department of the War Office was formed in September, 1916, for the purpose of co-ordinating the various branches of transportation. In this new department the Inland Water Transport branch was developed into a separate Directorate of Inland Waterways and Docks under the D.G.M.R. with responsibility covering inland water transport operations, the equipment and working of docks overseas and the supply of personnel and material for such purposes. It might incidentally be added that the Prussian Military Authorities did not establish a separate inland water transport department until March, 1917.

At the commencement of 1917 the Directorate of Inland Waterways and Docks was in a more or less embryonic state, as its constitution was still in process of formation. While provisional establishments had been authorised to cover the preliminary stage, it was quite impossible to frame the establishment on adequate lines owing to the impracticability of forecasting the growth of the work. During the year the scope of the new Directorate was extended to cover inland water transport and dock working in Egypt, Salonica and other theatres, and this required the provision of an augmehted establishment. Up to December, 1917, over 1,100 officers and nearly 30,000 men were transferred or enlisted to the new Directorate.

Meanwhile, the Richborough development scheme was put in hand. In addition, a constant stream of drafts, both officers and men, was sent to the various war theatres, whilst the building up of the canal and river fleets at home and abroad was energetically continued. The reinforcements furnished to the transportation personnel of the Expeditionary Forces might be shown by means of the following table, which indicates that over 600 officers and 8,000 men were drafted overseas from the United Kingdom during the year 1917:—

	Theatre of war.			Officers.	Other ranks.
France	..	..	..	87	5,787
Mesopotamia	..	..	..	465	1,394
Salonica	..	..	..	12	171
Mediterranean L. of C.	..	..	34	607
Egypt	..	..	..	29	94
East Africa	..	..	..	6	127
				633	8,270

The personnel sent to the M.L. of C. was mainly employed at Cherbourg and Taranto, and it might be added that the European personnel in Mesopotamia was supplemented by the recruitment of over 42,000 natives from India, Egypt, West Africa and China.

Towage of Craft.

The Inland Waterways and Docks Directorate was responsible for the towage of craft to the various theatres of war, and in order to ensure the most economical use of tug power in this connection, comprehensive arrangements had to be made. With regard to Mesopotamia, for example, the barge voyage was divided into six definite sections for relay tug purposes, the stages being Glasgow-Fowey-Gibraltar-Malta-Port Said-Aden-Muscat. The executive work in connection with the despatch of craft to Mesopotamia was performed at Glasgow, where a depôt was formed at the beginning of 1917, as the majority of new vessels were being built on the Clyde. At Muscat the other end of the tug link, the craft were taken over by the Mesopotamian Directorate.

Nearly 700 vessels were taken from this country to Mesopotamia by Inland Water Transport personnel during 1917, and whilst a few vessels were lost, the result must be regarded as reflecting the highest credit on the marine branch, particularly when it is remembered that they navigated craft, frail in the extreme, thousands of miles, in all weathers, through submarine-infested waters. This statement will be appreciated when it is observed that, generally speaking, the craft taken out to Mesopotamia comprised shallow-draught vessels, and small passenger steamboats, such as those which used to ply for hire for the L.C.C. on the Thames.

Richborough, the War Port.

The development of the Richborough Transportation Depôt has been remarkably rapid. In 1916 it was merely a small station formed for the purpose of supplying personnel and stores for inland water transport work, while it soon became a large and well-equipped seaport, 2,200 acres in extent, replete with all modern conveniences and capable of handling 30,000 tons of traffic per week.

Originally established before the inception of a separate Directorate of Inland Waterways and Docks as a depôt from which barges, acquired for service on the French waterways were equipped, manned and despatched, it was soon decided that the convenience of dealing with these matters under one control rendered it desirable to extend such functions. Accordingly, the depôt commenced to provide personnel and stores for the Directorate of Docks and the Directorate of Port Construction in France. The former was responsible for the proper control and co-ordination of dock working at the ports allotted for the use of the British Forces, whilst the latter dealt with additions to and maintenance of wharfage and dock accommodation.

Barge erection and construction.—The next step in the development of Richborough arose owing to the increasing difficulty of obtaining suitable barges to meet the needs in France, and it was therefore decided to undertake the erection of barges at Richborough. These barges were constructed at works where water and slipways were not available and forwarded in plates and angles to Richborough, where slips were constructed and the barges erected, equipped and despatched. As the shipping position became more acute, the work was extended to the complete construction of barges at Richborough, the material being supplied direct from the rolling mills. By this means alone was it possible to keep pace with the increasing demand for craft, and it necessitated the erection of workshops, power plant and a large barge-building yard, with slips and fitting-out wharves. These were laid down on the higher reaches of the River Stour, and were subsequently enlarged in order that construction of tugs, sea-plane carriers and other small craft might be undertaken for the Admiralty. The first re-erected barge was launched in January, 1917. During the year 97 keels were laid down and 92 vessels launched, whilst 619 vessels were overhauled, this figure being exclusive of minor repairs which did not put vessels out of commission for more than 24 hours.

Slipways, machine shops and power station.—Before the end of 1916 10 re-erecting slipways, complete with pneumatic riveting plant, were in operation, and by the end of 1917, 22 slips were available. The shops (fitters, smiths, carpenters and saw mill) were situated at the end of the Richborough Stores Yard, and were capable of dealing with all classes of machine repairs for the type of craft then in use. The shops were electrically driven, current being obtained from an adjoining power house, which contained two generating sets, boilers and the usual equipment. Current was distributed through sub-stations to the camp for lighting and to the new wharf for general purposes.

Personnel.—The adoption of these schemes of development necessitated the employment of skilled personnel. At the commencement, men were obtained from drafts awaiting despatch overseas, and the training and employment of these men very materially enhanced their value when finally despatched. As, however, it soon became apparent that the great expansion of the work could not be met by obtaining personnel in this way, the development of the craft construction programme coincided with the arrangement of a permanent establishment at Richborough.

Special personnel for this purpose was enlisted in the corps, but the highly-skilled trades were not largely drawn upon, although a nucleus of skilled men was engaged. The majority of the personnel consisted of totally unskilled or semi-skilled men who were trained by means of schools of instruction and gradually turned into skilled tradesmen. This resulted in a sort of "dilution upwards" and materially helped to solve the problem of man-power in relation to skilled labour, and the series of training classes indicated below proved of exceeding value :—

Course.				Class opened.
Shipbuilding	..	..	..	September 11, 1916
Marine motor drivers	..	..	..	November 20, 1916
Surveyors' assistants	..	..	..	March 8, 1917
Crane drivers	..	..	..	March 21, 1917
Divers	..	..	..	April 26, 1917
Pile driving	..	..	..	May 17, 1917

This method of intensive training was considerably developed on the expansion of inland water transport work both at home and in the various theatres of war. Many of the men so trained were drafted overseas, particularly shipwrights and motor boat drivers for the Mesopotamian campaign ; others were drafted to France for port construction and dock work, whilst skilled men were similarly provided for aerodrome and national shipyard construction in various parts of the country. At the end of 1917, nearly 1,000 men were undergoing courses, the specialities including, in addition to those previously mentioned, instruction for fitters and turners, smiths, wood machinists, carpenters, toolmakers, triggers, tinsmiths, riveters, platers, drillers, painters and plumbers.

Development of facilities.—During the year 1917 building operations at Richborough were pushed on as rapidly as possible. The engineering works were extended, shipyard facilities greatly augmented, additional shops built and equipped, the barge wharf extended, a train-ferry terminal established, and many other works executed, whilst power and light was provided for a large area. The extensive development of facilities, originally designed merely for barge construction, made it possible for the civil engineering shops to be relieved of much urgent work, and assisted them to meet the demands of the Ministry of Munitions. At Richborough, therefore, a large amount of work was subsequently performed that would otherwise have been placed in civilian shops, in connection with the maintenance of docks, wharves and canals in the various theatres of war. In fact, Richborough speedily partook of the character of a base workshop, for urgent work such as tractor and locomotive repairs which could not be carried out in the war area, owing to military operations, was performed there. It might also be mentioned that 632 side and end-tip wagons were built at Richborough, whilst nearly 10,000 vehicles were repaired.

Richborough new wharf.—The necessity of providing additional wharfage accommodation for the use of cross-Channel barges and other craft was met by the decision to construct a new wharf. There was a horse-shoe bend in the river opposite the point selected for the new wharf and in order to provide suitable facilities, it was decided to divert the river across the neck of the horse-shoe. This was effected by cutting a new channel and damming the two ends of the curved section. The water was subsequently pumped out of the old channel. which was filled with spoil dredged from the river. The work of cutting the new channel involved a total excavation of 200,000 cubic yards of material, but as, owing to the nature of the river, it gave an additional one and a-half hours workable tide at the wharf, whilst it also saved about three-quarters of a mile, it was a project well justified by the result.

The length of the wharf was 2,300 ft. and the depth of the canal below wharf level 24 ft., giving 18 ft. of water at H.W.O.S.T. and 6 ft. at L.W.O.S.T. The average clear width of the basin at the wharf was 112 ft. The wharf was built of interlocking steel piling, filled in behind from ground level to a height of 4 ft., with concrete platform walls and was provided with six electric 2-ton transporter cranes specially designed for the work, these having a range of travel of 63 ft., 44 ft. being inboard. Originally, the wharf was designed to accommodate 10 barges, but it was subsequently extended until at the conclusion of hostilities 24 berths were in operation.

Railway facilities at Richborough.—Naturally, the establishment and development of a port comprising an area of 2,200 acres required the construction of an extensive railway system, and adequate connections with the main railway serving the district. At Richborough, therefore, about 60 miles of line were laid down, the track consisting of 70-lb. F.B. rails.

The system comprises five distinct yards, whilst there is a through main line connecting these yards and giving access to the South Eastern & Chatham Railway. The military railway system leaves the South Eastern & Chatham main line at Minster B Junction, a point about 1 mile distant from Minster—the exchange station for the Margate and Ramsgate branch. Proceeding in a south-easterly direction towards the River Stour, the railway crosses the Sandwich-Ramsgate highway to Weatherlees, and continues towards the train-ferry berth.

The five yards, particulars of which are given below, were built at different periods and subsequently linked together for through working by a line 3 miles in length running from Minster B Junction to Stonar Camp :—

Name.	Wagon standage accommodation.	Use.
Weatherlees	1,150	Reception, marshalling and despatch of trains.
Train Ferry	360	Traffic for shipment by train ferry.
Saltpans	950	Traffic for cross-Channel barge service.
Richborough	325	Handling and storage of material to order or for internal work.
Salvage Transit Depôt	500	Reception, storage, sorting and despatch of battlefield salvage.
Total	3,285 wagons.	

The through line crosses the main Sandwich-Ramsgate highway on the level at three different places, and at these points hand-worked crossing gates are provided. No block-signalling system has been introduced, so the traffic is passed forward by groundsmen posted in cabins, connected with the local telephone circuit, at the entrance to the several sections. Generally, it might be said that trains are worked on the telephonic line-clear system, and whilst this arrangement might appear somewhat crude, it was found quite satisfactory, and there is no record of any accident or collision arising owing to the absence of more adequate signalling system.

Rolling-Stock.—There was naturally a very heavy internal traffic between the yards, stores, workshops, shipyards and camps, and for use in this way some 35 locomotives and 519 vehicles were provided. The wagon stock comprised low-sided and side-tip wagons, though there were some 19 ft. 6 in. flat wagons, several high-sided wagons, a few double-bolster wagons and one or two covered vans. The use made of this stock may be gauged from the fact that during August, 1918, the internal movement of material and miscellaneous stores totalled nearly 90,000 tons, ballast sand and filling accounting for 8,000 tons. The passenger stock in use comprised one inspection saloon, one first-class and two second-class four-wheeled coaches, one brake third, and 12 G.E. six-wheeled third-class coaches. These were used for the conveyance of men between the camps and the works, eight trips being run daily for this purpose, the average load on each journey being 500 passengers.

Traffic Figures.—One of the most striking features of the rapid progress of Richborough was the smooth working of railway traffic. Over 1,000,000 tons of traffic were handled over the military railways during 1917 and not a single serious accident occurred. This was an important factor in rendering practicable the constructional schemes which had to be carried through in such a short time. The Richborough railway traffic statement for 1917 is interesting as showing the great development during the year. While less than 30,000 tons was handled in " foreign " wagons and 6,000 tons in I.W.D. wagons during January, these figures increased to 100,000 and 34,000 respectively during December. Total traffic handled in " foreign " wagons during the year was 820,462, whilst 233,260 tons were moved in I.W.D. wagons.

Working.—The running of trains was facilitated by the installation of a central control at the Weatherlees crossing, this being connected with the five yard controls by a local telephone circuit. A regular service of trains was run from the South Eastern line and, on a train leaving Minster B Junction over the military line—and under the direction of a military pilotman—it was advised to the central control at Weatherlees, from which place the yard control concerned was informed.

On arrival in the inwards reception sidings at Weatherlees, the main line locomotive was uncoupled and returned light, or with empties, whilst the wagons were examined both by the military railway staff and the South Eastern & Chatham staff. The work of allocating the wagons for the various yards proceeded at the same time, and on this being completed, the train was shunted and the wagons marshalled in roads allotted to their destination. The yard controls were then advised of the traffic on hand for their respective sections, and the usual practice was for them to send a yard engine with any empties and loaded wagons on hand through to Weatherlees departure sidings, whence the locomotive, having disposed of its load, ran to the inwards sidings and picked up the traffic for the yard. This arrangement had the advantage of ensuring a steady flow of traffic to the various yards, a regular clearance of the inward reception roads and the prompt return of empty wagons to the South Eastern line. Prior to the armistice the average number of wagons handled daily in the Weatherlees yard was about 1,500.

With the exception of ammunition, all traffic for the new wharf was worked " rough " into the Saltpans yard from Weatherlees, and subsequently sorted for the 24 berths, a group of sidings accommodating 290 wagons being available for this purpose. A census of the stock taken two or three times each day furnished information for a position chart which was used by the military railway staff, which had to work on a daily shipment programme.

The new Salvage Transit Depôt at Richborough was served by a group of sidings capable of storing 500 wagons ; this yard had a special connection with the South Eastern & Chatham system at Sandwich A Junction, a point about 2 miles north of the passenger station. The loaded traffic transferred from craft was worked into these sidings, where it was off-loaded and sorted into various dumps, according to nature, and then reloaded for despatch.

The Cross-Channel Barge Service.

When the shipping position began to assume a serious aspect, it was realised that a good deal of relief might be afforded by using barges and tugs for the transport of war material to France. A special type of barge was, therefore, designed and built. This had to be of a sufficiently seaworthy construction to stand the cross-Channel passage and yet be of suitable dimensions to enter the French canals and so supplement the existing inland water transport there.

The remarkable development of this service was an outstanding feature in connection with the traffic for the British Forces on the Western Front. Apart from the actual relief to sea-going ships, the following advantages accrued on the inauguration of the cross-Channel barge service :—

(a) Dispersal of both marine and war risks into smaller units.
(b) Relief of dock congestion owing to the fact that barges could pass right through into the interior.
(c) Avoidance of double handling, as barges were discharged at inland depôts.
(d) Saving of railway carriage in France, and
(e) Comparative immunity from enemy torpedo attack owing to their shallow draught ;

and the provision of barges and additional wharf accommodation was therefore urged.

The first barge in connection with the service was towed from Richborough on December 1, 1916, and during that month 2,090 tons of traffic were transported to France, 21 barges then being in service. The shipment of war material by this service steadily increased, and in the middle of 1917 a scheme of development was planned by which the export tonnage would be 6,000 d.w. tons per day. This naturally demanded the provision of additional craft, but owing to certain difficulties the anticipated improvement was not effected. To some extent, however, this is explained by the fact that the deadweight programme originally planned was based on such traffic as railway material and ammunition, whilst the barge service was very quickly utilised to a large extent for the carriage of light supplies such as hay, aeroplanes and other light traffic which gave a very poor deadweight result, although the service rendered was quite as useful.

Growth of barge service.—The traffic conveyed across Channel by the barge service naturally increased as additional craft were placed in the service. By June, 1917, 105 barges were in commission and during that month export traffic amounted to 48,000 tons, whilst 10,000 tons of traffic, principally salvage, was imported. By the end of the year over 150 barges were in service and, during the 12 months, 500,000 tons of traffic—four-fifths passing direct to inland depôts on French waterways—was exported, and 35,000 tons imported by cross-Channel barges. The number of sailings from Richborough during 1917 was over 3,000 whilst 570 barges returned carrying loads.

A later development of the barge service was the decision to use 1,000-ton barges, and by the conclusion of hostilities 10 such barges were in service in addition to 232 other barges. The large barges were unable to proceed down the canals in France and had to be discharged in the docks, the special object of their introduction being to relieve ordinary shipping across the Channel. If the war had continued for a longer period, a very considerable proportion of traffic for the British Forces in France would have been transferred to these high-capacity barges, as the intention was to supplement the fleet until it comprised 79 units of this capacity.

In all, over 10,000 barges loaded with war material, weighing over 1,300,000 d.w. tons, were despatched from Richborough between December, 1916, and the end of 1918. The record tonnage for one day was 6,833 tons on October 1, 1918. Over 1,000,000 tons of the traffic passed direct to inland water transport depôts and thus immensely relieved the docks. Over 1,800 loaded barges were received from France between April, 1917, and the end of 1918, these craft conveying well over 150,000 tons of import traffic. The principal items exported were 750,000 tons of ammunition, 70,000 tons of supplies, 25,000 tons of R.F.C. material and 18,000 guns, carriages and limbers. The import traffic mainly comprised salvage, and material for repair purposes. It is of interest to note that, whilst over 20,000 barge trips were made across the Channel, no craft was lost as the result of enemy action, the few casualties which occurred being the result of collision or inclement weather.

Cross-Channel craft and traffic.—The following table indicates the growth of craft controlled from Richborough :—

	1916.	1917.	1918.
Tugs	26	59	67
Barges	23	161	155
Launches	3	16	22
Train ferries	—	3	4
Various craft	13	60	38
	65	299	286

In addition to cross-Channel vessels, this table includes port auxiliary craft, dredgers, &c. All the craft were designated by a letter code to facilitate reference, and were kept in repair at Richborough.

In January, 1917, the tonnage conveyed to France by cross-Channel barges averaged 1,904 per week, rising in that year to a maximum in September of 14,640 tons per week whilst in August, 1918, exports increased to 24,977 tons per week. Since the armistice. owing partly to the suspension of the exports of ammunition, the tonnage dropped considerably, the weekly average for December, 1918, being only 7,588 tons.

The general development of cross-Channel barge traffic is shown in Fig. 38, but it might here be added that the total tonnage carried to France by this service during the past two years was as follows :—

	Total tonnage.		Proportion to inland destinations.	
	1917.	1918.	1917.	1918.
January to March	33,823	180,059	32,785	138,276
April to June	106,663	264,206	95,883	170,313
July to September	173,901	311,604	156,045	208,401
October to December	135,186	207,739	117,024	154,134
Total	449,573	963,608	401,737	680,124

Other services.—It should be added that there was a certain amount of traffic sent to France by barge from other places, although this was relatively small as compared with the Richborough exports. The total traffic so exported—mainly from points on the Thames—was 130,000 tons, whilst traffic imported amounted to 40,000 tons. The Directorate of Inland Waterways and Docks also controlled barge work on the canals in the United Kingdom, the total weight of traffic moved during 1918 being 150,000 tons. The majority of this traffic was along the Forth-Clyde Canal, over which 130,000 tons of oil were transported.

Salvaged material.—The decision to return salvage to this country by means of the cross-Channel barges that would otherwise return empty or very lightly loaded was reached early in 1917, and whilst miscellaneous cargoes of this salvage arrived at Richborough during May, the transport of this traffic did not reach a substantial flow until September. In that month the Inland Waterways and Docks Directorate took over the whole of the work incidental to the unloading, sorting, storage and reloading of salvage, and by the end of 1917 the salvage problem was placed on a well organised basis with steadily increasing financial benefit to the country. During last

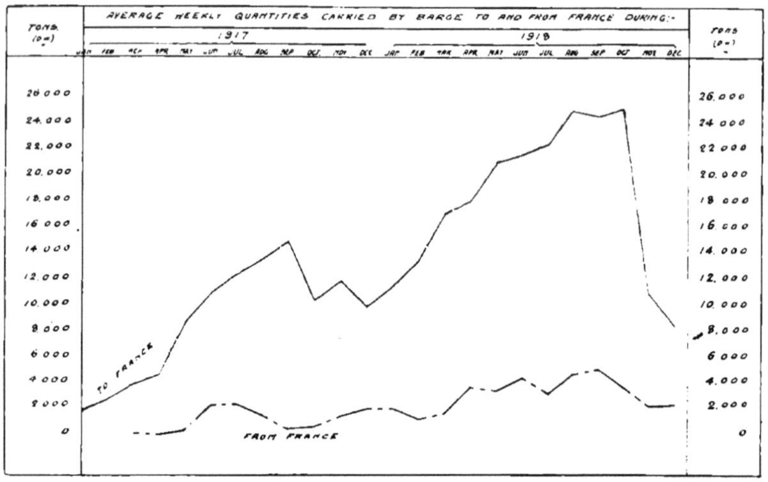

Fig. 38.— **Chart showing Traffic carried by Barge between England and France.**

year 46,642 tons of salvaged material were brought to Richborough in 700 barges, whilst nearly 40,000 tons were loaded to various inland factories and depôts. The total weight sorted and despatched by the salvage depôt was 65,000 tons, and as many as 120 wagons were forwarded in one day. The whole of the work at the depôt was performed by female labour brought in from the surrounding districts. The return traffic to the United Kingdom for the year 1918 totalled 156,086 tons, being just under three and a-half times greater than the total for 1917.

Southampton and Poole.—In June, 1918, provision was made for the evacuation of Richborough in the event of the enemy capturing the Channel ports, and the town quay at Southampton and Poole harbour were selected as suitable places from which the supply of war material could be sent by means of the barge service. The prospect of a large fleet of 1,000-ton barges also demanded the provision of additional accommodation to Richborough, and these ports were decided upon as either useful in an emergency, or suitable for the working of the big barges. The barge service at Southampton commenced in July, 1918, but utilisation of Poole was not carried into effect, although certain alterations were made to the town quay, and wharves and a railway connection with the London & South Western main line constructed.

The Cross-Channel Train-Ferry Service.

The suggestion to establish a train-ferry service between England and France was first made towards the end of 1916, when the shipping question was developing into a serious problem, owing to the enormous losses sustained by the mercantile marine as a result of enemy submarine activities. At this period also, there arose an increased demand for traffic facilities, and, whilst everything possible was done with the means at disposal, considerable delays occurred owing to the inadequacy of facilities for the handling of cargoes aggregating such a huge tonnage and also of big guns and other consignments of exceptional weight.

The necessity for additional transport facilities therefore became evident, and a scheme was submitted to the War Cabinet for the provision of a train-ferry service as an urgent war measure. To show the great utility of such facilities, a report on train-ferries as a means of transportation in other countries was prepared, and whilst it was appreciated that such services had been extremely successful on the inland waters of the United States, between Sassnitz and Trelleborg on the Baltic, and at other places, it did not follow that they would operate equally well in the Channel with its tidal range and peculiar characteristics.

Eventually, however, it was decided that the advantage of being able to rush through any particular war material direct from the works in England to the fighting forces in France without trans-shipment and consequent double handling, the ease of transportation of heavy concentrated loads such as locomotives, tanks, heavy guns, &c., and their return to England for repair, outweighed the disadvantages, and the scheme was adopted. On January 17, 1917, therefore, instructions were issued for three ferry steamers to be built, terminal ports selected and the necessary berths and other works pressed forward. At the same time arrangements were entered into for the prompt return of wagon-stock used in the service. It was evident that British rolling-stock could not indefinitely be passed into France and arrangements were made for the wagons to be returned promptly, and where possible given loads of salvage or material for repair.

Towards the end of 1917 the first trials of the train ferry were made. They proved satisfactory and led to great developments during the following year. The terminals at Dunkirk, Calais and Dieppe were completed early in 1918, and the inaugural service between Richborough and Calais was run on February 10, whilst the Southampton-Dieppe service commenced on February 22. Since that time a regular service has been maintained by three ferry steamers—and, latterly, four, an additional steamer being placed in service between Southampton and Cherbourg—and has proved of great value.

Construction of train-ferry berths.—The employment of train-ferry steamers, which furnish what amounts to a through railway connection between railways separated by sea, required the provision of special berths. These had to be arranged in connection with a well-planned series of sidings to serve the steamers, in order to afford the maximum expedition in loading and discharging traffic, and supplied with specially-designed conveniences to make an easy connection between berth and boat.

The selection of Richborough as a terminal necessitated the dredging of the entrance to a depth of 10 ft. below L.W.O.S.T., and the cutting of a new channel 200 ft. wide at the bottom. The site chosen for the berth is situated between the end of Richborough Wharf and the sea, and whilst its original distance from the sea was about 5,000 yards, this was reduced by the dredging of a new channel to 3,200 yards. A turning basin with a width of 500 ft. was provided close to the berth in which to swing the steamers (which have to enter the berth stern first), and the berth itself was dredged to a sufficient depth to accommodate the vessels at all states of the tide.

The berth is a timber jetty with arms on each side of the ship ; that on the port side is 420 ft. long and 26 ft. wide, while the arm on the starboard side is 130 ft. long and 50 ft. wide. These arms are splayed outwards towards the sea so as to facilitate the backing-in of the ship. They follow the shape of the ship as they approach the stern, but do not meet each other, since a gap has to be left for the communication bridge, which will subsequently be described. Bollards are provided for warping the vessel in and mooring her, and two bollards are also fixed on shore about 75 ft. from the stern on each side on the communication bridge. When the ship has been worked in, she fits snugly into the timber berth and lies central with the communication bridge.

A system of sidings for dealing with the train-ferry traffic was laid in close to the berth and connected to the main Richborough system by means of a short length of single line. Each set of ferry sidings accommodates a complete boat-load of inwards or outwards traffic, and two shunting engines work between the sidings and the boat. Opposite the sidings, four oil-fuel tanks were erected, each capable of storing about 525 tons of oil. A small pumping station was

built close by, and a pipe-line laid to the port side of the jetty, by which means the oil tanks on the steamer could be filled in 30 minutes.

At Southampton the natural conditions were better than at Richborough. Access to the site was good and the only dredging necessary was in a triangular area leading to the berth, accessible at all states of the tide which has a range of 13 ft. The berth was constructed on the same general lines as Richborough with certain modifications to suit the site. The long arm was arranged on the starboard side of the vessel to permit of easy access from Southampton Water ; it is 450 ft. long and 35 ft. wide, whilst the port arm is 110 ft. long and 35 ft. wide. The piles were arranged to admit of the future widening of the starboard jetty so that accommodation could easily be provided for a second boat on the opposite side of the first one. This second berth was subsequently provided in connection with the Cherbourg service, and it should be mentioned that at this berth no communication bridge had to be provided, the special construction of the steamer making the connecting link.

The land end of the communication bridge to the original berth is situated about 1,000 ft. seaward of the existing foreshore wall, the special consideration being that if the berth had been built nearer the shore, constant dredging would have been necessary to keep it free from silt. As a war measure, the intervening gap was bridged by a timber viaduct, 630 ft. long and 24 ft. wide which carries a footpath in addition to two railway tracks. The sidings were extended over the embankment and along the site of the obsolete West Quay and several small slips and yards. They are about 600 ft. long and comprise four tracks, two for outwards and two for inwards traffic. Between these sidings and Southampton West Station, two reception roads were laid in, each of these being 1,100 ft. long and able to hold a complete boat-load of traffic and main line engine. Four oil-fuel tanks were provided opposite the sidings, with pumping station and pipe line, as at Richborough, whilst water supply and electric cables for power and light were installed.

Whilst these works were proceeding at Richborough and Southampton, terminals of a somewhat similar design—certain modifications being essential to meet the conditions at each location—were being built at Dunkirk, Calais and Dieppe, and, subsequently, at Cherbourg. The works at all the French ports were carried out by military labour with the assistance of Chinese coolies. Very few of the soldiers were skilled men, and practically all the personnel employed in the constructional work had to be trained to their duties as the work progressed.

The work at the various terminals was pushed on so rapidly that by the end of 1917, when the train ferry steamers were ready for service, the construction was in a sufficiently advanced state to permit of trials being undertaken. These proved satisfactory and, as already noted, the train-ferry service soon commenced to run regularly and make its exceedingly useful contribution to the transportation effort. The routes operated are shown in Fig. 39, which also indicates barge routes.

Communication bridges.—The problem of providing a smooth and uninterrupted track between land and ship at varying tide levels was solved by the construction of a specially-designed communication bridge. The bridges at all five ports were built on the same principle and differed only as regards length, this being governed by the tidal conditions. The various spans, measured from centre to centre of bearings, were as follows :—

						Feet.
Southampton and Dieppe ..			..	..	..	120
Richborough			..	..	..	100
Dunkirk ..	..	..	..	..	..	80

Each bridge carries two railway tracks set to 11 ft. 6 in. centres, the gauge being the ordinary English standard gauge which will take both British and Continental stock. The structure was designed to clear the modified Berne or standard Continental loading gauge.

The bridges weigh anything up to 200 tons, extend from the recessed end of the berth to the shore, and consist of steel girders, the joints being given sufficient flexibility to allow the bridge to adapt

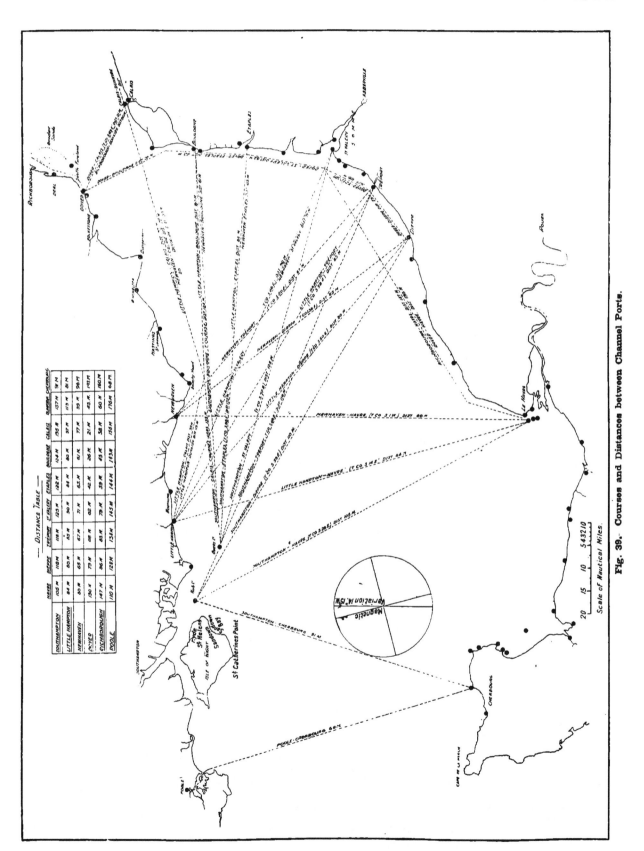

Fig. 39.- Courses and Distances between Channel Ports.

itself to a list of about 5 deg. in either direction in the steamer. The bridges are suspended from huge towers, consisting of two legs 42 ft. high and 5 ft. 6 in. square, placed 36 ft. 6 in. apart between centres. The outer ends of the bridges are supported by four steel wire ropes working on counterweights suspended in the tower legs, in which timber rubbing pieces are provided to prevent fouling.

The operating machinery comprises a winding drum revolved by an electric motor of 20 b.h.p., and this, driving through worm and spur gearing, lifts or lowers the outer end of the bridge which hinges about the pin connections on shore. By this means the rails at one end of the bridge are maintained at the same level as the rails on shore, while at the outer end rail level is adjusted to a varying rail level on the ship. Hand gearing which can easily be operated by two men is provided to meet any breakdown in the electrical machinery.

This design of communication bridge was not provided at the second train-ferry berth at Southampton, nor at Cherbourg, between which places the train-ferry transferred from the St. Lawrence River was in service. In this case, the railway tracks on the vessel could be lifted by hydraulic gear, and the connection with the shore tracks was effected by means of this elevating deck arrangement.

Ferry steamers.—The three vessels comprising the original cross-Channel ferry fleet were designed by Sir W. G. Armstrong, Whitworth & Co., Limited, Elswick, in conjunction with the I.W.D. Directorate. Two of the vessels were also built by this firm, whilst the third, owing to the urgency, was constructed by Messrs. Fairfield, of Govan, Glasgow. All three were built of mild steel in accordance with Lloyd's requirements for Channel service steamers under their special survey and official inspection. Details are given in Fig. 40.

The principal features of the vessels are as follows :—Overall length, 363 ft. 6 in. ; width, 61 ft. 6 in. ; mean draught with full load, 9 ft. 6 in. ; displacement, 3,654 tons ; cargo capacity, 850 tons ; speed, 12 knots ; cargo accommodation, 54 fully loaded 10-ton wagons or their equivalent in other stock, or as many guns, tanks, locomotives and other vehicles as could be arranged upon the available track, amounting to 1,080 ft. The total deadweight capacity, including stores, spare gear, water and oil fuel, is 960 tons.

A fourth ferry steamer was added to the fleet in 1918. Although built in this country, she was formerly in service on the St. Lawrence River for the transport of passenger and freight trains between Quebec and Levis. She is constructed of a framework of girders from bow to stern and has four funnels—two on each side. The wagon capacity is less than that of the other steamers as she has only three tracks against their four. As, however, the three tracks can be lifted by hydraulic gear within a range of 18 ft., space is provided for cargo other than rolling-stock. This vessel was employed on the Southampton-Cherbourg service, but was not found very suitable for cross-Channel work.

Working.—The control of the traffic, berthing and loading, was a responsibility of the I.W.D. Directorate at home and of the Docks Directorate in France, whilst the class of traffic to be carried was agreed upon monthly by the Director of Movements in consultation with the Director of Docks. The sidings at each of the ports were used for marshalling the wagons in accordance with the order in which they were required for transfer, and immediately the train-ferry was berthed, a complete boatload would be ready to run aboard. The usual practice at the English ports was to unload simultaneously the two outside tracks of the steamer, load them with out-going traffic, and then unload and reload the two inside lines, the actual time taken for the whole operation being about 20 minutes. At the French ports, where siding accommodation was restricted, only one track could be unloaded and reloaded at one time, and the operation was necessarily a longer one.

The method of working is as follows :—The train-ferry backs into her berth—stern end to the shore—and is moored to the staging. The communication bridge is then lowered until the ends of the girders rest upon the deck. These engage with a mooring pin bolted to the deck and thus centre bridge and boat, keep the rails in alignment and prevent the boat moving away in the event of the hawser snapping. As soon as the bridge has taken its seat on deck,

the motor and winding drums are disconnected and thereafter the bridge rises or falls with the movement of the vessel, the balance weights being so proportioned that only a few tons of the bridge-weight is borne by the boat. In practice it is usual to work within a tidal variation of 10 ft.; i.e., 5 ft. up or down. Thus, with the bridge 120 ft. long, there might be a down grade of 1 in 24 from ship to shore at high water or an up grade of 1 in 24 at low water. To safeguard the movement of traffic, special signalling arrangements are in operation. After the bridge has taken up its correct bearing on the steamer, a sequence of signalling operations follows before any traffic is moved across the bridge, and when the bridge is raised, it is mechanically impossible to run traffic on to the bridge.

The train-ferries have been especially useful in regard to the transfer into the war area of heavy siege guns on their own mountings, as they have carried these intact and avoided the previous necessity of dismantling on this side and re-erecting in France. On May 26, 1918, for example, two 14-in. guns on railway mountings, each weighing 296 tons and measuring 87 ft. over-all length, were taken over and safely unloaded at Calais. Owing to the great weight involved, it was found impossible to load the guns complete at Richborough, but the railway mountings were put on board at that port, and the guns subsequently placed in position at Chatham. A third gun of similar type and two heavy locomotives were unloaded at Calais on September 23, 1918, in the presence of M. Poincare, President of the French Republic, whilst a similar gun was off-loaded carried across the Channel during October.

The following details of special traffic conveyed by means of the train-ferries will be of interest :—

Description.	Richborough—Calais.		Southampton—Dieppe.		Total.
	Forwarded.	Received.	Forwarded.	Received.	Forwarded and received.
	No.	No.	No.	No.	No.
Armoured cars	3	—	—	—	3
Guns, &c.	28	2	8	6	44
Locomotives and tenders (standard gauge) ..	164	14	8	9	195
Locomotives—Decauville (60 cm. gauge) ..	70	113	—	—	183
Lorries and cars	39	1	602	578	1,220
Tanks	658	—	206	—	864
Wagons for retention in France	7,142	—	3,670	—	10,812

It might also be added that, in the transport of heavy cargo such as tanks, guns, motors, ammunition, &c., the three train-ferries were expected to release six 8,000-ton ocean-going steamers hitherto employed exclusively on this traffic, whilst also effecting an enormous economy in the avoidance of double transhipment.

The train-ferry service commenced in February, 1918, and during that month handled 5,000 tons of traffic. The traffic rapidly increased, and four months later 28,000 tons were exported and 12,000 tons imported. The total dealt with by means of the train-ferry to the end of 1918 was 240,000 tons, 220,000 tons being export traffic. The chart in Fig. 41 indicates the monthly movement of traffic, and it might be added that the working of the train-ferries, despite the abnormal conditions and difficulties which have prevailed, has been satisfactory in every way. It is of interest as justifying this remark to quote from Sir Douglas Haig's despatch, dated January 7, 1919, in which he said :—

" During the period following the great defensive battles up to the final triumph of the Allied cause, the Channel ferry has proved of inestimable value."

One of the outstanding features of the working of train-ferries is the ease and rapidity with which they are loaded and unloaded, which averages less than 30 minutes per trip—the average during November last being 18 minutes. As a war measure, the service has been justified by the results and, apart from the maintenance

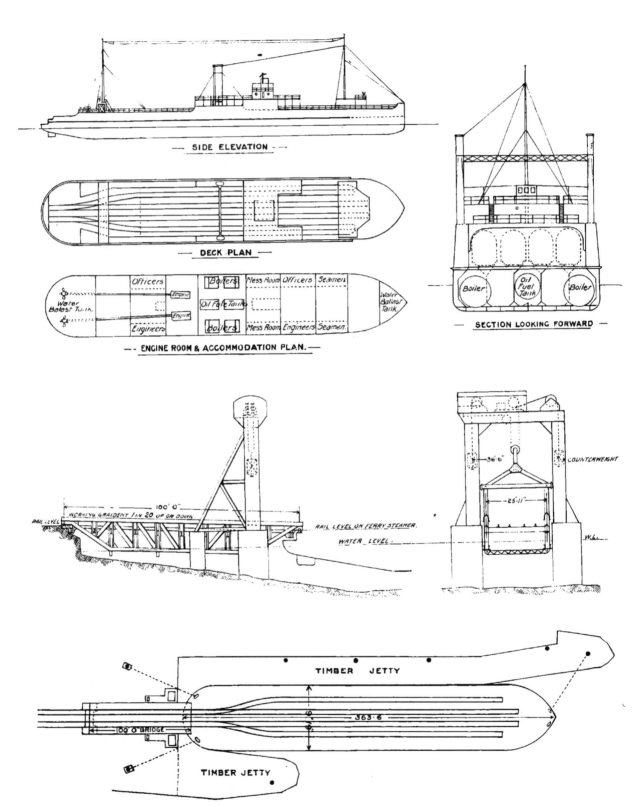

— SIDE ELEVATION —

— DECK PLAN —

— ENGINE ROOM & ACCOMMODATION PLAN. —

— SECTION LOOKING FORWARD —

Fig. 40.—Details of Train Ferry, Loading Bridge, Jetty and Railway Deck.

of a rapid and efficient means of transportation, has very considerably relieved shipping and port working. Under normal conditions of free and unrestricted working, when it would be possible to run a regular " shuttle " service and thus secure the maximum

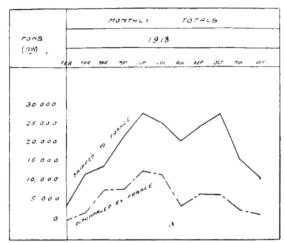

Fig. 41.—Chart showing Stores Shipped to France and Salvage, &c., Received from France on Train-Ferries.

economy in operation, there should be great scope for the development of train-ferries for cross Channel work, which would be of the greatest commercial value, pending the completion of the projected Channel Tunnel.

General Survey.

Within the limits of reasonable space it is impossible to do more than briefly sketch the manner in which this new Directorate helped the transportation effort. It might, however, here be appropriate to summarise the work actually performed, whilst mentioning certain special activities.

Apart altogether from the enormous development of Richborough, traffic passing through which is shown at Fig. 42, the Directorate did much valuable work in connection with the building of aerodromes and national shipyards, whilst it relieved the civilian establishments very considerably after the inauguration of shipbuilding yards and shops at the war port. Richborough, in fact, became a gigantic workshop as well as an important transportation depôt. Its workshops and shipyards cover an area of 47 acres, 4½ acres being under cover. There are 26 slipways in operation, and the good use made of these facilities will be marked from the fact that since the beginning of 1917, 142 barges have been re-erected, and five barges, one tug and 32 seaplane lighters have been built, whilst hundreds of vessels have been overhauled during the period. Other interesting points are that the length of the wharf is 2,180 ft., with 20 berths, and 13 electric gantry cranes and 12 electric transporters are in operation.

The Inland Waterways and Docks Directorate, moreover, performed much useful work in designing special plant to meet the peculiar conditions obtaining in the various theatres—and, especially with regard to cranes, filtration plants, &c.

Cranes.—It was early realised that successful working depended to a great extent on the provision of adequate craneage facilities wherever ships or barges had to be discharged. There was a great scarcity of available cranes in the country, and when the supply of

secondhand cranes became exhausted special consideration had to be given to the question. Cranemakers' works being fully occupied, quick delivery was almost impossible, and it was therefore decided to design and construct a standard crane. The various parts were manufactured wherever facilities offered and were assembled together and tested at Richborough, and up to the end of April, 1918, 200 cranes were supplied to various quarters by the new Directorate.

A special feature of the design of the Inland Waterways and Docks standard crane is its ability to be used as a locomotive, fixed, floating or gantry crane without alteration to the machinery, the jib and balance weight only being altered to suit the location and duty to be performed. When the crane is required for dock use it can be mounted on a barge or. gantry, and is capable of a 10-ton lift at 20 ft. radius, as 5 tons at 39 ft. radius or lighter loads at greater radii. Steam was adopted as a motive power in order to render the crane self-contained and independent of local power. The diagram in Fig. 43 shows a few applications of the I.W.D. standard crane which has been supplied to many departments outside the Directorate, and, quite recently, to the American Army for use in France.

Craft.—The enormous development of river craft in the various theatres of war will be appreciated from the fact that the number of vessels in service increased from 1,172 at the end of 1916 to 2,346 at the end of 1917, and subsequently rose to 3,113 before the conclusion of hostilities. These figures are exclusive of craft controlled or hired by the Government, which in 1918 were numbered in the thousands. Fig. 43 indicates the general increases in the fleets both at home and overseas. Such a great advance was not achieved without considerable difficulty. Not only was there much trouble in getting craft built by civilian workshops, which were all extremely busy on work for the Ministry of Munitions, but as in many cases specially designed craft were essential this intensified the problem of quick supply.

Personnel.—As indicating the extensive development of this Directorate, the following table showing the growth of personnel

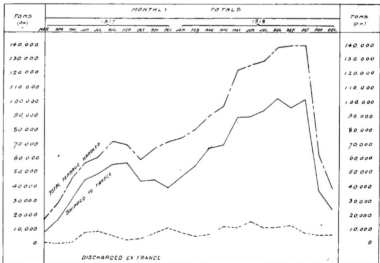

Fig. 42.—Chart showing Traffic Handled at Richborough.

during the three years is of interest. Officers and other ranks have been grouped together to facilitate reference :—

		1916.	1917.	1918.
Home	.. ..	12,247	27,232	17,538
France	..	3,533	9,073	11,166
Mesopotamia	..	1,501	2,950	2,940
Salonica	..	—	278	384
Egypt	..	—	119	410
M.L.O.C.	..	—	564	714
East Africa	..	—	133	308
		17,281	40,349	33,460

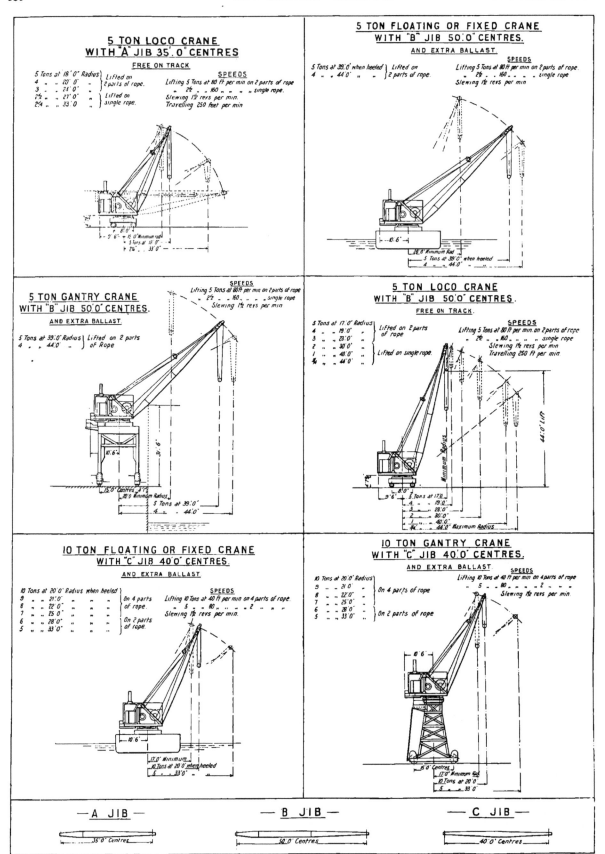

Fig. 43.—Some Applications of the Standard Steam Crane.

Conclusion.

From this brief survey it will be seen that the Directorate of Inland Waterways and Docks played a great part in the extensive development of communications which, it must be admitted, had a great influence on the successful conclusion of hostilities. The most effective working of the various transport agents, and

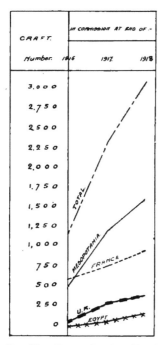

Fig. 44.—Chart showing Total Number of Craft in Commission in various Theatres of War in Yearly Periods.

their successful co-ordination is obviously a matter calling for the most complex organisation and for the specialised devolution of responsibility. It was by realising this in the fullest sense, and by the creation of a separate Directorate to deal exclusively with matters relating to docks and waterways, that the Directorate of Movements and Railways achieved great success in this sphere.

Salonica.

Compared with the other theatres of war, the functions of the Inland Waterways and Docks Directorate in the Macedonian campaign were relatively small. There was no river transport, and the whole of the work performed was that appertaining to a Docks Directorate.

Until the middle of 1917 the work of discharging ships at Salonica was in the hands of a P.N.T.O. and staff, but, following Sir Francis Dent's investigation of the transportation situation in this theatre of war, it was decided that the port handling work should be transferred to a Director of Docks, who would have control over discharge from ship to quay, clearance from quay and loading into truck. Lieut.-Colonel J. B. Parkhouse was appointed Director of Docks, and, accompanied by a staff of technical officers and men, arrived in Salonica during July, 1917.

During the period of Inland Water Transport control, almost one million tons of traffic was handled at Salonica, Stavros, Itea and Dedeagatch, 90 per cent. of this total being dealt with at Salonica, the principal base. The majority of the traffic was naturally imported, the exports amounting to less than 100,000 tons. The quantity of inwards traffic handled increased from 83,000 tons during the quarter ending September, 1917, to 150,000 tons twelve months later. The heaviest quarter was June, 1918, when 172,000 tons were handled. At the end of 1918 the Inland Water Transport personnel in Macedonia comprised about 400 officers and other ranks.

East Africa.

There was very little inland water transport work in connection with the East African operations, and the small amount that was done on the lakes was organised and conducted by the Marine Department of the Government of Uganda.

In September, 1917, however, it was decided that there should be considerable development of coastal shipping, and a more definite control of port work in this theatre of war, and it was decided that an Inland Water Transport section should be despatched from this country to assume control and development of dock work, landing facilities, &c., at the East African ports. Four officers and eight N.C.O.'s sailed during the month, whilst a further draft was despatched before the end of 1917 to bring the strength to 6 officers and 127 other ranks.

Early in 1918 this section established itself and took over all piers, cranes and loading facilities; stevedoring ex ship; clearing lighters on shore and the checking of all military stores. In addition, it assumed responsibility for all transport on the river between Lindi and Mingoyo, and commenced to develop the various ports.

By the end of 1918 the establishment had been augmented to 37 officers and 271 other ranks, and valuable work was done at the ports of Dar-es-Salaam, Lindi, Mozambique, Kilindini, Quilimane and Port Amelia. During the quarter ending June, 1918, the traffic handled amounted to 130,000 tons, 82,000 imports and 48,000 exports. In the following quarter 250,000 tons were handled, whilst in the last quarter of 1918 the traffic dropped to 225,000 tons. Of the 600,000 handled Dar-es-Salaam and Port Amelia accounted for 400,000 tons, the former place being the principal traffic point with 300,000 tons, or 50 per cent. of the total traffic handled up to the end of the year.

DESCRIPTION OF FERRY STEAMERS.

The three original ferry steamers were provided with propelling machinery consisting of triple-expansion engines, supplied with steam at 180 lb. pressure by four single-ended boilers, and fitted with Howden's forced draught arrangement and oil-firing appliances. The boilers are arranged in pairs on each side of the vessel, with two oil-fuel tanks between them on the centre line of the ship. These tanks have a total capacity of about 80 tons at 38 cubic ft per ton. The vessels are provided with two funnels, one on each side of the vessel, and are fitted with twin screws.

There is a single deck on which rails are laid and near the stern this deck is cut away square to provide room for the seatings on which the ship end of the communication bridge rests. The main bridge is situated amidships and carries chart and wireless rooms, together with captain's quarters, the captain's bridge and wheelhouse being situated above. The wheelhouse contains steam steering gear, telemotor control standard, wheel and compass, and is fitted with a searchlight. A docking bridge is also provided aft in order to control the transfer of traffic. This bridge, as well as the captain's bridge, is fitted with telegraphs, control standard and other apparatus. Two steam capstans are installed forward and two aft for mooring the vessel, and in case of need, for assisting wagons on and off the boat; each is capable of exerting a pull of 20 tons.

Accommodation is provided below deck for officers, engineers and crew, the side structure on deck being utilised for companion ways, cooking galley, &c. The personnel on each vessel comprises a captain, three executive officers, four engineer officers, one wireless operator, and about 37 petty officers, gunners and men. Four 12-pounder guns are provided on each vessel, whilst various anti-submarine devices are carried. Magazines are arranged below the water line and are fitted with trunks and ammunition hoists.

INLAND WATERWAYS AND DOCKS OVERSEAS.

A Review of the Development and Work of the Directorate of Inland Waterways and Docks in Mesopotamia, France and Egypt.

The description in the previous pages of the special activities at home of the Directorate of Inland Waterways and Docks leads the way to a general review of the development of inland waterways and docks overseas.

Apart from France, Mesopotamia and Egypt, it might be said that there was little or no river transport performed, and that the functions of the Directorate were confined to handling work at docks. In Mesopotamia, however, and to a lesser degree, in France and Egypt, inland water transport work was of the highest importance ; indeed, in Mesopotamia, the rivers were the only highroads for supplies until the campaign was well advanced. In the Far Eastern theatre, therefore, the rivers always formed the principal means of communication, whilst in France and Egypt they immensely relieved the railways and roads, and so contributed extensively to the success of the transportation effort.

Mesopotamia.

It was in the Far Eastern theatre of war that the Inland Waterways and Docks Directorate performed its greatest work. Whilst railways were eventually developed on an extensive scale, river transport was always the governing factor and was required for the movement of every single ton of supplies between Basra and Baghdad. Although a through railway route is now in process of completion, there was throughout the campaign a gap in the railway connection between Basra and the advanced base (and subsequently general headquarters) and the necessity for careful arrangement and extensive development of the river service will, therefore, be appreciated.

Commencement of Inland Waterways and Docks Control.—Subsequent to the surrender of General Townshend and the fall of Kut-el-Amara, the British forces in Mesopotamia were re-organised and, as strong reinforcements were being provided in view of renewed operations then being planned under General Maude, consideration was given to the problem of improving the river service from the British base at Basra to the advanced base, then at Sheikh Saad. It was about this time that the General Staff decided to send out an experienced officer to investigate the transport situation and, very soon after his arrival, it was decided to transfer the whole organisation and working of river transport in that theatre to the I.W.D. Directorate with Colonel Grey as D.I.W.T. at Basra.

Craft Requirements.—On being given full charge, as from September 4, 1916, Colonel Grey's first business was to investigate the general position, and he subsequently cabled full information as to the types of craft most suitable for work on the Tigris, together with an estimate of the additional craft requirements. Prompt attention was given to this report. Over 100 firms in England were approached with a view to ascertaining what craft could be despatched to meet immediate needs on the Tigris, and all those in any way suitable were inspected and despatched, the fact having to be kept in mind that the vessels had to go out under their own steam. By the end of 1916, moreover, the necessity for increasing the floating medical accommodation was met by the placing of orders for a large fleet of hospital vessels, provision being made for over 5,000 cots. Inquiries were meanwhile made regarding river vessels on the Nile and Niger, as well as in South America, Ceylon and Canada, and, from every possible source, craft were secured to augment the fleet and put river transport in Mesopotamia on a sound working basis.

The necessity of wholesale alterations to the majority of the craft sent to Mesopotamia after their arrival in that theatre in order to enable them properly to navigate the tortuous Tigris impelled the shipment of personnel and material for repair work.

By the end of September, 1916, over 7,000 tons of stores, consisting of complete workshops for carpenters, platers, fitters, &c., general engineering stores, cranes, heavy timber for wharves, &c., were despatched. Arrangements were also made for the despatch from Calcutta of the ss. *Abydos*, which was fitted up as a complete floating workshop. This vessel arrived at Basra during November, 1916.

In order to meet the additional demands for craft and material, a conference was held in London between representatives of the I.W.T. and some of the largest shipbuilding and navigating firms in India. As a result the resources of that country were consolidated to assist in the programme. The effect was to create (under the Indian Government) a Rivercraft Board to act in conjunction with the Indian Railway Board in the establishment of a subsidiary base at Karachi for craft sent from home and building in India.

Workshops and Depôts.—One of the most urgent aspects of the situation was the necessity for workshops to deal with the running repairs of vessels, and a site for this purpose was selected by Colonel Grey at Magil, 4 miles above Basra. Rapid developments followed the arrival of the material sent from England, and by February, 1917, the repair shops at Magil were doing excellent work, 56 barges being repaired there during the second week in that month. A floating landing stage was also provided. Bases and depôts were speedily established by the I.W.T. at Ashar, Kurna, Esra's Tomb and Nasiriyeh, where the necessary workshops and living accommodation were built by the personnel of the Directorate.

Developments in Mesopotamia.—Great strides were made in Mesopotamia during the latter part of 1916 and the early part of 1917. At Magil, near Basra, docks, wharves, warehouses, jetties and workshops were commenced, and the foundations laid for what has now become quite a modern port, replete with berths for ocean vessels and electrical handling equipment. The shallow stream of the Tigris was always a difficulty, and in order to maintain the deepest draught possible an efficient dredging service was commenced to clear the recurring formation of shoals of sand during the period of high levels. Surveys of the river were also put in hand and a system of daily charting was instituted, while pilots were put through an intensive course of training to prepare them for the fullest use during forthcoming operations.

The arrival of skilled and unskilled labour, recruited in India, Egypt, West Africa, China and elsewhere, helped materially to facilitate transport developments, and by the end of October, 1916, the traffic capacity of the waterways had so improved that the G.O.C. Mesopotamian Forces cabled to the following effect : " Owing to the improved state of river transport, I am able to send an increasing number of drafts to the front. Can you accelerate the despatch of men ? " The actual improvement will be appreciated by the fact that, whilst in July, 1916, only 222 tons daily were being conveyed up the Tigris, this figure was increased to 680 tons daily during October, and 1,000 tons daily by the end of the following month, whilst during the first month of 1917 the traffic up river had increased by 1,000 per cent. as compared with the previous July.

The Development of Basra.—Basra was the key to the whole situation. For purposes of administration it is bounded in the south by Suraji and in the north by Nahrumar, an expanse of river some 21 miles in length. Until the opening of the campaign in Mesopotamia, the river frontage, in common with the entire area subsequently occupied by Basra Base, consisted of swamp, date-palm groves and desert, subject to inundation and intersected by innumerable creeks, and it immediately became evident that the first requirement was the reclamation of certain areas on the river front. Whilst at that time the port was merely a river anchorage, where ships discharged to native craft, the limited personnel and material then available did not allow of much improvement being effected in the method of discharging, the whole of the resources being engaged in the reclamation and bunding of the Basra area, the construction of roads and other important undertakings.

In the early days of the campaign the force to be maintained in the country was small and a relatively low tonnage of shipping sufficed to supply the requirements. Whilst, therefore, it was apparent that transports suffered considerable delays, the situation

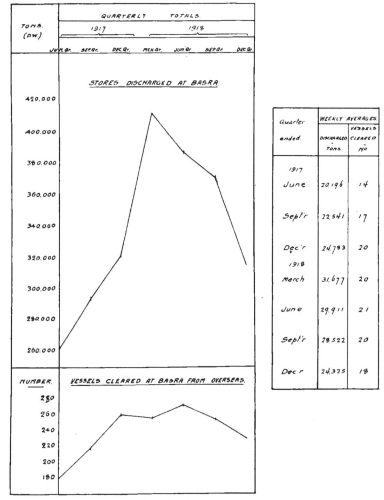

Fig. 45.—Traffic Handled at the Port of Basra, and Vessels Cleared.

was one in which port development had to be subordinated to the urgency of local and up-river undertakings more intimately connected with the immediate prosecution of the campaign. Until the middle of 1916, port development was a negligible quantity, though craft discharging jetties were erected on the river front to serve the depôts which had somewhat fortuitously developed there. Following the battle of Ctesiphon and the investment of Kut, however, the urgent necessity for satisfactory port arrangements came prominently under notice, as, with the very large accession of force following those events, it became apparent that a considerable increase in shipping would be required, and that the facilities at Basra must be developed on proper lines.

The problem was first taken in hand by Sir George Buchanan, who had made a survey of the situation at the request of the Indian Government towards the end of 1915. . Considerable improvement followed the arrangement of a definite form of organisation for the performance of the various phases of work. For example, by the end of 1916 the capacity for discharging ships had increased by 20 per cent., whilst the long delays formerly sustained by vessels were greatly reduced.

On the I.W.T. assuming control, considerable re-organisation took place, the result being to form a Docks Directorate (as at Salonica) with control of quays and the area immediately behind them, together with the regulation and distribution of all traffic passing over the quays. The placing of these functions into the hands of one department naturally expedited the discharge of vessels and utilised to the maximum the quay frontage facilities.

The following figures will afford some idea of the improvement effected in port working :—

Six months ending—	Weight discharged at Basra. Tons.
December, 1916	330,484
June, 1917 ..	529,879
December, 1917	620,263
June, 1918 ..	814,447
December, 1918	687,010
	2,982,083

The port working always suffered to some extent owing to the bunching of ships, and although efforts were made to avoid this as far as possible, the exigencies of war prevented the application of a complete remedy. The general improvement in the rate of discharge will more clearly be appreciated from the fact that whilst less than 40,000 tons were discharged during July, 1916, more than 80,000 tons were being cleared by the end of that year. By March, 1917, nearly 100,000 tons of traffic were being discharged monthly, this figure increasing to more than 160,000 twelve months later, and thereafter until the conclusion of hostilities fluctuating in the neighbourhood of 150,000 tons. The arrangement of a more effective system of handling obviously had a beneficial effect on the shipping position, and whereas, during July, 1916, the average detention of store ships at Basra was 46 days, this was reduced in 1918 to 6·2 days on an average. The development of Basra is shown in Fig. 28.

Ocean Wharves.—The first wharf to be constructed at Basra was completed in October, 1916, a second during April, 1917, and three more by the end of that year. In addition, three other wharves were under construction, whilst a further wharf, used for the accommodation of river vessels, was also available for ocean vessels.

The necessity of extending the wharfage accommodation impelled the development of Nahrumar, near Basra, as a further outlet for the discharge of ocean vessels, and arrangements were made to construct a subsidiary port consisting of six ocean wharves. The first, which was 353 ft. long and 34 ft. deep, was completed during November, 1917, and two others were ready by the end of the year. Additionally, the areas behind the wharves were protected from floods, sites for depôts cleared and a system of railway sidings introduced to connect the wharves and depôts with the concentration yard at Makina. The equipment of the port included three shunting engines, 200 port wagons and electric wharf cranes.

In reviewing the progress of Basra up to the end of 1917, it should be borne in mind that construction and other work was carried out under conditions of extreme difficulty. Development was constantly hindered by a rapidly increasing volume of traffic and an inadequate supply of material, whilst progress was constantly hindered by the great climatic difficulties. Much, however, was accomplished in the way of clearing and reclaiming the hinterland of the foreshore, but it was not until after the decisive battle of Sanna-i-yat at the end of February, 1917, and the big drive along the Tigris in which Baghdad was captured, that the cessation of urgent undertakings associated with operations in the forward areas afforded opportunity for developing the port. The wonderful results achieved in a comparatively short time will indicate the assiduity of those responsible for these developments. Whereas, in July, 1916, less than 40,000 tons (deadweight) were discharged at Basra, this increased to well over 112,000 tons monthly by the end of 1917. As the handling figures improved, so the vessels turned round more rapidly—a matter of great importance in view of the shortage of shipping. Fig. 45 shows traffic handled at Basra.

By the end of 1918 Basra had been developed into an up-to-date port. The unloading capacity had increased to 6,000 tons per day, and 12 ocean-going vessels could be berthed at permanent berths, 8 of which were fitted with electric cranes. As General Marshall well says in his final despatch : " The port has been planned so as to be capable of further extensions on the most modern commercial lines, and should prove a considerable asset to the future trade of the country." The wharves are equipped with first-class mechanical appliances, gantry cranes (50 at Basra), elevator conveyors, gravity runways, and so forth, whilst an extensive dockyard, several slipways and marine workshops with power-driven machinery have been constructed and equipped. From July 29, 1917, to March 29, 1919, the total weight discharged from sea transports at Basra exceeded 2,245,000 tons, whilst more than 1,600 sea-going vessels were berthed and unloaded. The number of men employed at the port was about 1,500 on the average.

River Conservancy.—Very careful attention had at all times to be paid to measures designed to improve river communication, owing to the many difficulties in the way of navigation. A comprehensive system of pilotage and buoyage was put into operation and this had a very good effect in reducing the number of craft which grounded.

The conservancy of the river in so far as the marking of fairway by buoys and the erection of transit marks on shore were concerned, was performed by experienced I.W.T. officers. Stationed on various reaches of the river, which are shallow and very unreliable, they made daily surveys and reported to Basra the result of their investigations. This enabled the draught of steamers and barges to be increased or reduced in accordance with the prevailing conditions, and facilitated the carrying of the maximum capacity with safety.

Bandalling.—During the low water season of 1917 a system of bandalling was introduced in the shallow reaches beyond Kut. This is a process of river training adopted extensively on Indian rivers. The best channel in a particular reach is selected by observation and a temporary wall of male bamboos and matting is erected in such a position as to guide the main flow of the river into the fairway which it is desired to keep open. The work can only be carried out on a falling river, but as it often enables a channel to be deepened as much as 18 in. to 20 in. in 24 hours it is of decided assistance on difficult sections of the waterway.

The Narrows.—Navigating difficulties were most marked in the stretch of river called the Narrows, which extends for a length of 28 miles from Ezra's Tomb to Qualet Saleh, where navigation becomes very difficult owing to the narrow and tortuous nature of the fairway. Navigation over this particular section proved so difficult that it had to be suspended during the night, and many attempts were made to improve the channel to enable transport to be conducted throughout the day. This, however, met with little success, and it was not until an independent system of control was instituted in the Narrows, and the channel illuminated by electric light, that navigation could be carried on continuously by all craft.

Improved Navigating Conditions.—Between June and November, 1917, much was done in the direction of river conservancy to improve navigating conditions. The Shujar Bund, which was wrecked by the Turks prior to their retreat, was repaired, and water from the Chahala Canal was deflected to the Tigris by the sinking of a hulk of

a steamer, this forming a groyne for a distance of 150 ft. The repair of the Shujar Bund was an extensive operation, and involved the excavation of 15,000 cubic metres of soil, the filling in of 44,000 cubic metres, and the facing of the Bund with 25,000 sandbags.

In order further to swell the river during the low level period the Majar Kebir was partially closed, and this had the effect of considerably improving navigating conditions. The flow of water in the treacherous " Narrows " was also increased, this greatly assisting navigation by permitting larger steamers to be employed between Kurna and Basra. The Turks themselves materially, though unintentionally, assisted navigating conditions on the Tigris when they cut the Saklawiah Bund in March, 1917, as this let a large quantity of water from the Euphrates into the Tigris below Baghdad, and thus raised the river level in the Tigris.

The net results of the extensive river conservancy work resulted in the maintenance during 1918 of a level sufficient to permit vessels with a draught of 5 ft. to ply between Basra and Baghdad. The work involved the placing in position of 557 buoys and the marking of 112 crossings, and an inspection at the end of 1917 disclosed that this work had been so well done that not a single vessel was aground.

Bridges over the Tigris.—A very great deal of important constructional work was performed by the Directorate of the Inland Waterways and Docks in Mesopotamia. The whole of the river front from Basra to beyond Baghdad was very fully equipped with jetties and wharves to meet the fullest possible requirements of the fleet, whilst workshops, hospitals and many other necessary establishments were provided. Of special interest in this connection was the construction of two bridges over the Tigris, one at Amara and the other at Baghdad.

The road bridge over the Tigris at Amara was opened on August 15, 1917. It is 750 ft. long and 20 ft. broad, and consists of a pile bridge with a floating section 270 ft. long and 2 girder ramps, each 62 ft. long, connecting the pile portion of the bridge with the floating section. The bridge, which is able to carry a weight of 8½ tons travelling at 15 miles per hour, can be closed in 2½ minutes. It replaced an old Turkish bridge of inadequate design and capacity. The second construction was completed towards the end of 1918, and comprises a floating bridge across the Tigris connecting the two parts of the city of Baghdad. The bridge, which is named after the late Lieut.-General Sir Stanley Maude, is 1,159 ft. long between abutments, and provides a roadway 9 ft. 6 in. wide and two footpaths each 3 ft. 6 in. wide. There is an opening portion of 260 ft. operated as a single leaf by power driven winding-gear, and a vessel can be passed there and the bridge laid again for road traffic in four minutes.

River Traffic and Craft.—The development of river transport was very rapid. In November, 1916, the total number of craft in service was 443 (exclusive of native craft), whilst the freight carried weekly amounted to 12,000 tons as compared with less than 5,000 tons weekly during the previous month. At that time the average distance cargo carried was 160 miles.

By February, 1917, the number of craft in commission had increased to 663, whilst the troop steamers had been made more comfortable by the fitting of awnings and side curtains to afford protection from the sun. The personnel employed on Inland Water Transport work also increased—from 7,000 in September, 1916, to 21,000 in January, 1917. Naturally, this assisted in the greater development of river transport. During the week ending February 10, 1917, the daily average weight conveyed was 2,400 tons, or an increase of 1,000 per cent., as compared with the 222 tons for the week ending July 20, 1916.

When Baghdad became a possible objective it was found essential to estimate the ultimate weekly tonnage requirements, and it was decided that this would be equal to 5 million river ton-miles, the figure being based on a river head near Baghdad. During March, 1917, the ton-miles increased to 4½ millions, a very large increase over previous periods, whilst the average haul was 230 miles, the advanced river head at that time being situated 453 miles from Basra. Two months later the traffic carried by river measured 6½ million ton-miles, the average length of haul being 254 miles, but in June and July the ton mileage rapidly declined to the neighbourhood of 4 millions, this reduction being largely due to the fall of the river, and also to a diminution in the tonnage awaiting transportation.

The wonderful improvement in river transport during 1917 will be evidenced from the fact that the late General Maude, in his despatch dated October 15, 1917, referring to the operations during the six months ending September 30, made some very gratifying remarks on the work in Mesopotamia. " Our communications," he said, " by water and by land, have been thoroughly overhauled to meet the new situation ; additional ships and barges have been placed on the river, and our railway system has been developed as rapidly as existing conditions have permitted. The ever-increasing needs of this Army have rendered expansions as regards port facilities at Basra necessary, and this has been successfully met by the opening of a subsidiary port in its vicinity, this being further developed as the result of the recommendations of a Committee assembled to report on the matter."

" The abnormally low river during the flood season gave rise to some anxiety that this might be followed by correspondingly low river during the summer months, and though the river did not fall beyond its lowest record, it reached as low as it had touched within reasonable recollection. The work of the I.W.T. was, however, from June onwards one of considerable difficulty, and it was due to the skill and ingenuity of the personnel of the I.W.T., and to the admirable buoying of the channels, that the number of serious groundings was almost negligible, and that the service of maintenance in front of the base was carried on unimpaired."

Following the occupation of Baghdad temporary workshops for I.W.T. purposes were established at Baghdad and a landing stage constructed near the arsenal for the handling of heavy guns. The mahela fleet under the protection of an armed launch moved further up stream in order to take part in the forward operations beyond Baghdad, whilst special efforts were made by the I.W.T. to deal with transportation around Baghdad. In May, 1917, except for the Baghdad-Samarra Railway, which was short of locomotives and rolling-stock, there was no railway communication at all and special tugs and barges were therefore earmarked for the transport of ammunition in case of sudden emergency. These were always in readiness at Baghdad, the arrangements being such that 500 tons

daily could be transported by water to a point 110 miles beyond Baghdad if occasion required. Early in 1918 it was reported that no further river craft would be required, as those in commission, together with those on order, would meet all necessities, assuming that no large increase in the Mesopotamian Forces were made. During the period in which the I.W.T. had performed the work of transportation on the Mesopotamian rivers the traffic figures had increased appreciably, 464,000 tons of freight, with a ton-mileage of 91,000,000, now being handled in a quarter (March, 1918) as compared with 120,000 tons, and the ton-mileage of 20,000,000 for the corresponding period during the previous year. The wide disparity between the increase in tonnage and ton-mileage is, of course, due to the greatly extended length of haul. The following table will indicate the general growth of traffic, whilst Fig. 46 shows the development of the fleet :—

STATEMENT OF TRAFFIC DEALT WITH ON MESOPOTAMIAN RIVERS, YEARS 1917 AND 1918.

Half-year ended—	Personnel (Troops, Camp followers, &c.)	Animals.	War Department stores.		
			Total tonnage dealt with.	Daily averages.	
				Tonnage dealt with.	Ton-mileage.
	No.*	No.			
June, 1917	236,861	15,959	477,142	2,636	538,730
December, 1917	281,267	17,338	759,239	4,126	715,062
June, 1918	154,931	18,574	949,628	5,246	1,059,045
December, 1918	144,546	11,134	747,649	4,062	745,237
	817,605	63,005	2,933,658	4,018	764,510

* Including 112,394 sick and wounded and 26,152 prisoners of war carried down river.

Conclusion.—That the Inland Water Transport Directorate performed very valuable work in Mesopotamia must be admitted. Whereas, in July, 1916, the weekly tonnage conveyed by river was less than 2,000 tons, this increased in 1918 to a weekly average of 40,000 tons conveyed over much longer distances. Additionally, the detention to store-ships at Basra, which in 1916 averaged 46 days, was reduced during 1918 to an average of 6·2 days. The craft in service, moreover, was increased from 346 to 1,621, and included floating filtration plants, hospital vessels and every convenience required by the troops. The extensive character of the development in inland water transport work will be further appreciated from the fact that whilst the total ton-mileage of river traffic during 1917 was 225 millions—which was an enormous increase over 1916—this figure increased to 330 millions during the year 1918. And, but for the armistice, this would have been considerably higher. At the end of 1918 the length of waterways operated was about 1,000 miles.

Unlike every other theatre of war, where waterways were developed to supplement railroad links, the rivers of Mesopotamia furnished the only means of communication available from the inception of the campaign until the first railways were opened at the end of 1916. Even then the absence of a through railway line from Basra to Baghdad necessitated the use of the river for all through traffic, though after the completion of the Kut-Baghdad line it was the general procedure to terminate the river conveyance at Kut and there transfer traffic to the railway. Throughout the campaign, however, it must be admitted that the rivers furnished the principal line of communication, and the fact that navigation was carried on with regularity and reliability, in

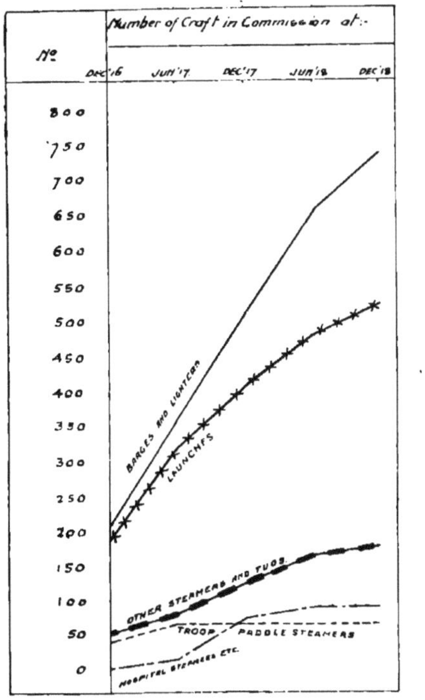

Fig. 46.—Chart showing River-Craft Development in Mesopotamia.

spite of many difficulties and troublesome climatic conditions, had much to do with the success of our forces in that theatre.

France.

Very soon after the outbreak of war the utility of inland water transport as a second line of communication in France was definitely recognised, and steps were taken to utilise this means of communication to the fullest extent. It was for this purpose that the original Inland Water Transport Section of the Royal Engineers was formed. This section performed much valuable work, and, especially after the inauguration of a separate directorate in France, developed inland water transport to such an extent as to afford considerable relief to the railways and the roads.

Towards the end of 1916, when 300 miles of waterways were operated, it became apparent that considerable development of inland waterway and dock work would be essential in the future to meet the ever-increasing quantity of war material and supplies going into France, and the capacity of the various French ports was thoroughly investigated in order to ascertain whether they could deal with the anticipated import tonnage of 200,000 tons per week during 1917. It was finally decided that it would be possible to meet the demands by a reorganisation of the work and an augmentation of the existing equipment. This was taken in hand so energetically that whilst, during the four weeks ending November 26, 1916, the aggregate weight of traffic discharged at French ports for the British Army was 470,000 tons, this figure increased during the four weeks ending February 25, 1917, to 604,000 tons, an improvement of 30 per cent. In order further to increase the capacity of certain ports, arrangements for delivering overside to craft were developed, and it was hoped by this means to relieve dock quays to the extent of over 4,000 tons per day. An establishment was provided during 1916 of 99 officers and nearly 3,000 other ranks for inland water transport work in France, whilst further numbers were in training or in reserve in England. In addition to working traffic for the canals which were then available, they were trained and prepared to restore the canals in Belgium as the army advanced. The cargo-carrying capacity of the barges then in use was 76,000 deadweight tons, and the possibility of utilising this capacity to its maximum extent was carefully considered. Further barges were being provided, and it was assumed that the cargo-carrying capacity would then be 110,000 deadweight tons.

The requirements of the waterways occupied subsequent to any advance through Belgium were carefully considered. Sections of lock gates were provided for the construction of 24 locks with double-leaf gates, and 12 gates with single-leaf gates, 6 up and 6 down-stream. Several special gates were also provided. The sections then in France were of great value, but in the event of an extensive advance it was obvious that they would not suffice to replace the number of locks that might be damaged by the enemy in the course of a retreat. Arrangements were consequently made to provide for the replacement of one-third of the locks on selected lines of advance with transversals up to a line from Ghent to Maubeuge.

As an example of Inland Water Transport activity in this direction, it might be mentioned that, after the battle of Arras, the Inland Water Transport restored to navigation the River Scarpe between Arras and Fampoux. Additionally that portion of the Somme which fell into British hands after the German retreat of March, 1917, was rendered available by the reconstruction of canal banks, locks, sluices and the removal of all obstacles to navigation.

Dock Working.—The greater part of the requirements for the

British Armies in France had to be imported from overseas, and as the demands for 1917 were considerably greater than those for previous years it became of importance to ensure that the programme of importation could effectively be handled by the various ports. In view, moreover, of the necessity of economising shipping by accelerating the rate of discharge it was essential to provide additional equipment and facilities, and, during 1917 and 1918, the accommodation allotted to the British was greatly developed and the whole system of working thoroughly reorganised.

At the commencement of 1917 imports averaged 150,000 tons per week, but during the period from March to June very rapid development was effected, especially at the northern ports. During May, for example, imports averaged 223,746 tons per week, the greatest tonnage handled in any one week being 240,000. This was in excess of the existing allocation, and proved that the facilities then available at the ports were sufficient to deal with the whole of the requirements for the British Armies.

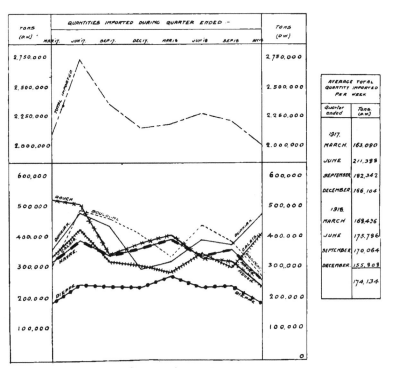

Fig. 47.—Chart showing Division of Traffic sent to France between Principal Ports.

The imports naturally fluctuated to a considerable extent from week to week. During November and December, 1917, for instance, severe weather was experienced and this adversely affected the sailing of ships, whilst the submarine activities of the enemy accounted for a number of loaded vessels intended for France. During 1918 the persistent attacks of the enemy on the various ports, by aircraft and long-range guns, caused some difficulty in coping with the work, whilst the considerable advance of the enemy in March and April, 1918, and the critical military situation that ensued, dislocated port working to some extent, and impelled the transfer of a large proportion of the imports from the southern to the northern ports.

During the last quarter of the year the rate of importation greatly diminished, as the transport of ammunition was wholly discontinued after the signing of the armistice, and all other traffics were reduced as far as possible. In consequence, the majority of the accommodation at the southern ports was given up and the traffic handled at the northern ports, the tendency being shown by the fact that whereas, during the first three months of the year, imports were equally divided between northern and southern ports, these proportions in December, 1918, were 76 per cent. to northern and 24 per cent. to southern ports.

The total imports for the years 1917 and 1918 were as follows :—

	1917. Dw. tons.	1918. Dw. tons.
January to March	2,120,168	2,225,325
April to June	2,748,050	2,317,580
July to September	2,370,452	2,255,644
October to December	2,159,350	2,070,943
	9,398,020	8,869,492

and were divided between various points as shown in Fig. 47. During the period of active operation, imports of ammunition were very heavy, and reached record figures for the second and third quarters of the year 1917. The total imports of ammunition, included in the above figures, amounted in 1917 to 2,109,735 tons and in 1918, 2,068,314 tons.

While the return traffic from France to England was relatively small as compared with the import traffic, this also was considerably developed especially after the introduction of the cross-Channel barge service. During the first week of January, 1917, 3,560 tons were despatched to England, this quantity increasing to a weekly average of 4,445 tons during March. Towards the end of 1917, the question of developing the return traffic in connection with salved material was taken in hand and a programme for 12,000 tons per week was agreed upon, but certain difficulties were experienced in maintaining this figure. The following figures indicate the great improvement in the shipment of material to the United Kingdom during the two years :—

	1917. Dw. tons.	1918. Dw. tons.
January to March	22,225	64,456
April to June	89,999	111,004
July to September	126,491	142,195
October to December	87,443	93,031
Total	326,158	410,686

In order to handle the great increase of traffic, port working had to be re-organised and the equipment and facilities greatly extended. Some idea of this expansion will be gathered from the fact that the number of cranes working at berths allotted to the British increased from 126 at the end of 1916 to 290 at the end of 1917 and 369 at the end of 1918. In addition, very extensive improvements were effected in the way of additional railway facilities, the construction of depôts, &c.

As a result of improved port equipment and organisation, the operating efficiency of the ports increased to a remarkable degree. The average tonnage per hour discharged from vessels during January, 1917, averaged 12·5, this rising in September, 1917, to 25·8. This figure was maintained until January, 1918, when improved facilities and additional personnel enabled the figure to be continuously increased until July, when the rate was 34·4. This increase in the rate of discharge represents a great economy in shipping owing to the quicker turn-round of vessels ; in fact, the improvement was so good that in the latter part of 1918 there was actually a decline in the rate of discharge, owing to the inability of the railways to supply rolling-stock to meet the traffic unloaded ex ship.

Inland Water Transport.—With the object of relieving the railways and roads, every effort was made to develop traffic on the waterways. The main operations were carried out on the waterways from Calais and Dunkirk, and at these ports a considerable proportion of the tonnage arriving was discharged by barge as from the beginning of 1917.

The length of waterways operated at the end of 1916 was 229 miles, but during the following year, 46 additional miles were brought under control, and so increased the total length to 346 miles. The larger portion of the waterways operated by the British, however, was lost to use owing to the enemy advance in the spring, and in April the mileage fell to 247, but, from that point, it increased until at the end of 1918 it amounted to 474 miles.

In order to handle the greatly augmented traffic, personnel and craft had to be increased, and the following table will indicate the

growth of personnel and craft, and the increase in transport capacity during the three years :—

INLAND WATER TRANSPORT.—PERSONNEL, NUMBER OF CRAFT EMPLOYED, AND LENGTH OF WATERWAYS OPERATED.

Position at end of year.	Personnel employed.	Craft employed.				Length or waterways operated.
		Self-propelled and dumb barges.		Other craft, i.e., tugs, water barges, &c.	Total craft.	
		No.	Approximate carrying capacity.	No.		
	No.		Tons (dw.).	No.		
1916	3,609	333	72,061	235	568	299
1917	6,913	463	102,630	346	809	345
1918	7,711	591	130,833	389	980	474

During the year 1917 traffic by cross-Channel barge from Richborough to inland depôts in France was developed on an extensive scale. In January the traffic carried by this means averaged less than 2,000 dw. tons per week, but this figure rose in September to nearly 15,000 tons per week. This large increase was largely accounted for by heavy consignments of ammunition which, during August and September, was conveyed through to inland depôts at an average rate of 7,000 tons weekly.

In the course of time, several inland quays were developed for the handling of traffic in and out by the cross-Channel barge service. At the end of 1916 only Zeneghem and Soquence were erected and the traffic was relatively small, but as will be shown from the following particulars this expanded to a remarkable degree during 1917 and 1918 :—

	Traffic dealt with (in and out)	
	1917.	1918.
Zeneghem	649,893	733,139
Vendroux (main wharf)	159,252	473,210
Les Attaques	—	126,209
Soquence	175,737	196,351
La Colme	179,880	102,607
Other quays	146,256	79,936
	1,311,018	1,711,452

A feature of the working was the extent to which assistance was afforded to the Allies. Tug trips were made up and down the coast for the French, and tugs and barges operated by British crews were lent to the Americans on the Seine. In order to supplement rail movements from the north to the south, a service of coastal barges was also instituted to ply between the northern canals and the Seine, and inland water traffic on the Seine was developed considerably.

The traffic carried during 1917 and 1918 was as follows :—

	1917.	1918.
Tonnage conveyed, dw.	2,307,424	2,842,418
Ton-kilometres	68,352,794	93,262,044
Sick and wounded (carried in ambulance barges)	13,270	25,545
Troops carried	171,761	44,454
Horses and mules carried	8,366	11,614

The movement of freight traffic on inland waterways in France includes traffic carried across Channel by the barge service working from Richborough. The weight carried in such barges, which worked through the rivers to inland depôts, is included in the above figures. The extensive improvement that was effected will be remarked from the fact that, in the 12 months ending June, 1916, no more than 500,000 dw. tons was carried on the waterways. In the early portion of this period, the average monthly figure was only 15,643 tons, but it rose to 65,000 tons towards the end of the 12 months.

Engineering and Construction Department.—The repair and maintenance requirements for so large a fleet, together with the operating facilities that were required, caused considerable expansion in the Mechanical and Marine Engineering Department in France. Additional workshops and yards were provided, these being essential not merely to meet the increase in the craft in service, but for the greater incidence of repair work which was to be expected from the extended period over which many of the vessels were operating.

The construction department for their part carried out many works of considerable importance ; they built and equipped wharves, and provided the necessary camps for personnel to work them at Vendroux, La Colme, St. Momelin, Les Forts, La Mailleraye, whilst they extended facilities at the depôts established at Zeneghem and Soquence. The workshops at Arques and dry docks at Arques and Abbeville for the repair and maintenance of Inland Water Transport craft were also constructed during 1917, whilst the No. 3 Transportation Stores Depôt at Aire, including stores sheds, wharves, roads, railways, &c., was erected during the same year.

In addition, the enemy offensive in March, 1918, caused a number of inundation and construction works to be undertaken, these involving extensive bridging over inland waterways. Subsequently, the successful counter-offensive of the Allies led to the necessity of the rapid opening up of waterways for navigation.

Egypt.

Considerable developments took place in Inland Water Transport work in Egypt at the beginning of 1917. Previously, conveyance by water had been in the hands of the R.A.S.C. and the Egyptian Public Works Department, but, following the visit of Sir Francis Dent on a Special War Office Mission of investigation, all inland water transport work was vested in the Directorate of Inland Waterways and Docks. Colonel Coysh assumed control in Egypt early in March, 1917.

The work included the extensive utilisation of the Nile and the canal system of Lower and Upper Egypt, together with the lighterage of ships at ports such as Alexandria and Port Said, and, subsequently at Kantara, which became the Base from which the Palestine Army obtained supplies. Personnel was sent out to build up an Inland Water Transport organisation in Egypt and to operate fleets on the Suez and Ismalia Canals. These fleets included large numbers of native craft which were hired by the Government.

Owing to the shortage of rolling-stock, particularly on the Egyptian State Railways, it became necessary for the greatest possible amount of traffic to be carried by water, and arrangements were accordingly put in hand. It was also decided that all tugs and lighters, except those for sea-going ships, required by the various departments should be obtained through the Inland Water Transport Department, which was instrumental in reducing the rate of lighter hire at Port Said by 25 per cent. and thus saving £6,000 per annum. As indicating the rapidity of development under the new control, it may be remarked that during the quarter ending September, 1917, the tonnage carried by water showed an increase of 60 per cent. as compared with the previous quarter.

The rivers and canals principally operated were the Delta, Suez Canal and Upper Nile, and one of the chief cargoes transported was cereals, &c., from Assouan. In fact, the Inland Water Transport undertook to convey all cereals for the military authorities, this traffic aggregating a quarter of a million per annum ; 200 additional native boats were specially hired during the season for this traffic.

Towards the end of 1917, when the craft in service numbered 891, an advance in Palestine somewhat diminished the weight carried by water. By this time the regular service of lighters between Cairo and Kantara which, in June, 1917, was conveying about 500 tons daily, was supplemented by a service of Inland Water Transport craft between Cairo and Alexandria, which proved very useful. During the year 1917 the pressure on the railways was very considerably relieved by the development of traffic on the waterways, which carried 1,328,842 tons (daily average of 4,520 tons), equivalent to a ton-mileage of over 35 millions, in addition to 42,896 passengers. The personnel supplied from England for Inland Water Transport purposes during the year comprised 29 officers and 94 men. In the first week of 1918 traffic by inland water transport reached a weekly total of 52,412 tons as compared with 5,000 tons weekly during March, 1917, whilst a large number of passengers were carried. It was then computed that the Inland Water Transport saved 150 wagons per day on the Egyptian State Railways. It was expected that the advance into Palestine and the arrangement for ships to be discharged at Kantara would reduce the tonnage to be handled by Inland Water Transport about one-half, and be the means of releasing a large number of craft for use on the Nile and Delta waterways, where they were urgently required. This expected decrease in Inland Water Transport activities was, however, not realised, as it became necessary to develop them still further in order to provide additional relief to the railways, particularly as regards foodstuffs from Upper Egypt. With this object in view and also to reduce import tonnage and enable Egypt to be more self-supporting, the traffic in cereals and tibben from Upper Egypt to the Delta was developed. In March, 1918, twelve Nile tourist steamers were requisitioned for the purpose of transporting compressed tibben from districts between Cairo and Assouan.

To cope with the new situation, moreover, and to increase the existing inland water transport services, arrangements were made about this time to increase the flotilla by the transfer of 17 high-power tugs and 3 barges intended for Mesopotamia, and to construct 27 barges in England for re-erection in Egypt. This increase in the fleet enabled the waterways to extend the relief afforded to the railways which were hard pressed for locomotives and rolling-stock.

A very considerable amount of lighterage work was performed by the Inland Water Transport in Egypt. For the quarter ending September, 1917, this amounted to just over 200,000 tons, which figure increased in six months to over 400,000 tons. During the last quarter of 1918 the lighterage work was represented by nearly half a million tons, and was actually much higher than the tonnage conveyed by river and canal.

Military traffic on the rivers and canals only slightly declined after the armistice, the weekly averages in the September and December quarters being 24,900 and 23,270 tons respectively.

The growth of the fleet is shown below :—

	1917.	1918.
Government-owned craft	72	157
Government-controlled craft	31	—
Hired craft	841	2,019
Loaned craft	—	6
	944	2,182

whilst the tonnage handled during 1918 was three millions, or more than double that of the previous year. The total river ton-mileage in 1918 was nearly one hundred millions, as compared with 35 millions during the preceding year, whilst the number of passengers carried during 1918 was over 80,000.

BELGIAN PORTS.

As a result of negotiations with the Belgian and French Governments, a fully representative international conference was held at Havre on July 10, 1917, to decide the main principles governing Allied action with regard to Belgian Ports and Railways after enemy evacuation. Inter-Allied Commissions, both military and technical, were formed to carry these principles into effect and to agree upon the measures to be taken to attain this end.

A Port Construction Department was formed and this collected a great deal of information concerning the pre-war and actual condition of the ports ; this served as a basis for estimating the probable damage that might be done by the enemy before evacuation, and schemes of repair were drawn up. Large quantities of plant and materials for this purpose, and to facilitate reconstruction, were passed into France during 1917, and principally stored in a special depôt at Les Forts near Bergues. During the year 1918, however, the military situation became so critical that no further preparations were made, and, in April, when the enemy advance was at its height, orders were given for the evacuation of the material from the depôts at Les Forts. The whole of the plant and materials was consequently despatched, mostly by barge, to Richborough and Zeneghem.

In October, 1918. it was decided by the War Cabinet that repairs to Belgian ports should be carried out by the Admiralty, and the plant and material acquired for the purpose, together with a section of the personnel from the Port Construction Department, were transferred to the Civil Engineer-in-Chief of the Admiralty.

THE WORK OF THE MINISTRY OF MUNITIONS TRANSPORT BRANCH.

An Account of the Development and Organisation of a Large Department concerned with Inland Transport during the War.

Having regard to the colossal amount of transport to which the creation of the Ministry of Munitions led, and, also, to the wide range of technical and other questions that naturally arose on such matters as transport facilities, traffic regulation and the working of the munitions traffic generally, it was inevitable that the Ministry would have to arrange at an early stage of its existence for a section specially designed to take charge of these and kindred subjects, thus greatly facilitating the work of the Ministry itself and of the railway companies, and avoiding those chaotic conditions which, otherwise, must inevitably have resulted. A transport branch was formed accordingly. It began on a very small scale, and, under the directorship for the greater part of its history of Mr. Howard Williams, C.B.E., whose appointment as General Manager of the Central Argentine Railway has recently been announced, it eventually became an organisation responsible for a long list of duties, limited, however, by the fact that the functions of the branch in respect to munitions ceased upon completion of manufacture, at which point the War Office assumed control over their despatch to final destination.

"C.M. 8."

The branch came into existence on September 15, 1915. It was created by Mr. Lloyd George, then Minister of Munitions, as a forwarding and delivery department under the Director-General of Munition Supply, Sir F. Black. That gentleman had four sections of his own department. These were known as "A," "B," "C" and "D" respectively, and each was under the control of a Deputy-Director-General. Mr. Eric Geddes—as the present Minister of Transport then was—had charge of Section "C," and this, in turn, was divided into eight sub-sections. Each was called "C.M," with a number from 1 to 8, inclusive. "C.M. 8" was the said "forwarding and delivery department"; but for some months it was known only as "C.M. 8." Its original staff consisted of four persons. The director of the sub-section was Lieutenant-Colonel, afterwards Brigadier-General, R. L. Wedgwood, then Chief Goods Manager of the North Eastern Railway, and he was assisted by Mr. Howard Williams, then Mineral Traffic Manager of the London & North Western Railway, who succeeded him as director when he joined the staff in France of Sir Eric Geddes on the appointment of the latter as Director-General of Military Railways.

The original function of "C.M. 8," as defined by the Director-General of Munitions Supply, specified that the department was to "communicate with the War Office, the Railway Executive Committee, or with the railway companies direct in reference to all special services required from the railways by the Ministry, such as construction of sidings, special train facilities, requests for special transit arrangements, and, generally, all technical railway matters"; but the scope of the sub-section's activities began almost at once their process of expansion, and they had undergone a substantial growth even before the end of 1915. By that time "C.M. 8" had been actively concerned in, among other things, advising as to layout, location, &c., of new sidings on behalf of various sections of the Ministry in conjunction with the railway companies; choice of location, from a traffic point of view, for munition stores; issue of priority certificates for urgent Government traffic; preparation for the Railway Executive Committee of statistics showing prospective amount of munitions traffic to be carried within a given period, and a variety of measures designed to facilitate munitions transport in general. Many other matters of a technical character were also referred to the branch.

From the beginning of 1916 the general functions of "C.M. 8" underwent further expansion. There was, for example, every indication of an early and a very great increase in the production of munitions, and the question arose as to whether the railways would be equal to the task of conveying them. The Railway Executive Committee replied that no difficulty in handling the increased traffic was anticipated—provided that certain conditions were fulfilled. These conditions included the carrying out of an effective organisation designed to ensure the off-loading of wagons without delay; the detection, reporting and investigation of cases of misuse and detention of stock in connection with factories and stores; regulation of the forwarding of traffic; economical use of wagons; avoidance of unnecessary haulage, and so on. It became the duty of "C.M. 8" to take an active part in the fulfilment of these conditions, and among many other measures adopted towards the attainment of this end was the issue, in the name of the Ministry of Munitions, of an extremely practical eight-page pamphlet of "Instructions to Boards of Management, Stores Officers, &c., in regard to Railway Working."

"Munitions Railway Transport Branch."

The development of the scope and functions of "C.M. 8" led, at the end of February, 1916, to a change in its designation. It became the "Munitions Railway Transport Branch," and an intimation was given that thenceforward it would deal with, among other matters, transport facilities for munition workers, whether by rail, tram or road vehicle, and also with questions of road transport generally so far as these affected, or might relieve, rail transport. So the organisation at headquarters was further expanded, and before the end of May, 1916, sections had been set up to deal with the following phases of munitions transport work; (1) Railway and canal transport; (2) railway transport permits; (3) traffic regulation at factories and stores; (4) railway rates, rules and regulations; (5) sidings and new works; (6) transport of munition workers; (7) road transport; (8) staff, equipment and registry.

The arrangements made in regard to transport requirements of the various branches of the Ministry varied according to circumstances and conditions. Certain of the branches, such as the Trench Warfare Supply Department, the Department of Explosives Supply, the Mechanical Warfare Department and the Gun-ammunition Filling Department, had in each instance a transport organisation of its own, subject to submission of matters of principle to the Transport Branch. In certain other branches members of the Munitions Transport Branch staff were allocated to them to co-ordinate requirements and deal with matters of detail. In some instances an organisation was set up which applied exclusively to the special needs of one particular department. All other departments of the Ministry not provided for under one or other of these categories approached the Munitions Railway Transport Branch direct whenever they required guidance or assistance in transport matters. Nor was the work of that Branch restricted to departments of the Ministry of Munitions. Before long it became the general friend, adviser and helper in regard to transport for Government Departments in general, as well as for establishments dealing with contracts for any of such departments.

Area Organisation.

In proportion as the manufacture of munitions spread throughout the country, involving multifarious transport questions which called for local inquiries, investigation or treatment, the fact became increasingly evident that a headquarters staff alone would not suffice to meet the necessities of the case. At first there were travelling inspectors who were sent out to inquire into such matters as provision of sidings, acquisition of buildings and sites from railway companies, detention of wagons at national and other establishments, congestion of traffic, supply of wagons, and a great variety of other matters of a kindred type. Then an "Area Transport Officer" was appointed for the Birmingham district, and this new departure was found to be of great advantage, not alone to the Munitions Transport Branch, in facilitating local inquiries and local arrangements, but also to the munitions establishments and to the railway companies. Area Transport Officers were subsequently established at Leeds, Manchester and elsewhere, and assistant officers were appointed, so that eventually all districts directly concerned were provided for by the local arrangements, and there was no longer any need for travelling inspectors at the London headquarters.

Many advantages are claimed as having resulted from the work undertaken by these Munitions Area Transport Officers. Special and successful efforts, for example, were made to secure the better loading and the earlier release of wagons. Improvements were secured in the rate of discharge at the ports. Much was done with a view to relieving the continued and increasing pressure on the railways by securing the diversion of short-distance traffic from rail to canal or road. In one area alone the transfer to canal of 300,000 tons of traffic which would otherwise have been put on rail was arranged. Munitions Transport Officers sought to effect a greater use of road motors for traffic flowing regularly between given points, and in the case of one firm a saving of 500 railway wagons per week was gained. Road transport in the various areas was under the jurisdiction of the Munitions Transport Officers, and in one of these areas the traffic conveyed between April, 1917, and December, 1918, by lorries belonging to the Ministry amounted to over 787,000 tons. About 143,000 tons consisted of short-distance traffic which had been diverted to the roads in order to relieve the railways. The Munitions Transport Officers were responsible, too, for the working of some of the motor controls established in various parts of the country, and they were especially successful in obtaining the maximum loading and the best use of vehicles. In one instance the officers concerned secured the transport of over 1,000 tons of munitions per week in road motors which otherwise would have run empty in one direction.

Headquarters' Work.

The Branch was constantly on the look-out for means by which transport could be saved or facilitated. It was as the result of a suggestion made by the Branch that arrangements were made for testing certain large articles at the place of construction instead of conveying them to another point for this purpose. The result was a saving of 67,829 miles of haulage, with the further advantage to the railway companies that they were in a better position to meet demands for wagons. Economy was obtained in the use of special trucks. Such trucks were being used for the forwarding of certain completed articles; but the Munitions Transport Branch found that, by despatching the articles in a nearly completed state, involving very little extra work at the base overseas, the traffic could be loaded on ordinary railway wagons. Exceptional steps were taken from January, 1916, to secure the most efficient user of tank wagons, of which the number available was below war-time requirements. A system of traffic organisation carried out in connection with the Central Stores Department led to the prevention of much wasteful haulage, to the obviating of congestion, to avoidance of detention of wagons, sheets and ropes, and to a better user of the wagons in general. Wasteful haulage was avoided by the drawing up of a geographical chart as a means of ensuring the most advantageous storage of materials in the closest proximity to ultimate destination. A specialised system of loading cartridge cases led to a saving in the case of 18-pdr. cases, for example, of over 6,000 wagon loads per

month. Use of returnable boxes necessitating a double journey for the rolling-stock was avoided by a system under which the cases could be packed loose and still be carried in perfect safety.

The Munitions Transport Branch initiated and carried through the establishment of the Railway Tranship Shed which effected a vast improvement in conditions at the Royal Arsenal, Woolwich. It represented the interests of the Ministry of Munitions in the carrying out of requirements for the provision of sidings and new works, and this in itself was a big piece of work, as sidings were essential to the efficient working of the very numerous factories and stores which sprang up all over the country. By the end of December, 1918, the Branch had under its supervision no fewer than 2,054 motor transport vehicles, including petrol lorries, light vans, steam lorries, trailers, light cars, cycles and cycles with side cars for passengers or goods. The work performed by the fleet during the 12 months ending October, 1918, included: Miles run loaded, 2,533,001; miles run empty, 1,958,525; total miles run, 4,491,526; tons carried, 1,903,259; number of loaded journeys, 559,008.

Much was done in one direction or another in securing increased travelling facilities for munition workers alike by railway, tramway, motor omnibus services, and ferry services to and from their work.

The fact that the Branch was taking so active and prominent a part in the development both of road and of canal transport led to still another change of title in October, 1917, when "Munitions Inland Transport Branch" was substituted for "Munitions Railway Transport Branch."

Final Organisation.

The eventual organisation of the Branch was as follows:—
Director: Mr. Howard Williams.
Section Director: Mr. F. C. A. Coventry.
Headquarters Staff (each with a Sub-section Director and staff):—
(1) Railway Transport, Air Board Office, Explosives Department; (2) Transit permits; (3) Liaison Section with Central Stores Department; (4) Free Conveyance of Ministry Traffic, Claims, Sidings; (5) Munition Workers' Travelling Facilities; (6) Motor Transport; (7) Staff, Office equipment, Supervision of Branch Registry, Typists.
Area Organisation:—Munitions Transport Officers and Staffs; Area No. 1, Newcastle, Sub-office, Middlesbrough; No. 2, Manchester, Sub-offices, Liverpool, Carnforth and Whitehaven; No. 3, Leeds, Sub-offices, Sheffield and Bradford; No. 4, Birmingham, Sub-offices, Coventry, Nottingham and Lincoln; No. 5, Cardiff; No. 6, Bristol; No. 7, London; Nos. 8 and 9, Glasgow.
Departments to which staff was loaned or placed under the control of: Central Stores Department; Explosives Department; Munitions Inventions Department; Finance Department; Trench Warfare Supply Department; Director of Forwarding; Salvage Department.

Development of Staff.

The following figures show the development of the staff of the Branch from the time of its creation to the signing of the armistice:—

	Headquarters.	Areas	Total.
September, 1915...	4	—	4
May, 1916	44	11	55
May, 1917	65	60	125
November, 1918	90	106	196

Of the 196 members of the staff on the last-mentioned date, 84 were members of the Ministry of Munitions staff, and 112 had been loaned by various railway companies and the Railway Clearing House.

Lightning Source UK Ltd.
Milton Keynes UK
UKHW050945300421
382900UK00008B/251